JUTLAND

AN ANALYSIS OF THE FIGHTING

JUTLAND

AN ANALYSIS OF THE FIGHTING

JOHN CAMPBELL

with a preface by
ANTONY PRESTON

The Lyons Press

This edition first published in Great Britain in 1998 by
Conway Maritime Press
a division of Batsford Communications PLC
583 Fulham Road, London SW6 5BY

This edition first published in the United States by the
Lyons Press, 31 West 21 Street, New York, New York 10010.

ISBN 1-55821-759-2

A CIP record for this book is available from the Lyons Press.

Book design and charts by John Mitchell
Typesetting and page make-up by Witwell Ltd, Liverpool
Printed and bound by Biddles Ltd, Guildford, UK

CONTENTS

PREFACE

There have been many books about the Battle of Jutland. With the exception of Trafalgar, no other sea battle has inspired so many 'last words'. Yet, unlike Trafalgar, this great fleet action in the North Sea at the end of May 1916 spawned controversy from the moment the firing stopped, and because it was superficially indecisive it will continue to fascinate naval historians.

Yet, surprisingly, when John Campbell's masterpiece appeared in 1986, it was the first comprehensive analysis of the fighting to make full use of technical records. Other naval historians had theorised about what might have been, but Campbell took as his starting point the question of what had actually happened to the various ships.

Working at the National Maritime Museum thirty years ago, I was in an unusual position to observe John Campbell at work. Month after month I would get out the detailed building drawings of the major warships of the Grand Fleet, the beautifully executed 'as fitted' plans of HMS *Indefatigable*, HMS *Invincible* and HMS *Queen Mary* and others. It was also my privilege to discuss with John his progress in other areas, notably the Public Record Office and the German naval archives at Freiburg im Breisgau. Thus I learned that Captain Meusemann had finally unearthed the drawings of damage-repairs to the High Seas Fleet ships, unseen by any historian since before the Second World War. Another 'find' in the Museum's manuscript collection was a snapshot taken of the battlecruiser HMS *Princess Royal* taken on the way back to Rosyth next day, confirming the shell-hits on her hull and superstructure.

Once the weighty manuscript had taken shape, the long struggle to find a publisher began. At times it was very dispiriting, but I took heart from a plea by the head of the naval archives at Freiburg, the late Dr Gerd Sandhofer. During a visit to Germany he said to me with great feeling, 'Mr Preston, this is a book which must see the light of day.' Since it's first publication in Britain the book has come to be seen as the standard work on the subject, and fortunately the Lyon Press, understanding the merits of the book, are now able to reissue it. In doing so they enable John's book to bring the last great clash of battlefleets in European waters to a wider readership, including wargamers and all who are fascinated by the mighty dreadnoughts of the past.

Antony Preston,
March 1998

CHAPTER 1

Introduction: North Sea Fleet Operations, 1914 to Jutland

NO NAVAL BATTLE has attracted so many attempts at its description as the Battle of Jutland fought on 31 May and 1 June 1916 between the two largest fleets of the time, those of Britain and Germany. The actions and supposed motives of the Admirals of both sides have been examined in many works. Far less attention, however, has been paid to the actual details of the fighting and to the damage and losses inflicted and these matters are fully described for the first time in this book.

In the era of the armoured battleship Jutland stands alone, the fleets engaged being so much more powerful than those of the Russian and Japanese Fleets at Tsushima, the second greatest battle of the period fought 11 years earlier. By the time that the greatest battles of World War II – Midway, the Philippine Sea and Leyte – were fought, the battleship had yielded pride of place to the aircraft carrier, and Britain to the USA as the chief naval power. From the British declaration of war on 4 August 1914 until Jutland little fighting was seen between the main fleets of Britain and Germany in the North Sea, known respectively as the Grand Fleet and the High Seas Fleet. The British were not willing to hazard their sea supremacy and the long range blockade of Germany, which were vital to them and their allies, by seeking a battle in unfavourable circumstances, as a major victory over the German fleet would not necessarily win the war, and a great disaster to the British fleet would certainly lose it.

The Germans did not realise that certain defects in British dreadnought battleships and battlecruisers, which are discussed on later pages and mainly concerned the ammunition, gave their own ships an individual superiority over their opponents of the same date, and did not wish to seek battle with the whole British fleet until the numerical superiority of the latter had been reduced by mines or submarines or by a successful action against an isolated part of the fleet. This was the Germans' great error of judgement; their chances of winning a fleet action were far better in the early part of the war than by mid-1916.

On 16 December 1914, when the Germans raided Scarborough, they had their best opportunity of defeating an important detached part of the Grand Fleet; the latter if concentrated, would have had twenty-two dreadnought battleships, and four battlecruisers against their fourteen and four. At Jutland the figures were twenty-eight dreadnought battleships and nine battlecruisers versus sixteen and five, respectively, and six of the British battleships had 15in guns compared with none in 1914. In addition, the Grand Fleet was short of destroyers in the early part of the war though the German destroyers in service in 1914 were far inferior to most of theirs at Jutland. Furthermore, the extremely valuable intelligence source provided by the deciphering of German wireless signals had not yet been developed. The origin of this was the German naval cyphers and other documents recovered by the Russians from the light cruiser *Magdeburg* wrecked in the Baltic on 26 August 1914.

Although the Grand Fleet, based on the north and east of Scotland, had the advantage of a better geographical location, and the bases in use were not identified by the Germans for some time, there were initially few facilities for a large fleet in this area, as the main dockyards were in southern England. The new dockyard at Rosyth was not useable until 1916, and the anchorages at Scapa Flow, Cromarty and Rosyth had no defences against submarines until October – November 1914, so that for a time the Grand Fleet used Loch Ewe in the north-west of Scotland and then Lough Swilly in the north of Ireland and Loch Na Keal in Mull. Permission was even given by the Admiralty on 20 October 1914 to withdraw to Berehaven in the extreme south-west of Ireland but this was not found necessary. In the southern part of the North Sea the British had the Harwich Force of light cruisers, destroyers and submarines, and some of the pre-dreadnought battleships were at times stationed at the Nore.

The High Seas Fleet was based on the principal German dockyard at Wilhelmshaven in the Jade, and the estuaries of the Elbe, Weser and Ems, as well as the outpost of Heligoland, could provide anchorages for some units, while a canal ran from the Elbe to the other main dockyard at Kiel in the Baltic. The Flanders flotilla of small submarines based on Bruges, Ostend and Zeebrugge, was developed by the Germans from 1915, and some destroyers were subsequently included in this force.

2

The danger from submarine attack seriously restricted the Grand Fleet's activities throughout the war and the range of the screening destroyers became the limiting factor in the operations of both fleets. However, no dreadnought battleship or battlecruiser was sunk by a submarine in World War I, and no British one was damaged, though British submarines made a total of five torpedo hits on German ships of these types, four in the North Sea and one in the Baltic. German submarines might well have had more success against the capital ships of the Grand Fleet if the greater part of their effort had not been directed at merchant shipping.

Submarines capable of operating at sea, had not been in existence in previous major wars, but mines had had great success in the Russo-Japanese War of 1904–5, and had been used effectively in the Confederate War of 1861–5, and their neglect by the British navy in the years before World War I was unfortunate. The *Audacious* struck a mine 28 miles from Lough Swilly on 27 October 1914 and sank, but she was the only dreadnought battleship or battlecruiser to be lost from this cause in 1914–18, and in the North Sea and waters round the British Isles only two other such ships, both German, were damaged by mines.

Of the four Admirals on whom the responsibility for the decisions in the Battle of Jutland mainly fell, three had held their command since the outbreak of war: Admiral Sir John Jellicoe, C in C of the Grand Fleet; Vice Admiral Sir David Beatty, in command of the battlecruisers or Battle Cruiser Fleet, as it was officially described from February 1915; and Vice Admiral Hipper, commanding the German Scouting Forces. Vice Admiral Scheer, the C in C of the High Seas Fleet, was, however, the third Admiral to hold this position since August 1914. Initially, Admiral von Ingenohl had been in command, but after the Battle of the Dogger Bank, 24 January 1915 he had been replaced in February 1915 by Admiral von Pohl, and on the latter's retirement from ill health in January 1916, Vice Admiral Scheer had been appointed.

Scheer was a better choice than either of his predecessors, and together with Jellicoe, Beatty and Hipper can be considered as sufficiently able, and though the spark of genius was lacking in all four, the conditions of Jutland were singularly unsuited to the display of this quality.

Dissatisfaction in Britain over the result of Jutland subsequently caused a virulent paper war between the supporters of Jellicoe and Beatty, but there was far less difference between the views of the two Admirals than Beatty's partisans were willing to believe. Jellicoe was cautious in seeking battle for the strategic reasons given previously, and also in his intended tactics when the High Seas Fleet might be encountered, as he feared that the Germans would turn away with the intention of leading him over mines and submarines and he would decline to be so drawn. The difficulties of close co-operation between a fleet and its submarines were not appreciated, and much unrewarding effort was expended by the British from 1915 to 1918 in the construction of the notorious 24-knot steam-driven *K* class submarines in the hope that they could work closely with the fleet.

With regard to mines the Japanese had lost two of their meagre total of six battleships on one day, 15 May 1904, to Russian mines laid in one of their probable tracks off Port Arthur, and among other mining successes of the Russo-Japanese War, Jellicoe probably knew that the old Russian battleship *Navarin* had been finally sunk in the night after Tsushima by one of twenty-four mines dropped close ahead of her by three Japanese destroyers. There was no reason why the Germans should not have developed such techniques.

Jellicoe was much keener to fight a battle with the High Seas Fleet than the foregoing might indicate, but it was impossible to tempt the Germans to an action with the whole Grand Fleet unless quite unacceptable risks were taken. A major attempt was made on 4 May 1916 to draw the High Seas Fleet out, and in preparation on the previous night, 80 mines were laid south of the Vyl lightship and 530 about 35–40 miles north-westward of Borkum, the ninth occasion that the Heligoland Bight had been mined. Three submarines were stationed off Terschelling and seven off the Vyl and Horns Reef lightships. The bait was to be provided by a raid on the Tondern airship sheds by eleven seaplanes from the *Vindex* and *Engadine*, 5 miles north of Horns Reef and escorted by a light cruiser squadron and a destroyer flotilla. The bait was however non-existent as only one seaplane took off successfully and dropped its bombs in Danish territory, so that the Grand Fleet battleships spent the morning of 4 May manoeuvring about 75 miles to the north-westward of the seaplane launching position with the battlecruisers c30 miles to the southward of the battleships, and at 1400 Jellicoe turned for home followed by Beatty. Some of the British ships had been reported, but the situation was not clear to the German command, and preparations were made to meet an attack on 5 May. Details of these were intercepted by the Admiralty, and wirelessed to Jellicoe between 1630 and 2030 but his destroyers were too short of fuel for him to return to the vicinity of Horns Reef at daylight on 5 May.

With the Grand Fleet based in the north, the English east coast was an obvious target for raids by the German battlecruisers. The most serious was on 16 December 1914. Hipper's battlecruisers (the *Seydlitz, Moltke, von der Tann, Derfflinger*), the fast armoured cruiser *Blücher*, four light cruisers of which the *Kolberg* carried 100 mines, and eighteen destroyers, were to reach the Yorkshire coast at dawn when the heavy ships would separate into two groups to bombard Hartlepool and Scarborough, while the *Kolberg* laid her mines off the coast. The main High Seas Fleet under von Ingenohl with fourteen dreadnoughts (the *Grosser Kurfürst*, five *Kaisers*, four *Ostfrieslands*, four *Nassaus*), eight pre-dreadnoughts, two armoured and seven light cruisers, and fifty-four destroyers, was to be in 54° 40′N, 3°00′E, about 130 miles east of Scarborough at daylight.

The Admiralty knew from deciphering intercepts of some of the orders, that the German battlecruisers would be out for two days, but they drew the dangerous conclusion that the battleships were very unlikely to come out, and their dispositions, based on this conclusion, might have led to irretrievable disaster. It was intended to intercept the raiders on their return, and the following ships were to concentrate at 0730 in 54° 10′N, 3°00′E, only 30 miles south of the High Seas Fleet's dawn position: the 2nd Battle Squadron (the *King George V, Centurion, Ajax, Orion, Monarch, Conqueror*), the four available battlecruisers (the *Lion, Queen Mary, Tiger, New Zealand*), four weak armoured cruisers, four light cruisers, and seven destroyers. Vice Admiral Sir George Warrender was in command in the *King George V*. The Harwich Force was to concentrate off Yarmouth at daylight to await events.

At 0515 the British destroyers made contact with the starboard wing of the screen ahead of the High Seas Fleet, and though the Germans had the better of the resultant fighting, von Ingenohl believed that his screen was in contact with the destroyer screen of the whole Grand Fleet and, too mindful of orders from the Kaiser against risking the battle fleet, turned 16 points to port to a reciprocal course at 0542, and 40 minutes later made for home. The port wing of the German screen had been less than 10 miles from the 2nd Battle Squadron.

It is not necessary to describe subsequent events on this day and whether the High Seas Fleet would have destroyed the 2nd Battle Squadron at small cost to itself and thus obtained superiority over the Grand Fleet, if von Ingenohl had pressed on, must remain a matter of conjecture, but at least there would have been a chance of so doing. It has been sometimes maintained that Beatty was unlucky in not meeting Hipper, at one time 12 miles away, but the four German battlecruisers were superior in fighting power to Beatty's four and it was probably fortunate for the British that Hipper was not engaged. Of the Grand Fleet's battlecruisers three including *Princess Royal* had been detached to deal with von Spee's armoured cruisers.

The next German operation resulted in the Battle of the Dogger Bank, an action in which the British had considerable success, though on closer examination matters were not so satisfactory. It was decided to make a reconnaissance of the Dogger Bank to discover the supposed British method of watch. Serious opposition was not expected and battleship support not considered necessary. The Germans were weak in the North Sea at this time as the *König* and *Kaiser* classes had gone to the Baltic for exercises, and the only dreadnoughts available were three *Ostfrieslands* and four *Nassaus*. The *von der Tann* was repairing defects, and Hipper's force comprised the *Seydlitz*, *Moltke*, *Derfflinger* and *Blücher*, four light cruisers and eighteen destroyers.

Orders wirelessed to Hipper were deciphered by the Admiralty at 1115 23 January, 5½ hours before the Germans left, and indicated that he was to be on the SE side of the Dogger Bank at dawn next day. Hipper requested extensive air reconnaissance for the early morning of 24 January, and three airships were ready but did not go up in time.

The Admiralty dispositions were as follows. Beatty with the five available battlecruisers, the *Lion, Tiger, Princess Royal, New Zealand, Indomitable*, which were now based at Rosyth, and four light cruisers, was to meet the Harwich Force of three light cruisers and thirty-five destroyers at 0700 24 January in 55° 13'N, 3° 12'E and endeavour to locate and engage the enemy. Six *King Edward* class pre-dreadnoughts and three weak armoured cruisers, also at Rosyth, were to be in 55° 35'N, 2° 00'E at 0745 in case the Germans came north, and the main body of the Grand Fleet from Scapa, and units from Cromarty, were to concentrate in 57° 00'N, 2° 20'E at 0930 and proceed southward. For this operation twenty-one dreadnoughts were available.

The first contact between the British and German light cruisers was at 0705, and by 0800 the German battlecruisers were in sight from the *Lion* in exceptionally good visibility with a slight sea and a north-easterly breeze. Beatty made for a position on their starboard quarter and at 0837 settled to a long chase. Hipper had turned to 122°* at 0735 as smoke clouds thought to come from eight large ships had been sighted to the north-westward, but it was not until 0840 that the British

---

*All courses and bearings are true unless otherwise stated (Variation c13°W), and Greenwich Mean Time is employed throughout.

battlecruisers were seen from their opponents, due mainly to the German funnel smoke and windward position.

The *Lion* fired her first shot at 0852 when the range was over 20,000yds, and although Beatty's ships chased for an hour at their highest speed, it never fell much below 16,000yds. The *Tiger* opened at 0900, the *Princess Royal* at 0907 and the German ships between 0911 and 0920, while the *New Zealand* opened at 0935 when Beatty gave the order to engage corresponding numbers, but the *Indomitable* which could not keep up and was handicapped by old type shell that restricted the guns to 16,300yds did not open until 1045. Fire distribution was irregular on both sides and the most visible target tended to be engaged. The Germans do not seem to have exceeded 23kts, while the *Lion* probably attained 27kts. The *Tiger* kept station, but the *Princess Royal* and *New Zealand* fell somewhat astern, and at 0952 Beatty reduced to 24kts so that his ships could close up.

In this first hour of the action the British shooting was considerably better than that of the German ships which were handicapped by their own funnel smoke. The *Seydlitz* and *Derfflinger* were each hit twice, the *Blücher* once and the *Lion* twice. Except for one hit on the *Seydlitz* at 0943 by the *Lion* which put two turrets out of action from a very serious ammunition fire, none was of much importance.

Beatty increased speed again at 1010 but in the period of the battle between 0952 and 1030 only one hit was obtained on the *Seydlitz* which had little effect, while four damaging hits were scored on the *Lion*. At 1030, however, the *Blücher* was hit by the *Princess Royal* and a disastrous ammunition fire occurred as well as damage in a boiler room which reduced her speed to *c*17kts so that she fell astern. It is not known how many hits were made on her in the next half hour, but they were probably not numerous. The German battlecruisers now had the *Lion's* range and from 1035 to 1051 ten hits were scored on her and she was put out of action. The *Tiger* which overtook the *Lion* at 1045 was also hit twice and only one hit was scored on the *Derfflinger* in return.

An imaginary submarine was now sighted on the *Lion's* starboard bow at 1054, and on Beatty's orders the *Tiger, Princess Royal* and *New Zealand* turned 90° to port together at 1102. This turn caused the cancellation of a German destroyer attack, and Beatty intended that these three battlecruisers should continue the chase under Rear Admiral Sir Archibald Moore in the *New Zealand* while the *Indomitable* dealt with the *Blücher*. His signals, however, were misunderstood and all four engaged the *Blücher*, while Hipper after some hesitation made off. Since the 90° turn four hits had been scored on the *Tiger* and a final hit on the

Lion. The *Blücher* proved very hard to sink, and eventually capsized at 1213 after about fifty hits from the battlecruisers and two torpedoes from the light cruiser *Arethusa.* She made one hit on the *Tiger* and one on the *Indomitable* and put the destroyer *Meteor* out of action.

The *Lion* eventually reached Rosyth in tow of the *Indomitable* at 0635 on 26 January with a screen which at one time after the Grand Fleet had come up, numbered fifty-five destroyers. British casualties were extraordinarily small at 15 killed and 32 wounded, while the Germans lost 954 killed, 80 wounded and 189 prisoners. Very few hits were scored on the German battlecruisers, a total of three each on the *Seydlitz* and *Derfflinger* and none on the *Moltke*, as against 16–11in or 12in hits on the *Lion* and six on the *Tiger*, and it was probably just as well for the British that the chase was broken off, as Hipper's three ships were superior to Moore's three.

Under von Pohl the High Seas Fleet showed little activity, but Scheer was more aggressive, and on 6 March 1916 the battlecruisers came as far as Brown Ridge, and the battleships to a position off the Texel. The presence of German battleships off the Dutch coast was not known to the Admiralty until 0700, 2½ hours before they turned back.

The bombardment of Lowestoft and Yarmouth on 25 April 1916 was intended as a demonstration in aid of the Irish rebellion, Hipper was ill and Rear Admiral Boedicker was to carry out the raid with the *Seydlitz, Lützow, Derfflinger, Moltke* and *von der Tann*, six light cruisers and two destroyer flotillas, while the rest of the High Seas Fleet, which included 17 dreadnoughts, was in support to the west of the Texel and about 70 miles from the English coast. The *Seydlitz* struck a mine on the afternoon of 24 April and was sent back, Boedicker transferring to the *Lützow*. It was clear to the Admiralty by 1900 on 24 April that the Germans were coming westward, but Jellicoe had only returned that morning from his latest sweep, and the Grand Fleet needed to refuel. The weather was good in the south but there was a heavy southerly gale in the north and it was doubtful if the destroyers could face it.

The Harwich Force of three light cruisers and eighteen destroyers sighted the battlecruisers shortly before 0400, but the latter first shelled Lowestoft and then Yarmouth and did not open fire on the Harwich Force until 0449. The light cruiser *Conquest* and one destroyer were damaged, but the British ships scattered, and Boedicker broke off the action after 7 minutes and started for home while Scheer turned back at 0520.

The various units of the Grand Fleet which included twenty-eight dreadnoughts and eight battlecruisers put to sea from Scapa, Cromarty and Rosyth between 2110 and 2300 on 24 April, and proceeded southward as fast as possible against the gale, but at 0500 the battlecruisers were still about 10 miles north of the latitude of Newcastle, and the leading battle squadron in the latitude of Aberdeen, and it was impossible to catch the Germans.

CHAPTER 2

Jutland preliminaries and forces engaged

THE NEXT MAJOR German operation led to the Battle of Jutland, and its origins lie in an attempt by Vice Admiral Scheer to force an action against part of the British Fleet under conditions of local German superiority. A second unrestricted submarine campaign against merchant shipping had begun on 1 March 1916 but was discontinued as a result of pressure by the United States on 25 April, and its cessation allowed the High Seas Fleet submarines to be included in the force available, as Scheer refused to sanction their use under prize law conditions.

As originally planned, the German battlecruisers, with the modern light cruisers of the 2nd Scouting Group and the three fastest destroyer flotillas, were to be off Sunderland at dawn and carry out a bombardment. This was expected to draw out a part of the British fleet, and to help the battlecruisers destroy it, the remainder of the High Seas Fleet comprising the dreadnought battleships with the rest of the light cruisers and destroyers, would be in a position between Flamborough Head and the S W Patch of the Dogger Bank. The High Seas Fleet submarines would be stationed off Scapa Flow, the Moray Firth and Humber and to the north of Terschelling, while the submarines of the Flanders flotilla would be off the Thames, and the channels to some bases would also be mined by minelaying submarines. All airships were to take part, to guard against a surprise from the Grand Fleet.

On 13 May it was discovered that the start of the operation would have to be postponed from 17 to 23 May on account of condenser troubles in some of the battleships of the 3rd Squadron, and changes were made in the disposition of the submarines. It was now decided that ten of the larger boats should first search for and attack warships in an area of the North Sea centred approximately in 57° 20′N, 3° 50′E, and extending from a position near the Norwegian coast to a line about 130 miles ENE of the Forth. This area, which was about 100 – 120 miles wide, was usually entered by the Grand Fleet when covering operations in Heligoland Bight or when expecting to counter a German advance. The submarines were to patrol this area from 17 or 18 to 22 May when it was intended that they were to take up their positions off the coast after the fleet operation had been completed so that they might attack British ships returning to harbour after the expected battle.

In the event, nine submarines arrived in the North Sea area between 17 and 19 May and duly left on the afternoon of 22 May, having seen nothing of importance. By 23 May they had all taken up their second positions with the *U43* and *U44* to the eastward of Pentland Firth, and the other seven off the Forth in order from north to south – the *U66, U63, U51, U32, U70, U24,* and *U52*.

The *U47* had meanwhile reconnoitred Sunderland on the night of 21/22 May and then proceeded to a position eastward of Peterhead, arriving on 24 May, while the *U67* and *U46* took up their positions to the north-westward of Terschelling on 22 May.

In addition three small submarines reached their stations on 23 May, the *UB21* and the *UB 22* a little to the northward of the Humber, and the *UB 27* off the Forth which she was to attempt to enter. The sectors allotted to the other boats off Scotland extended up to 80 or 90 miles from the entrances to the bases, and they were free to move within their sectors according to circumstances.

The start of the main operation against Sunderland was, however, postponed again, due to delay in completing the repairs to the *Seydlitz* which had struck a mine on 24 April when on the way to raid Lowestoft. Wilhelmshaven dockyard reported her ready for service on 22 May, but a flooding test on the night of 23/24 May showed that the broadside torpedo flat was not water-tight, and that its longitudinal and transverse bulkheads required further repairs. Scheer was unwilling to put to sea without this ship, and the earliest date she could be ready was 29 May. The submarines were due to leave their stations on the evening of 1 June except for the *U47* which was to stay another 24 hours, so that if they were to take part, only a few days remained.

Another difficulty now arose. It was considered essential that airships should take part in the Sunderland operation to guard against surprise by the whole Grand Fleet, but the weather was unsuitable for extended flights by airships, and showed little sign of improvement. Accordingly, on 28 May Scheer decided that if there was no change in the weather by 30 May, the Sunderland operation would be abandoned in favour of an advance to the Skagerrak for which airship scouting was less essential. At 1500 on 30 May it was reported that airship reconnaissance could not be counted on for the next two days, and the Sunderland operation was finally abandoned in favour of a sortie towards the Skagerrak. The pre-arranged signal '31 Gg.2490' announcing to all forces that the Skagerrak operation would begin on 31 May was made at 1540 and Bruges had already notified all submarines at sea at 1004 that the German fleet would be out on 31 May and 1 June.

Meanwhile the submarines stationed off the British bases had had an unprofitable wait, and had frequently to avoid patrols, particularly off the Forth and in the Pentland Firth. No capital ships had been sighted and only a single torpedo, which missed, had been fired up to 30 May. On that day the *U43* fired a torpedo at a number of minesweeping sloops to the eastward of the Pentland Firth, and the *U63* another at the destroyer *Trident*, attached to the Blyth submarine flotilla, off the Forth, but neither hit. By this time twelve of the fifteen boats were still on station. The *U66* which had been particularly harassed by patrols, changed her position on 30 May to one about 60 miles to the eastward of Peterhead, and on the same day *U46* had to return as her only periscope was unserviceable. On 24 May two torpedoes had been unsuccessfully fired at her by the *E23* which then surfaced and opened fire, but the gun (12pdr/8cwt) jammed after the first round, and the *U46* dived at once. Some hours later the *E37* sighted both the *U46* and *U67* but her torpedo also missed, and that evening the *E23* again fired two torpedoes at the *U46* without success. The *E23* had another chance at the *U46* on 28 May but both her torpedoes passed astern. The other submarine to leave her station was the *UB27*, which had had her port propeller put out of action in getting clear from nets in the Firth of Forth on 25 May.

Three minelaying submarines, the *U74, U72* and *U75* had been sent to lay 22 mines each in the Forth, Moray Firth and to the westward of the Orkneys, respectively. The *U74* left as early as 13 May but it is not certain if she laid her mines as she was sunk with all hands by four armed trawlers on 27 May. The *U72* had to return on 26 May with a leaky oil tank without laying her mines, but the *U75* was successful and laid her mines on 29 May in a channel used ordinarily by fleet auxiliaries and about 2 miles to the west of the Orkneys. It was in this minefield that the *Hampshire* was lost with Lord Kitchener on 5 June.

It was known in Britain that a considerable number of submarines had put to sea, but nothing definite had been discovered about their movements . At one time it was thought that some of them might be making for the White Sea to attack ships on the Archangel route. On 30 May, however, attacks were made off Scapa and off the Forth as noted above, and a submarine was sighted off Aberdeen, so that the presence of some of them near the British bases was certain. A major operation by the Grand Fleet had been planned to take place at the beginning of June, to try and bring at least part of the High Seas Fleet to action. Two light cruiser squadrons were to reach the Skaw by dawn on 2 June, and then sweep down the Kattegat to the Great Belt and the Sound. A battle squadron would be in support in the Skagerrak, with the rest of the battleships and the battlecruisers ready to attack any German heavy ships that put to sea. The *Abdiel* was to lay a minefield to the south-westward of the Vyl lightship, and the seaplane-carrier *Engadine*, escorted by light cruisers and destroyers, was to be ready to attack airships off Horns Reef. In addition three submarines would be stationed to the westward of the Vyl lightship and two more to the east of the Dogger Bank. This plan, which was bolder than any yet carried out by the Grand Fleet, was never put into operation as the Germans moved previously. On the morning of 29 May a signal from Scheer made the previous evening, and directing all forces in harbour to be ready from 0700 in accordance with orders for readiness of 30 March, was deciphered. At first it was thought that only a small sortie in support of returning airships was to be expected. Other intercepted signals indicated that some German operation was likely on 31 May–1 June, and soon after 1700 on 30 May it was known that an apparently important operational signal, '31 Gg.2490' had been sent to all sections of the High Seas Fleet, and though this could not be deciphered, it seemed that a major German movement might be about to take place. Accordingly at 1740 the Admiralty informed Jellicoe and Beatty that the Germans intended to carry out an operation on 31 May, apparently lasting two days, and ordered them to concentrate their forces as usual to the eastward of the 'Long Forties' (which extended about 100 miles east of Aberdeen) to be ready for eventualities.

Thus by 2230 on 30 May the Grand Fleet had put to sea from Scapa, Cromarty and Rosyth, 2½ hours before the High Seas Fleet battlecruisers left Schillig Roads. Under the German plan Hipper was to leave the Jade early on 31 May with the battlecruisers (1st Scouting Group), the light cruisers of the 2nd Scouting Group, the *Regensburg* (2nd Leader of Destroyer Forces) and the 2nd, 6th and 9th Destroyer Flotillas. He was to proceed northward out of sight of the Danish coast, and carry on cruiser and commerce warfare in and off the Skagerrak up to the Norwegian coast until the early morning of 1 June. The appearance of the German ships in this area would cause the British fleet to put to sea, and it was hoped that the submarines off the British bases would have opportunities of attacking. If Hipper met British forces in superior strength, he was to try and draw them towards the German battle fleet without counting on airship scouting. The battle fleet under Scheer, would comprise the dreadnoughts of the 1st and 3rd Squadrons, the light cruisers of the 4th Scouting Group, the *Hamburg* (Leader of Submarines), the *Rostock* (Leader of Destroyer Forces) and the 1st, 3rd, 5th and 7th Destroyer Flotillas. Scheer intended to arrive at a position 45 miles southward of Lindesnes at 0400 on 1 June when he would be joined by Hipper and further action would depend on circumstances.

At the last moment Scheer altered the plan to include the pre-dreadnoughts of the 2nd Squadron, and the battlefleet was now to put to sea directly after Hipper's forces, as the probable absence of air reconnaissance made it necessary to keep the German fleet as concentrated as possible. Accordingly the battlecruisers left Schillig Roads at 0100 on 31 May, and the dreadnought battleships followed between *c*0215 and 0230 while the 2nd Squadron in the Elbe left at 0145 and joined astern of the dreadnoughts three hours later.

The submarines of the Flanders Flotilla had begun to leave Zeebrugge at about 2300 on 30 May. The *UC10, UC6* and *UC1* (each twelve mines) were to mine the exits from Harwich and the Thames during the night of 31 May – 1 June. The *UB17, UB29, UB19, UB12, UB10* and *UB6* were to occupy patrol lines off the Suffolk coast from 0300 on 1 June until 1600 on 2 June, while the *UB18* and *UB23* would scout along the Dutch coast as far as Terschelling, and later join the patrol lines. The *UC1* developed an engine defect and had to remain in harbour.

On the British side, Jellicoe intended to be off the Skagerrak in 57° 45′N, 4° 15′E at 1400 31 May when he would be joined by the forces from Cromarty. He had with him the following squadrons from Scapa – the 1st and 4th Battle Squadrons, the 3rd Battle Cruiser Squadron, the 2nd Cruiser Squadron, the 4th Light Cruiser Squadron and also the 4th and 12th Destroyer Flotillas, and part of the 11th. The Cromarty ships comprised the 2nd Battle Squadron, the 1st Cruiser Squadron, and the greater part of the 11th Destroyer Flotilla. The forces from Rosyth under Beatty were to be in approximately 56° 40′N, 5° 00′E at 1400, that is, 69 miles bearing 161° from Jellicoe. Beatty had with him the 1st and 2nd Battle Cruiser Squadrons, the 5th Battle Squadron, the 1st, 2nd and 3rd Light Cruiser Squadrons, the 13th Destroyer Flotilla and parts of the 1st, 9th and 10th Flotillas. He also had the seaplane-carrier *Engadine*, while the minelayer *Abdiel* was with Jellicoe. If there was no further news by 1400 Beatty was to turn towards the battle fleet to get in visual communication with Jellicoe who would be steering for Horns Reef. The 3rd Battle Cruiser Squadron with two attached light cruisers, might be sent on to Beatty's 1400 position. This Squadron was part of the Battle Cruiser Fleet sent to Scapa for exercises, being temporarily replaced by the fast battleships of the 5th Battle Squadron which normally acted as a free wing squadron with the battlefleet.

The light cruisers and destroyers of the Harwich force, and the seven *King Edwards* of the 3rd Battle Squadron together with the 3rd Cruiser Squadron (two *Hampshire* class) which were based at Sheerness, were kept back until more was known of the German movements. Submarine patrols were maintained by the Harwich Flotilla off Terschelling and by the Blyth Flotilla between 54°00′ –54° 40′N and 2°30′–3°30′E. The *E16*, *E23*, *E37* and *H9* were on the Terschelling patrol from 24 to 30 May, and as previously noted the *E23* and *E37* unsuccessfully attacked German submarines. The *D3*, *H10* and *V1* sailed at noon on 1 June to replace them. Of the Blyth Flotilla the *G3* and *G4* were on patrol from 24 to 28 May, and were then relieved by the *G6* and *E43*, while the *G1* left Blyth on 2 June to replace the *G6*. In addition to these regular patrols, the *E31*, *E53* and *D6*, accompanied by the *Lurcher*, left Harwich on the evening of 30 May for positions to the east of Southwold, about halfway to the Dutch coast. The three submarines returned on 1 June, and the only incident of note was that the *E53* collided with the *Lurcher*, and although little damaged herself, holed the destroyer badly enough for the *Firedrake* to replace her.

The *E55*, *E26* and *D1* also left Harwich on the evening of 30 May for positions off the Vyl light, while the *G2*, *G3*, *G4* and *G5* accompanied by the *Talisman*, left Blyth at noon 31 May for a position off the south east side of the Dogger Bank in 54° 30′N, 4°E. The *G10* and *E30* of the Blyth Flotilla were off southern Norway from 28 May to 31 May and 1 June, respectively, in the hope of attacking German submarines thought to frequent that area. There were no British submarines in the Kattegat between 28 May when the *G1* left and 7 June.

On paper the Grand Fleet had a very marked superiority over the High Seas Fleet. The battleships present, in order as deployed, were:

2ND BS: 1ST DIVISION – *King George V* (Vice Admiral Sir Martyn Jerram) *Ajax, Centurion, Erin*

2ND DIVISION: – *Orion* (Rear Admiral Leveson). *Monarch, Conqueror, Thunderer*

4TH BS: 3RD DIVISION – *Iron Duke* (Admiral Sir John Jellicoe), *Royal Oak, Superb* (Rear Admiral Duff), *Canada*

4TH DIVISION – *Benbow* (Vice Admiral Sir Doveton Sturdee) *Bellerophon, Temeraire, Vanguard*

1ST BS: 5TH DIVISION – *Colossus* (Rear Admiral Gaunt), *Collingwood, Neptune, St Vincent*

6TH DIVISION – *Marlborough* (Vice Admiral Sir Cecil Burney) *Revenge, Hercules, Agincourt*

5TH BS: *Barham* (rear Admiral Evan-Thomas), *Vsaliant, Warspite*, Malaya

3RD SQ: 5TH DIVISION – *König* (Rear Admiral Behncke), *Grosser Kurfürst, Markgraf, Kronprinz*

6TH DIVISION – *Kaiser* (Rear Admiral Nordmann), *Prinzregent Luitpold, Kaiserin*

1ST SQ: 1ST DIVISION(including Fleet Flagship) – *Friederich der Grosse* (Vice Admiral Scheer), *Ostfriesland* (Vice Admiral Schmidt), *Thüringen, Helgoland, Oldenburg*

2ND DIVISION – *Posen* (Rear Admiral Engelhardt), *Rheinland, Nassau, Westfalen*

2ND SQ: 3RD DIVISION – *Deutschland* (Rear Admiral Mauve), *Pommern, Schlesien*

4TH DIVISION – *Schleswig-Holstein, Hessen, Hannover*, (Rear Admiral Baron von Dalwigk zu Lichtenfels)

The *Hannover* led this Division initially, but took station at the rear at 1450 31 May, so that there would be a flagship at each end of the battle line.

The battlecruisers were:

1ST BCS: *Lion* (Vice Admiral Sir David Beatty), *Princess Royal* (Rear Admiral Brock), *Queen Mary, Tiger*

2ND BCS: *New Zealand*, (Rear Admiral Pakenham), *Indefatigable*

3RD BCS: *Invincible* (Rear Admiral The Hon H L A Hood), *Inflexible, Indomitable*

1ST SG: – *Lützow* (Vice Admiral Hipper), *Derfflinger, Seydlitz, Moltke, Von der Tann.*

As the German 2nd Squadron was of little value and would have been better left behind, the British numerical superiority in battleships was virtually 28 to 16, in battlecruisers 9 to 5. The one weakness was that if (as actually occurred) Beatty engaged Hipper in the absence of the 3rd BCS, and in circumstances where the 5th BS was not able to come into action immediately, his numerical superiority would be only six to five and in fighting power he would be appreciably inferior, though this was not realised in 1916.

Three of the most powerful British ships were absent; the *Royal Sovereign* of the 1st BS which had joined the fleet on 25 May, too recently to be ready for battle, the *Queen Elizabeth* of the 5th BS and the *Emperor of India* of the 4th BS, which were both in dockyard hands. The *Australia* of the 2nd BCS, was also absent as a result of a collision with the *New Zealand* in thick fog on 22 April, while the *Dreadnought* was refitting and on completion would join the 3rd BS, ceasing to belong to the Grand Fleet. The German also lacked two important ships of the 3rd Squadron; the *König Albert* which had condenser trouble, and the new *Bayern* which had been commissioned on 18 March, but was still working-up in the Baltic, and only available in the event of a direct attack on the German coast. It was fortunate for the British that the *Bayern* was not ready for battle, as her 15in shells could have had a disastrous effect. The *Preussen* of the 2nd Squadron was also absent on duty as guard-ship in the Sound at the entrance to the Baltic.

Details of the battleships and battlecruisers engaged in the battle are given in the tables below.

German dreadnoughts and battlecruisers all carried a secondary armament of 5.9in guns while the pre-dreadnoughts had 14–6.7in. The *Royal Oak, Barham* and *Iron Duke* classes the *Tiger, Erin, Canada* and *Agincourt* had 6in, but other British dreadnoughts and battlecruisers had only 4in.

The thickness of the belt armour is taken between end barbettes, and from water-line to main deck, while that of the upper belt is taken from main to upper deck. In all German and some British ships, the lower edge of the belt, well below the water-line at fighting draught, was reduced in thickness, and the belt was always thinned forward and aft, the maximum here in any of the dreadnoughts being 8in, but 6in – 4in was more usual, while in some British ships the thickness aft did not exceed 2½in, and the *Invincible* class had no side armour abaft the sternmost barbette. The British 15in ships were much over their designed displacement so that in the *Royal Oaks* at a fighting draught of 32ft 6in, the 13in belt extended from 9ft below to 3ft 9in above water, while in the *Barhams* at 32ft 9in, the top of the 13in armour was only 6in

Battleships

	Displacement (tons of 2240lb)	Main Armament	Belt Armour	Upper Belt	Barbettes (max)	Turret Faces	Turret Crowns	Speed (kts)
Royal Oak, Revenge	28,000	8-15in	13in	6in (i)	10in	13in	4¼(iv)	22
Barham, Valiant, Warspite, Malaya	29,150	8-15in	13in-6in	6in	10in	13in	5in Malaya 4¼in (iv)	23½-24
Canada	28,600	10-14in	9in-7in	4½in	10in	10in	4in-3in	23-23½
Agincourt	28,840	14-12in	9in-6in	6in (ii)	9in	12in	3in-2in	22
Erin	22,780	10-13.5in	12in-9in	8in	10in	11in	4in-3in	21
Iron Duke, Benbow, Marlborough	25,820	10-13.5in	12in-9in	8in	10in	11in	4in-3in	21
King George V Ajax, Centurion	23,000	10-13.5in	12in-9in	8in	10in	11in	4in-3in	21
Orion, Monarch, Conqueror, Thunderer	22,200	10-13.5in	12in-9in	8in	10in	11in	4in-3in	21
Colossus, Hercules	20,225	10-12in	11in-8in	nil	11in, 10in	11in	4in-3in	21
Neptune	19,680	10-12in	10-8in	nil	10in, 9in	11in	4in-3in	21
St. Vincent, Collingwood, Vanguard	19,560	10-12in	10-8in	nil	10in, 9in	11in	4in	21
Bellerophon, Superb, Temeraire	18,800	10-12in	10in-8in	nil	10in, 9in	11in	3in	20½-21
König, Grosser Kurfürst, Markgraf, Kronprinz	25,390	10-12in	14in	8in	12in	12in	4.3-3.15in	22
Kaiser, Kaiserin, Prinzregent Luitpold, Friedrich der Grosse	24,330	10-12in	14in	8in	12in	12in	4.3-3.15in Prinzregent Luitpold	21½ 21
Ostfriesland, Thüringen, Helgoland, Oldenburg	22,440	12-12in	12in-6¾in	(iii)	12in-10¾in	12in	4in-2¾in	20½-21
Posen, Rheinland, Nassau, Westfalen	18,570	12-11in	12-6.3in	(iii)	11in, 10in	11in	3½-2.4in	19½-20
Pre-dreadnoughts of 2nd Squadron.	13,000	4-11in	9½-5½in	(iii)	11in, 10in	11in	2in	18

(i) Did not extend to aftermost barbette.
(ii) Did not extend to foremost or aftermost barbette.
(iii) These ships had a main deck battery, the armour being: *Ostfriesland* class 6¾in, *Nassau* class 6.3in, German pre-dreadnoughts 6¾in-6in.
(iv) The turret crowns in the *Royal Oak* class, and in the *Malaya*, were of a tougher steel than in the other *Barhams*.

	Displacement (tons of 2240lb)	Main Armament	Belt Armour	Upper Belt	Barbettes (max)	Turret Faces	Turret Crowns	Speed (kts)
Tiger	28,430	8-13.5in	9in-5in	6in-5in	9in	9in	3¼-2½in	28½
Queen Mary	26,770	8-13.5in	9in-5in	6in-5in	9in	9in	3¼-2½in	27½
Lion, Princess Royal	26,270	8-13.5in	9in-5in	6in-5in	9in	9in	3¼-2½in	27-27½
New Zealand	18,500	8-12in	6in-5in	nil	7in	7in	3in	25½-26
Indefatigable	18,470	8-12in	6in-4in	nil	7in	7in	3in	25½
Invincible, Inflexible Indomitable	17,340	8-12in	6in	nil	7in	7in	3in	25-25½
Lutzow, Derfflinger	26,250	8-12in	12in	12-9in	10¼in	10¾in	4.3-3.15in	27
Seydlitz	24,600	10-11in	12in	12-9in	9in	10in	4-2¾in	26½
Moltke	22,620	10-11in	10¾in	8in	9in, 8in	9in	3½-2.4in	26½
von der Tann	19,070	8-11in	10-6in	(i)	9in, 8in	9in	3½-2.4in	26

(i) This ship had a main deck battery, the armour being 6in, but not extending to end barbettes.
      The displacements quoted are 'actual normal for British ships as given in official lists, and designed for German. Displacements when putting to sea, were greater, in most ships by about 8-15%.

above water and the belt then tapered to 6in at 5ft above water. In the *König* class at 29ft 6in the 14in belt extended to 4ft above water, while in the *Seydlitz* at 30ft draught the top of the 12in armour was 18in above water, and the side armour then tapered to 9in at 8ft 3in above water.

Except where noted above as being on the main deck, most or all of the secondary battery of 5.9in or 6in guns was on the upper deck and protected by armour, usually 6in-6¾in. 4in guns were carried higher, and unarmoured in most ships.

In all ships barbette armour was reduced, sometimes drastically, whenever it was behind other armour.

With a few exceptions, the armour deck was from 1in to 2in thick amidships and the upper protective deck from ¾in to 2in in the ships of both fleets, though occasionally thickened locally, and in the case of the armour deck, often thicker at the ends of the ship, particularly over the steering gear. The most important exceptions were in the *Nassau* and *Ostfriesland* classes, and the German pre-dreadnoughts where the armour deck slope amidships was from 2.3in to 3in, being thickest in the oldest pre-dreadnoughts, and in the *Invincible* class and the *Indefatigable*, where there was no continuous upper protective deck.

19

The foregoing data shows that the dreadnoughts of the two fleets were well matched individually, the heavier British guns being compensated by thicker German armour, though in battlecruisers the German ships had the advantage. The British ships suffered from inferior armour-piercing shells, and from propellant charges which were very dangerous if an ammunition fire occurred, and their fighting value was thus reduced. The German dreadnoughts and battlecruisers were also superior in protection against mines and torpedoes, though the pre-dreadnoughts were very ill protected in this respect.

In German dreadnoughts and battlecruisers, the main feature of this protection was a longitudinal torpedo bulkhead extending between end barbettes and from 1in to 2in thick (to 0.8in in *Nassau* class), while the detailed construction below water was determined in a long series of trials. Similar bulkheads were fitted in the British 15in battleships, but very few trials had been carried out to determine the best construction. The *Erin, Neptune* and the *St Vincent* and *Bellerophon* classes had 1in–2in bulkheads between end barbettes, thickened to 3in by the wing turrets of the 12in ships, but the bulkheads were so far inboard by the forward and after turrets that they only served here as magazine screens. Other British dreadnoughts and battlecruisers had 1in to 3in discontinuous screen bulkheads protecting the magazines, and in the *Iron Duke* and *King George V* classes the middle engine room in addition, though not the wing engine rooms.

German dreadnoughts and battlecruisers were more subdivided below the armour deck, and in this part of the ship damage control and pumping arrangements were more complete, though these did not always work as intended. The metacentric height was also greater, ranging from *c*7ft to 10ft, while 7ft was about the maximum in British ships, and 5ft–6ft the usual figure at fighting draught, though in the 12in battlecruisers, the *Agincourt* and the *Royal Oak*s, the metacentric height was nearer 4ft at this loading, and in the latter it fell to 2.8ft at 28,000 tons.

The German dreadnoughts and battlecruisers all had small tube Schulz-Thornycroft boilers, while the British had large tube Babcock or Yarrow, and this saved a considerable amount of space and weight in German ships, as did the more compact engine rooms and lighter turbines, so that their battlecruisers had an appreciable advantage in fighting power for a given displacement over their British contemporaries.

The British were, however, further advanced in the use of oil fuel, the *Royal Oak* and *Barham* classes burnt oil only, and the other dreadnoughts and battlecruisers coal and oil, while the German ships were coal-fired, with a small amount of tar oil also carried, except in the *König* and *Derfflinger* classes where three or four of the boilers burnt oil only.

There was no previous evidence on which to compare the resistance of the rival dreadnoughts to heavy gunfire, but some was available from the Dogger Bank battle for the battlecruisers.

In this action three hits had been made on the German battlecruisers' armour by 13.5in shells at *c*16,500–18,000yds. Two on 12in belt-armour had been resisted with up to 4in displacement while the third shell struck the 9in armour of *Seydlitz's* aftermost barbette at 33° to the normal. The shell burst in holing the armour, and no shell splinters entered, but armour fragments did so, and a very serious ammunition fire occurred, which put two turrets out of action, and is disscussed with other such fires on a later page.

British 9in side armour had been hit three times by 11in or 12in shells at *c*17,000–18,000yds, without much effect, but a 12in on *Lion* at *c*18,000yds displaced the 9in armour by up to 3ft with great damage to the hull plating, opened the port feed tank to the sea, and put the port engine out of action. The discharge pipe from the air pumps to the feed tank was badly distorted but fortunately held, as there was no stop valve between this pipe and the feed tank, and if it had failed, the port engine room would have flooded, and the ship would have probably been lost.

An 11in shell burst on the *Lion's* 8in barbette armour with little damage, but 5–11in struck *Lion's* 5–7in armour at 16–18,000yds and of these, four had pierced causing much damage, while the other had driven in 6in armour by up to 2½ft. The effect of the six shells noted above as causing serious damage to the *Lion*, was sufficient to put the ship out of action, and as salting of the boilers eventually stopped the starboard engine. She had to be towed home.

An 11in on *Tiger's* 3¼in turret crown jammed 'Q' turret and put it out of action, but most of the shell burst had been kept out.

The evidence on the resistance of capital ships to underwater explosions, was not favourable to the British. The *Moltke* had been hit by an 18in torpedo from the *E1*, but far forward so that the effect was small. The *Seydlitz* had struck a British mine (300lb wet gun-cotton) and the *Goeben* two Russian (220lb TNT) within 2 minutes, all in important positions, but without crippling damage.

The *Inflexible*, withstood a Carbonit mine (176lb TNT) as well as could be expected, but the *Audacious* of the *King George V* class capsized 12 hours after striking a 180lb wet gun-cotton mine.

Water-tight integrity and damage control were poor but no such ship should ever have been sunk by so small a mine.

The British had many more cruisers and light cruisers present, with eight armoured cruisers and twenty-six light cruisers as against eleven light cruisers only.

1ST CS: *Defence* (Rear Admiral Sir Robert Arbuthnot) *Warrior, Duke of Edinburgh, Black Prince*

2ND CS: *Minotaur* (Rear Admiral Heath), *Hampshire, Cochrane, Shannon*

1ST LCS: *Galatea* (Commodore Alexander-Sinclair), *Phaeton, Inconstant, Cordelia*

2ND LCS: *Southampton* (Commodore Goodenough), *Birmingham, Nottingham, Dublin*

3RD LCS: *Falmouth* (Rear Admiral Napier), *Yarmouth, Birkenhead, Gloucester*

4TH LCS: *Calliope* (Commodore Le Mesurier), *Constance, Comus, Caroline, Royalist*

ATTACHED TO 3RD BCS: *Chester* (3rd LCS), *Canterbury* (From 5th LCS, Harwich).

WITH 1ST DESTROYER FLOTILLA: *Fearless*

WITH 11TH DESTROYER FLOTILLA: *Castor* (Commodore Hawksley (Commodore F))

WITH 13TH DESTROYER FLOTILLA: *Champion*

ATTACHED TO BATTLE SQUADRONS: *Active* (to Fleet Flagship), *Bellona* (1st BS), *Boadicea* (2nd BS), *Blanche* (4th BS)

2ND SG: *Frankfurt* (Rear Admiral Boedicker), *Pillau, Elbing, Wiesbaden*

4TH SG: *Stettin* (Commodore von Reuter), *München, Frauenlob, Stuttgart*, – attached *Hamburg* (Captain Bauer, Leader of Submarines)

LEADER OF DESTROYERS: *Rostock* (Commodore Michelsen).

2ND LEADER OF DESTROYERS: *Regensburg* (Commodore Heinrich).

The British armoured cruisers were not suitable for fleet work. They were little faster than the dreadnoughts and made huge quantities of funnel smoke at full speed. They were also extremely vulnerable to the gunfire of capital ships. The four light cruisers attached to the Battle Squadrons whose principal duty in action was to repeat visual signals, and also the *Fearless*, were weakly armed with 4in guns only, and the latter was too slow to be satisfactory as a flotilla cruiser.

These shortcomings were less serious than those in the German light cruisers. All five ships of the 4th Scouting Group were slow by 1916 standards and they, as well as the *Rostock* and *Regensburg*, only mounted 4.1in guns. Of other modern German light cruisers, the *Graudenz* and *Stralsund* were both in dockyard hands repairing damage from a mine and rearming with 5.9in guns, respectively, and the *Strassburg, Kolberg* and *Augsburg* were in the Baltic. The new minelaying light cruiser *Brummer* was ready for service at the end of May, but did not take part in the battle. The older *Berlin* of the 4th SG was also in dockyard hands.

Of Grand Fleet cruisers, the *Achilles* was refitting, and the *Donegal* had been detached for intercepting shipping off the Norwegian coast. Both belonged to the 2nd CS. The *Blonde* attached to the 4th BS was refitting, and the *Chatham* which was due to join the 3rd LCS, had struck a mine on 26 May and was under repair.

Data for the cruisers which took part in the battle are given in the table below.

In the armoured cruisers the 9.2in and 7.5in guns were in turrets with 8in or 7½in max armour, and the 6in guns were protected by 6in battery or casemate armour, but in the light cruisers the open-back shields did not exceed 3in max thickness in any ship. The twelve *Carolines* and *Galateas* and the *Chester* burnt oil fuel only.

The newer light cruisers of both fleets had proved to be tough ships for their size, and had a good chance of surviving a mine or torpedo.

In destroyers the British superiority was less marked, and the flotillas were being re-organised, with many new destroyers recently joined, and further exercising was needed. The allocation of destroyers to Beatty's force was unfortunate, as there were twenty-seven as against thirty with Hipper, and of the twenty-seven, thirteen were too slow for satisfactory work with the battlecruisers.

Attached to Fleet Flagship: *Oak*

1ST FLOTILLA (Part): Nine 'I' class (*Acheron, Ariel, Attack, Hydra, Badger, Goshawk, Defender, Lizard, Lapwing*).

4TH FLOTILLA: *Tipperary, Broke:* one 'Admiralty M' class (*Ophelia*): sixteen 'K' class (*Achates, Porpoise, Spitfire, Unity, Garland, Ambuscade, Ardent, Fortune, Sparrowhawk, Contest, Shark, Acasta, Christopher, Owl, Hardy, Midge*).

9TH FLOTILLA (Part): Four 'L' class (*Lydiard, Liberty, Landrail, Laurel*).

10TH FLOTILLA (Part): Two 'Admiralty M' class (*Moorsom, Morris*); two *Talisman* class (*Turbulent, Termagant*).

11TH FLOTILLA: *Kempenfelt:* 11 'Admiralty M' class (*Ossory, Mystic, Magic, Mandate, Minion, Martial, Milbrook, Marne, Manners, Michael, Mons*); Three 'Yarrow M' class (*Morning Star, Mounsey, Moon*).

Armoured Cruisers

	Normal Displacement (tons of 2240lb)	Armament	Maximum Side Armour	Speed (Kts)
Defence, Minotaur, Shannon	14,600	4-9.2in 10-7.5in	6in	22-22½
Warrior, Cochrane	13,280	6-9.2in 4-7.5in	6in	22-22½
Duke of Edinburgh[1]	12,600	6-9.2in	6in	22-22½
Black Prince		10-6in (i)	6in	22-22½
Hampshire	10,100	4-7.5in, 6-6in	6in	22½

Light Cruisers

	Normal Displacement (tons of 2240lb)	Armament	Maximum Side Armour	Speed (Kts)
Canterbury, Castor, Constance, Calliope, Champion, Caroline, Comus, Cordelia	3900/3970	2-6in, 8-4in	3in Champion	27½-28 28½
Galatea, Phaeton, Inconstant, Royalist	3720	2-6in, 6-4in	3in	27½-28
Chester	5190	10-5.5in	3in	26½
Birkenhead	5240	10-5.5in	3in	25
Birmingham, Nottingham	5280	9-6in	3in	25½
Southampton, Dublin	5290	8-6in	3in	25½-26
Falmouth, Yarmouth	5090	8-6in	Nil	25½
Gloucester	4850	2-6in, 10-4in	Nil	25½
Active, Fearless, Blanche Boadicea, Bellona	3275/3440	10-4in	Nil	25
Frankfurt, Wiesbaden	5100	8-5.9in	2.4in	27-27½
Pillau, Elbing	4320	8-5.9in	Nil	27-27½
Regensburg	4830	12.4.1in	2.4in	27
Rostock	4820	12-4.1in	2.4in	27
Stettin	3430	10-4.1in	Nil	24-24½
Stuttgart	3420	10-4.1in	Nil	23
Hamburg, München	3230	10-4.1in	Nil	22
Frauenlob	2660	10-4.1in	Nil	21

(i) *Duke of Edinburgh* 2-6in removed.

12TH FLOTILLA: *Faulknor, Marksman:* fourteen 'Admiralty M' class. (*Obedient, Maenad, Opal, Mary Rose, Marvel, Menace, Nessus, Narwhal, Mindful, Onslaught, Munster, Nonsuch, Noble, Mischief.*)

13TH FLOTILLA: Nine 'Admiralty M' class (*Nestor, Nomad, Narborough, Obdurate, Petard, Pelican, Onslow, Moresby, Nicator*); one 'Yarrow M' class (*Nerissa*).

Of the 11th Flotilla, the last four named 'Admiralty M's came from Scapa with the light cruiser *Castor*, and the others from Cromarty. The *Moon* had been on patrol, and did not join until about 1345 31 May. The destroyers of the 9th and 10th Flotillas and the *Defender* of the 1st Flotilla were normally part of the Harwich force. The *Tipperary, Broke, Kempenfelt, Faulknor* and *Marksman* were classed as Flotilla Leaders. None of the Grand Fleet Flotillas was at full strength, the following being in dockyard hands, or remaining in harbour.

Part of the 1st Flotilla assigned to Grand Fleet: *Botha* (Leader) and four 'I' class.
4th Flotilla: three 'K' class.
11th Flotilla: one 'Admiralty M' class, one 'Yarrow M' class.
12th Flotilla: two 'Admiralty M' class.
13th Flotilla: six 'Admiralty M' class (of which four had been completed on 29/31 May 1916).

Units of the German 2nd Flotilla, were at least as powerful as flotilla-leaders, but the boats of the 5th and 7th Flotillas were small by British standards.

1st Flotilla: 1st ½ Flotilla only: *G39, G40,* .
2nd Flotilla: *B98* 3rd ½ Flotilla - *G101, G102, B112, B97.*
4th ½ Flotilla - *B109, B110, B111, G103, G104.*
3rd Flotilla: *S53* 5th ½ Flotilla - *V71, V73, G88.*
6th ½ Flotilla - *S54, V48, G42.*
5th Flotilla: *G11* 9th ½ Flotilla - *V2, V4, V6, V1, V3.*
10th ½ Flotilla - *G8, G7, V5, G9, G10.*
6th Flotilla: *G41* 11th ½ Flotilla - *V44, G87, G86.*
12th ½ Flotilla - *V69, V45, V46, S50, G37.*
7th Flotilla: *S24* 13th ½ Flotilla - *S15, S17, S20, S16, S18.*
14th ½ Flotilla - *S19, S23, V189.*
(*V186* was sent back to Heligoland at 0715 31 May with a leaky condenser).
9th Flotilla: *V28* 17th ½ Flotilla - *V27, V26, S36, S51, S52.*
18th ½ Flotilla - *V30, S34, S33, V29, S35.*

The following modern destroyers belonging to the High Seas Fleet flotillas were in dockyard hands or otherwise absent:

3rd Flotilla: *V74, G85, V70, S55.*
6th Flotilla: *S49, V43.*

In addition one older boat was absent from the 7th Flotilla, as well seven as others forming the balance of the 1st Flotilla.

Details of the various classes of destroyers present in the battle are given in the table below.

The total number of torpedo tubes in the British destroyers was 260–21in as against 326–19.7in in the German but the British 'I' and 'K' class destroyers each carried a spare torpedo so that the actual German advantage was less than that indicated by the number of tubes. Omitting 18in tubes which were of little importance, the British battleships and battlecruisers had a total of 84–21in TT compared to 4–23.6in and 76–19.7in, but for the light cruisers, which had a better chance of using their torpedoes effectively, the figures were 60–21in and 16–19.7in. The number of torpedoes per capital ship was in many instances as high as 16, while in light cruisers the outfit of torpedoes varied from 5 to 10. The total number of 21in torpedoes carried by British capital ships at Jutland was 364, and by British light cruisers 180.

Although the use of mines by the German fleet was viewed with apprehension by the British, the only ship so armed was the *Abdiel*, attached to Jellicoe's flagship. She was a flotilla leader of the *Marksman* class, and carried 80 mines, her torpedo tubes and two––4in guns being removed.

The seaplane-carrier *Engadine* (2550 tons 22kts), a converted cross-channel steamer, was with Beatty's force, but the much larger *Campania* (20,570 tons 21kts) missed the signal to put to sea from Scapa and left nearly two hours late. She was ordered back though she might in fact have caught up before the battle. At that time the *Campania* carried seven Sopwith single-seater and three Short two-seater seaplanes as well as a Caquot kite-balloon, and her orders, dated 15 May, emphasised the use of this last item for short range reconnaissance and observation of enemy movements, with spotting as a secondary function, while her seaplanes would search for hostile submarines or minelayers near the battle area and attack airships. It is impossible to say if her kite-balloon would have provided information of value in the visibility conditions of the battle fleet action, and under the above orders, all her seaplanes could have done would have been to attack an

Destroyers

	Normal Displacement (tons of 2240 lb)	Guns	Torpedo Tubes	Speed (kts)
Kempenfelt, Marksman	1605	4–4in	4–21in	34
Tipperary, Broke, Faulknor (i)	1694/1737	6–4in	4–21in	31–32
Talisman class	1080/1098	5–4in	4–21in	32
Yarrow M class	883/898	3–4in	4–21in	35
Admiralty M class	997/1042	3–4in	4–21in	34
L class	965/1000	3–4in	4–21in	29
K class	898/1000	3–4in	2–21in	29–32
I class	745/799	2–4in, 2–12pdr	2–21in	27–30
Oak	765	2–4in, 2–12pdr	2–21in	32
B97, B98, B109—112 (ii)	1352	4–4.1in	6–19.7in	35½
G101—104 (ii)	1245	4–4.1in	6–19.7in	32
G41, G42, G86—88	945	3–3.5in	6–19.7in	33½
V48, S53, S54, V69, V71, V73	904–909	3–3.5in	6–19.7in	33½–34
V44—46	839	3–3.5in	6–19.7in	34½
V26—30, S32—36, G37—40, S50—52	789/809	3–3.5in	6–19.7in	33½–34
V1—6, G7—11, S15—20 S23, S24	559/564	2–3.5in	4–19.7in	32–32½
V189	655	2–3.5in	4–19.7in	32

(i) These ships were taken over and not designed for Britain.
(ii) *B97, B98, G101—104* taken over and not designed for Germany. *B109—112* were built to use turbines ordered by Russia.

The above destroyers burnt oil fuel only, except for the *Tipperary* class and the small German destroyers of the 5th and 7th Flotillas.

The *G101—104* were only capable of about 27kts with full fuel, and in consequence at times operated separately from the 'B' destroyers of the 2nd Flotilla. The *G42* was limited to 25kts during the battle from trouble with newly fitted feed pumps, and it may be noted that some and probably all of the small destroyers of the 5th and 7th Flotillas had 15-20 tons coal stowed on deck.

airship on 1 June. The *Campania*'s action station was about one mile on the disengaged side of the battle line, abeam of the ship three ahead of the *Iron Duke*.

The German submarines did not fulfil expectations. Only four boats received the warning signal initially: the *U67* off Terschelling, the *UB22* off the Humber, and the *U70* and *U32* off the Forth. Of these only the *U32* sighted any units of the British fleet. At about 0350 31 May, she attacked the *Galatea* and *Phaeton* and fired two torpedoes at about 1000yds at the former without success, but had to go to 50ft in a hurry to avoid being rammed by the *Phaeton*. On returning to periscope depth she could just make out the 2nd BCS and its destroyer screen, and reported them as two dreadnoughts, two cruisers and several destroyers steering 122°, in a wireless signal which was received by Wilhelmshaven 3rd Entrance, controlling W/T traffic in the German Bight at 0537. Meanwhile the *U66*, about 60 miles to the eastward of Peterhead received a later transmission of the warning signal at 0100 31 May, and at 0500 sighted an armoured cruiser of the 1st Cruiser Squadron. Shortly afterwards the *Boadicea*, then the 11th Destroyer Flotilla, and finally the eight battleships of the 2nd Battle Squadron came into view. The *U66*, however, was forced to go deep by the near approach of a destroyer, and though not detected, was unable to attack as she had dived under the escort on an opposite course. Her wireless signal reporting eight dreadnoughts with light cruisers and destroyers, steering 32°, was received by Wilhelmshaven 3rd Entrance at 0648.

Just previously, information obtained from intercepted signals by the deciphering office at Neumünster had been received and this stated that two large warships or squadrons, with destroyers, had left Scapa, but in spite of these three reports it was concluded that a connection between the forces sighted and the German fleet's movements was improbable. No further sightings of the British forces on their outward passage were made by German submarines, though a periscope was reported by the *Yarmouth* at 0819 and another by the *Turbulent* at 0908 but both were imaginary. The *Yarmouth*'s report caused Beatty to order a 90° turn to port, and it was *c*20 minutes before the previous course was resumed.

The weather was unsuitable for airships early on 31 May, and it was not until about 1130 that the *L9*, *L14*, *L16*, *L21*, and *L23* went up. They were to reconnoitre a sector between the Skagerrak and a position 80 miles eastward of Flamborough Head, but it was soon found that the weather was very hazy and the cloud base at 1000ft. By 1430 all were still far short of their positions and of those of the British fleet. A further indication of British activity was received by Wilhelmshaven 3rd Entrance at 1155 from Neumünster, in the form of an intercepted weather report for the Firth of Forth, of a type only put out as a rule when the fleet was at sea.

On the British side, reliable information as to the extent of the German operation was lacking. A signal timed at 1741 on 30 May to the effect that the head of the 3rd Squadron would pass the Jade war lightship 'A' at 0330, and that the 2nd Squadron would take part in the operation from the beginning and join up astern of the 1st Squadron, was intercepted but a new cipher, restricted to the surface vessels and airships taking part in the operation and to the principal shore wireless stations, had been used and it was not deciphered until 1840 on 31 May. This signal also stated that Wilhelmshaven 3rd Entrance would control wireless traffic in the German Bight. When so doing Scheer's harbour call-sign 'dk' would be used, and another call-sign 'rä' would be adopted by the fleet flagship at sea. Although there was a long delay in deciphering the above signal, two others that were deciphered on the evening of 30 May, revealed that the 2nd Squadron were putting to sea, and that Scheer's call-sign was being transferred at 2100 30 May. The transfer of Scheer's call-sign when the fleet was about to leave harbour, was well known to the British deciphering experts in Admiralty Room 40, but there was a very serious lack of contact with the Operations Division and, when the Director of Operations asked Room 40 on the morning of 31 May where the directional stations placed 'dk', he was told 'in the Jade' and made no further enquiries. Thus in ignorance that 'dk' was always 'in the Jade', the Admiralty sent a signal to Jellicoe timed at 1230 31 May, stating that there was no definite news of the enemy, and though it had been thought that the High Seas Fleet had sailed, directional wireless placed Scheer's flagship in the Jade at 1110 the delay being apparently due to inability to carry out air reconnaissance.

CHAPTER 3

First contact between the fleets

MEANWHILE, HIPPER'S AND Beatty's forces were approaching, unaware of each other. The 1st Scouting Group was in line ahead steering 347° at 16kts with the 9th Flotilla as submarine screen, and the light cruisers and other destroyers, disposed about 8 miles ahead on an arc of a circle bearing 302° to 32° from the *Lützow*. At 1415 the latter was about 65 miles westward of Lodbjerg, with the battle fleet about 50 miles astern steering 347° at 14kts.

Beatty's forces had been steaming at 19 or 19½kts course 86°, zig-zagging with speed of advance about 18kts. The 1st and 2nd BCS and the 5th BS were each in line ahead with the 2nd BCS 3 miles bearing 32° from the *Lion*, and the 5th BS 5 miles 302°. The *Champion*, with the 13th Flotilla and the *Turbulent* and *Termagant*, formed a submarine screen to the 1st BCS, the other six destroyers of the 9th and 10th Flotillas similarly screened the 2nd BCS, and the *Fearless* and 1st Flotilla the 5th BS. The three light cruiser squadrons were spread over 25 miles on a line running 32°–212° with the centre of the screen 8 miles bearing 88° from the *Lion*, except the *Yarmouth* acting as linking ship. At 1330 Beatty altered the position of his various units in preparation for the turn northward to join Jellicoe. The 2nd BCS was now to be 3 miles bearing 55° from the *Lion*, and the 5th BS 5 miles 325°, while the centre of the light cruiser screen was to be 8 miles 145°, and it was to spread on a line 55°–235°. Beatty was late in reaching his 1400 position and was about 13 miles short of it. At 1415 he turned to 358° to join the battle fleet. The 1st Scouting Group was now about 45 miles to the eastward of the 1st BCS, and 16 miles separated the nearest ships of the light cruiser screens.

The 2nd BS from Cromarty had met Jellicoe at 1115 while the 1st

CS had joined the cruiser line 2 hours previously, but the fleet was late in arriving at the 1400 rendezvous and, according to her reckoning, the *Iron Duke* was 19½ miles away though her actual position was 4 miles further on, in 57° 54½'N, 3° 52'E. The battle fleet's course was 117°, zig-zagging with a speed of advance of 14kts.

Contact between the rival fleets was brought about by the chance presence of a Danish tramp steamer, the *N J Fjord*. At about 1400 she was sighted to the westward by the *Elbing*, and the *B109* and *B110* were sent to examine her. While laying to blowing off steam, the *N J Fjord* was sighted by the *Galatea*, which closed to investigate accompanied by the *Phaeton*. The *Galatea* at first took the two destroyers to be cruisers, and at 1420 wirelessed to Beatty 'Urgent. Two cruisers, probably hostile, in sight bearing 100°, course unknown. My position 56° 48'N, 5° 21'E' (which was some miles too far to the south-westward). At 1428 the *Galatea* and *Phaeton* opened fire at about 11,000yds at the two ships now recognised as destroyers. The latter had previously sighted the light cruisers' mastheads, and signalled their direction to the *Elbing* which sighted the light cruisers' smoke and reported to Hipper, and the *Elbing* then made a report at 1420 (? 1423) by searchlight regarding British recognition signals, which was read in the *Frankfurt* and *Lützow* as if 24–26 battleships were in sight. The *B109* reported the presence of several enemy vessels to the *Regensburg*, added that they were steering 77° and subsequently, that the British recognition signal was 'PL', and she and the *B110* replied ineffectively to the *Galatea* and *Phaeton*, before turning towards the *Elbing*. The latter had turned towards the smoke and, as she closed the British light cruisers, at first mistook them for battlecruisers and so reported them at 1427 bearing 268° in a wireless signal to Scheer and Hipper, though in some versions their position is given as *c*57° 09'N, 5°30'E, about 15 miles too far north. At 1432 the *Elbing*, now steering *c*145°, opened fire for a few minutes at 14,000–15,000yds at the *Galatea*, which with the *Phaeton* was on a north-easterly course, and had now been correctly identified, although the *Elbing* does not appear to have reported that light cruisers were in sight until 1446. The British ships replied without success, while the *Elbing* scored one hit on the *Galatea* at 1436. At 1435 the *Galatea*, which had meanwhile amended her first signal to read destroyers instead of cruisers, and had correctly reported the *Elbing* as a cruiser, wirelessed to Beatty that she had sighted a large amount of smoke, as though from a fleet bearing 55°. The *Galatea* and *Phaeton* turned to the north-westward to lead the enemy ships in that direction, while the *Inconstant* and *Cordelia*, and the 3rd LCS closed in support.

The smoke came from the *Frankfurt* and *Pillau* and their destroyers, working up to full speed to join the *Elbing* which had turned north-westward to follow the British ships. The *Wiesbaden* and *Regensburg* were also steering to close the *Elbing*.

Meanwhile Hipper on receiving the *Elbing*'s first report of sighting smoke, turned his battlecruisers together at 1427 to 235° and increased to 18kts. He then formed line ahead, course 190°, increasing to 21kts and calling for full speed, as an action was thought to be imminent due to the *Elbing*'s misread signal but at 1443 turned his ships together to 235° and reduced to 18kts, while the 9th Flotilla took station on the *Lützow*'s port bow. Hipper had also wirelessed to Scheer, timed at 1427, that strong enemy forces, or, as the message taken in by the fleet flagship stated, several smoke clouds from enemy vessels, were in *c*56° 39'N, 5° 30'E the position given by the *B109*. This was at least 10 miles too far south.

At 1425 Beatty made a warning signal by flags to his destroyers to take up position as a submarine screen when the course was altered to 145°. By first steering in this direction Beatty intended to get sufficiently far to the southward to cut off the German forces from their base by a subsequent run to the east. At 1432 he made a General signal by flags to alter course to 145°, leading ships together and rest in succession, and then called for 22kts and also to raise steam for full speed. The two battlecruiser squadrons conformed, but the 5th BS continued northward until 1440 and at 1432 turned together 23° to port on the first leg of the usual zig-zag. The basic reason for this lapse which increased the distance of the 5th BS from the battlecruisers by about 5 miles, was the failure to repeat by searchlight, a signal made by flags at too great a distance to be seen. This should have been done by the *Tiger* in accordance with a signal from Beatty at 0428.

The *Elbing* continued to follow the *Galatea* and *Phaeton* to the north-westward, but shortly after reopening fire at 1448, steered more to the northward, so that the range increased and until 1507 when she ceased fire, the *Elbing* only engaged the two British ships intermittently, while the latter did not reply, though at about 1500, they also altered course to the northward. The *Cordelia* tried four rounds from her 6in but these fell short. The *Frankfurt* and *Pillau* were now closing at 26kts, and at 1450 sighted several imaginary torpedo tracks. In a signal to Scheer, timed at 1451, the former reported four light cruisers steering north-westwards, not battlecruisers (as previously reported by the *Elbing*) and this correction was confirmed later by Hipper. A total of eight light cruisers gradually came into sight, and at

1512 the *Frankfurt* and *Pillau* opened fire on the *Galatea* and *Phaeton* at their maximum range of 16,300yds. The shots fell short, and they ceased at 1517 as the range increased.

At 1451 the *Galatea* which had just sighted an imaginary torpedo track passing astern and heading for the *Phaeton* wirelessed that the smoke reported at 1435 seemed to be seven vessels besides destroyers and cruisers, which had turned to 347°. In fact she could only have seen the German light cruisers and destroyers as the battlecruisers were about 19 miles away, and only the *Elbing* and her destroyers were steering 347°, yet by good fortune the *Galatea's* report did indicate with fair accuracy the 325° course of the German battlecruisers between 1459 and 1510. Further reports of the German cruisers and destroyers were made by the *Galatea* and *Falmouth* between 1505 and 1508.

The seaplane-carrier *Engadine* whose station had been with the 3rd LCS, was told to take cover near the battlecruisers when the action began, and at 1447 Beatty ordered her to send up seaplanes to scout in direction 10° and also ordered the *Champion* to send two destroyers (*Onslow* and *Moresby*) to her. The *Engadine* had to keep clear of other ships and was delayed in hoisting out, so that her Short type 184 seaplane did not take off until 1508.

Over an hour had gone by since the *N J Fjord* had been brought to and neither side had yet located their opponent's battlecruisers. Beatty was much better off for light cruisers than Hipper, but the 2nd LCS was too far to the south-west to be able to help, and the 3rd LCS was being uselessly disposed in luring the German light cruisers to the north-westward, for which the four ships of the 1st LCS would have been adequate.

At about 1445 Hipper had turned his battlecruisers together to 257° and increased to 21kts. Five minutes later they turned together to 280°, and just before 1500 Hipper reformed line ahead, course 325°, and increased to 23kts. At 1510 he altered course to 302° and then called for 25kts, chasing after the light cruisers. The 9th Flotilla was now on the *Lützow's* starboard beam, with the *Regensburg* and her four *G101* class destroyers further off on the same bearing, while the *Wiesbaden* was ahead but still some way from the three leading light cruisers. The two British battlecruiser squadrons turned to 122° at 1452, at 1501 to 77°, and at 1513 to 32°, increasing to 23kts. The 5th BS steered 145° at 22kts until 1505 and then altered course to 100°, and to 77° at 1514. Thus at 1515 the 2nd BCS was about 3 miles from the *Lion* on her starboard bow, and the 5th BS approaching, about 7 miles away on the port beam. The destroyer screens were ahead of their respective squadrons, while the *Nottingham* and *Dublin* were near the 2nd BCS, and the *Southampton* and *Birmingham* about 4 miles astern of the *Lion*. The remaining light cruisers were well ahead, following the *Galatea* and *Phaeton* to the northward.

At 1515 the rival battlecruisers were thus approaching at right angles though the *Lützow* was still at least 18 miles bearing c65° from the *New Zealand*, the nearest of the British battlecruisers. At 1520 smoke from two rapidly approaching columns of large vessels was sighted from the German battlecruisers, and 2 minutes later the *Seydlitz* could make out the tripod masts of the *New Zealand* and *Indefatigable*, about 15 miles away, while the 5th BS seems to have been first recognised from the German battlecruisers at 1535 at about 17 miles. The smoke of five ships was observed at 1524, bearing starboard 40 from the *New Zealand*, while the *Princess Royal* made a signal by flags at 1523 calling Beatty's attention to 66°. The *Nottingham* in a wireless signal timed at 1522, reported five columns of smoke bearing 55°, but these sightings do not seem to have been identified as the German battlecruisers until about 1530. The *Galatea*'s wireless signal, recorded as timed at 1515 and sent at 1525, reporting smoke, apparently from a squadron astern of the cruisers bearing 100°, referred to the *Wiesbaden*. Visibility was at this time excellent for the Germans towards the west, and rather better than for the British.

When the British battlecruisers were first sighted, it was not possible to determine details of their formation and course though it appeared that six large ships were steering northward. Hipper decided to accept action in this direction, and at 1529 ordered distribution of fire from the right, having a few minutes previously reduced to 23kts and altered course to 313°.

Beatty had called for 24kts at 1520, and at 1530, because he was getting too far north to cut off his opponents, altered course from 32° to 77° and increased to 25kts. Hipper, on observing this, turned his line to starboard in succession to 122° at about 1533 and reduced to 18kts to allow the light cruisers to catch up. At 1540 Hipper ordered distribution of fire from the left, and at 1545 turned his squadron together to 145°. It was not until 1534 that Beatty ordered the 2nd BCS to take station astern so that all six battlecruisers would be in a single line, and a minute later he reduced to 24kts to assist in carrying out the manoeuvre*. At 1545 he made signals by flags to form on a line of

---

*According to a diary kept in the *Lion*, Beatty had just previously signalled the 2nd BCS to prolong the line ahead, but this must have been negatived almost at once.

bearing 302°, to alter course together to 100° and a minute later, for the *Lion* and *Princess Royal* to concentrate on the enemy's leading ship.

The 5th BS had altered course to 32° and increased to 23kts at 1521, and, on receipt of a searchlight signal from Beatty at 1535, altered course to 77°, Evan-Thomas calling for 24 and then 24½kts both beyond their speed. At 1545 they were still about 7½ miles bearing 291° from the *Lion*, and as events turned out it was unfortunate that Beatty had not previously concentrated his forces.

Of the light forces present, the 2nd Scouting Group had been ordered to close on the German battlecruisers at 1530 and just previously the *Frankfurt* and *Pillau* had fired on the *Engadine*'s seaplane flying at 1000ft. The latter saw the light cruisers turn and made four wirelsss reports, but the *Engadine* did not succeed in passing them on. The seaplane had been directed too far north to see anything of great value, and at 1545 alighted with a broken petrol pipe, and was hoisted in. No further use was made of the *Engadine*'s four aircraft. The ships of the 1st and 3rd light cruiser squadrons did not turn until about 7 or 8 minutes after the 2nd Scouting Group, and thus removed themselves from participation in the action about to begin to the south-eastward. The 2nd LCS, however, was placed to take up a position ahead of the *Lion*. The 13th Flotilla had been ordered to take station 2 miles away, 23° before the *Lion*'s starboard beam, and the 9th Flotilla to take station ahead, while the 1st Flotilla was still ahead of the 5th BS.

On the German side the 9th Flotilla was close on the *Lützow*'s port bow, and the *Regensburg* with the four 'G' boats of the 2nd Flotilla, on the *von der Tann*'s port quarter. The rest of the 2nd Flotilla and the 6th Flotilla, except for the *G37* which had dropped far back as her foremost boiler had cut out for some minutes from water entering through the ventilator, were astern near the *Wiesbaden*, and the other three cruisers of the 2nd SG were further to the rear, about 7½ miles from the *Lützow*.

At 1545 when the duel between the battlecruisers was about to begin, both battle fleets were steering towards the scene of action, but the *König*, leading the German line, was about 46 miles from the *Lützow*, and the *Iron Duke* about 53 miles from the *Lion*. The nearest airship, the *L23*, was still astern of the German fleet, and both Scheer and Jellicoe had to rely on wireless signals from their advanced forces. The German battleships were in line ahead with the 3rd Squadron leading, followed by the Fleet Flagship, and the 1st and 2nd Squadrons. The light cruisers, each with a destroyer ahead, were at 5 to 8 miles distance with the *Stettin* and the *V48* ahead of the *König*. The other destroyers were disposed as a submarine screen to the battleships.

On receiving the first contact signals, Scheer ordered the 1st and 2nd Squadrons to close, but otherwise continued at 14kts, course 347°. At *c*1510 he signalled 'General Quarters' and increased to 15kts, and 15 minutes later fixed the distance between ships as 770yds. At 1530 and 1535 signals came in from Hipper, reporting six large enemy ships in sight in *c*56° 51′N, 5° 18′E steering 347°, but as yet Scheer made no further increase in speed. The *Kaiserin* had to stop her centre turbines at 1519 as a leak had developed in the condenser, but they were restarted shortly before the 3rd Squadron came into action.

The Grand Fleet battleship divisions were in line ahead disposed abeam, in numerical order from port to starboard. The seven large armoured cruisers were spread at 5 mile intervals on a line of direction 27°–207°, 10 miles ahead of the *Iron Duke*. The *Hampshire* and *Active* were linking ships, and the 4th LCS were in line abreast 3 miles ahead of the *Iron Duke* as submarine screen and lookout. The 3rd Battlecruiser Squadron was about 10 miles ahead of the armoured cruiser screen with the *Canterbury* a further 5 miles ahead, and the *Chester* as linking ship with the screen. Most of the destroyers were disposed as a submarine screen to the battleship divisions but four from the 4th Flotilla: – *Shark, Acasta, Christopher* and *Ophelia* – were screening the 3rd BCS, and three from the 4th Flotilla and one from the 12th: – *Owl, Hardy, Midge* and *Mischief* – screened the cruisers of the 2nd CS, though the 1st CS had no screening destroyers, as Jerram had considered there were too few with the Cromarty forces.

When the first signals from the *Galatea* were received, Jellicoe continued on course 117° at 15kts, zig-zagging with speed of advance 14kts. At 1435 he ordered steam to be raised for full speed, and at 1443 following the *Galatea*'s report of smoke in 55°, ceased zig-zagging and increased to 17kts, signalling guides to bear 43° from guide of fleet. At 1455 he increased to 18kts and 2 minutes later ordered steam for full speed to be raised with all despatch. This was qualified at 1500 by a signal that destroyers were to bank fires in boilers not required for 21kts, and at the same time complete readiness for action was ordered. At 1502 Jellicoe altered course to 133°, and at 1510 ordered the armoured cruiser screen to increase their distance ahead to 16 miles with 8 miles between ships, though it does not appear that they succeeded in getting any further ahead, due to insufficient speed and decreasing visibility. At 1516 the battleship columns were ordered to be one mile apart, and 2 minutes later speed was increased to 19kts followed at 1522 by a signal for destroyers to raise steam for full speed.

Meanwhile at 1521 Beatty had wirelessed his 1515 position as 56°

48′N, 5° 17′E, course 32° (received as 27°), speed 23kts, and at 1527 Jellicoe wirelessed his 1515 position to Beatty as 57° 50′N, 4° 15′E, course 133°, speed 19kts. In a further signal timed at 1530 and intercepted by the *Iron Duke*, Beatty gave his course and speed as 77°, 25kts, and this was followed by two more signals to Jellicoe, timed at 1535 and 1545, reporting that five enemy battlecruisers and a large number of destroyers were bearing 32°, course 112°, the *Lion's* position at the latter time being 56° 53′N, 5° 33′E*.

Jellicoe did not order the 3rd BCS to join Beatty, as it was in a favourable position to intercept any German light forces which might try and escape by the Skagerrak. At 1500 the *Invincible* was ahead of station, 25 miles on the *Iron Duke's* port bow, and at 1513 Hood increased to 22kts on his own initiative steering 100° and at 1545 altered course to 141°.

As the battlecruisers were about to engage in a south-easterly direction, Scheer would be able to intervene long before Jellicoe, but it would be about an hour before the German battlefleet could take part and during that time the action would be between Hipper's and Beatty's forces, and initially between the battlecruisers only.

---

*These positions were all somewhat in error, but this was of no great importance at this juncture.

CHAPTER 4

Action between capital ships
First phase 1548–1654

Hipper was apprehensive lest the British opened fire outside the maximum range of the German battlecruisers. Allowing for wear of the guns, this was about 19,000 to 21,000yds, except for the *von der Tann* which could reach *c*22,400. Wear also affected the British guns, but the 13.5in battlecruisers could range to about 23,500yds at 20°, and 'super-elevation' 6° prisms added to the Director sights and to the centre position sights of turrets, now permitted the full elevation of the mountings to be used, whereas the sights had only been graduated to 15° 21′ at the Dogger Bank. The British 9ft range-finders were not satisfactory at such distances, and in addition the *New Zealand* and *Indefatigable* could not range much over 18,500yds at 13½° elevation. Beatty thus intended to close to within the latter distance, but the *Lion*'s range-finders over-estimated the range by more than 2000yds and it had sunk to about 16,000yds when the Germans opened fire at 1548.

In several ways conditions favoured Hipper. The visibility was better for the German ships, though by no means bad for the British, and the lighter grey German colour was less distinct against sea and overcast sky. The British ships were to windward, and the light W by N breeze would carry smoke between them and the enemy, while the Germans were freer from such interference. There were also fewer last minute orders in the German Squadron. Hipper had been steaming 122° since about 1533 at 18kts. At 1540 distribution of fire from the left was signalled, and 2 minutes later the distance between ships was ordered to be 550yds. At 1545 the 1st Scouting Group were signalled to turn together to 145°, a simple manoeuvre to increase the rate of closing. In contrast to this, Beatty made three important signals by flags at 1545/46: to change from line ahead, which the 2nd BCS had only just joined, to a line of bearing 302° so as to take up the most favourable disposition with regard to funnel and cordite smoke; to alter course together from 77° to 100°; the *Lion* and *Princess Royal* to concentrate on the leading enemy ship. The exact formation of the British ships at 1548 is not known, but the *Lion* was steering 93° when her first salvo was fired at the *Lützow* 42° on the port bow, and from the direction of the first shell to hit the *Tiger* at 1550/51, the *Moltke* was then only about 30° on the *Tiger*'s port bow. The *Lion* replied to the Germans at 1548½ and the other 13.5in ships apparently opened fire within the next minute, but the *New Zealand* did not join in until 1551, and the *Indefatigable* may have been later, as it was believed they were initially out of range. It is clear that the *Tiger* could only have fired her forward turrets at the outset, and from the *Lion*'s ammunition records her first salvos were also fired from forward turrets only.

Mistakes were made in the British distribution of fire. The *Lion* and *Princess Royal* engaged the *Lützow*, but the *Queen Mary* missed out the *Derfflinger* and fired at the *Seydlitz*, while the *Tiger* and *New Zealand* concentrated on the *Moltke* and the *Indefatigable* engaged the *von der Tann*. This was of less importance than might appear, as the *Derfflinger*'s initial salvos were not effective, and the first German ships to score were the *Lützow* and *Moltke*, on both of which two British ships were concentrating! The four leading German battlecruisers engaged opposite numbers; *Lützow* v *Lion*; *Derfflinger* v *Princess Royal*; *Seydlitz* v *Queen Mary*; *Moltke* v *Tiger*; but the *von der Tann* missed out the *New Zealand* and engaged the *Indefatigable*.

On both sides the initial range was over-estimated by most ships, and the closing rate under-estimated, but the German errors were less, and more quickly corrected. The German opening salvos were fired at the following ranges: *Lützow* 16,800yds, *Derfflinger* and *Seydlitz* 16,400yds, *Moltke* 15,500yds, *von der Tann* 17,700yds; all were over except the *Moltke*'s, which was short. The *Lion* and *Tiger* seem to have fired their opening salvos at 18,500yds, the *Princess Royal* at 16,000yds, and the *New Zealand* at 18,100yds and, except for the *Princess Royal*, were far over, the shells from the *Lion* falling near destroyers of the 9th Flotilla to port of the German line. There are no figures for the *Queen Mary* and *Indefatigable*, though the senior surviving Midshipman of the former mentions about 17,500yds.

The German initial rate of fire is generally supposed to have been faster than the British, and it is certainly true that they fired more shells in the opening minutes, as the British were late in bringing all their turrets into action. The *Lion*'s records, however, show that her first five salvos were fired in 2½ minutes, but according to Commander Paschen, the *Lützow*'s gunnery officer, the *Lion* did not straddle until the 9th salvo, which was fired 5½ minutes after opening. The *Princess Royal* appears to have fired her first five salvos in 3 minutes 40-seconds, and in the *Tiger* 'Q' turret only fired one round per gun up to the time that this turret was hit, *c*4½ minutes after the *Tiger* had opened fire, though this was at least in part due to her after turrets being unable to bear initially. It is clear that Beatty did not think the rate of fire sufficiently high, as about 1555 he made a General signal calling for an increase.

The *Lützow*'s first salvo was well to the left as the inclination of the *Lion* towards the 1st SG was under-estimated, but she seems to have fired her first five salvos in 3 minutes and hit with her fifth salvo. The *Derfflinger* also fired five salvos in 3 minutes, but then had a period of firing short, and does not appear to have scored a hit until 10 minutes after opening fire, while the *Moltke* made two hits in the first 3 minutes, and continued hitting in one of the most accurate spells of firing in the whole battle. According to the officer of 'Q' Turret in the *Tiger*, the *Moltke*'s first salvo appeared to fall about 300yds short, and she straddled the *Tiger* very soon afterwards. The spread for range was estimated as 100–150yds, and for deflection as 'nil'.

With the exception of the *Lützow*, the German ships fired APC shell with salvos of one gun per turret, but the flagship fired her four forward and four after guns alternately and used uncapped semi-AP. One full salvo was tried but it fell mostly short, obscuring the *Lion* with its numerous water columns. The British ships fired salvos of one gun per turret, and the 13.5in ships all used APC. The *New Zealand* apparently began with CPC, but on straddling changed to nose-fuzed HE.

Since opening fire the *Lion* had been gradually turning to starboard, and by 1554, when the range between the leading ships had fallen to about 14,000yds, she was on a divergent course of about 156°, and at 1557 turned further away to about 164°. British charts of the battle show Beatty's ships returning to line ahead at about 1552/53, but it was probably later than this. As Beatty's battlecruisers were making 24 or 25kts, Hipper increased speed at 1553 to 21kts, and one or two minutes later reformed line ahead. From the *Derfflinger*'s list of target bearings the 1st SG then turned away until they were steering 122°, but at 1559/1600 Hipper turned his ships together to 133°.

In this opening stage of the battle the German firing was far more effective than that of the British ships which mostly fired short after their earliest salvos. The *Lion* was hit by the *Lützow* at 1551 and 1552 and then again at 1600. The latter hit put 'Q' turret, which had fired a total of 12 rounds, out of action, and might well have caused the loss of the ship. The *Princess Royal* was not hit until 1558 when she was struck on her armour by two shells from the *Derfflinger*, one of which pierced. The shock put the Argo fire control tower temporarily out of action so that 'B' turret had to take over fire control, and at about 1600 she received another damaging hit near 'B' barbette. The *Tiger* is believed to have been hit nine times by the *Moltke* prior to 1600. The first two hits at 1550–1551 were on the forecastle and shelter deck, and at 1554 both 'Q' and 'X' turrets were hit and put temporarily out of action. A minute later serious damage was caused by a shell which pierced the hull armour aft of 'Q' turret. It is impossible to say whether any hits were made on the *Queen Mary* or *Indefatigable* in the first 12 minutes, but it is probable that the former was hit by the *Seydlitz*, and the *von der Tann* claimed a hit on the *Indefatigable*. In any case without counting the two ships later blown up, there are estimated to have been fifteen hits up to 1600 on the British ships, and there were only four on the German, two on the *Seydlitz* from the *Queen Mary* and two on the *Lützow*, probably from the *Lion*. The first of these hit the *Seydlitz* at 1555 and did considerable damage forward of the battery armour. By this time the power training of the *Seydlitz*'s after super-firing turret had failed, and at 1557 the barbette armour of this turret was holed and the turret put out of action with a serious ammunition fire, though nothing like that at the Dogger Bank. The two hits on the *Lützow* were on the forecastle from a salvo at 1600 and apparently had little immediate effect.

During this period as the range fell, most, if not all, of the German ships brought their 5.9in batteries into action but although a few hits were made, the damage caused was not worth the interference to the main armament. At 1554 the *Seydlitz*, and 8 minutes later the *Moltke* and *von der Tann* shifted their 5.9in guns to a group of destroyers on the engaged side of the British line.

These included three of the 'L' class destroyers which were trying to reach a position as ordered, ahead of the battlecruisers, but they lacked sufficient speed to do so without making quantities of oil-fuel smoke, which seriously added to the difficulties of some of Beatty's ships. According to Commodore Heinrich in the *Regensburg* steaming up the disengaged side of the German line about 2200yds away, with the four 'G' boats of the 2nd Flotilla, the British shell splashes at first lay very badly. When the *Regensburg* was approximately abreast of the *Moltke*, one ship, most probably the *Tiger*, trained on her for about 10 minutes; in considerable danger from the heavy shells, she increased her distance from the line. The *Tiger* had a difficult time under the *Moltke*'s very accurate fire, with two of her turrets temporarily out of action. She also appears to have been particularly affected by the destroyers' funnel smoke. It is doubtful whether any ship fired at the *Derfflinger* before 1617.

By 1600 the range had already increased to about 16,500yds between the two leading ships, and in the next 10 minutes rose to about 21,000yds. It is not clear how far this large increase was intentional, as at 1601/02 an error was made in handling the *Lion*. As related by A E M (later Lord) Chatfield who was then her captain, he told the Commander (N) to order an alteration of 5° to starboard to stop the range closing when 'Q' turret was hit, but the chief quartermaster misheard and maintained 5° port helm so that the *Lion* swung rapidly to starboard, and had to be brought back, and her speed increased, to resume station ahead of the *Princess Royal*, which appears to have taken about 10 minutes. From the *Lützow* which was at that time hitting repeatedly, the *Lion* was seen to sheer out of the line and at times seemed to disappear behind the other ships in a thick cloud of smoke, while the *Princess Royal* went ahead.

The *Lion*'s target bearing records show that she turned away through a little more than 30°, while the other battlecruisers probably turned away by about half this amount, and there seems no doubt that the *Lion* and *Princess Royal* were later confused by the *Lützow*. The *Lion* continued firing during her turn, and when regaining her station, but only with 'X' turret at the apex of the turn away. The German battlecruisers meanwhile turned together to 145° at 1604, and after a few minutes gradually altered course to starboard before turning together to 178° at 1611.

Between 1600 and 1610 the only certain score by the British was a near-miss on the *Moltke* at 1602 or just afterwards, probably by the *Tiger*. It is thought that the *Queen Mary* also made a similar hit on the *Seydlitz* during this period. The *Lützow* scored three hits on the *Lion* between 1601 and 1603, and her claim of six hits between 1548 and 1607 when she temporarily ceased firing at her, is thus correct. In the first 19 minutes of the battle, the *Lützow* fired 31 salvos at ranges of 14,300 to 18,300yds, and her shooting was clearly of a high order, though not as good as that of the *Moltke* for the same period. Fires were started in the *Lion* which expended twenty-three salvos up to 1607, but no very serious damage was done except by the hit on 'Q' turret at 1600, though the *Lion*'s main wireless went out of action at about 1605. Ten years later Paschen still regretted that the *Lützow* had not fired

APC in the first hour of the battle, and thought that the *Lion* would scarcely have survived if this had been done. No hits are recorded on the *Princess Royal*, to which the *Lützow* shifted at 1608 during this period, but the *Tiger* was hit once on the forecastle. It is not known whether any hits were made on the *Queen Mary* between 1600 and 1610, but she was certainly hit during the first half-hour of the battle.

At the rear of the line, the *Indefatigable* was hit at 1602/03 by two successive salvos from the *von der Tann* at about 15,500–16,000yds, the first of which caused a fatal magazine explosion. The details of her loss, as far as known, are given on a later page. The two salvos are each believed to have scored two hits and altogether the *von der Tann* fired 52–11in and 38–5.9in at the *Indefatigable* in 14 or 15 minutes, which does not give a high average rate of fire. Only two men were picked up 3¾ hours later by the German destroyer *S16*; 1017 officers and men were lost.

The *von der Tann* changed target to the *New Zealand*, but at about 1610 most of the German ships ceased firing for a short time as the British were drawing out of range. According to the *Lion*'s report in 'Jutland Despatches', more than one enemy ship was firing at her at about this time, and it seems that the *Lützow* and *Derfflinger*, which believed that they were engaging the *Princess Royal* between 1608 and 1616 when the range was not too great, were in fact both firing intermittently at the *Lion* from about 1610 to 1616.

As noted above the British fire was not effective in this period, and in addition to the disorganisation caused by the error in handling the *Lion*, smoke interference from the destroyers on the engaged side was a severe handicap and at 1611 Beatty ordered them to clear the range. The *New Zealand* shifted to the *von der Tann*, after the *Indefatigable* had sunk though her salvos soon fell short as the range increased. The German Official History states that by 1610 the *Tiger* was having great difficulty in keeping her guns on the proper target, as she frequently counted the *Regensburg*, ahead of the German line, as a battlecruiser, and thus from then onwards, often fired at the *Seydlitz* instead of the *Moltke*, but this is doubtful, as by 1620 the *Tiger* was firing at the *von der Tann*.

Fortunately for Beatty the 5th Battle Squadron was now entering the fight. At 1548 Evan-Thomas had altered course from 77° to 88° and at 1552 to 100°. The *Frankfurt*, *Pillau* and *Elbing* had been sighted, wide on the port bow, at about 1550, but they were difficult to make out owing to mist and to the presence of some of the 1st Flotilla to port of the 5th BS. The destroyers were ordered out of the way, and at 1558 the

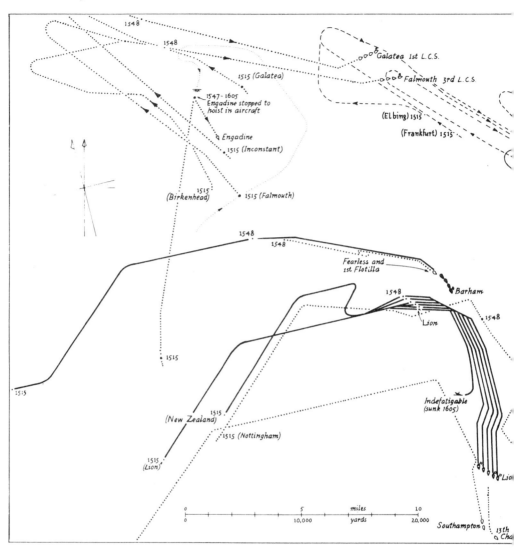

Barham opened fire on the *Frankfurt* at about 17,000yds followed by the *Valiant* and *Warspite* on the *Pillau*. The *Barham*'s first salvo was about 300yds short and the 3rd straddled, while other salvos fell within 100yds of the *Pillau*, so that the latter and then the *Frankfurt* made

44

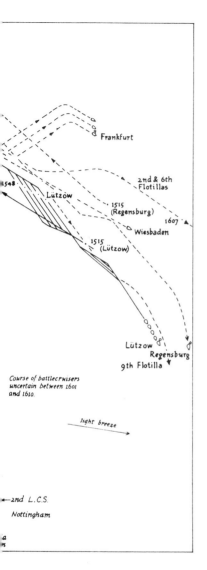

Chart I: Position at 1610

artificial fog as did the *G37*, and all three light cruisers turned away together and disappeared from view. A fog buoy dropped by the *Frankfurt* attracted the British salvos until 1605 when firing ceased. The *Pillau*'s report notes that the spread of the salvos fired at her and the

Frankfurt was extremely small at $c100 \times 50$yds. The German artificial fog was clearly most effective in enabling the light cruisers to escape. The 5th BS seem to have been mistaken for the 2nd BS before they opened fire. Evan-Thomas had received no orders from Beatty since the latter had opened fire, and the British battlecruisers had disappeared in the haze and smoke of the action, before their opponents could be made out from the 5th BS. At 1605 Evan-Thomas caught sight of the 1st Scouting Group about 10 miles ahead of the 5th BS, and then discovered that the British battlecruisers had turned southward. Accordingly, he altered course to 133° at 1605 and 3 minutes later to about 160°, when the *Barham* opened fire on the *von der Tann* with 15in CPC at about 19,000yds. It might have seemed that Beatty's troubles were now over, but such was not the case, though his position was much improved.

So far the only torpedoes fired in the action had been four by the *Moltke* at the *Queen Mary* between 1604 and 1608, and they had no chance of hitting, though it seems that the range was believed to be only about 11,000yds. At 1609 Beatty ordered the 13th Flotilla to attack, and 5 minutes later Hipper also ordered his destroyers to attack, but it would take time for these orders to be carried out. As usual imaginary torpedo tracks were sighted. At about 1611 supposed periscopes were reported to port and starboard of the British battlecruisers, as well as a torpedo track from each side. The track from port was noted by the *Landrail* as passing under her and then through the battlecruiser line, while that from starboard was recorded by the *Princess Royal* to have passed under her amidships! It was believed that the battlecruisers were passing a line of submarines, but none was near. At this time the *Moltke* also sighted three torpedo tracks, of which two passing astern were likewise imaginary, while the third, which was reported as running on the surface, and coming within 40yds of the ship, was perhaps a badly misrunning torpedo of her own. The four 'G' boats of the 2nd Flotilla hunted a supposed submarine, in fact a school of porpoises.

The next 20 minutes brought the action between Beatty's and Hipper's forces to a climax and gave the Germans their greatest success of the battle, when the *Queen Mary* was blown up at 1626.

When Beatty saw that the 5th Battle Squadron was coming into action, he altered course to near 145° at 1611 and at 1614 to 122°. Hipper had turned his ships together to 178° at 1611 and a minute later increased to 23kts. At 1618 he reformed line ahead to reduce the exposure of his rear ships to the 5th BS. The rival battlecruisers were thus on markedly convergent courses and at 1619, when the range between the leaders had fallen to about 16,000yds, Beatty turned away to 145°. Hipper altered course to about 169° at 1620, reduced to 21kts at 1625 and at 1628 when the range was down to about 14,000yds, turned his ships together to about 128°, while at 1627/28 Beatty altered course to 167°. The reasons for these turns away were to keep clear of the destroyer fighting which was now beginning, and to increase the range from the 5th BS and the German battlecruisers, respectively.

The 5th BS altered course to about 150° at about 1615 and at 1618 Evan-Thomas called for a slight reduction to a nominal 24kts, and for a distance of 600yds between ships. They held this course until 1630 when the subdivisions altered separately in succession 23° away. At that time the *Barham* was about 8 miles astern of the *Lion*, while the least range from the former to the German battlecruisers during the period had been 15,000–16,000yds.

The distribution of fire among the battlecruisers is not easy to determine. The *Lützow* fired at the *Lion*, and scored three hits in half a minute at 1624, though it appears that her target was thought to be the *Princess Royal*. At 1628 a serious cordite fire blazed up in the *Lion*'s 'Q' turret, hit at 1600, but fortunately the magazines had been flooded. The *Lion* had been previously emitting much smoke as at 1626 Beatty signalled the *Princess Royal* by auxiliary wireless to 'keep clear of smoke', and the *Derfflinger* which had fired a salvo at the *Lion* at 1616, shifted at 1617.20 to the *Queen Mary*, at which the *Seydlitz* was also firing, as the *Princess Royal* was presumably hidden in smoke.

At 1621 the *Queen Mary*'s 'Q' turret was hit and the right gun put completely out of action, and at 1626 it appears that two shells hit, one of which caused a disastrous magazine explosion forward, blowing the ship in two. The sequence of events as far as known, is given on a later page. The *Laurel* picked up seventeen survivors, the *Petard*, one, and the German destroyer the *G8*, two, but the rest of her crew, 1266, were lost.

When the *Queen Mary* blew up, the *Seydlitz* was firing at a range of 14,750yds, and the *Derfflinger* at 14,400, and the latter fired six salvos between 1623.45 and 1626.10 of which the last appears to have caused the disaster. A thick smoke cloud rose to perhaps 2000ft, completely hiding the *Tiger* and *New Zealand* as they steamed through it.

After the *Queen Mary* sank, the *Seydlitz* shifted to the *Tiger* and the *Derfflinger* to the *Princess Royal*, and the last named was hit at 1627 and again at 1632, while it is thought that a third hit was also made. The *Moltke* apparently reopened on the *Tiger* at 1619 and continued until 1630 when her target was much hidden by smoke, and only isolated salvos were fired. The *Moltke* claimed a hit at 1622 and another at 1624, and it is believed that she obtained a total of three hits in this spell of firing. The *von der Tann* first fired at the *New Zealand*, but at 1618 shifted to the *Barham* until 1624, when she had to return to the *New Zealand* as her forward and after turrets had been put out of action, and only two guns would bear on the *Barham*. She fired 34 rounds at the latter ship at 17,000–18,600yds, and made one hit on the armour belt at 1623. The *von der Tann* also made one hit on the *New Zealand* at 1626 on 'X' barbette which did not cause very serious damage. At 1635 there was a breakdown in her starboard wing turret and she was left with only two–11in guns which had very limited arcs of training to starboard. Her total expenditure of ammunition fired at the *New Zealand* up to this time was 55–11in shells.

The *Lion* fired at the *Lützow* and so did the *Princess Royal* which should be credited with the two hits scored on the her at 1615, one shell bursting between the forward turrets, and the other striking the armour belt. At that time the *Lion* was going far over, and had been continually going over for at least the previous 6 minutes, her gun range reaching a maximum of *c*23,000yds, while the *Princess Royal*, after a pause of 5 minutes, reopened at the correct range. The *Lion* fired two torpedoes at the *Derfflinger* between 1615 and 1630, but these cannot have crossed the German line. The *Queen Mary* engaged the *Seydlitz* until at least 1617, and then changed to the *Derfflinger*. The *Tiger* was supposed to be engaging the *Moltke*, but was actually firing at the *von der Tann*, and scored two hits on the latter. The first, at 1620, was on the fore barbette, and permanently disabled the turret, while the second at 1623, damaged the base of the after barbette, and put this turret out of action for more than 3½ hours, before it was got ready with hand training. After the *Queen Mary* sank, the *Tiger*'s report states that she engaged the '3rd ship from the left' which should have been the *Seydlitz*, but the *Seydlitz* was not fired at for about half an hour after the *Queen Mary* sank, and it cannot be determined whether the *Tiger* was in fact then firing at the *Moltke* or at the *Derfflinger*. The *New Zealand*'s reports indicate that she engaged the *von der Tann*, but shifted to the *Moltke* when shell splashes from the 5th BS (and the *Tiger*) obscured her former target. According to her record of ranges in 'Jutland Despatches' this was at 1622½ but the time is 5 or 6 minutes fast, and her range plot gives 1616. The *Moltke* was hit at 1623 and at 1626 by the 5th BS, but the *New Zealand*'s records show that she was then going over, and that it had not been realised how much the range was falling. According to the *V44*'s report, which is among the best of those from destroyers, the 11th Half-Flotilla were, prior to 1622, several times surrounded by shell splashes that were probably intended for the *Wiesbaden* further astern. The relative positions of the rear of the 1st SG, the *Wiesbaden* and the 11th Half-Flotilla are not known with sufficient accuracy for comment.

The firing of the 5th Battle Squadron was much more impressive than that of the British battlecruisers in this period. The German official historian, Captain O Groos, who was the *von der Tann*'s navigator at Jutland, says that their fire proved to be extremely effective, and that the rear ships of the German line were exposed to a regular hail of 15in projectiles. Salvos of closely spaced shells, fired at extremely short intervals, fell all about them, and many explosions close to the hulls, caused the latter to shake and reverberate. Both the *Moltke* and *von der Tann* made alterations of course and speed to throw out the British fire control, and from the *Malaya*'s reports, they were zig-zagging at very short and regular intervals, and were never far off the mean course. Groos remarks that the 15in salvos possessed almost too little spread.

As previously mentioned, the *Barham* opened fire on the *von der Tann* at about 19,000yds at 1608. At 1609 she scored a hit aft which did much damage and narrowly missed putting the steering gear out of action. A few minutes later the 5th BS were ordered to concentrate in pairs on the two rear ships, so that the *Barham* and *Valiant* engaged the *Moltke*, and the *Warspite* and *Malaya* the *von der Tann*. All four battleships were firing by 1615, and at 1616 the *Moltke* was hit by a shell which put a 5.9in gun out of action, while another shell hit near the stern at about this time. She was hit on the armour belt at 1623 and again at 1626 when the range was down to about 16,000yds, but a very smoky fire which broke out as a result of the *Tiger*'s hit on the *von der Tann* at 1623, obscured the latter so that she escaped hits from the *Warspite* and *Malaya*.

Conditions seem otherwise to have been fairly good for the 5th BS up to 1630. The *Barham* reported that the *Moltke* was a fair target at 18,000-17,000yds and was frequently straddled. Both the *Valiant* and *Malaya* reported that their range-finders gave good results during this period, and both apparently straddled at the 4th salvo, which in the *Malaya* was fired at 19,200yds, 2½ minutes after opening fire. The *Barham* began with CPC and changed to APC after firing for some time at the *Moltke*, but the *Valiant* fired APC and very little CPC. Data is lacking for the other two ships. The 5th Battle Squadron had the advantage over the battlecruisers of better range-finders – 15ft as against 9ft – and were far less exposed to German fire.

Meanwhile a fierce destroyer action had begun between the lines.

The leading British group had crossed ahead of the battlecruisers at about 1620, and at *c*1626 the German 9th Flotilla also steamed out to attack. It had been intended that each destroyer of the latter should fire two torpedoes in an 'inconspicuous' (unauffällig) attack, in which the flotilla edged down gradually towards the hostile line, but this plan was abandoned on the advance of the British destroyers. These comprised the 13th Flotilla, less the *Onslow* and *Moresby* which had been detached to the *Engadine*, and the four units of the 10th Flotilla. The *Nottingham* and *Dublin* had been ordered to support the attack, but the latter could not cross ahead of the battlecruisers in time, and the *Nottingham* was not engaged for long. Judging from her ammunition returns, the 13th Flotilla's light cruiser *Champion* took little if any part, and of the total of 12 destroyers, neither the *Narborough* nor the *Pelican* opened fire. The *Tiger* fired her 6in guns for some minutes from 1634, but none of the other British heavy ships appears to have fired at the destroyers. On the German side the eleven destroyers of the 9th Flotilla were supported by the *Regensburg* and the four units of the *G101* class. The British were not all in regular formation as the *Obdurate* and *Morris* had been on the engaged side of the battlecruisers since the beginning of the action, and the *Nottingham* had cut through the flotilla causing some disorganisation, but they had the better of the fight. The *Nomad* whose speed had been reduced by trouble in her main bearings, was hit at least once, and then brought to a stop by a shell in the engine-room, but otherwise only the *Obdurate* seems to have been hit by 2–4.1in which had little effect. Of the German destroyers, the *V27* was hit twice in the forward engine room and disabled when her main steam pipe was destroyed; the *S36* was damaged by splinters which caused a temporary reduction in speed. The *V29* was hit aft by a torpedo from the *Petard* fired at about 2000yds, and set to run at high speed and 6ft depth, and her stern was soon under water, though her bows remained afloat for *c*30 minutes, and she managed to fire four torpedoes at the British line. The *V26* took off *V27*'s crew, and then fired a torpedo to scuttle her, but this ran in circles, so that *V26* had to sink *V27* by gun-fire. The *V26* then rescued most of *V29*'s crew, and the rest were taken on board the *S35*.

The above destroyer action began at *c*1630 and lasted for 10–15 minutes at ranges of *c*7500–1000yds, except that the *Regensburg* and the four *G101* class were firing at *c*11,000––8000 and 10,300–5500yds, respectively.

Meanwhile ten torpedoes (the *V28*, two: the *V27*, one before disabled: the *V26*, one: the *S51*, three: the *S52*, one: the *S33*, two) had been fired at the British battlecruisers at *c*9000yds. The time of firing was about 1633–1635, and the battlecruisers subsequent turn northward at 1640 took them out of the way of the torpedoes. In addition the *S52* fired one torpedo at the disabled *Nomad* at *c*1100yds which ran under her, while a second torpedo was also reported to have run under this ship and a British torpedo under the *S33*. The *Lützow* also fired a 23.6in torpedo at the *Tiger* at 1634, but it too had no success.

On the British side the *Nestor* and *Nicator* fired two torpedoes each at the German battlecruisers at 5/6000yds though the *Lützow*'s ranges indicate 7000yds. The time was about 1635. According to the German accounts, the torpedoes were fired at the *Lützow*, but the danger had been recognised in time and the battlecruisers had turned together to 105° at 1633 and to 77° at 1636 so that the torpedoes ran past. The British Torpedo School analysis has no details for the *Nestor*, but gives the *Seydlitz* as the *Nicator*'s target. The latter's 2nd torpedo mis-fired and slid out of the tube and broke in two. The *Lützow* which had fired her secondary armament at the *Obdurate* and *Morris* from 1620 to 1629 at 9000–14,000yds, engaged the *Nestor* and *Nicator* with 5.9in from 1631 to 1636 at 11,000 to 7000yds, but it is not clear whether any of the other battlecruisers did so, and neither destroyer appears to have been hit at this time. It would seem from the Torpedo School analysis that it was shortly after the above attack, that the *Petard* fired two torpedoes at the *Derfflinger* at 7000yds, neither of which hit. The *Derfflinger*'s secondary armament opened at 1637, and fired a total of eight salvos at two destroyers, the range being 6600–8100yds.

Further attacks by the British destroyers are described subsequently, as the situation was now completely altered by the arrival of the German battle fleet. When Hipper opened fire at 1548, Scheer was steaming 347° at 15kts. At 1554 a report from Hipper came in stating that he was in action with six battlecruisers, giving particulars of position, course and speed, and also requesting Scheer's position. At 1605 Scheer altered course to 302°, with the possibility of catching the British battlecruisers between two German forces in view. He wirelessed his position, course and speed to Hipper in a signal timed at 1609, closed the spacing between ships to 550yds and at 1618 altered course to 257°. The screening destroyers were ordered to assemble on their flotilla leaders, but at 1620 a signal from the *Frankfurt* reporting five ships of the British 2nd Battle Squadron was received in the *Friedrich der Grosse* and Scheer altered course back to 347° to intervene in the fight as quickly as possible.

At 1628 the *Stettin* signalled that she had observed firing in a direction 319°, distant about 4 miles, (the last figure being clearly in error), and at 1630 the *König*, leading the German battleships, sighted ships in action at *c*325°. It was soon made out that the 1st Scouting Group was approaching on the port bow, and further to port were four battlecruisers in action with Hipper, and also apparently light cruisers of the *Chatham* type, while destroyers were between the lines. Scheer wirelessed his position, course and speed to Hipper in a signal timed at 1631, and at 1635 ordered his destroyer flotillas to starboard. A minute later he called for an increase in speed to 17kts, and at just after 1640 it was reported from the *König*'s fore-top that the British battlecruisers were apparently turning northwards. Accordingly at 1642 Scheer ordered a 23° turn to port by Divisions, so that his battleships were in six columns steering 325°. The 4th Scouting Group proceeded to form a 7th column astern and to port (later to starboard) of the 4th Division, while the *Rostock*, with the 1st and 3rd Flotillas (the *S32* was transferred at this time to the latter) and the 9th Half-Flotilla, was to starboard of the leading 5th Division, the rest of the 5th Flotilla with the *S19* and *S23* to starboard of the 1st Squadron, and the remainder of the 7th Flotilla to starboard of the 2nd Squadron.

Thanks to the 2nd LCS which was about 2 miles ahead of the British battlecruisers, the German battlefleet was detected not long after the latter had first observed the action between Beatty and Hipper. At 1630 the *Southampton* made an urgent wireless report of one enemy cruiser, bearing 122° and apparently steering 32°. This was the *Rostock*, and after further cruiser sightings by the *Nottingham* and *Birmingham*, the *Southampton* signalled by searchlight to Beatty at 1633 that battleships bore 122°. This was followed at 1638 by a priority wireless signal that the enemy battlefleet had been sighted, bearing approximately 122°, course 347°, and at about the same time the presence of the battlefleet was confirmed by the *Champion*. There were considerable errors in the reported positions of the *Southampton* and *Champion*, but these did not affect Beatty as he was in visual touch, though they were of importance to Jellicoe. Beatty gradually altered course to port from about 1632 until he was steering 128° and, having sighted the leading dreadnoughts about 12 miles away, made a General signal by flags at 1640 to alter course in succession 180° to starboard.

As previously noted Hipper had turned away until the 1st Scouting Group were steering 77° at 1636. Two minutes later they turned together to 145° and at 1641 to 190°. The action between the battlecruisers had largely died away, and except for a hit on the *Tiger*'s forecastle, which appears to have been made by the *Seydlitz* at about

1635, there is no record of any hits since that time on the *Princess Royal* at 1632. The *von der Tann* fired four rounds at the *New Zealand* from 1637 at 21,900–22,700yds, which must have fallen far over. The *Derfflinger*'s records show that she fired a total of 49–12in salvos between 1548 and 1626, while the *Lützow* expended about 60 salvos in the same period. Of the *Derfflinger*'s salvos, it is believed that 25 or 26 were fired at the *Princess Royal* between 1548 and 1608 (or 1609); two or three at the *Lion* from 1608 to 1616; 11 at the *Queen Mary* from 1617.20 to 1636.10, and 10 at the *Princess Royal* from 1627 to 1636. On the British side, the *Lion* ceased firing at 1634 after expending 48 salvos, while the *Princess Royal* and *New Zealand* apparently continued until 1636, and the *Tiger* until 1639. None of the four reopened before 1649.

The 2nd LCS held on towards the German battlefleet in order to obtain more information, and did not turn north-westwards at 1640. At this time, or a minute or so later, the *Nottingham* fired an ER torpedo ('Extreme Range'; *c*17,000yds at 18kts) at the 7th German ship, the *Kaiserin*. The reported range was about 16,500yds but must have been greater, and no hit was obtained.

The 5th BS also did not act on Beatty's 1640 signal, as they were about 8 miles astern and flags quite invisible. At 1630 they had turned by subdivisions to about 173°, in anticipation of the German destroyer attack being directed against them, and at 1636 returned to line ahead on a course of approximately 156°. As with the rival battlecruisers, the firing of the 5th BS had largely died away, as the visibility worsened and the light grey German ships merged into the haze.

Astern of the fighting the 1st and 3rd LCS and the three rear ships of the 2nd SG had again come into sight of one another at about 1625. Shortly before this, the *Frankfurt* had opened fire to starboard at an imaginary submarine 650yds away, that was thought to have fired an equally imaginary torpedo passing a short distance astern. The only other incident was that the *G37*, which had fallen far astern of the other destroyers, fired two torpedoes without effect at the British light cruisers at a time given as 1644 and at a range of 10,300yds.

During the period of the battle between Beatty's signal to turn northward at 1640, and Evan-Thomas's turn at 1654, the British battlecruisers were only within the maximum range of the German battleships for a short time; the 5th BS never were, but their continued southward course subsequently placed them in considerable danger from the German 3rd Squadron. Scheer had signalled the German battlefleet to turn by divisions to 325° at 1642, and at 1645 he ordered distribution of fire from the right, ship against ship, followed a minute later by the order to open fire, though it was about 1648 before the first ships opened. At this time both the British battlecruisers and the 5th BS could be made out from the *Friedrich der Grosse*, though the 5th BS were well out of range, and the battlecruisers only doubtfully in reach of the leading ships. Scheer made no other alteration of course in this period, but called for a further increase in speed at 1654.

The *König*, now gradually working up to full speed, opened on the *Lion* but her shots were short, and she ceased firing at 1654 after four salvos. The *Grosser Kurfürst* fired at the *Princess Royal*, and the *Markgraf* at the *Tiger* but both were short. The *Prinzregent Luitpold and Kaiserin* also fired at the battlecruisers, the former choosing the most easily made out target, thought to be of the *Lion* class, and the latter the *New Zealand*. Both were short, though the *Prinzregent Luitpold* fired at up to 22,300yds, as her mountings had been altered to allow 16° elevation. Beatty had altered course at about 1644 from 302° to 347° and at 1651 to 325° so that he was on a parallel course, and at 1654 turned to *c*285° which increased his distance from the 3rd Squadron and also avoided the immediate vicinity of the *Queen Mary*'s wreck.

The 2nd Light Cruiser Squadron held on towards the German battlefleet until about 14,000–15,000yds away before beginning their turn at 1645. There was some doubt as to whether they were the 2nd Scouting Group, although the *Rostock* fired at one of them from 1645 to 1649, and the German battleships held their fire until the distinctive broadside appearance of the British light cruisers could be seen. The *Friedrich der Grosse, Kaiser, Kronprinz* and all eight ships of the 1st Squadron then opened fire between 1648 and 1652, so that eleven dreadnoughts were firing at the 2nd LCS. Only the *Kaiser, Ostfriesland*, and *Nassau* continued for long firing at the *Southampton*, and the *Kronprinz* and *Thüringen* at the *Dublin*.

The 2nd LCS managed to evade the German shells very skilfully, and escaped undamaged apart from an oblique hit on the *Southampton*'s port side aft, thought to have been by an 11in shell from the *Nassau* soon after she opened fire at 1650 at 20,100yds.

Prior to the German battlefleet opening fire, the 5th Battle Squadron and the 1st Scouting Group had been engaging each other at long range. The 5th BS steered near 156° from 1636 to 1647 and then between 178° and 173°. At 1648 Beatty signalled them by flags to alter course in succession 180° to starboard. He was then 3–3½ miles from the *Barham*, but the signal was not hauled down to give the executive order until after the two flagships had passed on nearly opposite courses about 2½ miles apart, so that the turn was not made until 1654.

The 1st Scouting Group, after turning together to 190° at 1641, turned together to 122° at 1645/46 and reformed line ahead, course 167°, at 1649. At 1652 they began to turn in succession 180°s to starboard, and took station ahead of the battlefleet.

The 5th BS seem to have reopened fire at about 1640 as at this time Evan-Thomas signalled them to concentrate in pairs from the rear. It is probable that they engaged the ships that could be seen most clearly, but visibility must have been fairly good as the *Malaya* reported a gun range of 21,500yds, at about this time. The 5th BS had to cease fire when Beatty's battlecruisers passed between them and the target just before their turn northward. The least range was about 18,000-19,000yds, and one 15in hit was scored on the *Seydlitz*'s forecastle at 1650, but it is not possible to say which ship was responsible.

Hipper ordered the 1st Scouting Group to open fire on the 5th BS at 1644 and about 2 minutes later the *Valiant* was severely shaken by a salvo which fell very close on the port side aft. The *Malaya* also reported salvos falling just ahead, and it was probably at this time the *Barham* received her second hit, presumably from the *Lützow*. The shell struck over the wing engine-room and caused much damage to light structures. The *Derfflinger* fired a total of seven salvos in 4 minutes 40 seconds from 1645 in spite of alterations of course, changing to semi AP for the last three of these which were fired in 50 seconds at 19,700yds. The *von der Tann* did not engage the 5th BS at this time, and the *Moltke* fired little, if at all, as the range was too great. The other German battlecruisers ceased firing at the 5th BS when they were masked by Beatty's ships, and the *Lützow*, *Seydlitz* and *Moltke* changed targets to the latter after turning ahead of the battlefleet.

The surviving British battlecruisers reopened from 1649. The *Lion* fired four salvos at a ship which was probably the light cruiser *Wiesbaden*. The *Princess Royal* fired four salvos at the *Regensburg* and then shifted to one of the battlecruisers, while the *Tiger* fired two salvos at an indistinct target, possibly the *Seydlitz*, and the *New Zealand* only fired briefly, if at all, as she was incorrectly believed to be out of range.

Beatty had recalled his destroyers at 1643, and at 1650 ordered them to close and take station ahead but these signals made by flags, were not seen by some of the destroyers, which carried out very gallant attacks at about this time. It is impossible to be certain over the details, but the following appears to have been the course of events. The *Nestor* and *Nicator* which had previously made one attack on the German battlecruisers, closed again to within 3000-4000yds of the *Lützow*, though if the *Lützow*'s 5.9in firing between 1639 and 1645 was at these destroyers as appears likely, her least range was 6600yds, and the *Derfflinger*'s report gives a minimum of 5500yds for her 10–5.9in salvos from 1642 to *c*1648. In any event the *Nestor* fired one torpedo at the *Lützow* which failed to hit, and the *Nicator* also fired a torpedo at the *Derfflinger* without success. One or both of the destroyers opened fire with their guns, as seven hits from 4in shells were scored on the *Derfflinger*. Both escaped disablement from the secondary batteries of the battlecruisers, and of the two or three leading battleships which engaged them at *c*13,000yds for a few minutes, but the *Regensburg* also took part, and though the *Nicator* got away unscathed, the *Nestor* was hit twice in her boilers and eventually came to a stop. A tow from the *Petard* was refused and the *Nestor* and also the *Nomad*, disabled in the first destroyer fighting, were later sunk by some of the German battleships.

The *Petard* also made another attack and, according to the Torpedo School analysis, fired her last torpedo at 6500yds at the second battlecruiser, the torpedo director being set for a target steaming 23kts on a similar course inclined at 120° to the torpedo track. This torpedo is usually credited as being the one which hit the *Seydlitz* at 1657, but the *Turbulent*, later sunk during the night, was apparently following the *Petard*, and probably fired torpedoes at this time. The German Official History states that she fired three in this phase of the battle, and this is partly confirmed by a statement from a survivor in Wilhelmshaven hospital that two torpedoes were fired from her after tubes. It appears that the 1st Scouting Group's alteration of course to 347° caused the *Seydlitz* to steam directly towards a number of torpedoes, and when it was too late to avoid them, the tracks of two were sighted to starboard, as well as another running on the surface, and several that had finished their runs. A few moments later at 1657, the *Seydlitz* was hit by a torpedo on the starboard part of the fore-turret. The torpedo bulkhead held, though bulged and leaking, and the *Seydlitz* was able to keep her place in the line and did not reduce speed.

The *Nerissa* fired two torpedoes at 7000yds which apparently passed by the *von der Tann* as she was turning to 347°, and the *Moorsom* made two attacks on the German battle-fleet, probably at a time subsequent to the 5th Battle Squadron's turn. In the first of these she fired two torpedoes at 8500yds at the *Grosser Kurfürst*, and although then hit by a 5.9in shell which damaged her oil-fuel tanks, fired two more torpedoes at the same range at the *Markgraf* and got away without

Chart II: Position at 1650

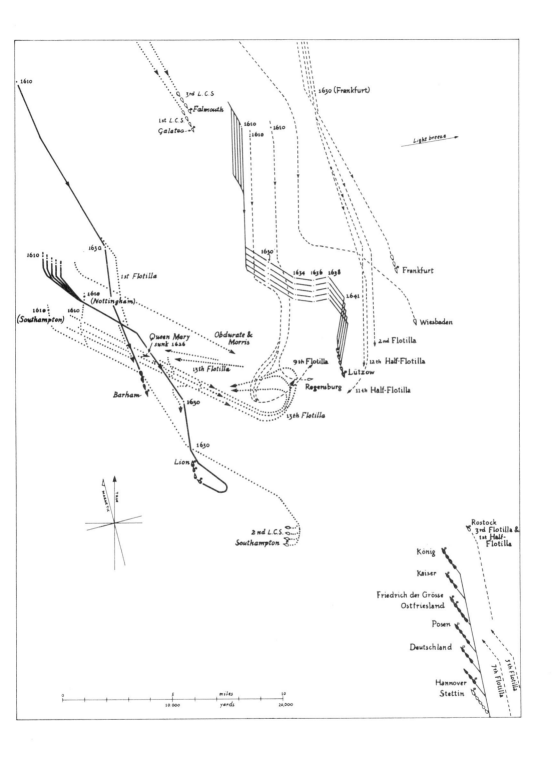

1610

1630 (Frankfurt)

3rd L.C.S.

Falmouth

1st L.C.S.
Galatea

1610
1610 1610

Light breeze

1630

1st Flotilla

1610
(Nottingham)

1630

1634 1636 1638

Frankfurt

1610
(Southampton)

1610 1610

1641

Wiesbaden

Queen Mary
sunk 1626

Obdurate &
Morris

2nd Flotilla

12th Half-Flotilla

9th Flotilla

Lützow

13th Flotilla

Regensburg

14th Half-Flotilla

Barham

1630

13th Flotilla

1630

Lion

1630

MAGNETIC

TRUE

2nd L.C.S.

Southampton

Rostock
3rd Flotilla &
1st Half-
Flotilla

König

Kaiser

Friedrich der Grösse
Ostfriesland

Posen

Deutschland

5th Flotilla

7th Flotilla

Hannover
Stettin

0   5   miles   10
                10,000   yards   20,000

further damage. None of her four torpedoes hit. The *König* reported firing 9–5.9in salvos between 1659 and 1706, and it would seem that the *Moorsom* was her target, while the *Grosser Kurfürst* claimed 3–5.9in hits at *c*9000yds on a destroyer which was also probably the *Moorsom*, as was the destroyer fired at by the *Rostock* from 1657 to 1704.

Altogether the destroyers of the 13th and 10th Flotillas had fired nineteen torpedoes, allowing three to the *Turbulent*, and made two hits, on the *Seydlitz* and the *V29*.

At about 1650 another torpedo attack was made by *G41* and the three boats of the 11th Half-Flotilla. The 5th BS and the battlecruisers were passing one another, and appeared to offer a good target. A total of seven torpedoes (the *G41*, *V44*, *G87*, two each: the *G86*, one) was fired at about 9000–10,000yds without success and it is not certain that any tracks were sighted from the British line, though there are unconfirmed reports of a torpedo passing ahead of the *Valiant* and of another passing astern of her, which may refer to this attack. At this time *G103* and *G104* also began an attack on the battlecruisers, but abandoned it as they were too far astern.

During this first phase of the battle which is often known as 'The Run to the South', Jellicoe had continued on 133°. In a signal timed at 1550, Beatty had reported that he was engaging the enemy, the *Lion*'s position being given as 56° 53′N, 5° 31′E, which may have been correct to within about 4 miles. At 1559 a signal from the *Galatea* was intercepted giving her position as 57° 03′N, 5° 27′E, which was probably 5–6 miles out, and stating that the enemy bore 100°, course 100°. This probably referred to the 2nd Scouting Group. Jellicoe at this time increased to 20kts, which was his greatest practicable fleet speed. Nothing had yet been heard of the 5th BS and at 1617 Jellicoe asked Evan-Thomas if he was in company with Beatty, a brief but satisfactory reply being sent at about 1630 'Yes, I am engaging Enemy.'

The *Southampton*'s signal reporting an enemy cruiser at 1630 was received in mutilated form, but her signal at 1638, reporting the German battlefleet bearing approximately 122°, course 347°, was correctly taken in. Unfortunately the *Southampton*'s signalled position, 56° 34′N, 6° 20′E was about 13 miles too far to the eastward. The *Champion*'s signal gave the bearing of the centre of the German line as 122°, but the course as 55°, and her position, 56° 51′N, 5° 46′E, was possibly as much as 14 or 15 miles too far to the northward. The *Champion*'s report was received in the *Iron Duke* about 6 minutes after the *Southampton*'s and it clearly had less weight with Jellicoe, who signalled to the Grand Fleet at 1647 that the enemy's battlefleet was coming north (347°), and at 1651 wirelessed the Admiralty that a fleet action was imminent. Further reports of the German battlefleet by the *Lion* via the *Princess Royal*, and by the *Southampton*, timed at 1645/46, were not received in the *Iron Duke* until 1700 or later.

Hood's 3rd Battlecruiser Squadron had taken in Beatty's signal that he was engaging the enemy, and at 1600 Hood increased to 24kts, and two minutes later altered course slightly to 145°. At 1605 Jellicoe ordered him to proceed immediately to support the Battlecruiser Fleet. Beatty's 1550 position was included, and also the last reported course of 112°, which was an estimate of Hipper's course at 1545. In a signal timed at 1606, Hood gave his position as 57° 39′N, 5° 35′E (probably 7 miles too far north), course 145° and speed 25kts. He was thus by his own reckoning, about 25 miles 85°, and nearly 49 miles 355° from the estimated 1606 positions of the *Iron Duke* and *Lion*, respectively. Hood had anticipated Jellicoe's order, and continued on 145° until 1650 when he altered course to 156° and 6 minutes later asked Beatty for his position, course and speed, but this signal does not seem to have been correctly received as a repeat was requested at 1730. Hood's courses later proved to have been very fortunate, and enabled the 3rd BCS and attached destroyers to intervene in the battle with an effect quite disproportionate to their limited strength.

In the first phase of the action, now concluded by the 5th Battle Squadron's turn to the northward, Hipper had scored a notable success. Outnumbered two to one in heavy ships, he had inflicted far heavier losses than he had suffered, and had brought Beatty's forces within reach of Scheer, though the four surviving British battlecruisers had already managed to get clear of the German battleships.

CHAPTER 5

Damage to capital ships 1548–1654

Dᴇᴛᴀɪʟꜱ ᴏꜰ ᴇᴠᴇɴᴛꜱ in the *Indefatigable* and *Queen Mary* are meagre, but there is little doubt that flash reaching a magazine from cordite charges ignited in a gunhouse, working chamber or trunk, was responsible for their destruction.

Rear Admiral Pakenham in the *New Zealand*, reported that two or three shells falling together hit the *Indefatigable* about the outer edge of the upper deck in line with 'X' turret. A small explosion followed and she swung out of the line sinking by the stern. She was hit again almost instantly near 'A' turret by another salvo, listed heavily to port, turned over and disappeared. Pakenham had seen the *Borodino* blow up at Tsushima, and was probably the only officer present at Jutland who had seen a large ship blown up by gunfire. He was on the *New Zealand*'s upper bridge during the battle, but it is not clear how much of the sinking of the *Indefatigable* was actually observed by him. The Navigating Officer of the *New Zealand*, Commander Creighton, who was stationed in the conning tower, stated that the Torpedo Officer's attention was drawn to the *Indefatigable* by the Admiral's Secretary, both of whom were also in the conning tower. The Torpedo Officer, Lieutenant-Commander Lovett-Cameron, crossed to the starboard side of the conning tower, and observed her through his glasses. She had been hit aft, apparently by the mainmast, and a good deal of smoke was coming from the superstructure aft, but there were no flames visible, and Lovett-Cameron thought that the smoke came from her boom boats. The *New Zealand* was turning to port at the time, and the *Indefatigable*'s steering gear seemed to be damaged, as she did not follow round, but held on until she was about 500yds on the *New Zealand*'s starboard quarter, and in full view from the conning tower. While

Lovett–Cameron still had his glasses on her, the *Indefatigable* was hit by two shells, one on the forecastle, and the other on 'A' turret. Both shells appeared to explode on impact. There was then an appreciable interval, said to be about 30 seconds, during which there was no sign of fire, flame or smoke, except the little amount formed by the shell-bursts. At the end of this interval, the *Indefatigable* completely blew up, apparently beginning from forward. The main explosion started with sheets of flame, followed immediately by dense, dark smoke, hiding the ship from view, while many objects were blown high in the air.

The *von der Tann*'s gunnery report states that four salvos straddled the *Indefatigable*, and she then began firing 5.9in in addition. After a further seven salvos, several heavy explosions occured amidships and aft. The *Indefatigable* was enveloped in dense smoke for some time, and when this had dispersed, she had disappeared. It was observed from the *von der Tann* that the great cloud of black smoke was twice the height of the *Indefatigable*'s masts.

The *B98*, which was some distance on the *von der Tann*'s port quarter, observed a hit at 1602, and immediately afterwards a second hit. There was a high column of flame, two heavy explosion clouds far above the masts and also jets of flame. The *B97* reported three heavy explosions following one another, while the *V30*, ahead of the *Lützow*, noted a serious fire at 1602, and 2 minutes later a high column of fire.

The two survivors, Able Seaman Elliott and Leading Signalman Falmer, picked up by the *S16* at 1950, were both stationed in the top, and thought that the *Indefatigable* had been torpedoed and sunk within 4 minutes. They tried to support Captain Sowerby in the water, but he was too badly wounded to survive.

Creighton's account, given in *The Fighting at Jutland*, is detailed, but it is not supported by a photograph taken by Captain W P Carne who was then a midshipman in the *New Zealand*'s after torpedo control station. This was taken just before the final explosion in the *Indefatigable*, and shows her sinking by the stern to port with the whole after part of the ship to near the middle funnel already under water. Whatever the cause of the final explosion in her, the loss of the *Indefatigable* was due to an initial explosion in 'X' magazines, probably from a shell striking 'X' barbette below the upper deck, and this could not have been seen from the *New Zealand*'s conning tower as the view astern was very restricted.

It is impossible to determine the number of hits on the *Indefatigable* with certainty, but it seems most likely that the *von der Tann* obtained one hit previously, and two from each of her last two salvos to give a total of 5–11in.

There is more data available on the loss of the *Queen Mary*. Midshipman Storey who was in 'Q' turret, stated that several hits were heard to strike up to about 10 minutes before she blew up, and at 1621 a heavy shell hit 'Q' turret on the sloping armour at the right side of the right gun. All training and elevating gear was smashed, and the right gun completely out of action. At that time 'Q' turret had fired 17 rounds per gun and the left gun fired three more, when there was a terrific explosion, forward, thought to be 'B' magazine. The explosion rocked 'Q' turret about and the shock broke the left gun in half just outside the gun-house. The left gun breech dropped into the working chamber, and the right gun came off the trunnions, and the breech was dropping down towards the working chamber when Storey started to get out. Some cordite caught fire in the working chamber and the fumes killed many in the gun-house. When he was on top of the turret, Storey could see where the ship had broken off by the foremast, and the stern was coming rapidly out of the water. Then the 'X' turret magazine blew up, and the survivors from 'Q' were blown into the water.

It is improbable that 'Q' left gun was broken in half by the shock of the explosion forward, but there is some evidence that a hit occured near 'Q' turret at the same time as the fatal hit near 'B', and it may be that this hit was on 'Q' left gun.

From 'X' turret Midshipman Lloyd-Owen survived, but his account is not as complete as that of Petty Officer (Gunner's Mate) Francis. Initially Francis did not notice any noise of hits, but soon afterwards a heavy blow struck, thought to be in the after 4in battery, as a lot of dust and pieces were flying around on top of 'X' turret. Another hit seems to have then occurred near 'X', as a man who went on top of the turret to clean the periscope glasses was killed or severely wounded. Shortly after this, another shock was felt, which did not affect 'X', and was perhaps the 1621 hit on 'Q'. A big explosion then shook 'X' turret and the hydraulic pressure failed. Immediately afterwards, a much larger explosion occured, and the floor of 'X' turret was bulged up and the guns made absolutely useless. Francis stated that the left gun had apparently fallen through the trunnions, and Lloyd-Owen that both guns were right off on their slides. Francis looked through the hole in the turret roof and saw that the after 4in battery was smashed out of recognition, and that the ship had a very heavy list to port. Orders were given to clear the turret, and the survivors got out, though there was none from the working chamber as water was right up the main trunk. Francis managed to reach the starboard side of the ship, and had swum some distance away, when there was another big explosion, and the air was full of flying fragments.

Lloyd–Owen stated that when he got out of the turret, the ship was heeling at about 45°, and the stern was in the air. Nothing could be seen forward, and all the side plating had gone, and the ship was on fire aft. There was a terrific lurch, a second explosion was heard forward, and he was thrown into the water. Just as he was in the water, another explosion was heard overhead.

Captain Pelly of the *Tiger* reported that he observed a salvo pitch abreast 'Q' turret, the first time he had seen the *Queen Mary* hit, and almost instantaneously there was a terrific upheaval, and a dense cloud of smoke, which could not be altogether avoided as the *Tiger* was only about 2 cables from the *Queen Mary*. As the *Tiger* passed through the smoke cloud, there was a heavy fall of material on her decks, but no sign of the *Queen Mary*.

Rear Admiral Brock, in the *Princess Royal*, also reported that the *Queen Mary* was hit by a plunging salvo near 'Q' turret which apparently penetrated the armoured deck and ignited the magazine. A bright flame was observed to shoot up as she was hit, followed almost immediately by a mass of cordite smoke in which she disappeared. This report may not be independent of the *Tiger's*, and it is not likely that a shell reached a magazine through the armour deck.

The *New Zealand's* Navigating Officer, Commander Creighton, saw a salvo hit the *Queen Mary* on the port side. A small cloud of what looked like coal–dust, came out from where she was hit, but nothing more happened until several moments later, when a terrific yellow flame with a heavy and very dense mass of black smoke showed ahead, and the *Queen Mary* herself was no longer visible. The *Tiger* hauled sharply out to port and disappeared in the smoke, and the *New Zealand* hauled out to starboard and passed the *Queen Mary* close on the *New Zealand's* port beam. The smoke had now blown fairly clear and the stern could be seen, afloat from the after funnel with the propellers still revolving, but the forward part of the ship had already vanished. There was no sign of fire or cordite flame and men were crawling out of 'X' turret and up the after hatchway. When the *New Zealand* was abreast and only about 150yds away, the after part of the hull rolled over and as it did so blew up. Masses of paper and much else was blown in the air, and before the *New Zealand* had quite passed, the *Queen Mary* completely disappeared.

In the *Petard*, when picking up Petty Officer Francis, part of the bilge of a ship was seen in the middle of an oil patch floating about a foot out of water.

The German Official History says that the *Queen Mary*'s masts and funnels were distinctly observed by several ships to fall inwards, while smoke and flames issued from the hull, and the former rose to 2000ft, at times completely obscuring the *Tiger* and *New Zealand*. The *Seydlitz* reported a small outbreak of fire in the *Queen Mary* shortly before she blew up, which was thought to be an ammunition fire as noticed in other ships. The *Derfflinger*'s official report notes that a dense black smoke cloud rose to several hundred yards without a considerable development of flame and in the after gunnery control a particularly violent explosion was seen to the right of the smoke cloud from the *Queen Mary* at a time given as 1630, and this presumably was the final explosion in her wreck.

The course of events would seem to have been as follows:

1 Several hits up to about 1615. Apparently including a hit in the after 4in battery, and perhaps another hit near 'X' turret. Possibly serious damage in the after 4in battery, including ammunition fire noticed by the *Seydlitz*.

2 About 1621. Hit on right side of 'Q' turret and right gun out of action.

3 1626. Hit on 'A' or 'B' turret or barbette, and perhaps on left gun of 'Q' turret. Explosion somewhere in 'A' or 'B' shook ship and hydraulic pressure failed in turrets. Immediately afterwards 'A' and 'B' magazines exploded. Forepart of ship broken off near foremast and probably destroyed completely. 'Q' and 'X' turrets wrecked, with cordite fire in 'Q' working chamber.

4 After part of ship listing heavily, stern in air and propellers still revolving.

5 As heel increased, an explosion blew up remainder of ship.

It is thought that the *Seydlitz* scored about four hits in the first half hour. The shells hitting at about 1621 and at 1626 are considered to have come from the *Derfflinger* and the estimate is thus: Up to c1615: 4–11in, c1621: 1–12in, c1626: 2–12in – giving a total of seven hits.

The *Lion* had nine certain hits from 12in SAP in this phase, all from the *Lützow*. By far the most serious hit was that on 'Q' turret at 1600 when the range was about 16,500yds. This shell which was estimated to have an angle of fall of about 20° to the horizontal, struck on the right upper corner of the left gun port, which was formed by the junction of the 9in centre face plate and the 3¼in roof. A piece of 9in armour was driven into the gun-house and the shell also entered and burst about 3ft from impact over the centre-line of the left gun, after being deflected slightly on the gun collars. Everyone in the gun-house was killed or wounded. The front roof plate was blown off, and lay upside down on the port side of the deck about 12ft from the turret, while the centre face

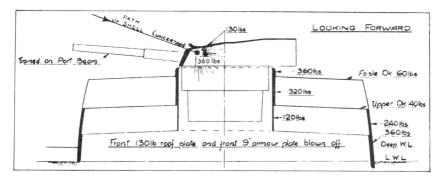

Lion: hit on 'Q' turret at 1600.

plate was also dislodged and came to rest about 15ft abaft the turret and close to the ship's side. The left gun was damaged and later condemned, and many light fittings were damaged inside the gun-house. The centre and left sights were destroyed, as was the left Director receiver, though the right sight and Director receiver were intact. Fragments pierced three pressure pipes but all the hydraulic machinery remained operative even after the subsequent cordite fire, except for the radial crane presses. A fire occurred in the gun-house which the fire party thought they had extinguished from above. At the time of the hit, the right gun was in the act of loading, with the shell rammed home and the rammer back. As No 1 fell back dead, he pulled the gun-loading cage lever to 'lower', and the gun-loading cage went down to 4ft above the working chamber with cordite in it. The left gun-loading cage was in the working chamber and loaded . Both waiting positions in the working chamber were loaded, while both central cages were down and loaded, and both magazine hoppers loaded with cordite.

Two or three minutes after the hit, the *Lion*'s Chief Gunner, Mr Alexander Grant, visited 'Q' magazine, and while there, one of the working chamber crew arrived in the handing room down the trunk, and told the Chief Gunner the state of affairs. Orders were given for the magazine doors to be closed and later for the magazine to be flooded. At 1628 the Chief Gunner was approaching the hatch to the handing room on the main deck, when a large sheet of flame came up the hatch killing several of the fire party in the vicinity. As soon as the smoke had sufficiently cleared, a party headed by the Chief Gunner went down to the handing room and other compartments, and found half the shell room crew in the shell room burned to death, as well as the magazine and half shell room crews in the handing room and switchboard flat. The paint in the handing room and shell room near the hoist was blackened and blistered but by no means all burnt, and the switchboard was blackened but intact.

It was conjectured that the fire had spread from the gun-house to the working chamber via the electric cables as they were the only things burnt as opposed to blistered or blackened. All that is certain, however, is that a smouldering fire in the gun-house spread in some manner to the working chamber and ignited the charges there. The effect of the ignition of the eight charges that were between the handing room and 4ft above the working chamber, was very violent, although vented by the absence of part of the turret roof, and by the handing room hatch being open. The flame went as high as the mastheads, and 'Q' magazine bulkheads were considerably buckled and bulged inwards although supported by the water in the magazine which had probably by then been completely flooded. If the magazine had still been open, the *Lion* would, without any doubt have followed the *Indefatigable* and *Queen Mary*.

The above account is largely taken from Jellicoe's memorandum of 16 June 1916 which contained notes on the more important damage to the battlecruisers and the *Warspite* and was later reproduced in Grand Fleet Gunnery and Torpedo Order No 15 on the lessons of Jutland. There is no mention in this of the part played by Major FJW Harvey, RMLI, the officer of the turret, except that he sent a messenger to the bridge to report that the turret was out of action. Major Harvey was awarded a posthumous VC for giving orders to close the magazine doors and flood the magazine when he was mortally wounded; in the event the order to flood the magazine came from the Captain to the transmitting station, and William · Yeo, Stoker 1st class, special messenger to the transmitting station, was the man actually sent to order 'Q' magazine to be flooded. The transmitting station asked for the order to be repeated, as the *Lion* had partially flooded 'A' magazine in error at the Dogger Bank battle, and Grand Fleet Gunnery Orders after the action had indicated that the person in charge of a magazine, if there was no fire there, should take steps to find out why the order to flood had been given, and inform a responsible officer of what was occurring.

In this case it was fortunate that 'Q' magazine was flooded in time, as tests later showed that magazine doors as then fitted, were by no means flash tight when closed. As it was, a venting plate admitted a tongue of flame into the magazine but no harm was done. At that date magazine venting plates were fitted in handing rooms, so that a sudden pressure rise in the magazine from spontaneously ignited cordite would vent into the handing room and thence up the space between the fixed and revolving turret structures, and also up the turret trunk. They were not flash-tight in the reverse direction.

Many lives might have been saved if orders had been given to clear the whole of 'Q' turret once the magazine had been flooded, and it is not clear why the charges between turret and magazine were not returned to the latter before closing the doors, which would have prevented the cordite fire. The other eight hits on the *Lion* in this phase of the battle were, in order from forward:

1 Hit about 115ft from bows and shattered starboard cable holder; passed through the $\frac{1}{2}$in forecastle deck, a $\frac{1}{4}$in water-tight bulkhead, and out through the $\frac{7}{16}$in side, making a hole of 30in × 20in, without bursting.

2 Passed through the 1in side plating between the forecastle and upper decks near the fore funnel, and struck the 1in upper deck making a scooped hole 15ft × 2ft. The shell was deflected up and passed through a $\frac{3}{4}$in ventilator side, and out through the 1in forecastle deck at its junction with the ventilator side. It then went through a $\frac{1}{2}$in blast screen making a hole 7ft × 3ft and finally overboard without bursting, though it may have subsequently burst in the air. This shell came from forward of the beam and passed through a total of about $4\frac{1}{2}$in of plate. Damage on the line of its path is described as 'moderate', but a considerable fire which was most troublesome to extinguish, was caused in the Navigator's cabin where the shell entered, and much dense smoke produced, some of which was drawn down by the boiler room fans.

3 Passed through a $\frac{1}{2}$in blast screen and $\frac{1}{4}$in funnel casing and burst on the $1\frac{1}{4}$in forecastle deck at base of the middle funnel. The funnel base was severely damaged with a hole 12ft × 15ft in the casing, but the draught was not reduced appreciably. The forecastle deck was displaced up to 10in for an area of 8ft × 20in and a fire started, while 'D' and 'B' boiler-rooms were filled with fumes and smoke. Practically no damage was done to the armour gratings which caught many fragments. This hit was also by a shell coming from forward of the beam.

4 Ricochet passed through a $\frac{1}{2}$in blast screen to the middle funnel, and dropped unexploded between screen and funnel.

5 Hit the 6in upper belt in line with the forward edge of 'Q' barbette. The shell coming from abaft the beam, struck a glancing blow near the joint between two plates and probably burst on impact. The surface of the forward plate was depressed over a 12in diameter circle with some spalling and concentric cracks, and the top corner forced in 3in. The surface of the after plate was little damaged and the top corner was driven in 1in. Plating and framing behind the armour were slightly deformed.

6 Passed through the roof of the after 4in control and out through the side of the control position, which was of thin plating, without exploding.

7 and 8 Two shells, coming from abaft the beam, struck about 5-6ft apart on the

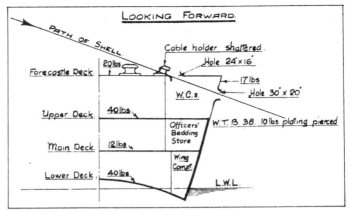

Lion: *hit No 1.*

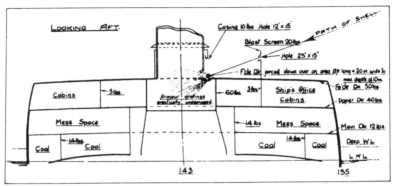

Lion: *hit No 3.*

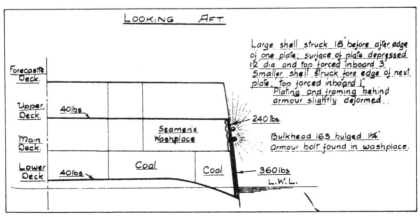

Lion: *hit No 5.*

¾in vertical plating between the forecastle and upper decks, aft of the after 4in battery. They passed through the starboard ¾in vertical plating also, and burst either just above or on the 1in upper deck 24ft from impact, making a hole 8ft × 8ft inboard of the canteen store roof. The ⁵⁄₁₆in main deck below was damaged, and many casualties caused among the 4in guns' crews, the approximate figures being 19 killed and 35 wounded.

Of the above eight hits, No 2 was at 1551, No 3 at 1552 and Nos 7 and 8 at 1624. The times of the other four hits cannot be given individually, but the *Lion* was hit at 1601, 1601.30, 1603 and 1624.30. It will be seen that apart from the hit on 'Q' turret, the *Lion* was far less severely damaged in this phase of the action than at the Dogger Bank. The number of 12in SAP which failed to explode should be noted.

The information on the *Princess Royal*'s hits is not satisfactory. Her report places the total for the whole battle at about nine heavy hits and Jellicoe's memorandum of 16 June gives a figure of about ten, without stating if they were all heavy. Only the six most interesting hits, of which three came from port, have been recorded in detail, but from photographs it is possible to identify three more on the port side, and it is thus considered that there were 6–12in hits in the first phase of the battle, all from the *Derfflinger*.

At 1558. One shell hit the 6in belt in line with the centre of 'B' barbette, and a little below the main deck. The range was about 15,500yds, and the shell struck somewhat obliquely at an angle of 25–30° to the normal. It pierced the armour, making a hole 13in in diameter and displacing the plate to some extent, and burst 5ft from impact in the port forward reserve bunker. The coal was not ignited, though hot fragments fired bags and gear on the main deck. A hole 6ft × 5ft was blown up through the ⁵⁄₁₆in main deck, and the coal passage bulkhead by the burst was blown away for a length of 8½ft. Water-tight bulkheads near the burst were much damaged, and the port forward reserve bunker was flooded for a length of 32ft, and 'A' upper bunker also flooded. The former bunker was intended to protect the forward magazines, and may well have prevented this shell from reaching them. In addition the fire main pipe, and the flood valve gearing to 'B' port magazine were wrecked.

The second shell at this time burst or broke up on striking the 6in upper belt below the bridge. The shock of these two hits caused the fuzes of the Argo fire control tower training motor to blow, set up the hand training gear, and jammed the range-finder transmitter. Splinters cut the voice pipes from the Argo tower to the compass platform and Director tower.

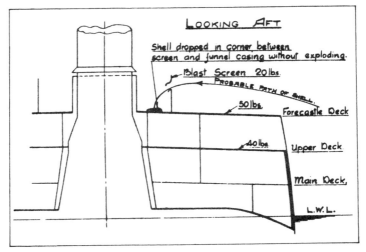

Lion: *hit No 4.*

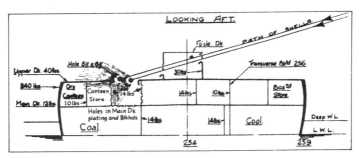

Lion: *hits Nos 7 and 8.*

At *c*1600. Shell struck a ½in port cover between the forecastle and upper decks 12ft abaft the centre of 'B' barbette. It passed through a coal trunk and two light bulkheads and burst 22ft from impact on the 1in upper deck in which a hole 5ft × 5ft was blown. Severe damage was caused to light structures, and the 8in barbette armour was forced back about 1in at the butt by the explosion *c*8ft distant, though the 3in armour below the upper deck was unaffected. Several small fires were started, and fumes and gas entered the fore dressing station, which had to be evacuated for a time, and also reached the transmitting station and lower conning tower. There were eight killed and thirty eight wounded from this hit, mostly from burns and gas.

Between *c*1627 and 1632. One shell struck the muzzle of the right gun of 'Q' turret and burst about 10ft off in the air, causing minor damage to the forecastle deck. The inner 'A' tube of the gun was cracked for 2in and the right trunnion bush scored, but the gun continued firing.

Another shell passed through the second funnel without exploding, and a third, which was probably a ricochet, burst on the junction of the 6in and 9in side armour in line with the fore funnel.

In addition to these hits, the *Princess Royal* had a serious breakdown in 'A' turret. On the left gun the stud axis crank pinion sheered with the breech closed, and it could not be opened for eleven hours. Considerable delay was also caused to the right gun in this turret by a bent retractor lever causing misfires.

In the *Tiger* both 'Q' and 'X' turrets were hit at 1554 at about 13,500yds range. The 3¼in front roof plate of 'Q' turret was struck close to the centre sighting hood, at an angle of about 22° to the plate face by a shell which burst on impact. The plate was lifted 2in at the right rear corner and most of the fastenings fractured. The centre sighting hood was knocked off and the side hoods shaken, the right one being sheared off its fastenings. The roof kept the shell out, but it was holed over an area of 3ft3in × 4ft8in, and there were eight casualties (three killed), while shell fragments made a hole 9in × 3in in the turntable centre girder. The centre and right sights and the centre position training gear were wrecked, and the range-finder was out of action, the left sight 'wooded', and all firing circuits cut. The air cock was blown off the right run in and out cylinder of the left gun, causing loss of water when the gun ran out. Both gun-loading cages were jammed, but after removing the cam rail actuating the cordite flash doors, the left cage could be used, though the right gun had to go to

Princess Royal: *hit at 1558.*

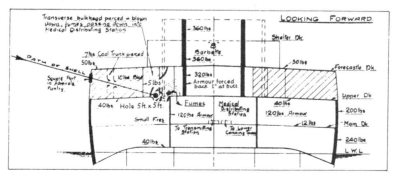

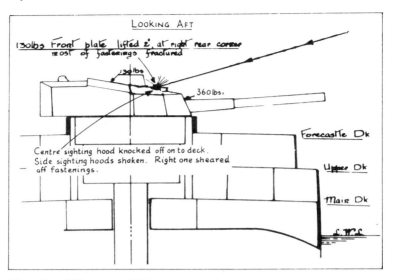

Tiger: *hit on 'Q' barbette at 1554.*

secondary loading for the rest of the battle. Both guns were soon brought back into action, and as the Director gear was undamaged, they were laid and trained by Director and fired by percussion on hearing the forward guns fire.

Cordite fumes caused some trouble as the compressed air supply failed as a result of Hit No 9 below, and in the whole action 'Q' only fired 32 rounds, of which two were before the hit, as compared with 109 rounds by 'B' turret.

'X' turret was hit on the 9in barbette armour near its junction with the 3in armour and the 1in upper deck. A piece of 9in armour 27in ×16in was broken off, the 3in armour dented in about 3in and the upper deck holed, while the 4in armour plate adjoining the 3in was also dented at the top corner. The shell entered the turret through the revolving structure about 3ft below the lower edge of the turret shield, but did not explode properly, though the bursting charge ignited with a partial burst and partial rocket effect just inside the turn-table, and the body of the shell without the point, remained in the lower floor of the gun-house between the guns in the centre of the turret, together with large fragments of armour. The centre sight-setter was blown against the roof and killed but there were apparently no other casualties, respirators preventing any gassing. The centre training shaft was smashed, one of the flash doors jammed, the left gun depression control valve casting fractured which led to water running down to the handing room, and the Director laying and firing circuits cut. After 7 minutes the turret began firing again, and both guns were able to continue in action with Director training, individual laying and percussion firing. A total of 75 rounds was fired by 'X' turret in the battle but some probably went very wide as at 1811 it was discovered that the turret was 19° off its correct bearing in Director training, and had to be lined up. The effect of these two hits was thus to reduce the *Tiger* to at best a 3-turret ship.

In addition to the above, 12 more 11in hits were made on the *Tiger*. In order from forward these were:

1 Struck the ½in forecastle deck 10ft from the port edge and about 107ft from the bows, coming from *c*50° abaft the beam, and burst 22ft from impact. Severe damage was caused to light structures and the fire-main wrecked. Fragments holed the ¼in upper deck, and also the ⁷⁄₁₆in starboard side at the top of the cable locker, 30ft from the burst. One small hole in the 1in main deck. This hit was at about 1605.

2 Struck and shattered inner starboard cable holder about 8ft aft of Hit No 1, at 1550/51 coming from *c*60° forward of the beam, and passed through the ½in forecastle deck, bursting 8ft from impact in the sick-bay. Severe damage was caused to light structures, and many holes were made by fragments in the ⁷⁄₁₆in starboard side, and a hole 5ft × 4ft blown in the 1in upper deck, though the ⅜in main deck was not holed.

3 Passed through a side scuttle in the ⁷⁄₁₆in side between the upper and forecastle decks about 14ft aft of Hit No 2, and burst 17ft inboard over the 1in upper deck. Fragments made holes up to 3ft × 2ft6in in the upper deck but did not pierce the ⅜in main deck. Considerable damage was done to all light structures near the burst of this shell which came from *c*25° abaft the beam and hit at about 1635.

4 Passed through the ⁷⁄₁₆in side plating just below a scuttle between the forecastle and upper decks, coming from a few degrees forward of the beam, and struck 8in armour on the fore side of 'A' barbette 1ft6in above the 1in upper deck, and about the same distance from a vertical joint between plates. The armour was holed to a depth of 2½in, with concentric cracks, and driven in about 6in at the lower edge where it joined the 4in armour at upper deck level. The amount of damage on the upper deck is uncertain, but the turret mounting was undamaged, though 'A' handing room was severely affected by gas and smoke. This hit was probably at about 1553.

5 This shell which came from somewhat abaft the beam, probably struck a few minutes after No 4, and pierced the 5in side armour at main deck level on a line 4ft aft of 'A' barbette, making a hole 13½in × 12¼in. It burst 4ft from impact, blowing a hole 10ft × 4ft in the ⅜in main deck, and wrecking the Chief Stokers' mess on this deck and the flour store on the lower deck.

6 Dented the 5in armour at the forecastle deck edge in line with CT, and deflected off. Probably came from somewhat abaft the beam and hit at a similar time to No 5.

73

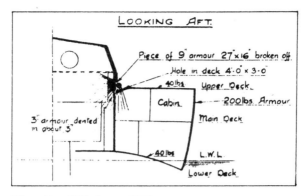

Tiger: hit on 'X' barbette at 1554.

7 Went through the middle funnel, coming from *c*17° forward of the beam. This shell which probably hit at about 1620, may have been a ricochet.

8 Struck starboard side of the shelter deck on a level between the 2nd and 3rd funnels at 1551, coming from *c*50° forward of the port beam. It made a hole *c*7ft6in × 3ft–2ft in the ⅜in shelter-deck and one of 7ft6in × 8ft–4ft in the starboard ½in vertical plating between the shelter and forecastle decks, bursting 16ft from impact over the forecastle deck, which was here 3in teak on 1½in steel. The planking was torn up but the 1½in plating was only indented and not holed.

9 This hit at 1555, pierced the 6in side armour a little below the upper deck, and 2ft forward of the after edge of 'Q' barbette. The angle to the normal was estimated at 5–10°, and the shell made a hole of 12½in diameter in the side armour with a piece 6in wide broken away to the edge of the plate, passed through a ⅜in bulkhead and burst against a second one, 22ft from impact and 8ft from the after 6in hoist. There were 2–6in charges near the top of the hoist which were set on fire, but the flash did not pass down the trunk to the shell room and magazine. Severe damage was done to light structures along the path of the shell and near the burst and some damage done well aft of the latter, and also to the middle line of the ship. Many holes were made in the ⅜in main deck, and the base of the shell also went through the 1in armour deck making a hole 10½in × 9in, and penetrated the ¾in thick web of the main steam pipe. Another fragment also went through the main deck, a ⅜in bulkhead and the 1in armour deck. The fire-main was perforated by small holes and the casualties were 12 killed and several wounded and gassed.

The after 6in magazine was flooded, and 'Q' port magazine, a relatively small compartment as most of 'Q' magazine was to starboard, also flooded through a ventilation pipe from the 6in magazine, as an attempt to close the 6in ventilation valve failed. When 'Q' port magazine was full, water leaked badly through the venting plates, and it appears that the after 6in shell room flooded, and water also entered 'Q' shell room. It does not appear to have been necessary to flood the after 6in magazine, and it was done by the Stoker PO of the flooding party after

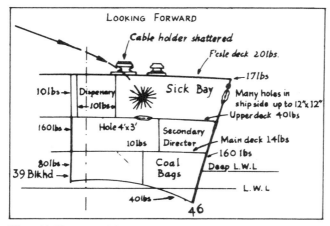

Tiger: *hit No 2 at 1550/51.*

consultation with the rating in charge of the magazine. Some water had previously entered from the cut fire-main.

10 This shell struck the 6in side armour c30ft aft of No 9, the plate being set in about 3in maximum, with some distortion of framing.

11 Struck the 9in side armour just aft of the forward engine room. The plate was indented and forced in about 4in maximum, with some buckling of the structure inboard of the armour.

These two shells probably hit between 1620 and 1630. They are said to have burst on impact but there was apparently no bulging in of the hull plating below the armour, which would be expected if this were the case in Hit no 11.

12 This shell was a ricochet, and probably hit in the first 10 minutes. It struck the 4in water-line armour c35ft from the stern, and indented it over an area of c5ft × 2ft

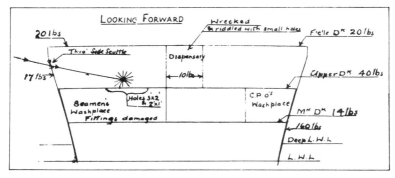

Tiger: *hit No 3.*

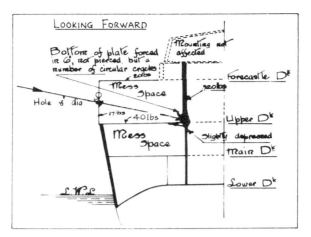

Tiger: *hit No 4.*

to a maximum of about 6in, with buckling and distortion of the framing inboard. A wing compartment 18ft in length, was flooded above the armour deck.

Of the total of 14 hits on the *Tiger*, No 3 above, is credited to the *Seydlitz*, and the others were from the *Moltke*.

The *New Zealand* was hit once by an 11in shell from the *von der Tann* at 1626 at a range of about 15,000yds. This struck the 7in armour of 'X' barbette about 1ft or 1½ft above the upper deck and burst outside the barbette. A cone-shaped piece of armour 11in diameter on the face and 30in at the rear, was displaced, and the revolving structure slightly bulged in, while fragments on the roller path jammed the turret for a short time, and the tilt of the roller path was slightly altered. A hole of about 3ft × 3ft was blown in the upper deck and a small fire started on the 1in main deck, which was also holed by fragments.

The *Barham* was hit twice in this phase. The first hit at 1623 was by an 11in at about 17,000yds from the *von der Tann*, which struck the armour belt below water apparently without effect other than to drive the plate in ¾in. The second hit was by a 12in presumably from the *Lützow* on the edge of the ½in forecastle deck over the port wing engine room and abeam of the after CT. The shell burst 14ft from impact in the gun-room and caused very severe damage to light structures. A large fragment of the shell carried on through the 1¼in upper deck, where it was sharply deflected downwards, and through the ½in main deck, stopping on the 1in middle deck about 20ft from the burst. A hole about

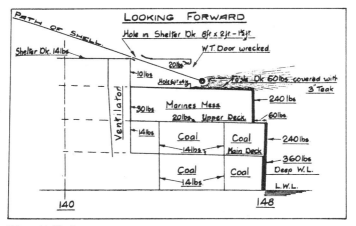

Tiger: hit No 8.

7ft in diameter was blown in the gun-room bulkhead and a fire started. The ventilation trunk to the wing engine room was destroyed, and large splinters wrecked a cabin on the starboard side of the ship.

There were no other hits on the hits on the 5th Battle Squadron during the 'Run to the South' but the *Malaya* had trouble with the alignment of the main cage and shell bogie in 'X' turret and had to use the auxiliary shell hoist for the right gun, when the turret was trained on the port beam.

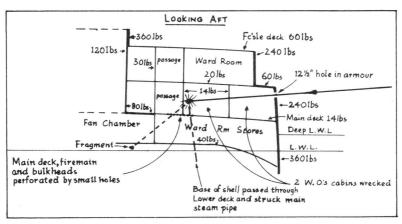

Tiger: hit No 9.

The number of 11in and 12in hits on the British ships from 1548 to 1654 is thus estimated as follows:

	12in	11in	Total
Lion	9	—	9
Princess Royal	6	—	6
Queen Mary	3	4	7
Tiger	—	14	14
New Zealand	—	1	1
Indefatigable	—	5	5
Barham	1	1	2
Total	19	25	44

The *Lutzow* is estimated to have made ten hits, the *Derfflinger* nine, *Seydlitz* five, *Moltke* thirteen, and *von der Tann* seven.

In addition there was one hit by a heavy shell on the *Southampton* probably an 11in from the *Nassau*.

The only 5.9in hits on capital ships for which records have been found were on the *Tiger*:

1 On side plating 58ft from the bows above the main deck. This hit is given in the *Tiger*'s list as 5.9in, but drawings show the plating dented over an area *c*5ft × 3ft and a hole 10in × 10in, which seem to indicate the head of an 11in.

2 On side plating near the stern, 3ft below the upper deck.

There were four hits by 1250lb 13.5in shells on the *Lützow* in this

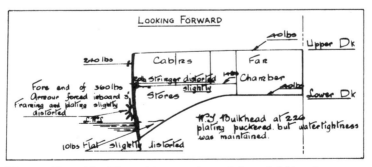

Tiger: hit No 11. Note: The 9in belt armour about 24ft forward of this station was struck similarly and the plate slightly driven in, the total damage being less than that shown above.

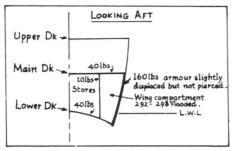

Tiger*: hit No 12.*

phase, but full details are lacking. The first two hits at 1600 where on the forecastle forward of 'A' turret, and together made a large or very large hole in the upper deck. The immediate consequences were not serious, but subsequently when the *Lützow*'s draught was increased forward by under-water damage, these hits allowed much water to enter the ship and spread above the armour deck. At 1615 there were two more hits, of which one struck the 1in upper deck between 'A' and 'B' barbettes and burst, wrecking the forward dressing station, while the other was on the belt armour below the water-line abaft the mainmast, and apparently caused little or no damage though the ship was severely shaken. The first two hits were probably from the *Lion*, and the second two from the *Princess Royal*.

Examination of the *Derfflinger*'s official damage report proves that no hits by heavy shells were made on her in this phase.

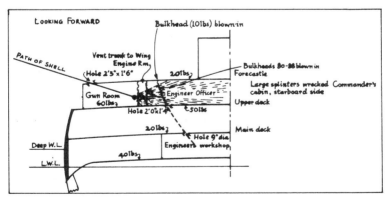

Barham*: hit at 1623. Explosion caused a hole about 7ft in diameter in bulkhead No 184 between Gun Room and Engineer Officer's cabin, and destroyed vent trunk to wing engine room. Fire started in Gun Room.*

For the *Seydlitz* detailed information is available. There were five heavy hits on the starboard side, all, except No 3 for which the direction is not known coming from within 10° of the beam, and in addition one torpedo hit. It is not possible to say which ship of the 5th BS scored hit No 1, but the other shell hits were from the *Queen Mary*, and the torpedo from the *Petard* or possibly the *Turbulent*.

In order from forward, the hits by heavy shells on the *Seydlitz* were:

1 15in hit at 1650. Struck and pierced the forecastle deck near the water-way on the starboard side over the broadside torpedo flat, and exploded immediately. There was a hole of about 5ft × 5ft in the forecastle deck and one of about 6½ft × 13ft in the upper deck about 10ft from impact. The side plating was bulged outwards, and fragments holed the battery deck and a section bulkhead. Splinter damage enabled water, which entered from subsequent hits, to spread through the forepart.

2 13.5in/1400lb hit at 1555. Holed the side plating about 5ft above the battery deck forward of the foremast, passed through a coal-shoot and exploded over the battery deck just outboard of the 0.8in longitudinal splinter bulkhead and forward of the 6in diagonal casemate bulkhead. The upper deck was bulged upwards and a hole about 10ft × 10ft torn in the 1in battery deck while the longitudinal splinter bulkhead was destroyed to a great extent, and a large fragment of the cap travelled across the ship and pierced the port longitudinal bulkhead. Much damage was done to cabins and light structures on the battery deck, and fires started, and damage was also done on the main deck. Small amounts of gas penetrated through voice pipes to the ship's control room. In conjunction with the subsequent flooding of the forepart and the torpedo hit, this shell enabled water to reach the main deck near 'A' barbette, and thence, largely via damaged ventilation trunks, to spread to compartments under the armour deck, so that by 2100 the forward electrical station was out of action, and subsequently 'A' turret magazines and then the torpedo transmitting station and the ship's control room flooded, while further water entered the broadside torpedo flat via the emergency escape and some also entered the foremost boiler room.

This was one of the only two hits on the *Seydlitz* in the whole battle, which showed a great explosive effect. It can be proved from fragments to have been an APC shell.

3 This shell, thought to be a 13.5in, burst under water near the skin plating below the starboard wing barbette. The skin plating was bulged in below the armour for a distance of 40ft × 15ft, frames bent and the starboard wing compartments flooded for 36ft. The time was most probably between 1600 and 1610.

4 13.5in/1400lb hit at 1617. This shell struck the hull plating immediately abaft the aftermost starboard 5.9in casemate, and then the junction between the 8in–9in port sill plate, (8¼in where hit) and the 6in transverse battery bulkhead. It burst in holing the armour, making a large hole in the 6in bulkhead plate, and breaking a large piece off the upper corner of the port sill plate which was also much cracked. The hit was about 1½ft above the battery deck, and a hole of about 20sq ft was

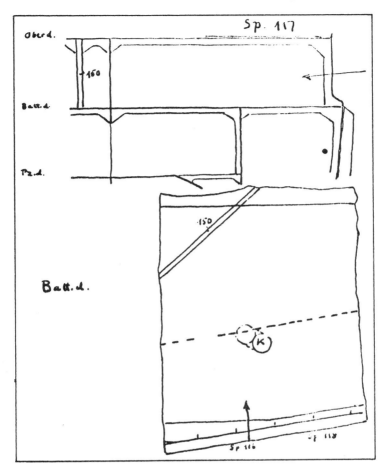

Seydlitz:*hit at 1555.*

blown in this where 1in thick outside the casemate. Armour fragments and shell splinters entered the casemate, and splinters pierced the 1.4in casemate roof, the battery deck, here 0.8in, and the 0.8in longitudinal casemate bulkhead. Much damage was done, ventilation trunks being wrecked, and shell fragments travelled across the ship abaft the battery, and holed the port side plating, wrecking five cabins and causing fires. The aftermost starboard 5.9in gun which was loaded, was put out of action, the ammunition hoist damaged, and all but one of the men in the casemate killed. There was no ammunition fire though the anti-flash flaps were pressed against the hoist trunk and badly bulged and a cartridge laying behind was crushed but not ignited. The magazine party felt the pressure and put a wooden

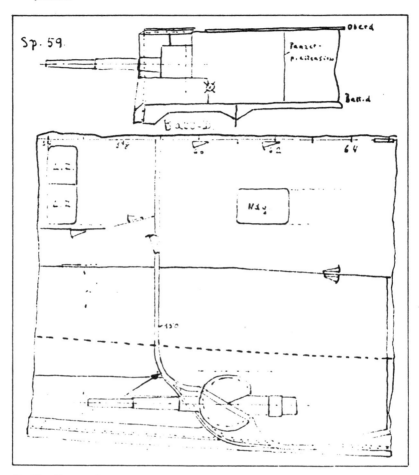

Seydlitz: *hit at 1617.*

cover on the lower opening of the hoist trunk. In the casemate ready base-fuzed shells were smashed but not detonated.

There was a serious danger from smoke and gas in the starboard HP and LP turbine rooms, and the latter had to be vacated for a short time. This shell was the only one, other than No 2 above, of those that struck the *Seydlitz*, to show a great explosive effect and, like it, was presumably APC. The range at the time was about 18,000yds.

5 13.5in/1400lb hit at 1557. This APC shell struck the 9in barbette armour of the after super-firing turret, about 6ft above the battery deck and very near a vertical

joint between two plates, though the 14in × 14in hole was confined to one plate, except for some damage to the other plate edge, and the armour plates were not displaced. The range was about 14,500-15,000yds. The shell, which struck at an angle of *c*33° to the plate normal, burst in penetrating, and fragments of armour and shell splinters tore a hole *c*5ft × 5ft in the ring bulkhead and entered the working chamber. The turret training and elevating gear, the hoists and cartridge transfer rails were put out of action, and two main and two fore charges were laying in the working chamber ignited. The flash entered the gun-house where the left gun was loaded, and two main and two fore charges lay in the cartridge loading trays but these were not ignited. It also passed down between the fixed and revolving structures of the turret as well as down the main trunk, but in one of the lower cartridge cages which was down, the main charge was only blackened and the fore charge not ignited, though the silk bag was singed. Only two fore charge magazine cases were open, and the charges in these did not ignite, though the paper labels of the fore charge magazine cases were in part burnt. Only two main and two fore charges were involved in the fire as compared with 62 at the Dogger Bank, and the regulations introduced after that action, prohibiting an accumulation of charges between magazine and gun, proved their worth. The magazine and shell room parties survived with the aid of gas-masks, but all those in the handing rooms were killed (except one who later died) as well as all in the working chamber and switchboard room. The power training gear had previously broken down, and one gun's crew were manning the hand training gear in the working-chamber. From the gun-house six managed to escape through an open manhole but they were badly burnt and three later died, while there were another ten survivors from the magazines and shell room.

The magazines were flooded by the shell room party, and emptied as soon as the fire was put out. About 3ft or so of water entered and some found its way through leaking voice-pipes and a ventilation trunk into the pump room below and put the after pump out of action, while water also leaked into the shell room of the aftermost turret.

Torpedo hit at 1657. This was below the forward part of the fore barbette and a short distance aft of the mine damage incurred on 24 April 1916. The starboard skin plating was holed below the armour belt over an area of about 40ft × 13ft, and an armour plate driven in by up to *c*9in. The torpedo bulkhead, which was here 2in thick, held, and was not holed though bulged and leaking considerably. The principal leaks appear to have been at the junction of the armour deck with the torpedo bulkhead, and also at the angle between the belt and armour deck. The column of water from the explosion lifted the muzzle of the foremost starboard 5.9in and jammed the gun so firmly in its mounting that it was out of action. The explosion was just abaft the broadside torpedo flat which was not affected directly and could be kept drained, though all electrical equipment in the torpedo transmitting station was put out of action. The starboard wing compartments were flooded for a length of

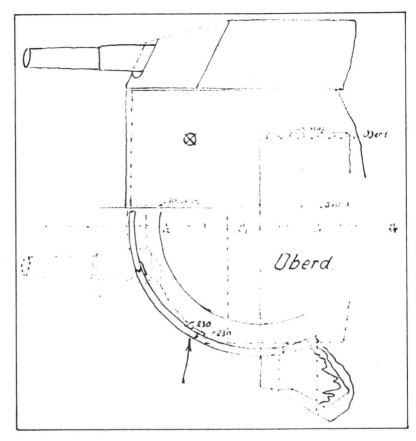

Seydlitz: *hit at 1557.*

91ft and later for a further 20ft, and the outer and protective bunkers for 83ft. The effects of the explosion wrecked equipment in the forward cooling engine room, and in the starboard forward switchboard room, and water leaked into these compartments, and by 2100, due to the increased immersion of the fore part of the ship, the effect of the torpedo hit, and of Hit No 2 above, the whole forward electrical station had flooded. Water gradually spread through leaky voice-pipes, ventilation ducts and faulty cable glands until many and eventually all compartments below the armour deck in the 64ft long section between the forward citadel and foremost boiler-room bulkheads were filled. For the moment, however, the ship only took on a slight list and was able to maintain full speed.

It is possible that the more forward of the starboard wing compartments, affected by the torpedo hit, had been leaking since the beginning of the battle and had caused some flooding, due to unsatisfactory repairs of the mine damage of 24 April 1916 which were unable to withstand the ship being severely shaken.

The surviving information on the damage to the *Moltke* is not as full as for the *Seydlitz*, but sufficient data exists to provide an accurate description of the five hits that were made.

The first damage inflicted was at 1602 or just afterwards, when a shell, probably from the *Tiger*, burst underwater near the forward part of the hull. The plating was forced inwards, and the *Moltke* was violently shaken while a considerable length of the double-bottom was flooded to starboard, some rivets burst loose in the bottom of one of the trimming tanks, and slight leakage, which was easily stopped, occurred in the bow torpedo flat.

The hit at 1616 was from a 15in at about 18,000yds range. This shell apparently APC, pierced the 8in upper side armour below No 5 starboard 5.9in gun and 8¾ft above the legend water-line, making a circular hole of 21in outer and 39in inner diameter. The after edge of the armour plate was forced 1¼in to 2in outwards, and the forward edge ⅜in to 1in, while the 6in casemate plate was displaced outwards by up to ⅜in. The shell burst in an outer bunker, and the armour deck, which was here 1in at main deck level with a high 2in slope, held and was not pierced, but splinters and armour fragments tore open the ¼in inner bulkhead of the bunker towards the main deck passage, the ⁵⁄₁₆in battery deck was bulged up and holed from below close in rear of the gun, and the 5.9in hoist was torn open by splinters. No 5 gun was out of action and immovable, and the ready ammunition caught fire so that all 12 men in the casemate were killed. Flash passed down the hoist to the magazine, badly burning two men of the magazine party, though two were unhurt. It also entered the main deck passage via the torn bunker bulkhead and caused some casualties there.

Both Nos 4 and 6 starboard 5.9in were temporarily out of action from smoke and gas, and after this cleared the leak was stopped and the only flooding was that of the outer bunker to the top of the armour deck slope for a length of 20ft. Exact details of the coal content of the bunker are lacking, but the *Moltke*'s outer bunkers were not full, though the coal was trimmed to give protection on the outboard side.

Another 15in shell which hit at about this time, struck the side plating a little below the upper deck about 50ft forward of the stern. It

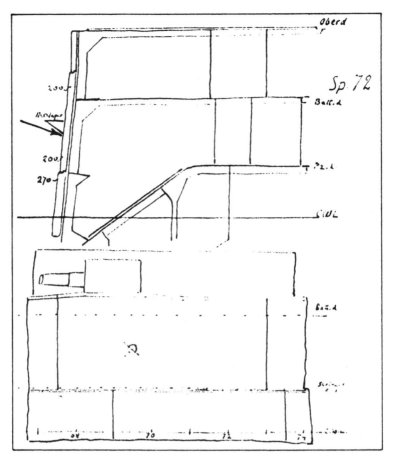

Moltke: *15in hit at 1616.*

passed through the ship and struck the 4in port side armour on the inside at lwl level. The shell does not appear to have exploded, but an armour plate was detached and fell off with a hole *c*6ft × 5ft in the hull plating inboard, and though the armour deck was intact, a considerable quantity of water entered compartments above this deck for nearly 120ft from the stern.

The hit at 1623 was again by a 15in. The shell burst on the $10\frac{3}{4}$in armour belt, 16in above lwl, but below the actual wl, and just abaft No 2 starboard 5.9in. A piece 9in × $12\frac{1}{2}$in ×$2\frac{3}{4}$in deep was broken off the plate surface, and at the 5in lower edge, the plate was driven in 8in with a 3in deep crack. The skin plating was bulged in by up to 14in for a length of 36ft and to a maximum depth of 8ft below the armour. It was also much torn and pierced in one place by a splinter, while the wing bulkhead was severely bulged. The starboard wings were flooded for 71ft, the protective bunkers for 53ft, the outer bunkers for 32ft to just above the crown of the armour deck at main deck level, and part of the double-bottom adjoining the wings for 16ft. A small amount of water also entered the protective bunkers for a further 33ft forward, but this was drained, and the bunker doors in the undamaged torpedo bulkhead which admitted a little water into Nos 3 and 4 stokeholds, were made tight. Above the water-line the torpedo-net stowage was much damaged, and the net, though undamaged, hung in the water.

The shell that hit at 1626 was also a 15in. This burst on the 10¾in armour belt, 12in below lwl and a little abaft the main mast. The hit was 28in from the after edge of the plate. There was some spalling of the surface, and the plate, which was *c*17½ft long, was forced 12in inwards at the after edge and 1½in outward at the forward edge. The next plate aft was forced in 6½in at the forward edge and 1¼in outward at the after edge. Both plates had vertical cracks in the centre area, and the armour deck slope was forced in by up to 10in for a length of 26ft. The hull plating was bulged in by up to 16in for a length of 40ft and to a maximum of 5ft below the armour, and was also torn. The starboard wings were flooded for 75ft, the protective bunkers for 63ft and, above the armour deck, the outer bunkers were flooded for 43ft to a little above the crown of the armour deck at main deck level. Small amounts of water entered the protective bunkers for some distance forward and aft of the flooding, but this was drained away. The torpedo bulkhead remained undamaged and prevented water reaching vital compartments of the ship. Above the water-line the torpedo-net stowage was torn away for 33ft, but the net was not damaged. The range of these shells which hit the main belt was about 16,500–15,500yds.

As a result of these hits the *Moltke* listed *c*3° to starboard which was corrected by counter-flooding the port wings. After this had been done, about 1000 tons of water were present in the ship with an increase in draught of *c*2ft 8in aft and a decrease of *c*8in forward, but the *Moltke* was able to maintain 25kts to the end. The 1616 hit by an APC shell should probably be credited to the *Valiant*, but it cannot be determined whether this ship or the *Barham* was responsible for the other 15in hits.

The three hits on the *von der Tann* were as follows: the first being a 15in from the *Barham*, and the second and third 13.5in from the *Tiger*.

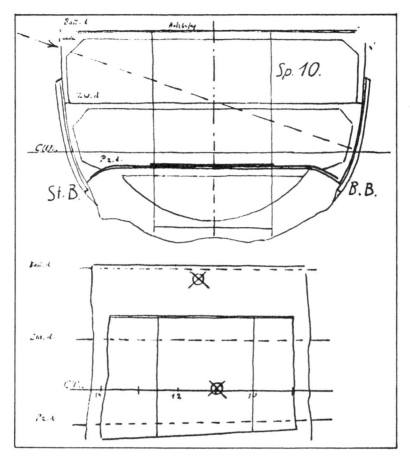

Moltke: *second 15in hit c1616.*

Hit at 1609. This shell was a CPC fired at a range of about 19,000yds, and hit 28ft from the stern at middle deck level, 3ft above the legend, and probably just below the actual wl. It struck the after side armour on the joint between the 3¼in upper and 4in lower strakes, and also on a joint between two upper plates, and 3ft from a joint between two lower plates. The shell burst on the armour and the explosive effect inside the ship was small, but a piece 20in × 28in was broken off the corner of an upper plate, and one 12in × 16in off the corner of a lower plate with two fractures 32in distant from it. The armour plates were

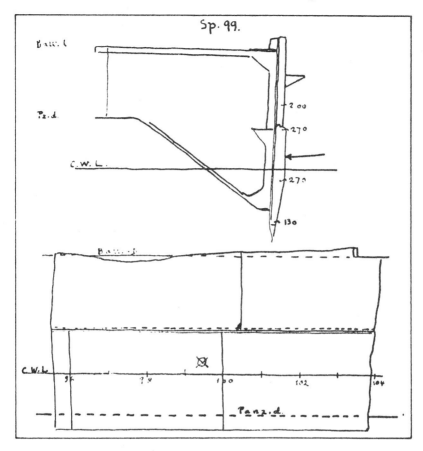

Moltke: *hit at 1623.*

bent inwards by as much as 32in and also displaced, while the hull plating inboard of the armour was destroyed for a length of 6ft to the main deck and driven 5ft inward. Below the armour the hull plating was bulged inwards to a maximum of 2ft with two vertical cracks 5½ft long.

The hull vibrated longitudinally like a tuning-fork, and the main deck was pierced and bulged upwards apparently by armour fragments, the lower support of a 3.5in gun torn away from the middle deck, and this deck damaged and the armour deck distorted at the hull side. Compartments on the armour deck and some on the middle deck

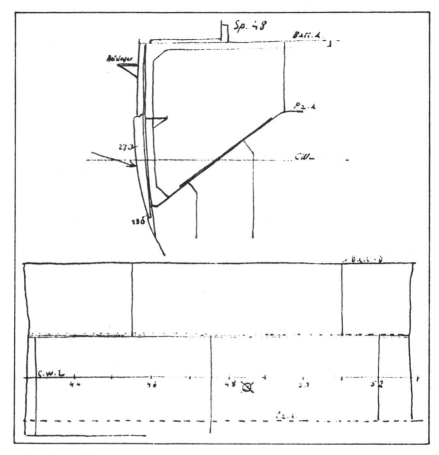

Moltke: *hit at 1626.*

flooded, while a considerable quantity of water entered compartments below the armour deck, and the stern torpedo flat was half filled. The steering-engine ran hot, and the steering compartments flooded, but complete failure of the rudder gear was averted and, after a short interval, the steering gear functioned again, while it was possible to shore the bulkhead leading to the after engine. The change in the ship's draught from 29ft (fore) 28ft10in (aft) before the battle to 28ft3in (fore), 31ft2in (aft), with a list of 2° to starboard, after the battle, shows that over 1000 tons of water were present in the ship.

Hit at 1620. This shell struck the fore barbette armour where it was 8in thick, at an angle of about 25° to the plate normal, and 9in below the

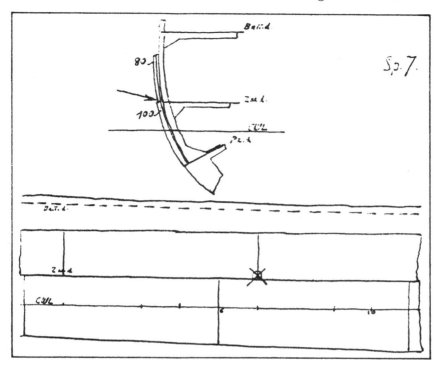

Von der Tann: *hit at 1609.*

upper edge of the barbette. The range was about 17,000yds. It burst on striking the armour, and made a hole 35in × 22in at the plate edge with concentric cracks over a large area and deep cracks running to the forecastle deck, while the armour plate was somewhat bowed though the armour fastenings were undamaged. The forecastle deck, 0.3in plus 0.6in reinforcement, distant 3½ft from the hit, had a hole 14½ft × 3¼ft blown in it, and the 0.3in upper deck was pierced by splinters. The turret was severely shaken, and a large piece of armour flew in and damaged equipment, so that the turret was jammed at 30° abaft the starboard beam, and was out of action for the rest of the battle. There was no fire in the turret and apparently little gas, but the magazines were at once flooded. A small fire occurred in a cabin, and the only casualties were some men slightly injured by flash from the shell burst.

Hit at 1623. The shell struck the recessed side of the hull just above the main deck and about 3ft forward of the centre of the after barbette. It passed through the side plating and 1in main deck, making holes of

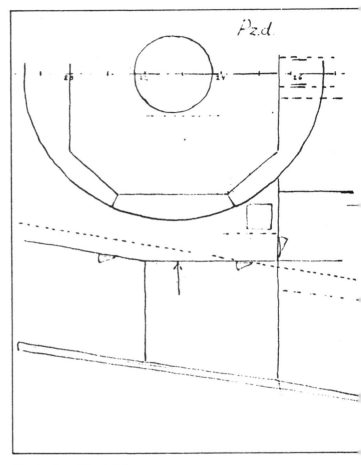

Von der Tann: *hit at 1623.*

*c*16in × 20in and *c*35in × 16in, respectively, and then through a cabin bulkhead and a bunker longitudinal bulkhead, before bursting 40in below the main deck and 50in above the armour deck, in front of the after barbette which was here only 1.2in thick. The barbette was holed for *c*12ft and from the main to the armour deck, and forced against the supporting structure of the turret guns. This structure was also bowed inwards and holed in places so that the turret was jammed, and splinters put the power training and elevating gear and the power drive for the lower hoists, out of action.

A fire was started among the practice targets stowed below the

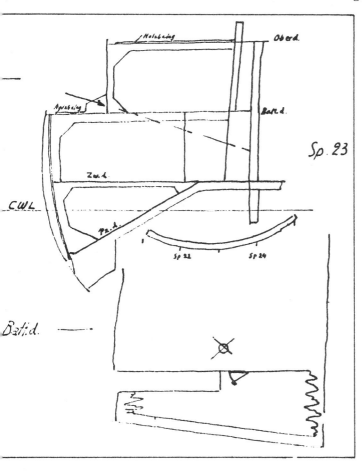

turret, and clouds of dense smoke were given off, which in addition to gas, entered both steering engine rooms through torn ventilation trunks, and made them untenable for 20 minutes. The fire smouldered for some hours, and enveloped the ship in smoke. The turret magazines could not be flooded at once as the valves were buried under wreckage, but no ammunition ignited and two main and two fore charges in the working chamber, between the main and upper decks, and 6 or 7ft from the hit on the barbette, were undamaged.

The effect of the burst was mainly in the direction of the shell, and a transverse bulkhead 10ft from the burst was relatively little damaged.

The 1in main deck was torn upwards for *c*6ft × 5ft by the barbette, and the 1in armour deck had two small holes and was bulged in close to the barbette, with two more small holes and slight bowing on the 2in slope. Among other damage the starboard longitudinal bulkhead was destroyed for 8ft, and the port one slightly bowed for 36ft, while part of the torpedo net was torn loose by the shell on entry, and trailed over the side, but was cut away before becoming entangled in the propellers. Water which entered through the hole in the side when steaming at high speed, and which leaked from damaged piping, caused some flooding on the armour and upper platform decks.

This shell which killed 6 and wounded 14, put the after turret out of action until 2000, and even then, hand operated training, elevation and lower hoists had to be used, though the upper hoists could be worked electrically.

In addition to the above damage, the 11in guns of the starboard wing turret, became hot and failed to run-out properly at 1635, and the trouble was not overcome until 1930, and it seemed probable that it would recur in further firing, while the right gun of the port wing turret began to give similar trouble at 1650.

The number of hits by heavy shells on the German battlecruisers from 1548 to 1654 is estimated as follows:

	15in	13.5in/1400lb	13.5in/1250lb	12in	Total
Lützow	—	—	4	—	4
Derfflinger	—	—	—	—	Nil
Seydlitz	1	4	—	—	5
Moltke	4	1	—	—	5
von der Tann	1	2	—	—	3
Total	6	7	4	—	17

The 13.5in hits are believed to have been all APC, and the 15in partly CPC and APC.

It is believed that the *V29* was hit by the *Petard*'s torpedo, and not by a heavy shell.

It is to be noted that the *Moltke* scored more hits in this phase of the action than the whole of the British battlecruisers. The Germans certainly had the better light conditions, but from the British point of view, one can only repeat Jellicoe's comment that the result of the first part of the battle 'cannot be other than unpalatable'.

A number of hits were made by the destroyers' 4in shells, including 7 on the *Derfflinger*. The most destructive burst below the bridge and tore an 8ft × 4½ft hole in the uppermost superstructure deck. The *Lützow* may also have been hit by 4in shells at this time, but details are lacking, while the *Seydlitz* was struck by one on the starboard side armour.

CHAPTER 6

Action between capital ships
Second phase 1654 – 1815

T HIS PHASE OF the Battle of Jutland extends from the 5th Battle Squadron's turn to the northward to Jellicoe's signal for the deployment of the Grand Fleet at 1815. The earlier part of this phase is generally known as the 'Run to the North', when the British battlecruisers were able to avoid further destruction until they could reopen the action in changed conditions of visibility. The 5th Battle Squadron also escaped disaster, and inflicted considerable damage on the German battlecruisers, though the *Malaya* suffered from the fire of the 3rd Squadron, and the *Barham* to a lesser degree from that of the *Derfflinger*.

Subsequently, due to the surprise approach of Hood's force from the eastward, and to the deteriorating visibility, Jellicoe's battleships were able to arrive undetected by the German fleet.

At 1657, when the range was about 17,500yds, Beatty altered course to 347° parallel to the 1st SG, but the *Lion* was soon hit by the *Lützow*, and at 1700 Beatty turned away to 325°, and after a few minutes to *c*320°. Hipper did not follow and at 1702 reduced speed for 4 minutes, and then turned the 1st SG together to 336° at 1708 and to 325° at 1712. As a result of these manoeuvres the *Lion* had increased her range from the *Lützow* to about 21,000yds at 1710, and Beatty then reduced from 25 to 24kts and at 1714 altered course to 336°.

Hipper had ordered his battlecruisers at 1657 to distribute fire from the right, ship against ship, but the *Derfflinger* actually fired at the *Barham* while the *von der Tann* opened with her one remaining heavy gun on the *Malaya* at 1700. The *Lützow* engaged the *Lion, Seydlitz – Tiger*, and *Moltke – New Zealand*. Visibility seems to have been good at first, at least for the *Lützow*, but smoke and haze soon made conditions difficult, and although the *Lützow* continued to engage the British battlecruisers until 1727, her firing at ranges of 19,000 – 20,800yds was latterly intermittent and ineffective. The *Seydlitz* fired at the *Tiger* until 1710, while the *Moltke* may have continued a little longer at the *New Zealand* without result. The *Lützow* made three hits on the *Lion*, one causing a cordite fire in the after 4in battery, and another wrecking the sick-bay, while the *Seydlitz*, whose ammunition records show an expenditure of *c*300– 11in shells between 1548 and 1710, scored one hit on the *Tiger* at *c*1658. An important defect also occurred in the latter ship, as the right gun of 'A' turret was disabled by the failure of an hydraulic valve casting.

Some of the 3rd Squadron including the *Markgraf, Prinzregent Luitpold* and *Kaiserin*, continued firing at the British battlecruisers for a time, but were out of range.

The British battlecruisers opened fire from 1657, but conditions were not good initially, though they were better for a short period after 1701, and the *Tiger* reported that the light improved and hitting seemed to be established and maintained on the 3rd ship, presumably the *Seydlitz*, which appeared to be down by the stem and to leave the line. The *Tiger* shifted to the 2nd ship (*Derfflinger*) shortly before ceasing at 1710 when the target became obscured. It has been sometimes maintained that the *Tiger* scored several hits on the *Seydlitz* at this time, but all the hits on her during the 'Run to the North' were 15in. The *Lion* expended a total of seven salvos at the *Lützow* between 1658½ and 1705, of which the last five were fired in 3½ minutes, but failed to find the range, and the *Princess Royal* which reported engaging the *Lützow* until 1708 when the target could no longer be made out, also had no success. The *New Zealand*'s records indicate that she fired at 1658, but this time is probably 5 or 6 minutes fast.

Hipper's failure to pursue Beatty as soon as the 1st Scouting Group turned north, allowed his opponent to escape from an action at ranges where further disaster to the British battlecruisers might well have occurred, and although Hipper subsequently steamed at 26kts for a time, he was unable to close the range sufficiently for effective firing in the decreasing visibility. By 1741 when Beatty reopened on the German battlecruisers, conditions had changed so much that his ships were almost or completely hidden from the 1st SG at a distance of 7 to 8 miles. However, if Hipper had chased immediately after Beatty at full speed, he would have been exposed to the fire of the 5th BS to a greater extent than was actually the case, and this could well have led to very serious damage to the German battlecruisers, and it was probably the risk of engaging the 5th BS without the support of the 3rd Squadron, which caused Hipper to reduce speed for 6 minutes at 1717, and further prejudiced his chances of engaging Beatty effectively.

On completing their 180° turn in succession, the three leading ships of the 5th BS steadied on course 360°, but if her track chart is correct, the *Malaya*, which had wisely been turned short of the others, was steering about 328°, and hauled out to port. At about 1707 Evan-Thomas altered course to *c*350°, and then turned further to port, so that he was steering about 291° at 1714. The *Valiant* and *Warspite* hauled out on to the *Barham*'s port quarter, and at about 1716 Evan-Thomas again altered course to approximately 313°. He had called for a speed of 25kts at 1710 but the actual speed cannot have reached 24kts.

At 1658 Scheer signalled for course to be altered to 302° and also called for utmost speed. At 1705 he signalled for a change back to 325° and at 1715 to 302°. The 5th Division did not comply with the earlier course signals, and steered 325° until about 1706, when course was altered to *c*344°. At about 1711 course was again altered to *c*322° and about 1715 to 302°. The 6th Division conformed approximately to Scheer's orders, and as a result of these divergent courses, and also of the 5th Division's higher speed, the distance between the *König* and *Kaiser*, which was a little over a mile at 1648, had increased by *c*3000yds at 1710.

Contrary to the usual accounts, none of the 3rd Squadron was firing at the 5th BS, while they were making their turn and the first ship to engage them in this phase was the *Derfflinger*. Altogether she fired 22 salvos, most if not all of semi AP, between 1655 and 1719. 20 at ranges of from 18,800 to 20,500 yds, and averaging 19,500. For most of this time she was engaging the *Barham*, but the *Valiant* may have been her target latterly. Four hits were made on the *Barham*, the times being approximately 1658, 1701, 1708 and 1710. The shell at 1658 struck the glacis near No 2 starboard 6in gun, and did a great deal of damage, while the others hit the after superstructure, the side aft, and about 20ft forward of the 1658 hit, respectively. Of the other ships of the 1st SG, the *von der Tann* fired 10 rounds from her one 11in still in action, at the *Malaya* between 1700 and 1713 at 18,200 to 22,700yds.

The 5th BS were offering a good, if distant, target to the 3rd Squadron and the *König* opened at 1710 on the *Malaya*, at *c*18,600yds, and fired her first 7 salvos in 5 minutes. Straddling salvos were reported, and a hit claimed at 1717 near the forward turrets. The *Grosser Kurfürst* had begun to fire at the *Valiant* at 19,000yds by 1700 or just afterwards, very quickly found the range, and at 1709 incorrectly claimed a hit after four straddling salvos, though she ceased firing at 1716 as the range was too great. It is not certain which of the 5th BS was engaged by the *Markgraf*, though it may have been the *Malaya* or perhaps the *Warspite*, but the *Kronprinz*, after firing at the *Dublin* from 1651 to 1700 at 18,600 to 20,300yds, reopened on the *Malaya* at 1708 at 18,600yds and continued until 1721 when the latter ran out of range at 21,300yds. The *Kronprinz* fired semi AP until she had the range and then AP. Her target was at first in clear contrast to the horizon, with perfect conditions for range-finding and spotting, and a hit was claimed in a similar position to the *König*'s 1717 claim.

The *Kaiser* fired 11 salvos at the *Southampton* in 8 minutes from 1648½ at 16,000 – 20,800yds, and a further four salvos at the same target from 1705 to 1708 at *c*19,000yds. She then opened on the *Malaya* at 1710½ at 17,900 yds, and continued engaging this ship, as did the *Prinzregent Luitpold* which began at 1708 at 19,100yds. It does not appear that the *Kaiserin* was firing in this period, but some of the 1st Squadron continued to fire at the 2nd LCS. The *Ostfriesland* had opened on the *Southampton* at 1651, but later checked and from 1712 to 1717 fired at the *Birmingham* and *Nottingham*. Her range to the 2nd LCS varied from 18,800 to 20,600yds. The *Nassau* fired at the *Southampton* and then apparently at the *Dublin*, between 1650 and 1710 at 20,100 to 22,900yds, while the *Thüringen* expended 29-12in at the *Dublin* in 8 minutes from 1650 at 18,600-20,800yds. The *Rheinland* and *Westfalen* also reopened, the former, which claimed straddle with her 2nd salvo, at 1705, on the *Birmingham* or perhaps the *Nottingham* at 21,000-21,500yds, while the latter, which expended 38-11in shells, fired from 1658 at 18,400 to 21,200yds on a target that was most probably the *Southampton*. No hits were made on the 2nd LCS in this period.

The *Barham* was hit four times by the *Derfflinger* as noted above, but the *Valiant* was not hit, though when she took up a position on the *Barham*'s port quarter at 1713, this caused the next four salvos to miss by 10yds ahead, and at this time the German fire was very rapid and accurate, the salvos which had a very small spread, being correct for range but missing for direction. The *Malaya* reported a salvo 50yds over at 1659, and others falling close at 1705 and 1712 – 1714, but it is doubtful if she was hit before 1720. There was a hit that did little damage on the *Malaya*'s side for which the time is not recorded, near the position of that claimed by the *König* and *Kronprinz*, but the *Kronprinz* noted a thick yellow explosion cloud and good incendiary effect, which indicates that it was the flash of the *Malaya*'s guns seen through haze and smoke, which gave rise to the claim.

Visibility was generally poor for the 5th BS and the Germans indistinct from the mist and smoke, though their gun-flashes were bright but too brief to lay on. At times one of the ships would show up more clearly, and the British fire was then effective, though any regular distribution was impossible, and the most visible target was selected. The *Barham* and *Valiant* engaged the battlecruisers, and the *Warspite* and *Malaya* the 5th Division. The *Barham* opened fire again at 1702, and at that time obtained very good ranges of 20,400yds, while the *Valiant* reported reopening fire at 1706 on a ship thought to be the second battlecruiser from the right, but which was probably the *Seydlitz*. The target was described as most indistinct, and occasionally obscured by mist and smoke, when another ship was selected. Nevertheless, the *Seydlitz* was hit by 15in shells at 1706, 1708 and 1710. The first of these struck the forecastle and the large hole torn in the far side by the burst, was the main cause of her subsequent troubles. The second hit was also on the forecastle, while the shell at 1710 struck the starboard wing turret and put the right gun out of action. The *Lützow* was hit by a 15in shell at 1713, and it would thus appear that conditions were better at this time for the two leading ships of the 5th BS than their reports indicate.

The *Malaya* reported opening fire at about 1700 on what appeared to be a ship of the *König* class at a guessed range of 17,000yds, which was very short. Spotting was very difficult owing to the haze, but the *Rostock*, on the *König*'s starboard bow, could be seen. Both the *Warspite*, whose report of this period is unreliable, and the *Malaya* had some success however, as the *Grosser Kurfürst* was hit at 1709 and the *Markgraf* at 1710. German reports indicate that the British opened fire at 1656, while the *Kaiser* noted at 1704 that heavy shells were falling ahead of the 5th Division at regular intervals of 1 to 2 minutes. A little later the *Kronprinz* noted that salvos fell close to her, but mostly on her quarter, while the spread was at times extremely small.

Of the lighter units present, the 2nd LCS were, at 1720, fine on the port quarter of the 5th BS, having escaped without loss, thanks to a combination of good luck and great skill in avoiding the German salvos. At this time the 1st LCS were to the north-eastward of the *Lion*, and the 3rd LCS to the northward of the 1st LCS, while the 2nd SG were wide on the *Lützow*'s starboard bow.

The destroyers *Onslow* and *Moresby*, which had been previously detailed to stand by the *Engadine*, joined the battle shortly before 1700 and attempted to attack the German battlecruisers, but were driven off by the *Frankfurt* and *Pillau* and the battlecruisers' 5.9in. The *Lützow* reported opening with 5.9in at 14,000yds at 1708, and fired for six minutes, the range not falling below 11,500yds. She claimed many straddling salvos, but neither destroyer was hit. The *von der Tann* shifted the fire of her only turret still in action, in which both 11in guns were now working, from the *Malaya* to one of the destroyers and expended six rounds, but at 1715 both guns failed to run out. The *Moresby* continued southwards and at shortly after 1710, fired one torpedo at the *Markgraf* at about 8000yds without success. The *Moresby* had been under heavy fire, but of the 5th Division, only the *Grosser Kurfürst* seems to have fired her 5.9in for a minute at extreme range at 1722, and the *Moresby* escaped undamaged.

The *Onslow* took up a position on the *Lion*'s starboard bow, but the other British destroyers with the *Champion* and *Fearless*, were on the battlecruisers' port quarter or on the 5th Battle Squadron's port beam, except for some which were still making for these positions. Of Hipper's flotillas, the 'B' boats of the 2nd were on the *Lützow*'s starboard bow, and the remainder, with the *Regensburg* on the *Lützow*'s starboard beam, or coming up to take station. The *Rostock* with the 3rd Flotilla and 1st Half-Flotilla, was on the *König*'s starboard beam, the 9th Half-Flotilla to starboard of the 5th Division and the rest of the older destroyers further astern.

The disabled *Nomad* and *Nestor*, the latter of which had been fired on, and probably hit once by the *Rostock* between 1705 and 1713, lay ahead and to port of the approaching German battlefleet, the *Nomad* being the nearer, and their remaining torpedoes, four apparently in the *Nomad* and one in the *Nestor*, were fired but no hits were made. The *Nomad* was engaged by the *Friedrich der Grosse*, *Prinzregent Luitpold*, *Kaiser* and *Kaiserin* with 5.9in. She was soon on fire and her fore magazine was hit and blew up about 2 minutes before she sank stern first at 1730. The *Nestor* was under fire from a total of eight battleships, comprising the *Prinzregent Luitpold* and the 1st Squadron except the *Westfalen*. The *Thüringen*, *Helgoland* and possibly *Oldenburg* and *Posen*, fired turret guns as well as 5.9in. Heavy explosions were seen just before the *Nestor* sank by the stern at 1735 after being fired at for 12 minutes, but it is doubtful if any main armament hits were made. Most of the crews were picked up by German destroyers (*G9*, *G10*, *G11*, *S16*, *S17*).

The four British battlecruisers continued on 336° at 24kts until 1727, when they altered course to 325°. At 1733 they turned in succession to 10°, and 4 or 5 minutes later to 21°, but at 1740 they again turned away to about 4°. At 1720 Beatty had ordered the 1st Flotilla to form a submarine screen, but the 'I' class destroyers could only get ahead very slowly, and the *Fearless* not at all, and the screen was never formed. Although Beatty made a signal for the battlecruisers to prepare to renew the action at 1725, it was not until 1741 that fire was reopened, and for 31 minutes the 5th Battle Squadron alone carried on the engagement with the 1st Scouting Group and 3rd Squadron.

The German battlecruisers had turned together to 325° at 1712 and were steaming at full speed, but at 1717 Hipper signalled for speed to be reduced. This was probably to avoid the risk of engaging the 5th BS without the support of the 3rd Squadron, but at 1721 Scheer ordered Hipper to take up the chase, and at 1723 the 1st SG accordingly increased speed, and at 1727 turned together to *c*305°. Ten minutes later they turned to line ahead, course 336°, and at 1739 altered course to 32°. At this time Beatty's ships were not more than 14,000yds away, but visibility was now very unfavourable for Hipper. The turn away at 1739 seems to have been made to keep out of torpedo range of the 1st LCS. This Squadron had been ordered at 1727 to keep touch with the German battlecruisers, and at about 1735 appeared likely to cross the latter's bows at about 14,000yds. They were apparently not fired at, and were only dimly made out. The *Lützow* intermittently engaged the British battlecruisers until 1727, but otherwise Beatty was left alone.

Although the 1st SG were at times steaming at 26kts, their average speed was only about 23kts. In addition to Hipper's reduction of speed from 1717 to 1723, the *Moltke* and *von der Tann* were finding it difficult to maintain high speed by about 1740, as their fires which had not been cleaned since 1500, had become very dirty due to stony coal, and stokers and trimmers were showing signs of exhaustion. In some ships the supplementary oil firing gave out, as sediment from the tanks choked the pipes to the burners, and the *Seydlitz*'s torpedo hit must have affected her performance. The *von der Tann*'s damage aft was also reducing her speed, as revolutions for 26kts were only giving 23.

For the period when the British battlecruisers had withdrawn from the action, the 5th Battle Squadron's track lay for the most part about a mile to the westward of Beatty's. It is not clear whether the *Valiant*, *Warspite* and *Malaya* were still on the *Barham*'s port quarter, or in line ahead. From about 1716 to 1736 Evan-Thomas steered between 313° and 336°, and then altered course to *c*350° and 2 or 3 minutes later back to about 336° before turning to 358° at 1742/43. Evan-Thomas had called for 25kts at 1710, and about a quarter of an hour later signalled for 'Utmost Speed', but the *Barham*'s average speed during this period can be taken as 23.8kts. The ships of the 5th BS were well over their original designed displacement and were never 25kt ships. After her repairs were completed, the *Barham* was tried over the measured mile on 6 July

1916. She was in approximately the same trim as at Jutland with 79% of her oil fuel, and drawing 32ft6in forward and 33ft aft with a displacement of 32,250 tons. The figures for four runs were 70,790shp = 23.9kts and the best run 71,730shp = 23.97kts. The *Valiant* was known to be slower than the *Barham* at this time, due to differences in her HP turbine nozzles, and dropped astern to some extent at Jutland.

The 1st Scouting Group were wary of approaching the 5th Battle Squadron too closely, and during the 'Run to the North' their range was at least 17,000yds with a maximum of around 20,500yds at about 1720. The 3rd Squadron however, tried very hard to close the 5th BS but without success. The 5th Division steered 302° from about 1715 until 1742 when they turned to 347°, while the 6th Division's course was *c*310° from 1718/19 until about 1731 when they altered to 296°. This course was held until 1743 when they turned to follow the 5th Division. The mean course of the 5th Division from 1710 to 1735 converged *c*18° on that of the 5th BS, and if taken from 1710 to 1742, *c*24°. The *König* was probably about 19,000yds from the *Barham* at 1735, and by 1742 she may have been 1000yds closer, but the British ships had become invisible in the haze. The intervals between the ships of the 5th Division had altered during the chase, and the *König* and *Grosser Kurfürst* were well ahead of the others by about 1740, and the *König* some way ahead of the *Grosser Kurfürst*.

In the *König* the order for 'Utmost Power' had been given as early as 1639, but it would take time to work up speed. At 1654 she was making 19kts, and 10 minutes later the supplementary oil burners were in use, so that at 1711 she was making 250revs, equivalent to about 43,000shp. The *König* maintained at least 240/245revs during the chase, and was at times steaming at over 22kts, while the *Grosser Kurfürst* reported that her own maximum during the battle was 22kts, though the *Markgraf* did not record a greater speed than 20kts. The *König* class were not all carrying their full supply of coal, as their mean draughts prior to the battle were: *König* 29ft8in; *Grosser Kurfürst* 29ft0in; *Markgraf* 29ft5in; *Kronprinz* no data; compared to a nominal full load figure 30ft6in. The *König* which made the best speed, had thus the greatest draught, but she reported about 1850/1900 tons of coal remaining at *c*0600 1 June, and can hardly have used more than 500 tons previously, whereas her full supply was 3540tons. The *Markgraf* reported 2350/2400 tons of coal on board at 0520 1 June. The *Westfalen*, last of the dreadnoughts, and the *Hannover*, at the rear of the 2nd Squadron, attained revolutions for 20 and 18kts, respectively.

Conditions for the 5th Battle Squadron were similar to those in the earlier part of the 'Run to the North', and for a few minutes at about 1735 their firing ceased, as the German ships were obscured by mist and smoke. The *Barham* and *Valiant* fired at the 1st SG, while the *Warspite* also shifted to this target for a time. The *Malaya* continued at the 5th Division, and at about 1725 reported shifting to what appeared to be the leading battleship, and as soon as a short salvo was spotted, broke into rapid Director fire as the *Malaya* was presenting a good target to several ships at this time. In spite of the difficult conditions, hits continued to be scored on the leading German battlecruisers. The *Lützow* was hit twice at 1725 and again at 1730, and the *Derfflinger* at 1719. The other three were not hit, but as previously noted, the *von der Tann's* last turret broke down at 1715, though she remained in the line, steering an irregular course to avoid further damage. No hits were recorded on the 5th Division, though the *König* was struck several times by splinters.

Visibility seems to have been still good for the leading German battleships until about 1735, except when the sun broke through and dazzled gun-layers and spotters, but it then changed very quickly as the 5th BS were obscured in the haze, and at 1740 the *König* could no longer make out her target. The bearing of the 5th BS was already very unfavourable, and only the *Malaya* offered a good target in this period, though the *Valiant* and perhaps the *Warspite* were also engaged.

The *König* fired ten salvos from 1726 to 1740 at the *Malaya*, but it was noted that only two ships of the 5th BS were in sight at 1727, and by 1730 the target bore 18° on the port bow, so that only the two turrets could fire. The *Grosser Kurfürst* reopened on the *Valiant* from her two fore turrets at 1722 and fired until 1730, but her shots fired at 19,900 – 20,700yds were spotted as short. The surviving accounts of the *Markgraf's* firing give few details, but here again only her two forward turrets were ultimately able to fire, and she checked at 1725 to avoid endangering the *Grosser Kurfürst* though a salvo was fired 2 minutes later at 19,800yds, one of the very few from the *Markgraf* for which any facts survive.

The *Kronprinz* resumed on the *Malaya* at 1730 and fired for 6 minutes, while the *Kaiser* expended 27 salvos at this target from 1710½ to 1735 when she ceased as the *Malaya's* bearing was unfavourable, spotting was very difficult and the *Kaiser's* fire appeared to be without effect. Many of the above 27 salvos were from two turrets only, and were at ranges of 17,500 to 20,300yds with an average of 18,900. The *Kaiserin's* report makes no mention of her firing in this period, but the *Prinzregent Luitpold* engaged the *Malaya* from 1708 to 1738 when the latter disappeared in the haze. As with the *Kaisser* many of the

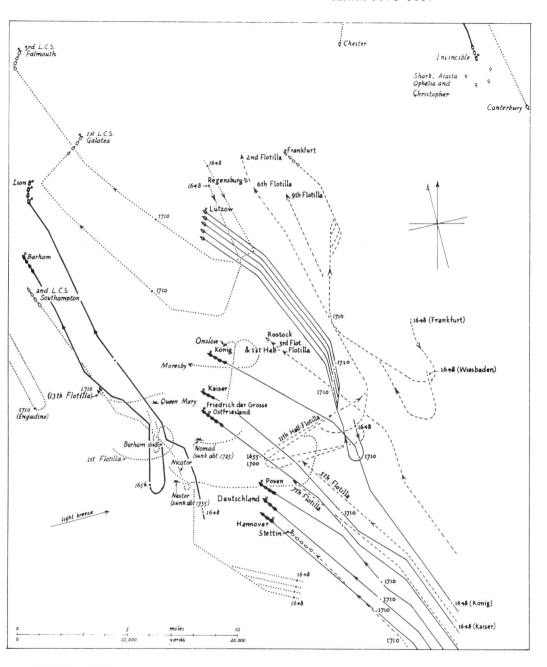

Chart III: Position at 1730

Prinzregent Luitpold's salvos were from only two turrets, but her firing was slower, as she expended 26 salvos in a longer time, maintaining one minute between salvos when she had the range, for which figures of *c*19,000 – 21,000yds are given.

Of the German battlecruisers, the *Derfflinger* had ceased firing at the 5th BS by 1720, but at this time the *Moltke* opened on the *Barham*, and incorrectly claimed hits, though her reported ranges of 18,800 – 17,500yds were short. At 1727 (? 1725) the 1st SG were ordered to engage opposite numbers in the 5th BS, but the *Lützow* had no success, and the *Derfflinger* only fired four salvos between then and 1742, though the *Moltke* noted that her own salvos at the *Malaya* were well placed. The *Seydlitz*, whose guns had been silent since 1710, reported a range of 20,200yds to the *Warspite*, and is believed to have made two hits.

Neither the *Barham* nor the *Valiant* was hit in this period, though at 1729 the latter noted a salvo falling just short and another just over. The *Malaya*, however, was hit seven times by the 3rd Squadron. She was under a very heavy constant fire from at least four ships of the High Seas Fleet. Only their gun-flashes were visible, and six salvos were falling round the *Malaya* per minute, and at one time, counting some which were probably meant for the *Warspite*, nine salvos fell in rapid succession. The *Malaya* was hit at 1720 on the lower edge of the main belt, and at 1727 on the roof of 'X' turret which remained in action. It was then decided to fire the 6in guns short to throw up a water screen, but before this could be done, two shells hit amidships at 1730, one of which put the whole starboard 6in battery out of action with a dangerous cordite fire that came near to causing the *Malaya* to blow up. At 1735 two more shells struck below the armour belt, flooding oil bunkers and resulting in a list to starboard of about 4°. The time of the remaining hit, which was on the 6in side armour, is not recorded, but at 1737, just before the firing on the *Malaya* died away, two shells passed over the ship and fell within a few feet of the port side abreast the forward 6in gun.

Until now conditions had favoured the Germans, but for the rest of the daylight action visibility was usually better for the British though it was seldom good and frequently poor. For the German conditions were often very difficult, but on the few occasions when they could see their targets clearly, their shooting was as dangerous as ever.

Beatty altered course at 1745/46 to 10° and at 1749/50 to 26° and

Chart IV: Position at 1800

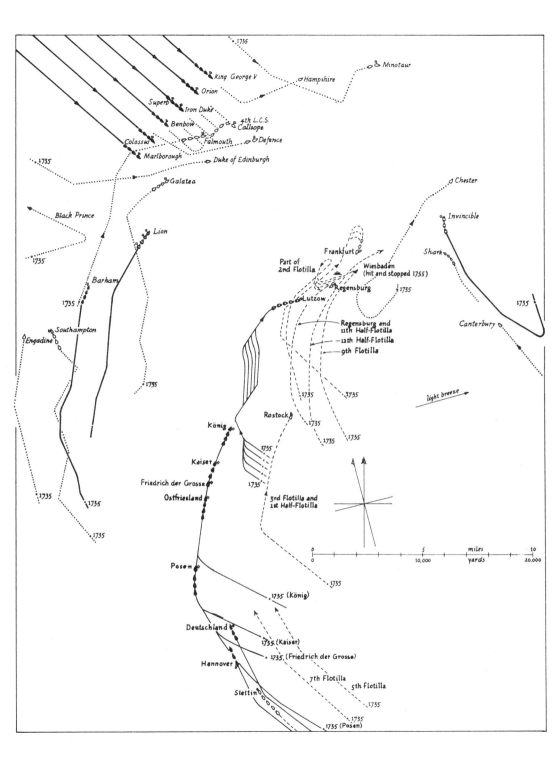

3 minutes later turned further to the eastward until he was steering 66° at 1757, and at 1804 turned to 77°. He called for an increase to 25 kts at 1755 and at 1756 sighted the leading battleships of the Grand Fleet about 5 miles to the northward. At 1747 he had ordered the 1st LCS to carry out a torpedo attack on the German battlecruisers, but this was not done, apparently due to the approach of the Grand Fleet and all the 1st LCS were able to do in the next 20 minutes was to fire a few 6in which fell short, at such German ships as appeared possible targets.

The 1st Scouting Group turned together to 10° at 1747 and at 1751 made a further turn together to 347°. Hipper intended, by thus closing the range, to bring his destroyers into action, but as yet only the 'B' boats of the 2nd Flotilla were far enough ahead, and they had already turned to starboard in pursuit of the *Chester*, while the attention of the German destroyers was now diverted to the rest of Hood's force. What appeared to be numerous cruisers and destroyers assembling for a torpedo attack, but which were probably the 1st LCS, were seen to the northward, and at 1753 the German battlecruisers returned to line ahead, steering 32°. Some units at least, of the 5th BS now added their fire to that of Beatty's ships, and at 1756 Hipper turned to 77°.

Hipper ordered the 1st SG at 1759 to turn together to starboard until the ships were in single line ahead in the opposite direction, and this was followed at 1800 by a signal to reduce speed, and by a report from the 2nd SG to the eastward, that they were under fire from enemy battleships. The 1st SG did not turn until about 1805, after heavy shells from the supposed battleships (the 3rd BCS) to the eastward, had begun to fall near. At this time the *König* was at least 6 miles from the *Lützow*, and though it was still possible to make out Beatty's battlecruisers and the 5th BS from the *von der Tann* as she turned, the supposed battleships to the eastward were invisible to the 1st Scouting Group, and it was time for the German fleet to concentrate. In fact only the *von der Tann* turned through 180°, and the other four battlecruisers steadied on course 201° which led more directly to the head of the 3rd Squadron.

The eastward course of the various units of Beatty's force helped to prevent any of the German ships from discovering Jellicoe's approach, but it was the unexpected appearance of Hood's small force *from* the eastward which distracted the 2nd SG and Hipper's powerful destroyer flotillas.

The *Lion* reopened fire at 1741, followed by the *Princess Royal*. Both ships engaged the *Lützow* for the most part, though other battlecruisers were also fired on. Visibility was at times extremely bad, the *Lion* noting soon after opening fire, that only the enemy's wake could be seen. The range between the leading ships varied from 14,500 to 16,500yds, but the *Lion* actually began at a gun range of 10,000yds, spotting up 4000yds in 5½ minutes, and with an opening rate in use, her gun range attained a maximum of 16,000yds at 1750. She expended 17 salvos in 13 minutes, and then checked for 5 minutes as the enemy disappeared in the mist, before firing a further five salvos between 1759 and 1803, probably at one of the battlecruisers astern of the *Lützow*. Hits were claimed but it is not believed that any were made.

The *Princess Royal* fired less that the *Lion*, but her ranges were more accurate, and a hit claimed at 1747 at 16,500yds, is probably that recorded on the *Lützow* at 1745. By 1803/04 the 1st SG had vanished into the mist, and the *Princess Royal* and then the *Lion* each fired a salvo at the disabled light cruiser *Wiesbaden*, which fell extremely short.

The *Tiger* recorded firing at the 3rd ship from the left (*Seydlitz*) from 1744 to 1805, and seems to have had a fair run, but made no hits and had to check at 1756 on account of interference from the 5th BS. The *New Zealand* engaged the second ship of the only two that could be seen, and reported firing intermittently from 1747 to 1758. She was handicapped by mist and smoke, and was initially going over. The *New Zealand* began again at 1806, and fired three salvos at an unidentifiable target at 16,000yds. The error in her times for this period is not certain, but those given may be as much as 5 minutes fast.

From the German ships, the British battlecruisers were almost or quite invisible, and the *Derfflinger* did not fire a shot from her heavy guns between 1742 and 1816, though the *Lützow* scored once on the *Lion* at 1805. The 1st and 3rd LCS and Jellicoe's wing armoured cruisers the *Black Prince* and *Duke of Edinburgh*, seem to have been dimly made out ahead of, and beyond, the *Lion*, and some shells were fired in their direction without result. Hipper had told the *Moltke* at 1740 to transfer the fire of her heavy guns to battleships and it was perhaps one of her salvos that landed just over the *Valiant* at 1753.

The 5th Battle Squadron steered a mean course of 10° between 1743 and 1758 with alterations of 11° either way, but at 1758 they turned to 21°, and at 1800 to 32°. They were still apparently steaming at full speed, but the 5th Division had abandoned the chase. They had turned to 347° at 1742 and 2 minutes later Scheer signalled that the choice of further courses was to be left to Behncke in the *König*, and the latter which was intermittently under a heavy fire at about this time, altered course to 10° at 1749 and reduced speed to 18kts, so that the rest could close up. Behncke's report notes that the high speed of the 5th Division had loosened the cohesion of the German line, and within this division the spacings had also increased, so that the *König* and *Grosser Kurfürst*, alone with the battlecruisers, stood opposite Beatty's outflanking forces. Behncke again called for 'Utmost Power' at 1755, and this was maintained for 10 mintues, but he altered course at 1800 to 32° and at 1803 to 55°. The other German dreadnought divisions came into line astern of the 5th Division from about 1746 to 1752, and Scheer reduced to 15kts, for 5 minutes to allow the 2nd Division and the old battleships to close up. The track of the 5th Division was not followed exactly, and the old battleships in particular altered course so that at 1815 they were on the starboard quarter of the 2nd Division and not in line, while at this time, the head of the 1st Squadron was steering 29°.

The 5th Battle Squadron did some effective shooting in this period, and as previously, the *Barham* and *Valiant* engaged the 1st SG and the *Warspite* and *Malaya* the 5th Division, though the *Seydlitz* noted that the *Warspite* was firing at the 1st SG at 1740. Unfortunately there are few details in the surviving British records. The *Barham* obtained very good ranges of 19,200yds at 1744, while the *Valiant* was engaging about the 4th ship from the right at 1740, as this was the only one sufficiently visible to fire at, and at 1748 there was a lull in the action as the target was most indistinct. At 1753 the light was much improved, and the *Valiant* reopened, continuing until 1802 when the enemy was lost to sight in the mist at a range of over 19,000yds. The *Malaya* reported that her 15in guns were firing for a short time at nearly 20° elevation to compensate for her list to starboard. The *Valiant* fired a torpedo at the *König* at 1800 or 1801, and the *Malaya* fired one at the *Markgraf* at 1805 but the range was too long for success.

The *Seydlitz* was hit by 2–15in shells at about 1755, and at this time the *Derfflinger* had two large armour plates torn away from her bows by one or more probably two shells of a 15in salvo. The range was about 19,000yds. Numerous 15in shells fell all around the *König* at 1740, and at 1747 it appeared as if at least three battleships were concentrating on her, while at about this time the *Grosser Kurfürst* noted that the British salvos, which had a very small spread, came in quick succession, and fell between her and the *König*. The latter was then well ahead of the other German battleships, and must have offered a fair target at perhaps 18,000yds, but, though heavily shaken, she received no hits from large calibre shells apart from splinters, and that recorded on the *Markgraf* at 1751 is based on an entry in her control room record which refers to the hit at 1710. When visibility was bad, some of the 5th BS were at times going far over, as at *c*1745 shells fell so close to the *Regensburg* 4600yds beyond the 1st SG, that she had to turn away, and at 1756 the first of several salvos fell very near the 3rd Flotilla on the *König's* starboard beam, forcing the destroyers to increase their distance, though only the *S32* was hit by splinters.

At about 1744 the *Southampton* and *Dublin* opened a brisk fire on the *König* with their 6in guns and scored four hits, but the first possible hit by a heavy shell on the *König* was not until 1803.

For the German 5th Division conditions seem to have been very difficult, though the *König* opened fire on the two light cruisers at 1754, and fired 6 salvos in 4 minutes, some of which straddled, at 15,000 – 16,500yds, followed by a single salvo at 1803 at an unidentifiable target to the north-eastward. The *Markgraf* began firing at one of the 2nd LCS about 3 minutes before the *König*, and at 1759 changed to a ship of the 5th BS, which was engaged ineffectively for 10 minutes under increasingly difficult conditions. Of the other ships of the 3rd Squadron, the *Kaiserin* fired 3 salvos at a 4-funnelled light cruiser at 20,800yds from 1755, and the *Prinzregent Luitpold* opened on a similar target at 1803 at 19,700yds but only got off 2 salvos. The 2nd Light Cruiser Squadron reported being under a very heavy fire at intervals until about 1805.

The activities of Hood's force during this phase must now be described. Hood continued on 156° at 25kts. until 1730, when he was about 21 miles 66° from Beatty, instead of in contact as hoped. Errors in estimating positions had led to this gap between the two forces, and Hood's wireless signal at 1656 requesting details of Beatty's whereabouts, was not correctly received, and a reply was not sent until 1806. The 3rd Battlecruiser Squadron were in line ahead with the four destroyers as a submarine screen, the *Canterbury* 5 or 6 miles fine on the port bow, and the *Chester* about 4 – 5 miles abaft the starboard beam.

At 1727 gunfire to the south-west was heard in the *Chester*. Visibility was rapidly decreasing to the westward, but gun flashes were soon seen as the *Chester* turned to investigate, reporting to Hood by searchlight. At 1736 a 3-funnelled light cruiser and one or two destroyers could be indistinctly made out. It was not certain that these ships were German, and as the *Chester* turned to starboard, the dim outlines of two more light cruisers appeared. In fact the vessels sighted belonged to the 2nd Scouting Group and 2nd Flotilla. The *Chester* was more clearly visible to the Germans, and at 1738 the *Frankfurt* opened fire at 7000yds, followed by the *Pillau, Elbing* and *Wiesbaden*, as well as by some of the 2nd Flotilla and 12th Half-Flotilla. The *Chester* turned north-eastward and retired at full speed with the 2nd SG and the destroyers after her. Fortunately, her engines remained intact, though she was hit about 17 times, and had 4 guns disabled, with three holes in her side armour and heavy casualties, she was able to reach safety on the *Invincible*'s starboard bow, the 3rd BCS having turned to a converging course.

According to the *Chester*'s report she was under fire for 19 minutes, though the *Frankfurt*'s war diary gives 13 mintues with a least range of 5900yds, while 7500yds was reported by the *Pillau*. In the first 5 minutes 3 guns were disabled, and severe casualties caused to some other guns' crews, but towards the end, the *Chester*'s zig-zagging was largely successful in avoiding hits. She only fired a total of 56 – 5.5in, not replying until after the 3rd salvo, and estimated the number of shells fired at her as about 400 though this is too high as the *Pillau* expended 90, and it is unlikely that the destroyers fired many rounds, while the *Wiesbaden* and *Elbing* were ordered to cease fire in order to make spotting easier.

In thus pursuing the *Chester*, Boedicker ran into a dangerous trap. The 3rd BCS had altered course to 167° at 1730, and though Hood turned back to about 156° at 1736, firing was then heard in the *Chester*'s direction and gun-flashes seen. At 1738 therefore, Hood led his squadron round to about 313° and at 1741 to about 302°. The *Chester* came into view shortly afterwards, and at 1745 Hood altered course to *c*319°. At 1752 he again turned to about 336°, at 1758 to 2° and at 1801 to about 26°. It is not clear when the 2nd SG were first sighted by the 3rd BCS, but at 1755 or just before, Hood's ships opened fire at about 10,000yds. The 2nd SG accordingly began a 180° turn away to starboard at 1756, but the *Wiesbaden*, which slightly delayed her turn, was hit and both engines disabled, so that she remained laying stopped, while the others made off under cover of artificial fog. The *Frankfurt* and *Elbing* each fired a torpedo without result at their barely visible opponents, while the *Pillau* was hit by a 12in shell at 1758 which exploded below the chart house. Much of the effect of the burst went overboard, but flash entered the 2nd boiler room via the starboard air supply shaft, and the funnel uptakes to the fore boiler room were torn. Of the *Pillau*'s 10 boilers, all six coal-fired ones were put temporarily out of action, but she could still steam 24kts on her four oil-fired boilers and escaped behind the artificial fog.

By just after 1800 the 2nd SG had vanished and the *Inflexible* ceased firing at 1759, but at least one of her sisterships must have continued for some minutes to account for the heavy shells falling near the 1st SG from the eastward at about 1805. In this action the *Inflexible* fired *c*15 rounds, the *Indomitable c*30 and, assuming that the *Invincible* fired at least as many rounds as the *Indomitable*, the total becomes about 80–12in. The *Inflexible*'s first two salvos at the *Pillau* were short but the 4th hit, and the 5th was apparently fired at the *Elbing*. The *Indomitable* opened at the *Wiesbaden* and her first salvo was well over, but it was thought that the 3rd or 4th hit shortly before the *Wiesbaden*'s engines were disabled, and the *Elbing* was apparently then taken as the target. The *Indomitable* fired CPC for her first four salvos and then HE. The *Invincible* also fired at the *Wiesbaden* for some of the time, and most probably scored the hit that disabled her. In all, one hit was made on the *Pillau* and perhaps two on the *Wiesbaden*, but this estimate is very uncertain.

Hood's three battlecruisers were never clearly seen from the 2nd Scouting Group, and were taken to be a squadron or four or more powerful dreadnoughts. As a result Boedicker signalled to Hipper at 1800, and again to Hipper and Scheer via the *Derfflinger* at 1802, that he was under fire from enemy battleships, and some minutes later gave their position (at least 7 miles too far north), followed by a signal that the *Wiesbaden* was disabled, and by a request to the *Regensburg* to send a destroyer to take the *Wiesbaden* in tow.

Hipper had intended that a torpedo attack should be made against Beatty's ships, and gave the order at 1758, but the leading destroyers were already involved with Hood's force. The 12th Half-Flotilla, to starboard of the 2nd Scouting Group, were signalled by the *Wiesbaden* to turn away at utmost speed, when the latter was hit, but they had sighted what appeared to be a fleet of 'many battleships' to the south-eastward of the *Chester*, on a north-westerly course, and made for the supposed battleships which were believed to be part of the main British battlefleet, approaching from the eastward. Of the three leading destroyers the *V69* fired two torpedoes at *c*6500yds, the *S50* one at *c*7500yds which apparently ran in circles, and *V46* did not fire as three torpedo tracks, of which one was circling, were seen approaching. The other two tracks were from the *Shark* which had meanwhile led the four British destroyers present with the 3rd BCS out to attack, and had been fired at by the 2nd SG. Haze and smoke prevented the leading German destroyers from seeing the result of their attack, and they made off to the westward, under heavy fire from the last shells fired at the supposed position of the 2nd SG which had disappeared from view. The destroyer attacks on the 3rd BCS were not detected as such, and it was thought that the torpedoes which later crossed their course, came from the German light cruisers. The *V45* and *G37* followed the first three destroyers, but only one torpedo was fired at the 3rd BCS by *V45* at *c*6500yds, as the 2nd SG approached the *G37*'s line of fire, and she thus fired a torpedo at the British destroyers at about 6000yds.

The 9th Flotilla then attacked, but they were hampered by the returning 12th Half-Flotilla, and only the *V28*, *S52* and *S34* fired one torpedo each at 6500 – 7500yds at the 3rd BCS, visible for a brief moment in the haze. The flotilla then engaged the four British destroyers, at which the *S36* had fired a torpedo at about 8000yds, and the *V28* also fired one at about 4500yds, but the 'B' boats of the 2nd Flotilla obscured the range. The latter had been to port of the 2nd SG, and had also turned away. The 'G' boats of the 2nd Flotilla began an attack on the 3rd BCS but the returning 12th Half-Flotilla obscured the target and only the *G104* fired a torpedo at the *Inflexible* at about 7000yds. The torpedoes aimed at the 3rd BCS appear to have all been fired within a few minutes of 1800 and none hit.

The 'B' class boats were about to attack, when the *Regensburg* which had the *G41* and the 11th Half-Flotilla with her, ordered them to follow, and led southwards to engage the four British destroyers. The 9th Flotilla also took part briefly as noted above, and the *G37*, *G103* and possibly others also joined in the action, while the *Canterbury* supported the British destroyers from the southward. The *Shark* which had already fired two torpedoes at the 2nd SG, was the principal target and fought most gallantly against heavy odds, but her oil-fuel pipe leads and steering gear were wrecked and she came to a stop, while at some time during the action her spare torpedo was destroyed by a shell which struck the air vessel. Help offered by the *Acasta* was refused, and both this destroyer and the *Shark* were sighted at about 1815 by the *Frankfurt* which fired several straddling salvos at 12,400yds, while the *G41* had previously fired a torpedo at *c*6500yds at a destroyer which was probably the *Acasta*. Though disabled, the *Shark* was not yet sunk and had one gun still in action, while the other three destroyers got away with relatively little or no damage, and the *Canterbury* was only hit by a blind 4.1in shell. On the German side the *B98* was hit on the after twin TT mounting at 1807, and in the *B97* the forecastle gun fell out from a jammed breech. The 'B' boats appear to have fired for the most part at *c*3500 – 5000yds, while the *Regensburg* engaged the *Shark* from 1804 to 1808 at 7400 – 2800yds, and then the *Canterbury* until 1817 at 7700 to 10,300yds. The passing of many vessels near to one another at high speed raised a considerable sea, and the *B97* class found gunnery difficult from rolling and from spray over the sights. In addition too many ships were firing at the *Shark*, and the failure to sink her by gunfire is not surprising. None of the torpedoes fired at Hood's destroyers at this time scored a hit. The 3rd Battlecruiser

Squadron did not remain for long on a north-easterly course, as at 1804 they turned in succession to 266°. This was probably done to join forces with Beatty, whose approximate location must have been known, though it was not until 1806 that Beatty signalled his position to Hood as 55°58′N, 5°37′E: course 77°: 25kts and this, if correctly recorded in *Jutland Despatches* p 458, gave an obviously incorrect latitude. The 3rd LCS then came into sight ahead, and Hood asked Napier by searchlight at 1812 where the *Lion* was. No reply is recorded, but the *Lion* must have been sighted almost immediately from the *Invincible*, fine on the latter's port bow.

Hood's westward course since 1804 brought the 3rd BCS towards the torpedoes fired by Hipper's destroyers. These had been aimed in the belief that the 3rd BCS were steering more to the westward at the time of firing than was actually the case, and it was not until about 1813, when the torpedoes were nearing the end of their runs, that they reached the target. Some of those reported were sighted by more than one ship or else were imaginary. The *Invincible* turned away and her helm jammed when put 'hard-a-port', so that she stopped, blowing off large amounts of steam. The trouble was quickly remedied and she went ahead again to resume station. The *Inflexible* turned towards the tracks of which she sighted three. One track ran under the ship and was seen to emerge on the other side. A second passed astern, and the third torpedo, near the end of its run and going very slowly, passed down the port side about 20ft off. The *Indomitable* which reported sighting about five tracks, turned away and increased to full speed. The first track was seen from the fore top to pass under the hull amidships, and to continue its course beyond, and three other torpedoes came near, two passing close to the *Indomitable*'s stern as she turned, and one running along the port side about 20yds away, but these three torpedoes were near the end of their runs and going slowly.

Disaster was thus narrowly avoided, and the 3rd BCS reformed line ahead and swung round to starboard at 1817 to take station ahead of Beatty. The latter had continued on 77° at 25kts until 1809/10, when he turned to 100°, and 3 minutes later 122° to regain contact with the German battlecruisers. At 1815, however, the *Defence* and *Warrior* cut across the *Lion*'s bows, as they advanced to attack the disabled *Wiesbaden* and the *Lion*'s helm had to be put hard over, so that she swung under the *Warrior*'s stern and cleared her by only 200yds. After this Beatty's battlecruisers steadied on course 62° to join Hood.

The withdrawal of the German battlecruisers to the south-westward did not last long, and at 1810 Hipper signalled them to turn together to starboard until they were in single line ahead in the opposite direction.

The *von der Tann* turned to port and the others as ordered, and all then steered to take their stations astern of the *Lützow*, whose course was 21°. Beatty's battlecruisers had lost sight of the 1st Scouting Group as the latter withdrew, and though the *Princess Royal* fired a salvo at 1812, the *Defence* and *Warrior* temporarily fouled the range 3 minutes afterwards.

The *Tiger* engaged the *Wiesbaden* with her 6in guns from 1807 to 1812, and it was perhaps shortly after this that the *Lion* fired two torpedoes, the first aimed to cross the line of the enemy battlefleet, and the second which was incorrectly thought to have hit amidships, at the *Wiesbaden*, but there is no record of the exact time of firing. The German battlecruisers appear to have fired little, if at all, at Beatty's ships at this time, though salvos were reported by the *Colossus* falling round the 1st BCS, and it does not seem that any of the 3rd Squadron were responsible. Behncke had been steering 55° since 1803 and at 1815 or a minute or two later, turned his squadron together to 32° and increased speed to support the battlecruisers.

The 5th Battle Squadron had meanwhile continued on 32° until *c*1806 when the *Barham* turned somewhat to starboard. The *Marlborough* was then sighted on the *Barham*'s port bow, and was thought to be steering 100°. Evan-Thomas altered course to *c*90°, and other ships of the *Marlborough*'s division were seen, but none of other divisions, so that she appeared to be leading the battle line. The *Marlborough*'s course was actually 122°, and at 1812 Evan-Thomas altered course to about 116° to take station ahead of her. The *Valiant* noted that the German battleships reappeared at 1806, but she does not seem to have opened fire again until 1815, one minute after the *Barham*. The formation of the 5th BS at this time is not certain, as at 1814 Evan-Thomas signalled them to form single line ahead.

Durng this period, gallant individual torpedo attacks were made by two British destroyers. The *Onslow*, on the *Lion*'s starboard bow, sighted the *Wiesbaden* at about 1805 in a favourable position, ahead and to starboard, for firing torpedoes at Beatty's ships. The *Onslow* closed and fired 58 rounds of 4in at 4000 – 2000yds, but at a little after 1810 the German battlecruisers appeared and the *Onslow* steered to attack, from a position on their port bow. One torpedo was fired at 8000yds, which failed to hit, and the *Onslow* was then struck by 2 – 5.9in shells from the *Lützow* in a boiler room, and by a third further aft, and turned away at greatly reduced speed. A torpedo was fired at the *Wiesbaden* at 3500yds which was thought to have hit below the conning tower, but appears to have hit far aft, and the 3rd Squadron then came into sight. Although the *Onslow* was well placed on their port bow, she was only capable of low speed, but again attacked and fired two torpedoes at the *Kronprinz* at 8000yds. One of these passed ahead of the *Kaiser* at 1825, running on the surface, and neither hit, but the *Onslow* managed to escape, as the 3rd Squadron were concerned with other targets. She was however hit twice by 4.1in shells from the *Rostock*, and was briefly fired at by the *König*'s 5.9in, but eventually reached home in tow of the *Defender*.

Some minutes after the *Onslow*, the *Acasta* also attacked the German battlecruisers, but from a position on their starboard bow. She fired one torpedo at about 4500yds at the *Lützow* which failed to hit,and came under a heavy fire from that ship and from the *Derfflinger*. The *Acasta* was hit by 2 – 5.9in shells in the engine-room, but she was then hidden from the *Lützow* in smoke, and though for a time unable to stop her engines or steer, she was not further damaged, and was able to make port after the battle with assistance from the *Nonsuch*.

Meanwhile, Jellicoe had been steering 133° at 20kts, and had received two reports of the German battlefleet. Unfortunately the *Southampton*'s report, sent at 1638, gave her position as about 13 miles too far to the eastward, and the *Champion*'s position was possibly in error by 14 or 15 miles to the northward.

Between about 1700 and 1715 four more reports came in. The *Lion*, in a signal timed at 1645 and sent via the *Princess Royal*, reported sighting the enemy battlefleet bearing 122°, and gave her position as 56°36'N, 6°04'E which was about 7 miles too far east. This signal was received correctly by some ships in the Grand Fleet, probably between 1705 and 1710, but it was not taken in by the *Iron Duke* which received it via the *Benbow*, stand-by ship on the wave-length as: 26 – 30 battleships, probably hostile, bearing 145°, steering 122° – the *Lion*'s position being given as in the original. The erroneous figure of 26 – 30 battleships was apparently taken by Jellicoe as indicating that the Germans were at their theoretical maximum strength with eighteen dreadnoughts and ten pre-dreadnoughts. The *Southampton* sent two reports. The first, timed at 1646 and possibly received after the *Lion*'s, was full: 'Course of enemy's battlefleet, 347°, single line-ahead. Composition of van *Kaiser* class. Bearing of centre 77°. Destroyers on both wings and ahead. Enemy's battlecruisers joining battlefleet from Northward. My position 56°29'N,6°14'E.' In fact Scheer's course was 325°, and his centre bore to the southward of 77°, but more serious was the error in the *Southampton*'s position, which was *c*9 – 10 miles too far to the south-eastward, and corresponded to the position of the German 1st Squadron.

The *Southampton*'s second signal, timed at 1700 and apparently received before the previous one, reported that the enemy's battlefleet was steering 347° and bore 77°, 10 – 11 miles away, the *Southampton*'s position being given as 56°33′N, 6°00′E. This placed the Germans about 6 – 7 miles too far to the eastward and again gave the course incorrectly, as the 5th Division were steering 325° and the 6th just turning to 302°. The *Southampton*'s positions given in her various signals were not self-consistent, and if plotted indicated an impossibly high speed.

The fourth report, sent at 1700, was an Admiralty intercept of Scheer's signal to Hipper timed at 1609, which had given his position as: 56°27′N, 6°18′E. Course 302°. Speed 15kts, the position being probably correct to within 4 miles. This indicated that Scheer might be further to the westward than given in the cruisers' reports, but Jellicoe was not inclined to give it equal weight, after the Admiralty's error in placing Scheer in the Jade at 1110.

Although three of the four British light cruiser squadrons were with Beatty, no further reports of the German battlefleet were received by Jellicoe until after 1740.

Jellicoe's one light cruiser squadron was employed as a submarine screen ahead of the battleship divisions, and the armoured cruisers of his scouting screen had never been able to spread as intended, due to the high speed of the battleships and to the decreasing visibility. At least one of the dreadnoughts had difficulty in maintaining 20kts, as shown by a signal from Jellicoe at 1717, telling the *Thunderer* to pass the *Conqueror* if able to do so. In addition to the errors in the reported positions of the *Lion* and *Southampton*, there was also an error in the *Iron Duke*'s calculated position. In a signal timed at 1713, Jellicoe gave Beatty his position as 57°25′N, 5°12′E. Course 133°. Speed 20kts. This was his calculated 1700 position, and the *Iron Duke* was at that time actually about 4½ miles ahead, which made the engaged forces appear still further away than they really were. This signal did not give any time for the position, but it was probably taken as that at 1700.

From the information available it appeared that Jellicoe's course was correct and the Grand Fleet continued on 133° at 20kts. The *Lion* had not given her own course in her recent signal, but it could be inferred to be somewhat to the west of the German battlefleet's course, erroneously given as 347° by the *Southampton*.

At 1733 Beatty's leading light cruiser, the *Falmouth*, then about 5 miles ahead of the *Lion* and the *Black Prince*, Jellicoe's western-most armoured cruiser, about 11 miles southward of the *Marlborough*, sighted one another, and it might be thought that the errors in reported positions would be quickly corrected. This, however, was not so, and the *Falmouth*'s searchlight signal at 1736 merely stated that battlecruisers were engaged in 190°, which was actually to the westward of the *Lion* and of the *Barham*.

As far as can be gathered from Appendix G to the Admiralty 'Narrative', Jellicoe on the evidence available to him, considered the van of the German battlefleet to be about 43 miles directly ahead of the *Iron Duke* at 1735, assuming their speed to be 20kts. The actual position of the *König* at this time was 29½ miles away, 29° on the *Iron Duke*'s starboard bow. Beatty probably believed the *Iron Duke* to be 27 – 28 miles distant at 1735, bearing 331°, whereas she was in fact 20 miles away, and bearing 356°. Such discrepancies were inevitable before visual contact between the two parts of the British fleet was obtained.

Further reports of the enemy soon began to come in. The *Black Prince* in a signal timed at 1740, reported enemy battlecruisers bearing 167°, distant 5 miles, her position being given as 56°59′N, 5°24′E, which was about 7 miles too far to the south-westward. As received in the *Iron Duke* the word 'enemy' was omitted, and in any event the battlecruisers were correctly taken to be Beatty's, but the report was disturbing as it placed part of the engaged forces much further west than had been thought, even though it was probably realised that the *Black Prince*'s reported position was wrong. The *Defence* also made a signal, timed at 1745, which reported ships in action bearing 190°, steering 32°, and gave her position as 57°07′N, 5°38′E which was only 2½ miles out. This was again a report of Beatty's battlecruisers but Jellicoe apparently thought that it might refer to Hipper. Visibility was at that time poor for most, if not all, of the Grand Fleet, the *Duke of Edinburgh* noting it as 3 to 4 miles and the *Colossus* as 6 miles.

Two reports of the German battlefleet now came in from the *Southampton*. The first signal, timed at 1740, said that the German battlefleet had altered course to 325°, and gave the *Southampton*'s position as 56°46′N, 5°40′E which was 5–6 miles too far to the south-eastward. The other, timed at 1750, stated that the German battlefleet had altered course to 347°, and that the German battlecruisers bore 212° from their battlefleet. The *Southampton*, this time, gave her position as 56°50′N, 5°44′E which was about 7 miles too far to the south-eastward. Neither course was accurate, though indicating the alteration to starboard begun at 1742, and a reciprocal bearing was given for the battlecruisers, which actually bore between 21° and 32° from the leading battleships.

Another report from an intercepted German signal was sent by the Admiralty at 1745. This was based on Scheer's 1631 signal to Hipper, and gave the German battlefleet's 1630 position as 56°31′N, 6°05′E:

course 347° speed 15kts, which was probably 4 miles too far to the north-westward. Neither the 1st nor the 3rd Light Cruiser Squadron sent Jellicoe any reports at this time, although the *Falmouth* made a searchlight signal to SO Cruisers at 1748, which was seen by the *Marlborough*, that two heavy enemy ships were bearing 145°, steering 32°. This referred to the 1st Scouting Group, and gave their bearing and course quite accurately, though the *Falmouth*'s actual position was about 5 miles to the south-westward of that given, which would affect ships out of sight of her, if the signal were repeated.

In addition to the above contact signals, the *Minotaur*, *Hampshire* and *Comus* reported gunfire being heard to the south at about 1740, and 10 minutes later gun flashes were reported in 190° by the *Calliope*, and on the starboard bow by the *Marlborough*.

None of these reports gave Jellicoe any certain information about the position of the German battlefleet, though the indications were that it was closer and more to the westward than had been thought. For an ideal deployment it was necessary to have accurate knowledge in advance of the enemy's position, course and speed, so that the Grand Fleet's course and the bearing of the divisional guides could be adjusted to bring the enemy battlefleet ahead with its course at 90° to the line of bearing of the guides and at 180° to the course of the Grand Fleet. If this could be done, a 90° turn together by the divisional guides, with the rest turning in succession, would bring all 24 dreadnoughts into line ahead across the enemy's advance in about 4 minutes, and the 90° turn could be made to port or starboard as desired. Visibility was no better than 10 minutes earlier, and at 1755 Jellicoe asked the *Marlborough* by SL what could be seen. The reply at 1800 said that the British battlecruisers were in sight, bearing 190°, (3 to 4 miles in some versions), steering 77° with the *Lion* leading. By then the latter could be seen from the *Iron Duke* and at 1801 Jellicoe asked by SL where the enemy's battlefleet was. It was now evident that the enemy was likely to be on the Grand Fleet's starboard bow, instead of ahead, and before a reply was received from Beatty, Jellicoe at 1802 altered course to 167°, leading ships together and the rest in succession, and reduced to 18kts to allow ships to close up. It was probable that the German battlefleet might be met 20 minutes earlier than anticipated, so that there was no time to alter the line of bearing of the divisional guides from 43°. The resultant formation was unsuitable for a deployment to the eastward which was becoming more likely as the battle in which Beatty was engaged was clearly moving that way, and at 1806 Jellicoe altered the course of his divisions to 122°. The *Lion* signalled by searchlight at this time that the enemy battlecruisers bore 122°, but they had actually just turned away and disappeared from view, so that their course was not known, and neither was the position of the German battlefleet. At 1807 the *Marlborough* signalled that the 5th BS bore 212° and at 1808 Jellicoe, who realised from the position of the German battlecruisers that he would have to deploy to the eastward, ordered his destroyers to take up dispositions for this.

Meanwhile, a further signal from the *Southampton*, timed at 1800, had come in. This reported that she had lost sight of the enemy's battlefleet, and was engaging the enemy's battlecruisers. Her position was given as 56° 57′N, 5° 43′E. Course 10°. Speed 26kts. But she was actually *c*5 miles to the north-westward of this, and her report of engaging battlecruisers referred to her firing on the *König*. There was still no news of the enemy's battlefleet and at 1810 Jellicoe repeated his question to Beatty. Before the German battleships came into view from the *Lion*, they were sighted by Evan-Thomas, who signalled at 1810 by flags and wireless that the enemy's battlefleet bore 145°. Unfortunately, the *Barham* was not in sight from the *Iron Duke*, and her wireless was out of action, so that the report had to be sent via the *Valiant* and was probably not received until after the German battlefleet was in sight from the *Lion*, though there is some conflict of opinion on this point. At 1814 Beatty signalled by searchlight that the German battlefleet bore 190°. On a basis of five miles visibility, this report placed the enemy battlefleet as 34° on the *Marlborough*'s starboard bow, and only 5 miles away, (the *König*'s actual distance was about 7 miles), and at 1815 Jellicoe made the signal for deployment on the port column, maintaining the speed of the fleet. There was no confusion-proof signal for such a deployment if the fleet's course were unchanged, and the leading division was thus to alter course in succession to 111°. The other divisions would turn to 43°, leading ships together and the rest in succession, and each ship would then turn in succession to 111° as she reached the point where the leading division had altered course. This was not a quick manoeuvre, and would take about 22 minutes to complete, though each battleship should have a clear field of fire in a fifth of that time.

Jellicoe's deployment has been criticised on various grounds, among them that it delayed the entry of the Grand Fleet dreadnoughts into the battle. The details of this controversy will not be discussed here, but in the circumstances of limited visibility and tardy and incomplete information, the deployment was probably the best that could be made, and it gave the Grand Fleet the very great advantage of better gunnery conditions than their opponents, as though for much of the time these were difficult, they were often nearly impossible for the Germans.

Apart from two shells half a mile or more from the *Iron Duke* at 1814, and some which fell near the *Agincourt* at the same time, the Grand Fleet battleships were not fired at previous to the signal for deployment, and did not open fire, though the *Marlborough* sighted the disabled *Wiesbaden*, fine on the port bow, at 1812, but the target disappeared in the haze. Some of the armoured cruisers were however engaged.

The *Defence* and *Warrior* sighted the 2nd Scouting Group, then in pursuit of the *Chester*, on the starboard bow at about 1747, and altered course to port, opening fire at about 1753. Both fired three salvos at about 16,000yds but all were short. The *Defence* then led round to starboard to close the German light cruisers which replied for a few minutes, and the two armoured cruisers, which were apparently taken by the 2nd SG to be two *Town* class light cruisers, fired a few more ineffectual salvos, and then opened on the disabled *Wiesbaden* at perhaps 8/9000yds. The second salvos of the *Defence* and *Warrior* hit according to the latter, and the *Duke of Edinburgh* noted that the *Wiesbaden* was on fire aft and was struck twice amidships by a heavy shell, but continued to fire her bow gun at intervals. The *Defence* and *Warrior* were now steering approximately 190°, and as previously mentioned forced the *Lion* to alter course at 1815. They were in fact heading straight for destruction.

The number of hits scored on the *Wiesbaden* is not known, but was probably about 6-9.2in or 7.5in, though the *Warrior* reported firing about 16 salvos, of which all but five were at under 9000yds, and thought that four or five of them had hit. The *Warrior* was hit by 2-5.9in shells from the 2nd Scouting Group, before they were in range of her own guns, and she and the *Defence* were straddled by heavy salvos from about 1813. The first capital ships to fire at them were the *König* which opened on the *Defence* with 12in, and the *Seydlitz* which fired for a considerable time with 5.9in.

The *Duke of Edinburgh* opened fire at 1808 on the *Wiesbaden*, but was prevented from following the *Defence* by the approach of Beatty's battlecruisers. Her report only mentions two salvos from her port 9.2in, but her returns give an expenditure of 20 rounds. The *Black Prince* was seen by the *Duke of Edinburgh* to turn about 135° to port at 1742, presumably to get out of Beatty's way, and her subsequent movements are unknown. She was lost with all hands during the night. The *Warrior* probably sighted her astern of the Grand Fleet at about 1900, and in a signal timed at 2045, the *Black Prince* reported an imaginary submarine to Jellicoe, and gave her position as 56°55′N, 6°11′E, which was about 17 miles astern of the *Iron Duke*. It seems likely that the *Black Prince*'s speed had been reduced by some machinery failure or damage from a stray shell, but nothing is known, though she appears to have been the armoured cruiser which the *Markgraf* took very briefly for her target at 1812 on a bearing 40° abaft the port beam.

In the 2nd Cruiser Squadron the *Shannon* and *Hampshire* had opened fire at various imaginary periscopes, and the *Hampshire* fired four salvos at the 2nd Scouting Group, which fell extremely short.

No use was made of the *Engadine*'s seaplanes to obtain information, though she was ready to hand on the disengaged side of Beatty's forces. None of the German airships was close enough to observe anything in the existing weather conditions, and the nearest, the *L14*, was about 35 miles from the *Iron Duke* at 1815.

The Harwich Force was held back by the Admiralty which still feared a possible attack by other German ships on the Thames or Channel, but Commodore Tyrwhitt was getting restive, and after requesting instructions at 1645, waited 25 minutes for a reply, and then informed the Admiralty that he was proceeding to sea. He accordingly sailed at 1712, just before instructions arrived to complete with fuel, as he might have to relieve light cruisers and destroyers in the Battlecruiser Fleet later. Tyrwhitt's force comprised the 5th Light Cruiser Squadron and 9th and 10th Destroyer Flotillas (totalling five light cruisers, two flotilla leaders and sixteen destroyers), but less than half an hour after leaving, the Admiralty wirelessed him to return at once and await orders. It was already too late for the Harwich Force to intervene in the battle as events turned out.

This phase had been far more satisfactory for the British than the 'Run to the South' as, apart from the German fleet having been brought within reach of Jellicoe without Scheer realising it, the 5th Battle Squadron had been able to inflict considerable damage on the 1st Scouting Group, and to escape from the 3rd Squadron.

CHAPTER 7

Damage to capital ships
1654–1815

T HE *LION* WAS hit by 3 – 12in shells from the *Lützow* between 1659 and 1702, and by a fourth at 1805. The shell at 1659 struck near the after end of the ½in superstructure side just above the 1¼in forecastle deck. It passed through both of these and burst 21ft from impact just across the centre-line in the galley. The explosion blew down and holed the 1in upper deck, and did much damage to light structure, though reinforced armour gratings prevented damage in the engine room below. Ready-use 4in cordite on the forecastle deck was set on fire, and was difficult to extinguish as fire mains had been cut. This shell also disabled 2–4in guns in the starboard after battery, but details are lacking.

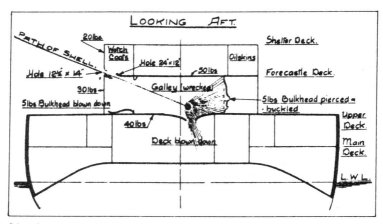

Lion: *hit at 1659.*

124

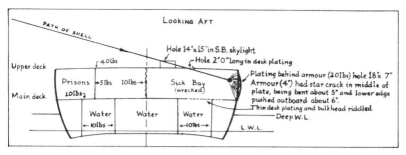

Lion: hit at Station 283 through skylight in sick-bay at 1701/02.

The next two hits were at 1701 and 1702. One shell struck the sick-bay skylight on the port side of the upper deck aft, pierced the 1in upper deck, and burst 13ft from striking the deck, against the inside of the port 4in side armour. The armour plate was hit near the lower edge, and was bent about 3in with a star crack through the plate, and was also forced about 6in outboard at the lower edge. The sick-bay was wrecked, with severe damage to light structure, the ¼in main deck riddled, and a large fragment rebounded and went through the ¼in C/L bulkhead. Smoke penetrated down from the sick-bay, and in consequence a fire was erroneously reported in 'X' port magazine. The cause of the smoke was suspected, but orders given not to flood unless certain that the magazine was on fire, were misheard, and six cordite cases damaged before flooding was stopped.

The other shell at this time passed through the mainmast without exploding, and caused it to be in danger of falling.

No adequate description has survived of the hit at 1805, but the shell struck the starboard hull plating a little forward of 'A' barbette, and burst on the port side which was holed. A small fire was also caused. According to the *Lion*'s damage control notes the only shores required in the battle were to block up a shot hole in 'A' turret lobby which must have been due to this hit.

The *Princess Royal* and *New Zealand* were not hit, but there was one 11in hit on the *Tiger* at about 1658 from the *Seydlitz*. This shell, which was possibly a ricochet, passed through the after funnel near the top, coming from far aft. There was also an important gunnery breakdown in the *Tiger*, as the right gun of 'A' turret was put out of action after firing 27 rounds, by a fracture in the valve-box and control plunger of the run-out cut-off valve, and temporary repairs were not completed until after the action was over. There was considerable leakage of water which got into the working chamber.

In the 5th Battle Squadron, the *Valiant* was not hit, but the other three were damaged to some extent. There were four hits on the *Barham*, all from the *Derfflinger*, and probably by SAP shells, though the last may have been AP.

The hit at about 1658 was one of the most destructive in the battle. The shell struck the 1¼in upper deck, where this formed the glacis near No 2 starboard 6in gun, in line with the aftermost part of 'B' barbette and about 7ft from the ship's side. The angle of descent was estimated at 30–35° which indicates that the shell was deflected downwards by $c5–10°$. It pierced the upper deck (hole 2½ft × 1½ft) and burst 15ft from impact at the ⅜in main deck over the medical store, which was completely wrecked, as was the auxiliary wireless office on the main deck. Very severe damage was caused to light structure and the shell had a very marked incendiary effect. The starboard 6in hand-ups and dredger hoist, as well as the port dredger hoist were badly holed by fragments between the main and upper deck, and the starboard hoists were also holed between the main and middle deck. The flash of the burst passed via the hand-ups to No 2 starboard 6in casemate, causing a serious cordite fire and putting the gun's crew out of action. The flash of the shell-burst also passed down a trunk to the dynamo room on the platform deck and burned all the men there.

Barham: hit at 1658.

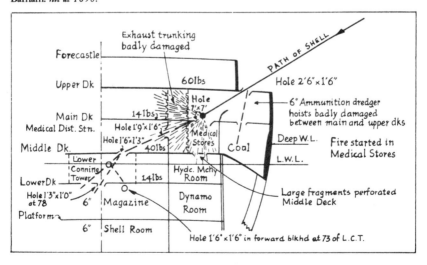

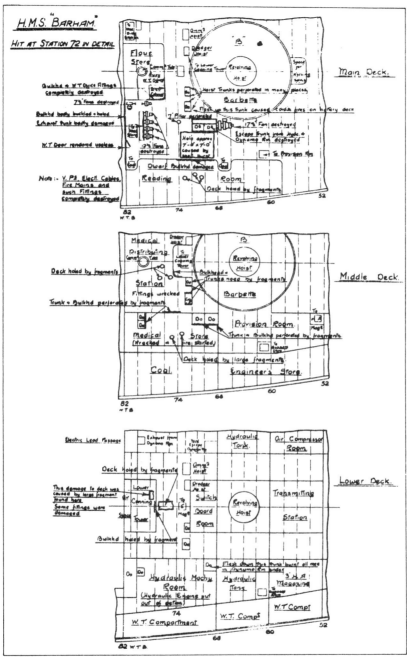

Barham: *details of hit at 1658.*

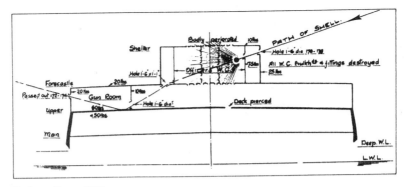

Barham: *hit at c1701.*

The explosion blew a hole 7ft × 7ft in the main deck, and part of the shell head went through the 1in middle deck and was found in the lower conning tower. The ⅜in lower deck, forming the roof of the forward 6in magazine directly below the lower CT, was holed and this magazine and the 6in shell room filled with smoke. Other fragments also pierced the middle deck, and the starboard forward hydraulic pump was put out of action by fracture of the pressure pipe to the hydraulic governor, though the remaining three pumps kept all four turrets going. The largest hole in the middle deck measured 18in × 15in and that in the lower deck over the 6in magazine 15in × 12in.

Barham: *hit at c1708.*

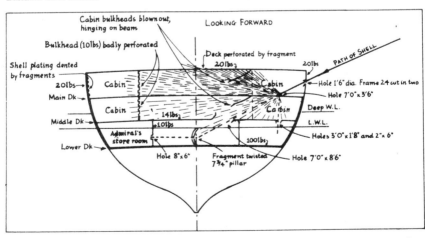

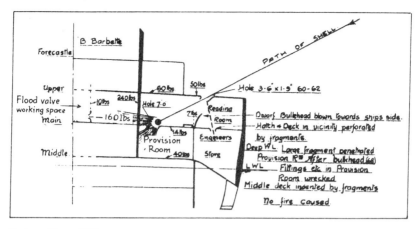

Barham: *hit at c1710.*

The shell at about 1701 went through the ⅝in superstructure side *c*14ft abaft the mainmast, and burst 10ft from impact between the shelter and forecastle decks. Very severe damage was caused to light structure and the main wireless put out of action by cut feeders, while the forecastle deck was badly holed, and fragments also pierced the 1¼in upper deck. One large fragment passed through two light bulkheads and the ½in forecastle deck. It then holed a ¼in bulkhead, was deflected upwards by the upper deck and went overboard through the ½in side plating, over 50ft from the burst.

The hit at about 1708 was on the ½in side plating aft, below the upper deck. The shell burst 6ft from impact on striking the 1¼in main deck in which a hole 7ft × 3ft6in was blown. Here again very severe damage was caused to light structure, to the main deck and to the ⅜in middle deck, while fragments holed the ½in upper deck near the C/L and the ¼in bulkheads of cabins on the port side, in which fires were caused. One large fragment passed down through the main deck, where this was damaged by the burst, and then went through a ¼in bulkhead, and the middle deck, in which a hole 7ft × 2ft6in was made, before striking a 7½in diameter pillar which deflected it to a horizontal path. It then holed a ¼in bulkhead and came to rest above the lower deck, about 40ft from the burst.

The last shell which hit at about 1710 struck the 1¼in upper deck, where it formed the glacis to No 1 starboard 6in gun, 4ft forward of the centre-line of 'B' barbette and about 9ft from the ship's side, and burst 14ft from impact, close to the ⅜in main deck. The hole in the upper deck

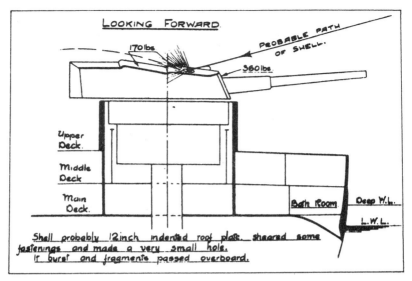

LOOKING FORWARD.

170 lbs

PROBABLE PATH OF SHELL.

360 lbs.

Upper Deck.

Middle Deck

Main Deck.

Bath Room

Deep W.L.

L.W.L.

Shell probably 12inch indented roof plate, sheared some fastenings and made a very small hole. It burst and fragments passed overboard.

Malaya: hit at 1727.

measured $3\frac{1}{2}$ft × $1\frac{3}{4}$ft, and that in the main deck had an area of 7sq ft. Severe damage was caused to light structure, and fittings in the provision room below the burst wrecked, but there was no fire, and the 1in middle deck was not holed by fragments, though dented. Many fragments struck the 4in barbette armour a little above the main deck and $4\frac{1}{2}$ft from the burst, but it was undamaged. The difference between the effect of this shell and that which hit in a similar place at 1658 is remarkable.

The *Warspite* was hit twice. The first hit by an 11in shell pierced the after 6in side armour 3ft above the flat part of the middle deck and about 4ft abaft 'Y' barbette. It made a calibre size hole in the armour and burst 6ft from impact in a cabin. Considerable local damage was done not affecting fighting efficiency, and a water-tight bulkhead was buckled and leaked through rivet holes. The $2\frac{1}{2}$in middle deck was not damaged, and no injuries were visible on the main deck which was here $1\frac{1}{4}$in.

The other hit was apparently through the fore funnel near the top, but details are lacking. The first hit must be credited to the *Seydlitz*, and probably the second was also from this ship. Both are believed to have occurred shortly after 1727.

There were seven hits on the *Malaya*, and for all but one, the time

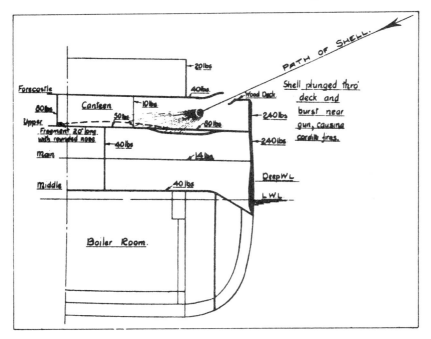

Malaya: *second hit at 1730.*

was recorded. They were as follows:

Hit at 1720. This shell struck the water and is thought to have burst 16ft–18ft from impact, just short of the 8in lower edge of the main belt, and just above the armour shelf 8ft abaft the centre-line of 'A' barbette. The armour was slightly driven in and the 1in hull plating bulged in, below the armour, but no very serious damage was done, though the wings immediately below the armour were flooded for a length of c80ft, with some flooding on the middle deck, the bar of the starboard forward TT was jammed, and the ship very heavily shaken.

Hit at 1727. The shell struck the 4¼in roof of 'X' turret at about 20° to the plate surface and apparently burst on impact. The roof was bulged in and a very small hole made, with some cracking, while many of the securing bolts were sheared, and the roof started up, clear of the turret walls. The range-finder was put out of action, but the turret was otherwise virtually undamaged, as the effect of the burst was outside and the shell fragments went overboard.

Two hits at 1730. One of these hits was unimportant, the shell striking the lower boom stanchion and causing damage to the starboard forward superstructure, but the other came near to bringing about the destruction of the ship.

This SAP shell which had an angle of descent of 20–25° pierced the 1in forecastle deck, 6ft from the ship's side, near No 3 starboard 6in gun, making a hole 5ft × 4ft, and burst 7ft from impact, seriously damaging the gun, which had to be replaced, and wrecking the mounting. The 2in upper deck was forced down several inches by the explosion and fragments wrecked the galley and canteen inboard of the battery. A large part of the head of the shell was deflected off the upper deck, went through the ¼in battery rear bulkhead and stopped against the 2in C/L bulkhead about 30ft from the burst. It was usual at this time to have 12 charges per 6in gun stowed in the battery in rectangular 'W' cases (each containing four charges) for which small racks were provided, and shell fragments penetrated some of these cases and ignited the charges. The resultant cordite fire involved other 6in cartridges in the battery, including those still in their cases which were made of soft-soldered sheet brass and were not fireproof. The whole starboard battery was put out of action for a time with 102 casualties, and all electric cables in the battery were destroyed. Two of the six guns were in action again by 1925.

The flash from the cordite passed down the 6in ammunition hoist into the 6in shell room and was only prevented from igniting a group of

Malaya: *first hit at 1735.*

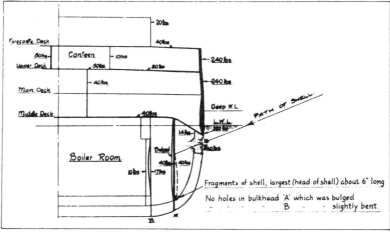

10–6in cartridges, hooked on ready for hoisting, by the prompt action of PO Day and L/S Watson in removing smouldering debris. If these cartridges had ignited, there is little doubt that the forward 6in magazine, above the shell-room, and with two handing scuttles open to the latter, would have exploded, and as this magazine was adjacent to the forward 15in magazines, the loss of the ship must have followed.

Flame and debris also passed down the starboard air supply trunk to the forward boiler room, damaging fittings and slightly burning one man.

Two hits at 1735. These two shells struck close together, abreast of the forward boiler room, and just below the armour shelf, about 10ft below the deep load line. One shell burst soon after impact with the 1in hull plating, and blew holes through the ⅜in inner bottom, with some distortion of the armour shelf and nearby plates, while a fragment was driven back and holed the hull plating. Some large fragments carried on and struck the 2 × 1in torpedo bulkhead, without perforating, falling to the bottom of the outer oil bunker, where several were found 18ft from the impact of the shell. The torpedo bulkhead was bulged but not holed, and the inner ⁷⁄₁₆in bulkhead somewhat distorted.

The other shell did not explode and passed out again through the double bottom, making a fairly large hole.

The wing compartments were flooded for a length of over 50ft and the outer and later the inner oil bunkers for 35ft, and some flooding also occurred on the middle deck. As a result the *Malaya* listed about 4°, but was gradually brought back to the correct trim by pumping oil from starboard to port bunkers. At about 1800 several burners were extinguished in the forward boilers by water which had become mixed with oil fuel, due to leakage into the starboard inner bunkers, and the latter had to be shut off and oil taken from the port side. Eventually oil began to leak into the forward stokehold, and at about 2000 on 1 June the burners had to be shut off. Owing to the list and the lack of stop and non-return valves in the hydraulic exhaust system, the port hydraulic pumps could not get enough water and sea water had to be admitted to the port supply tanks.

The hit for which the time is not known, was on the 6in side armour, just above the main deck and halfway between 'A' and 'B' barbettes. The shell which may have struck a glancing blow, and is said to have burst on impact, drove in the armour slightly and damaged and cracked the surface of the plate.

All seven hits were from the German battleships, but it is not possible to credit individual ships.

The trouble with the alignment of the main cage and shell bogie in 'X' turret continued, but it affected the left gun when the turret was trained on the starboard beam.

The estimated number of 11in and 12in hits on the British ships from 1654 to 1815 is given in the table below.

	12in	11in	Total
Lion	4	—	4
Tiger	—	1	1
Barham	4	—	4
Warspite	—	2	2
Malaya	7	—	7
Total	15	3	18

Of the total of eighteen hits, seven were made by the 3rd Squadron, four each by the *Lützow* and *Derfflinger*, and three by the *Seydlitz*.

There were five hits on the *Lützow*, the first four being 15in and the other 1250lb 13.5in. The hit at 1713 was on the armour belt below the water line, and a little forward of No 1–5.9in. The ship was violently shaken, but initially only two outer wing compartments were flooded and 85 tons water entered. However by shortly before 1800 No 1 port 5.9in magazine had flooded and had to be abandoned, while water also entered No 1 starboard 5.9in magazine, which was drained, and a port protective bunker and probably some other compartments. It is not clear how this latter flooding occurred, and it may have been due in part to cut fire hoses.

The two shells at 1725 hit the superstructure deck between the funnels, and then pierced the 1in battery roof deck inboard of the 5.9in casemates. A large hole was blown in the superstructure deck and considerable damage was caused, the wireless room and its environs being completely destroyed so that both the main and reserve wireless were out of action, but it does not appear that any of the 5.9in guns were disabled, although the hoist to No 6 starboard gun could only be worked by hand.

The hit at 1730 seems to have been on the port edge of the battery roof deck between Nos 4 and 5 – 5.9in. The shell probably burst above the 1.2in armour deck, which was little damaged, but the transmitting station was heavily shaken by the explosion overhead, and the order-transmission equipment put out of action temporarily. Smoke also penetrated the transmitting station and fire control was interrupted for a short time. The shell at 1745 was probably from the *Princess Royal* and appears to have hit the superstructure side below the CT, and to have caused minor damage inboard of the port forward 5.9in casemates.

The *Derfflinger* was hit by a 15in shell at 1719, coming from somewhat forward of the port beam, which holed the hull plating above the armour 68ft forward of the fore barbette, and burst on the port side of the lower main deck. The upper main deck was holed for 16ft × 16ft and the lower main deck torn up and split for a similar area, with another large hole in a transverse bulkhead. There were several holes in the forecastle, and shell splinters struck the starboard 4in side armour on the inside at lwl level and displaced a plate by ⅝in. Much damage was caused on both main decks and fittings destroyed, and fires started in the canteen on the upper main deck, and in the PO's mess on the lower main deck. The effect of the fires and also of smoke and gas was considerable, and the fore part of the ship was filled with smoke, which was blown away forward by employing the forced-draught turbo-blowers of the foremost boiler rooms, so that the fires could be reached. When steaming at high speed, water entered through the holes caused by this hit and spread to compartments on the lower main and armour decks, and eventually *c*1400 tons water entered the compartments affected by this hit, though it is not clear to what extent this was also due to the hit at 1755.

This was by one or more probably two shells of a 15in salvo, which struck the 4in port side armour near the water-line forward of the hawse-pipes, and completely detached both the 4th and 5th armour plates from the bows which together covered an area 17ft long and *c*21ft deep. The 3rd and 6th plates were bent and started away from the ship. All armour bolts of the detached plates were torn off at the plate, while some of those belonging to the 3rd and 6th plates were broken, and some pulled through the hull plating. The latter was much driven in from the keel to the upper deck, particularly inboard of the detached armour, where there was a wide longitudinal tear at about the water-line, and wide vertical tears at either end. Above the water-line the greatest effect was in the forward part of this area and the hull plating was, in addition, torn away above the after half of the 3rd armour plate. The upper and lower main decks were heavily buckled and the upper deck distorted, but there was no destruction within the ship, and the hull plating was nowhere pierced by splinters. The shock was however considerable as a torpedo laying behind the tube in the bow torpedo flat

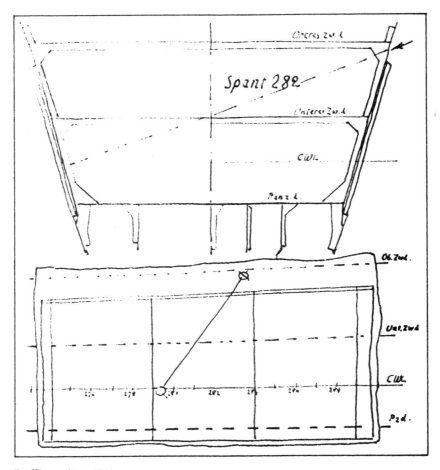

Derfflinger: hit at 1719.

was thrown $c1\frac{1}{2}$ft in the air. The amount of water taken in solely as a result of this hit, amounted initially to $c250$ tons in the bows of the ship, but it is not clear how much of the water noted under the 1719 hit should be added. At about 1930 the bow torpedo sluice room flooded, and later the trimming tanks aft of this, below the bow torpedo flat, slowly filled, so that a further $c300$ tons of water entered. The bow torpedo flat was however kept drained though the tube was out of action.

The total quantity of flood water present in the *Derfflinger* after the battle was calculated to be 3350 tons, but 1020 tons of this was in the

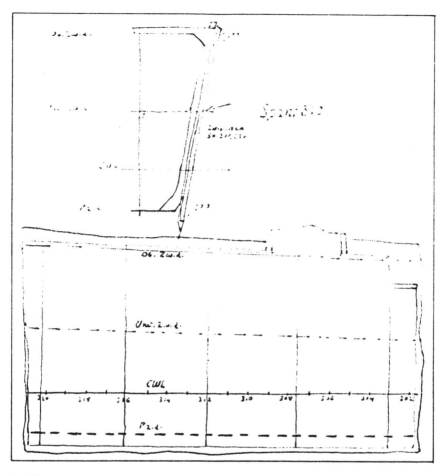

Derfflinger: 15in hit on the 4in port side armour.

magazines and shell rooms of the 2 after turrets which had been flooded after serious propellant fires, and had not been drained in order to prevent the ship trimming too much by the head. A list of about 2° to port eventually developed, and the starboard wings were counter-flooded 80% full for 130ft in the after part of the ship at 0525 1 June, which admitted 206 tons of water, included in the above total. The *Derfflinger*'s mean draught before the battle was 30ft 8in which would be reduced 7in by consumption of fuel, water and ammunition during the action, and her draught after the battle was altered by the above flood water to 37ft 11in (fore), 27ft 8in (aft).

The first hit on the *Seydlitz* for which the time is known, was by a 15in shell at 1706 which pierced the forecastle deck about 6ft on the port side of the midships line and 65/70ft from the bows. It exploded above the upper deck, and 6ft from the starboard side, tearing a hole *c*10ft × 13ft in the outer skin plating between the battery and forecastle decks. A hole *c*6ft × 6ft was blown in the upper deck, and the forecastle deck bulged over the point of explosion. Fragments also pierced the skin plating and the battery and forecastle decks. The hole made in the starboard side of the hull by this shell, was the chief cause of the subsequent very serious flooding which affected the *Seydlitz*. While under way, large quantities of water poured in through this hole, and aided by the damage from four other 15in hits, gradually spread to all forward compartments above the armour deck. This increased the immersion of the forward part of the ship, and by 2100 the hole in the starboard side caused by the explosion of this shell was only a little above the then water-line. As the *Seydlitz*'s forecastle continued to sink deeper, water was able to enter aft of the citadel bulkhead through damage in that part of the ship, and water also gradually penetrated into forward compartments, below the armour deck through leakage at cable joints, voice-pipes, ventilation trunks and hatches.

At 1708, another 15in shell pierced the forecastle deck on the port side about 20ft abaft the previous hit. This exploded immediately, blowing a hole 6ft × 6ft in the forecastle deck and a much larger one, measuring 20ft × 23ft in the upper deck directly below. Extensive damage was caused, and fragments holed the battery deck and the striking-down trunk for torpedoes, wrecking the forward torpedo winch and hoist. Splinter damage from this shell assisted water which had entered from the previous hit, to spread through the forepart.

At 1710 the starboard wing turret was hit by a third 15in shell at a range of *c*19,000yds. This struck the turret face to the right of the right gun and holed the 10in armour, although the shell burst in so doing, and the effect of the explosion was mostly outwards. The hole measured 14in × 10in with concentric cracks, as well as some spalling above the hole on the outside, and below it on the inside. The plate was apparently not displaced, but the whole turret, trained right aft, was violently shaken, and fragments of armour, a piece of the shell body, and part of the driving band entered the turret, striking the elevating gear and right cradle carrier of the right gun. The right elevation and training mechanisms were wrecked and the right cradle carrier and trunnion damaged, but it was possible to move the right gun by coupling it to the other. Fragments of armour plate thrown sideways struck the casemate

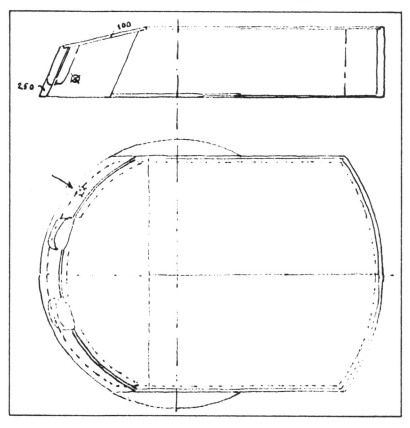

Seydlitz: *hit at 1710.*

range-finder, and others which entered the turret, seriously wounded one man, the only casualty apart from one slightly burned. Large amounts of gas entered the turret, but the gun-house crew put on gas-masks and were ordered to leave the turret for about 3 minutes until the gas had dispersed. No inconvenience was experienced in the working-chamber.

The *Seydlitz* is next known to have been hit by 2–15in shells at about 1755.

In order from forward they were:

1 An APC shell pierced the upper edge of the side armour (4¾in thick) above the

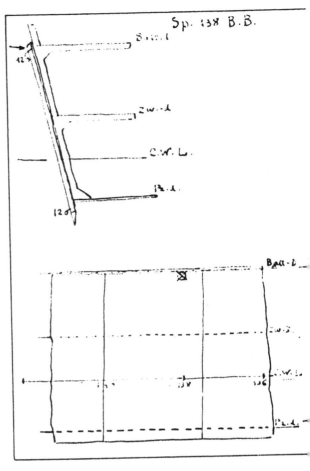

Seydlitz: first 15in hit at c1755.

forward end of the broadside torpedo flat, the hole measuring 28in × 16in. The shell glanced off a deck support, and burst against the capstan drum which was bent almost at right angles. Large holes c16ft × 23ft were torn in the battery and main decks close to the hull side and bulkheads damaged on these decks. Fragments of armour plate also tore up the battery deck.

When the shell burst, the nose carried on across the ship and penetrated the skin plating on the starboard side, between the battery and main decks, starting an armour plate outwards by 1½in at the upper edge and nearly holing it. Other large fragments were flung against the starboard skin plating inboard of the armour, and the main deck was also holed on this side. Water entered the cable-locker via the started armour plate, which by 2100 was on the then water-line, and damage to

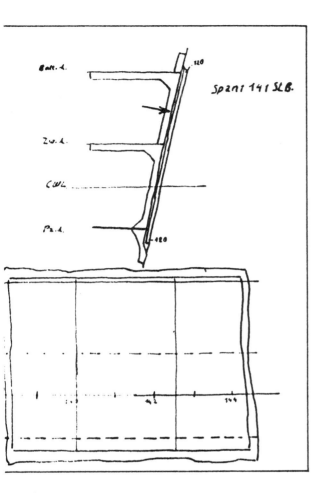

decks and bulkheads aided the spread of the flooding forward.

2 This struck the port windlass drum and exploded, blowing a hole in the forecastle deck and one measuring *c*6ft × 13ft in the upper deck directly below. Fragments holed the battery deck and the skin plating on the port side of the upper deck, as well as a transverse bulkhead. Damage to the decks enabled water to find new inlets into compartments, including the bow capstan room, and the capstan engines were eventually put out of action.

In addition to the foregoing five hits, the *Seydlitz* was hit during this phase by a 15in shell which burst under water near the hull, in line

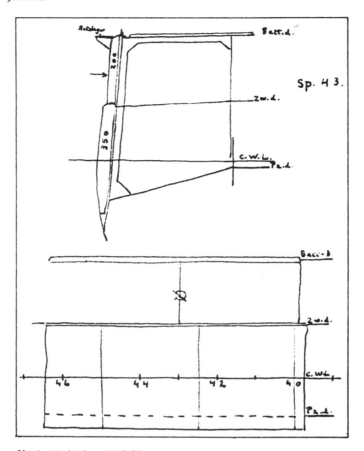

König: *6in hit from 2nd LCS.*

with the foremast. The nose of the shell without the cap pierced the outer skin about 1½ft–2ft below the armour belt and came to rest in a port wing compartment which was flooded for a length of 20ft. The direction of this hit is not known, but the others were all from within 10° of the port beam.

According to her war diary, there was a fire under the forecastle at 1757, and at 1803 it was noted that, because of water above the armour deck, the forward part of the ship had no longer any buoyancy, though flooding was not seriously affecting compartments below the armour deck in this part of the ship. Five minutes later, it was recorded that the *Seydlitz* was slowly taking up a list to starboard.

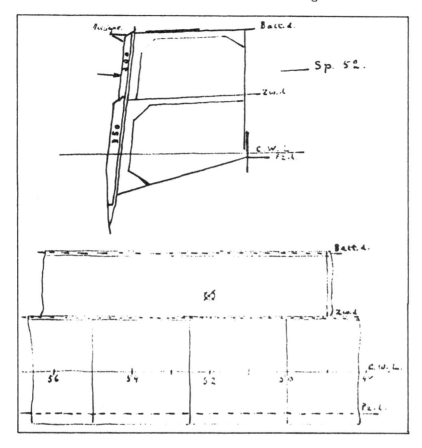

König: *6in hit from 2nd LCS.*

Neither the *Moltke* nor the *von der Tann* were hit, but in the latter, the last turret (port wing) broke down at 1715, as the guns jammed, and would no longer run-out after recoil, the right gun having previously done so for *c*20 minutes from 1650. The trouble was overcome by 1830 though it was liable to recur, and meanwhile the *von der Tann* had only her secondary battery.

One of the ten hits from heavy shells received by the *König* during the battle was at 1803, though this was apparently by a large fragment of a 15in short and not a direct hit. It made a hole *c*20in × 8in in the sheer-strake near the bows on the port side, and went overboard without causing further damage. Two other hits from fragments were

143

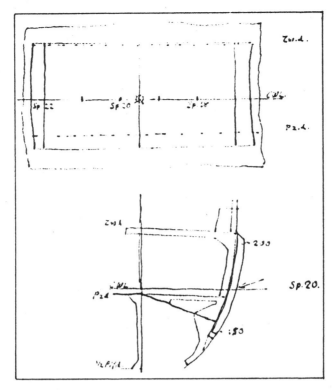

Markgraf: *hit at 1710.*

recorded at this time. The 4–6in hits on the *König* from the 2nd LCS were all on the side armour, two on 8in and two on 14in, between the after funnel and 'X' barbette, and had little or no effect.

The *Grosser Kurfürst* was hit once by a 15in at 1709, and the *Markgraf* three times by 15in shells during this phase, but the time of only one hit, that at 1710, is known. There is no detailed description surviving of the hit on the *Grosser Kurfürst*, but the shell struck the water 30–60ft from the hull. It is not clear whether it burst or ricochetted, but the former is probable, and the fragments apparently struck the 6in port side armour c85ft from the bows with little effect.

One hit on the *Markgraf* was by a shell which passed through the starboard derrick-post near the top without exploding, and another shell similarly passed through the foremast 60ft above water. At the date of the battle the *Markgraf* had a thin 'pole' foremast which was nearly cut in two, but remained standing.

The hit at 1710 was on a joint between two plates of the 8in after side armour, 77ft forward of the stern and on the lwl.

The shell burst had no effect inside the ship, but the armour was holed and large pieces broken from both plates, which were forced in 2¾in at the upper edge. The hull plating was bulged in under water for a length of 25ft, and to a depth of 8ft below the lower edge of the armour deck slope, and was also torn at the joints. The armour deck was undamaged but the main deck was buckled, and an armour fragment pierced two longitudinal bulkheads, the main deck and the starboard hull plating, a total of over 1½in in addition to cabin bulkheads. One compartment above the armour deck was flooded, and the wardroom and several cabins on the main and armour decks wrecked, while there was some further flooding below the armour deck, and about 400 tons of water remained in the ship as a result of this hit.

The number of hits by heavy shells on the German ships from 1654 to 1815 is estimated as follows:

	15in	13.5in/1250lb	Total
Lützow	4	1	5
Derfflinger	3	—	3
Seydlitz	6	—	6
König	1	—	1
Grosser Kurfürst	1	—	1
Markgraf	3	—	3
Total	18	1	19

In addition there were about three 12in hits on the 2nd Scouting Group from the 3rd BCS, of which one was on the *Pillau* and the remainder on the *Wiesbaden*. It is not possible to assign the 15in hits to individual ships, but the *Barham* and *Valiant* can be credited with those on the 1st SG, and the *Warspite* and *Malaya* with the others.

CHAPTER 8

Action between capital ships
Third phase 1815–1900

I N THIS PHASE of the action, Jellicoe's battleships briefly engaged the German 3rd Squadron in conditions such that no effective reply could be made, but the German fleet caused considerable loss to other British units, blowing up the *Invincible* and *Defence*, while in return the 3rd BCS, the oldest battlecruisers in either fleet, scored the most important British success in the whole battle, by inflicting the damage which ultimately proved fatal to the *Lützow*.

At 1815 when the signal for the deployment of the British battlefleet was made, the *Marlborough* and *King George V* were, respectively, about 6.8 miles bearing 332° and 9.4 miles bearing 360° from the *König*. The *King George V* led the 1st Division on 111°, while the other battleships came into line ahead, course 43°, and then turned in succession to follow the 1st Division. At 1826 when the rear of the 3rd Division had rounded the turning point, the *King George V* altered course to 88° to give more sea room between the battlefleet and Beatty's ships which were now level with the head of the line, and at this time or a little before, Jellicoe ordered a reduction to 14kts to help Beatty get clear. Considerable bunching was now occurring amongst the ships towards the rear of the line, and the *Marlborough* and others had to reduce to 8kts, while the *St Vincent* had to stop for a short time; some overlapping also took place in the 2nd and 3rd Divisions. At 1833 the battlecruisers were sufficiently far ahead for Jellicoe to signal for 17kts, and the *King George V* which maintained a higher speed than that of the fleet in order to reduce bunching, and averaged 18kts between 1800 and 1900, led back to 111°. By 1837 all 24 ships had rounded the turning point, and in a few minutes the line had straightened out. At 1829 Jellicoe had made a signal for subdivisions to alter course separately to

145° to close the range, but promptly negatived the order, as further thought convinced him of its impracticability before the deployment had been completed.

At 1817 the 5th BS altered course to 100°. It was then realised that the *Marlborough* was not leading the battle line as had been thought, but that her division was at the rear, and to avoid blanketing the fire of Jellicoe's battleships by attempting to take station ahead, Evan-Thomas turned about 90° to port at 1819. While making this turn, the *Warspite*'s steering jammed and she swung towards the German line under very heavy fire, and made about 1½ complete circles, before she was brought under control on a northerly course. The other three ships had meanwhile turned gradually to starboard until they were steering 43° at 1826. They reduced to 18kts, and subsequently to 12–16kts, as they followed astern of the 6th Division, and at 1839 turned to about 106°.

After clearing the *Defence* and *Warrior*, Beatty's four battlecruisers steered 62° until about 1823 when course was altered to starboard. Beatty had called for 26kts at 1821 to get clear of the battleships as quickly as possible, and by 1827 was steering 111°, which was held until 1837 when he altered course to 100° to clear the wreck of the *Invincible*. The battlecruisers' movement across the Grand Fleet's field of fire was unfortunate, but Beatty had no choice.

The 3rd Battlecruiser Squadron had turned in succession to starboard at 1817, and then steered *c*120° at about 20kts, leading the whole fleet. The two surviving ships hauled out temporarily to port to clear the *Invincible*'s wreck, and increased to 25kts, but they did not make any important alteration of course until 1844.

At 1815 the *Lützow*'s course was 21° and by 1820 about 32°, while the rest of the 1st Scouting Group were steering to take station astern. The 3rd BCS, which was quite invisible to the Germans, then opened a very heavy fire, and the *Lützow* turned away, as did the other German battlecruisers, so that by about 1828 the 1st SG was in line ahead, course 122°. At about 1834 the battlecruisers turned together to starboard, the *Lützow* was out of action at 1837, and withdrew at greatly reduced speed to the south-westward while, as it was seen that the battleships were beginning to turn 180°, the *Derfflinger*, *Seydlitz* and *Moltke* continued to starboard until they were steering about 280° at 1840. The *von der Tann* had not turned so far to starboard, and then turned to port and headed somewhat to the northward of the rest, but soon steered to close them. It appears that the *Seydlitz* was late in making the turn to starboard at about 1834, as her war-diary notes that the damaged *Lützow* was abeam to starboard, and that she had to be steered

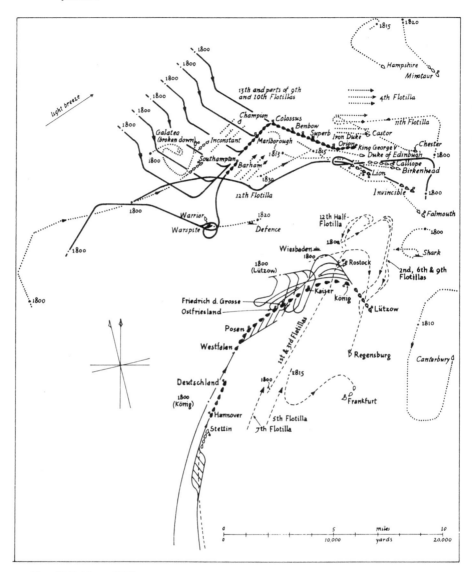

Chart V: Position at 1830

temporarily from the steering gear compartment, as the coupling at the upper steering engine had flown out due to the shaking from a hit.

The ships of the 3rd Squadron had turned together to 32° at 1815 or just afterwards, and increased speed, but at 1826 they returned to line ahead steering 55° and 2 or 3 minutes later 77°. The *Friedrich der Grosse* and the 1st Squadron turned together to 10° at 1818 but at 1821 came back into line ahead steering 32°. By about 1835, the *König* was under a heavy and accurate fire from the *Iron Duke*, and was slowly turning to starboard following the movements of the 1st SG, while the rest of the 5th Division were beginning to follow the *König* with the 6th Division still steering 77°, and the *Friedrich der Grosse* and 1st Squadron 32° so that there was a considerable curve in the battle line. Little or nothing could be seen of the British and Scheer believed them to be more to the eastward than they really were, so that at 1835, he ordered the battleships to make an 'about-turn' (Kehrtwendung) to starboard, in order to withdraw temporarily. In this manoeuvre as practised by the German Navy, the ships did not turn 180° simultaneously and the rearmost ship began to turn first. It should thus have been begun by the *Hannover* of the 2nd Squadron, but it was wisely initiated by the *Westfalen*, the rear ship of the 1st Squadron, which became Guide of Fleet when Scheer signalled course 257° at 1839. The *König* did not receive the signal to turn about as her short range wireless ('Z' station) aerial was temporarily out of action, and she had continued gradually turning to starboard until by about 1838 she was steering 167°. The ships astern of her were then seen to be turning about, and at 1840 the *König* altered course to 257°. The pre-dreadnoughts of the 2nd Squadron had also turned 180° and were now on the *Westfalen*'s port bow.

Of the other units present, the disabled light cruiser *Wiesbaden* was about 12,000yds 161° from the British deployment turning-point, while the rest of the 2nd SG were 9000yds or less southward of the *König* at 1820. They remained in this area, and the *Canterbury* engaged the *Frankfurt* for c6 minutes and scored 2–6in hits in line with the mainmast, and also 2–4in, between 1826 and 1829. The *Rostock* with the 3rd Flotilla and the 1st Half-Flotilla, was near the *König* but the *Regensburg* and the 2nd, 6th and 9th Flotillas, which were 6000–7000yds to the eastward of the *König* at 1820, then took up a position to the south-westward of the 1st SG, and for the last 15 or 20 minuts of this phase were near the *Lützow*. The *Regensburg* fired at the *Shark*, while the *Rostock*, after engaging the *Defence* and *Warrior*, fired at the *Onslow* and scored two hits as previously noted. The 9th Half-Flotilla were near the 1st Squadron, while the 4th SG, the rest of the 5th Flotilla and the 7th Flotilla remained in the vicinity of the 2nd Squadron.

The *Defence* and *Warrior* of the 1st Cruiser Squadron, headed 190° to attack the *Wiesbaden*, and after the *Defence* sank at 1820, the badly damaged *Warrior* got away to the westward and then north-westward. The *Duke of Edinburgh* steamed up the engaged side of the battlefleet and reached a position on the *King George V*'s starboard bow at about 1830, while the *Black Prince* was probably astern of the fleet. The 2nd CS with their four screening destroyers closed the *King George V* and then remained about 7000–10,000yds on her port bow. They had previously steered 21° for about 10 minutes, apparently to ensure that no minelayers were working to the eastward.

The 1st LCS had to get out of the way between the 4th and 5th Divisions before deployment, and at 1840 were still on the *Agincourt*'s port quarter, with the *Galatea* some way astern as a splinter had broken up a forced draught fan impellor, and put the after boiler-room out of action at *c*1815, reducing speed to 18kts. The 2nd LCS took up a position on the port quarter or beam of the 5th BS, while the 3rd LCS were able to reach the head of the line and at 1820 were close on the starboard bow of the 3rd BCS. The *Falmouth* and *Yarmouth* drew ahead, but the *Birkenhead* and *Gloucester* turned to the disengaged side to avoid fouling the range, and by 1840 the other two were crossing ahead of the *Inflexible* to join them. The 4th LCS were on the *King George V*'s starboard bow at 1820 and 2 miles clear at 1840.

The *Chester* was on the disengaged beam of the 3rd BCS and then steered to join the 2nd CS, while the light cruisers attached to the battle squadrons took station on their port side, as did the *Abdiel* and *Oak*, and the *Engadine* was clear of the action to the westward. The *Canterbury* was steering southwards about 8 miles south-eastwards of the *König* at 1820. She then turned north-eastwards and briefly engaged the *Frankfurt* as noted above. She was only about 4 miles to the eastward of the *Lützow* at 1834, but was not fired at, and eventually joined the 3rd LCS soon after 1900.

Of the Grand Fleet flotillas, the 4th, less four destroyers with the 3rd BCS and three with the 2nd CS, were ahead of the 2nd BS previous to deployment and then took station ahead of the *King George V*, on her port bow. The *Castor* and the 11th Flotilla were ahead of the 4th BS and on deployment also took station ahead and to port of the *King George V*, but closer than the 4th Flotilla. The 12th Flotilla, less one destroyer with the 2nd CS, were ahead of the 1st BS, and took station on the starboard beam of the 5th BS.

The *Champion* with the destroyers of the 9th, 10th and 13th Flotillas, less the crippled *Onslow*, took up a position on the port beam of the 6th Division and 5th BS, while the destroyers of the 1st Flotilla, after some difficulty in passing through the 12th Flotilla, went ahead on the port beam of Beatty's battlecruisers, and were later joined by the *Christopher* and *Ophelia* of Hood's screen. The *Shark* was disabled about 5 miles bearing 100° from the *Wiesbaden*, and the *Acasta* crippled near the British line. The *Fearless* lacked speed to follow her destroyers of the 1st Flotilla, and took station on the disengaged quarter of the Grand Fleet.

The foregoing shows how complex the battle situation was between 1815 and 1840, but little of the enemy could be seen from either the *Iron Duke* or *Friedrich der Grosse*. Of capital ships, only three or four *König*'s were seen from the *Iron Duke* for about 5 minutes, and only the *Warspite* appears to have been sufficiently visible for the *Friedrich der Grosse* to fire. Very little information was provided by the many British cruisers. The *Southampton* in a signal timed at 1820, reported that the enemy battlefleet bore 10–11 miles 145°, course 32°, which was correct except that they were about 2 miles closer, but her position was given as 56° 58′N, 5° 51′E, which was about 7 miles too far to the south-eastward. The *Lion* in a searchlight signal sent at 1827 via the 4th LCS and the *King George V*, and timed at 1818, stated that the enemy battlefleet was in sight, bearing 167°, the nearest ship distant 7 miles. The bearing was, however, that of the 1st SG, and the distance about 2 miles too great. The *Falmouth* engaged the *Lützow* at under 6000yds with her 6in guns and saw the German battlecruisers turn away at about 1834 but made no report, until Beatty later asked for the bearing of enemy battlecruisers. It was noted by the *Iron Duke*'s fire control that one of the *Königs* turned away *c*145°, but this was not seen by Jellicoe or anyone with him on top of the chart house. A note was also made on the *Benbow*'s range plot that at 1840 her target turned away and appeared to circle round to the right.

The only information received by Scheer was from the 5th Flotilla in a signal at 1825, stating that, according to prisoners from the *Nomad*, there were 60 large ships in the vicinity, including 20 modern battleships and six battlecruisers. It does not appear that the destruction of a capital ship was reported by the 1st SG when the *Invincible* blew up.

Visibility to the north-eastward was bad for the Germans in this period and did not in general exceed about 4 miles, though gun flashes could be seen at a greater distance, and the *Invincible* was clearly visible at nearly 5½ miles for a short time. To the north-westward conditions were better, and the *Warspite* was engaged at over 7 miles. For the British, visibility was about 5 to 7 miles, and occasionally more, as the *Valiant* reported a range of 19,000yds at 1817, and for a short time at about 1830, the *Thunderer* obtained ranges of 22,000-18,000yds from the foretop.

Interference was caused to the British by various ships between the battle lines. In addition to the passage of Beatty's battlecruisers and the 1st Flotilla, the *Duke of Edinburgh*'s dense funnel smoke obscured the range for the leading ships of the 2nd BS, and the latter were also affected by funnel and cordite fumes from ships ahead. Dense smoke from fires in the *Warrior* interfered with units in the centre and rear of the line, and the 12th Flotilla caused some interference to the *Agincourt*, while smoke from the *Wiesbaden* also contributed to the worsening conditions, and this unfortunate light cruiser distracted much of the British fire from the more difficult target of the German line.

The firing of the German battleships was quite ineffective against Jellicoe's line, though the *Hercules* was closely straddled at 1816 by a salvo of five shells which fell round her forecastle and deluged the bridge, conning-tower and foretop. Other ships of the 1st BS and also the *Vanguard*, reported shells falling near in the first 10 minutes of the deployment, and the *Royal Oak* was straddled once at 1833. The *Prinzregent Luitpold* reported firing 21 salvos from 1815 until the 180° turn was made, but had no success, and would have been over at her reported ranges of 18,800-17,500yds.

The *Defence* and *Warrior* of the 1st CS, and the *Warspite* offered better targets. The two armoured cruisers continued towards the German fleet, firing at the *Wiesbaden*, and at 1816 the *Defence*, already under fire from the *König*'s 12in, and from the *Seydlitz*'s 5.9in was sighted by the *Lützow* about 8000yds away. The *Lützow* fired 5-12in salvos in quick succession, of which three straddled, and also discharged a torpedo, while the *König*'s 5.9in joined in, and the *Grosser Kurfürst*, *Markgraf*, *Kronprinz* and *Kaiser* opened on the *Defence* at times variously given between 1814 and 1817, and were followed by the *Kaiserin*. The *Warrior* came in for some of the extremely violent fire from 12in and 5.9in guns that was concentrated on the *Defence*, and which from the *Valiant*, appeared to form a danger zone of 1000-1500yds.

The *Lützow* apparently fired no 5.9in, while the *Kaiser*, which fired 10-12in salvos at the *Defence* from her turrets that would bear, only expended 41 rounds of 5.9in in the whole battle. The *Kronprinz* fired only 2-12in salvos and no 5.9in, the *Markgraf* fired 12in and 5.9in and the *Grosser Kurfürst* and *Kaiserin* opened with 5.9in, the former then firing 2–12in salvos, and the latter only one. At 1819 the *Defence* which had altered course to starboard, was heavily hit aft, flame shot out of her after 9.2in turret, and was followed by a series of flames from the 7.5in turrets, working forward until there was a large burst of flame from the fore 9.2in turret, and in less than 30 seconds from being hit aft, she had completely blown up and disappeared with all 903 of her complement.

The *Lützow* changed target to the British battlecruisers after the *Defence* had blown up, and the *König*, which fired a torpedo that failed to hit at the *Warrior* at 9000yds at 1822, transferred her fire to the *Warspite* at this time. The *Kaiserin* shifted from the *Defence* to a target at 14,200yds, which was thought to be the *Tiger*, but had to cease after two salvos from lack of visibility. The *Markgraf* fired her 12in at Beatty's battlecruisers for a time after the *Defence* had sunk, but kept her 5.9in on the *Warrior*, while the *Grosser Kurfürst*, *Kronprinz* and *Kaiser* engaged the latter target.

According to the *Valiant* some of the German shooting at the *Warrior* was bad, and about 2000yds over, and several of the 18–12in salvos fired by the *Kaiser* between 1823 and 1835 at 12,000 to 9,000yds, must have gone over the *Warrior* and fallen near the 5th BS. The 2–12in shells which hit the *Princess Royal* at c1822 were not 'overs' at the *Warrior*, but from the *Markgraf* and aimed at the *Princess Royal*. They were from one salvo and did considerable damage, one putting 'X' turret out of action and the other piercing the 6in side armour. The *Warrior* was hit by c15 heavy shells, and violent fires broke out but, screened to some extent by the smoke from these, she was able to withdraw as her engines continued running, though both engine rooms were flooding rapidly. None of the German ships fired at the *Warrior* after 1835 as she was obscured by the *Warspite*, but she was too badly damaged to reach harbour, and after being towed by the *Engadine*, was abandoned on the morning after the battle in rising seas.

The exact details of the 5th Battle Squadron's turn at 1819, which resulted in the *Warspite*'s helm jamming, are uncertain, but it was probably made together without a signal, as stated by Evan-Thomas, though a signal was logged at 1818, ordering the 5th BS to alter course in succession 180° to port. The turn was, however, of about 90° only. The reasons for the *Warspite*'s helm jamming are discussed on a later page, but in the sequence of events, when the *Warspite* was turning northward, she appeared to be closing the *Malaya*; 20° of port helm were applied to bring her head to starboard and the steering then jammed. She passed close under the *Valiant*'s stern, and attempts to bring her back to port by her engines only resulted in closing the German line at decreasing speed. Full speed was then ordered and the *Warspite* continued round to starboard and, after making about one and a half complete circles, was brought under control and got away to the northward.

According to the German Official History, the *Kaiserin* opened fire on the *Warspite* at 1817 at 12,000–12,600yds, and scored a hit which damaged the latter's steering gear, but the failure of the *Warspite*'s steering was not due to a hit. The *Kaiserin*'s reports confirm that she fired at one of the 5th BS for 3 minutes or so, at the above range, before shifting to the *Defence*, but her target is described as the 4th battleship from the right, the *Malaya*, and it is not believed that she was firing at the *Warspite*. When the latter hauled out of line, she became the first reasonably visible capital ship target that several of the German battleships had yet seen. The *Friedrich der Grosse* opened fire on the *Warspite* at 1820, the *König* at 1822, the *Helgoland* at 1824 and the *Ostfriesland* and *Thüringen* at 1825. The *Friedrich der Grosse*, *König* and *Thüringen*, fired 5.9in as well as 12in, while the *Helgoland* and *Ostfriesland* only fired 12in. At 1826 the *König*, which had claimed straddling salvos at *c*12,000yds, lost sight of the *Warspite*, now bearing aft, while the *Thüringen* expended 21–12in and 37–5.9in in 5 or 6 minutes at 11,800–10,600yds and then shifted to the *Malaya*. The *Friedrich der Grosse* fired at 12,500 to 9600yds until 1834 when the *Warspite* was lost to sight, and the *Helgoland*, which reported firing slowly and intermittently as the target was at times hidden in haze and smoke, ceased a minute or two later. Her reported ranges were 15,300 to 12,000yds, and several straddling salvos claimed.

The *Nassau* meanwhile opened fire at 1833 (? 1835) at 15,300yds with 11in, but soon had to cease when the German line turned 180°, and the *Oldenburg* fired 12in, but her times are unreliable and the quoted ranges of 17,500–14,200yds do not agree with those of other ships, though a straddling salvo was claimed. Her firing was slow and intermittent as the *Warspite* was very difficult to make out in decreasing visibility. The last ship to cease firing at the *Warspite* was the *Ostfriesland* at 1845, but she only fired two salvos after the German 180° turn, as the *Warspite* was steaming away, and disappearing in the haze and smoke. The *Ostfriesland*'s ranges varied from 15,000 to 10,800yds, and hits were claimed from her 3rd and 4th salvos.

Altogether the *Warspite* was hit by 13 heavy shells in this period, and by at least 5–5.9in, one of which put the left gun of 'Y' turret out of action, but no vital damage was done, though considerable flooding was caused by a shell which pierced the belt just below the main deck, and by another below the waterline far aft.

The *Barham* and *Valiant* reported being under a heavy fire as they turned northward, and at 1824 several salvos fell just over the latter, but no hits of importance were made, though there may have been some from 5.9in.

As noted above, a good many 12in shells from the *Kaiser* must have fallen near the 5th BS, and the *Kaiserin* fired at the *Malaya* for a time. The *Derfflinger* fired four salvos at the *Barham* between 1816 and 1820 at 13,800–10,900yds, while the *Kaiserin* reopened for 5 minutes before the German 180° turn at a ship taken to be the *Malaya* with a single salvo after turning, at an unidentifiable target. The *Thüringen* also fired at the *Malaya* for *c*7 minutes before turning 180° and expended 20–12in shells at 14,100yds.

Owing to indifferent visibility, the presence of British ships between the lines, and the easier target offered by the *Wiesbaden*, it was not until 1830 that any of Jellicoe's battleships opened an effective fire on the German 5th Division, and in most cases the target disappeared in the haze before Scheer's 180° turn was made. Of the 24 dreadnoughts in the British line 12 and possibly only 10, engaged capital ships in this period and the 1st Division did not fire a shot. Any organised distribution of fire was impossible, and no attempt at this was made. For convenience the firing at capital ships will be described first, and then that at the *Wiesbaden*.

The first to engage was the *Marlborough* which dimly made out what were thought to be four ships of the *Kaiser* and four of the *Helgoland* class, and opened fire on one of the *Kaisers* at 1817. The range-finders could not get a range initially, and an estimated 10,000yds was used and later 13,000yds. The *Marlborough* fired seven salvos in 4 minutes and claimed hits from the 5th and 7th, but it is not believed that any were made. The target was then hidden by a cruiser on fire, which was perhaps the *Warrior*.

The *Revenge* opened fire at 1822 and checked 17 minutes later. Her firing was intermittent and it is not known how much was at the *Wiesbaden* and how much at battleships, but the latter were very indistinct, though her initial target was thought to be the leading ship of the second unit in the German line. No hits were claimed.

The *Agincourt* opened at 1824 at a target which could just be made out, and was thought to be a battlecruiser. It was believed that hits were obtained, but the target was then obscured by smoke from the *Warrior* and from the blowing up of the *Defence*. The *Agincourt* reported a range of 10,000yds which if correct indicates that she was firing at the *Wiesbaden*. At 1832 she again opened for a very short time at what was thought to be the same ship, and claimed another hit, but mist made it impossible to be certain of the fall of shot, and the line of fire was then masked by the 12th Flotilla. The *Hercules* opened fire at 1825 at 12,000yds on the most visible of three ships, thought to be of the *Kaiser* class, and seen indistinctly through the haze. She fired seven or eight salvos but had to check continually from poor visibility.

The *Iron Duke* opened fire at 1830½ on the *König* which was 12,600yds away and lit up by the sun. Nine salvos of CPC totalling 43 rounds, were fired in 4 minutes 50 seconds before the *König* appeared to turn away and was lost in mist and smoke. The first salvo was short to the right, and was corrected Left 4, Up 800, but the 2nd, 3rd and 4th were thought to have hit, and a total of at least six hits was claimed and seven made, which severely damaged the *König* forward and ignited a number of 5.9in charges.

The *Thunderer*'s report of engaging a capital ship target at this time refers to the next phase of the battle, but the *Conqueror* fired three salvos at one of the *Königs* at *c*12,000yds from about 1831, though the target quickly disappeared in the haze. The *Orion* opened fire at 1832, probably on the *Markgraf*, and fired four salvos of APC of which the last scored a hit at 13,300yds. The target was then lost in the mist and spray from a short salvo of another ship. The *Monarch* sighted three *Königs* and two *Kaisers* at 1833 and fired two salvos of APC at the leading *König*, the second of which appeared to straddle. The target was then lost to view, and a salvo was fired at one of the *Kaisers* but not spotted. One hit on the *König* can be credited to the *Monarch*.

Of the other battleships, the *Benbow* opened at 1830 and fired intermittently for over 10 minutes, but she was much hampered by the haze and only fired 6–2-gun salvos from her forward turrets. The *Bellerophon* may also have fired briefly at the German battleships at this time, while the *Colossus* opened at 1830 and fired three deliberate salvos at the German line which was difficult to see.

Lastly at 1839, the *Marlborough* again fired one salvo at a supposed *Kaiser* class ship which was then lost to sight, and at 1840 the *Neptune*, which had been badly masked by the *St Vincent* opened at 11,000yds, and fired two salvos which must have fallen very short at a battleship, indistinctly visible in the mist.

Only the *Iron Duke* was able to get a good run at a German battleship in this period, and gave a fine display of speedy and accurate firing.

The *Revenge* which fired intermittently from 1822 to 1839, engaged the *Wiesbaden* for some of the time, and at 1820, or a little afterwards, the *Hercules* also fired her first salvo at this ship. The *Iron Duke* opened on her at 1823 and fired four salvos of which one straddled, and at 1825 the *Bellerophon* joined in, and fired intermittently for 15 minutes, but she may have been firing at battleships for part of this time. The *Marlborough* also began firing on the *Wiesbaden* at 1825 and got off five salvos, during which the right gun of 'A' turret was put out of action by a premature. The *Superb* opened at 1826 and claimed hits from her third and fourth salvos, and the *Thunderer* began a minute later, but soon shifted to one of four battleships, though fire was not opened as the *Thunderer* was masked by the *Conqueror* and then by the *Iron Duke*. It was at this time that ranges of 22,000–18,000yds were obtained from the *Thunderer*'s fore-top, but it is not clear what ship was seen, though it may have been the *Regensburg* or one of the 2nd SG.

At 1829 the *Royal Oak* opened on the *Wiesbaden* and fired four salvos, claiming a hit aft with the 3rd, and at 1830 the *Monarch* joined in, firing three salvos. The *Vanguard* which reported previously sighting the German battlecruisers but had then been blanketed by Beatty's ships, opened at 1832 and in the next 13 minutes fired 42 rounds at the *Wiesbaden* and claimed several hits from her 4th and succeeding salvos. The *Colossus* began on the *Wiesbaden* at the same time and fired four salvos, and the *Collingwood* also opened fire on this ship at 1832, and from her expenditure of 84 rounds of 12in in the whole battle, fired about eight salvos. Shortly afterwards the *Conqueror* fired at the *Wiesbaden*, shifting from a battleship target, and the *St Vincent* opened at 1833 and fired a few salvos during the next 12 minutes. The *Agincourt* which may have engaged the *Wiesbaden* previously, reported firing very briefly on a cruiser, but the target was lost at 1834.

The *Temeraire* began at this time and fired five salvos of HE, claiming at least two and probably three hits on the *Wiesbaden* from her 3rd salvo. Her fire was slow and was checked temporarily after the 3rd salvo as several ships were firing at the same target. Finally, the *Canada* opened fire at 1840, but only got off two salvos and neither was seen to fall.

In addition to the above firing at the *Wiesbaden* from turret guns, the *Marlborough* and then the *Royal Oak* briefly fired 6in.

Too many ships were firing at the *Wiesbaden*, which was still afloat at 1845 and had just fired a torpedo, and the effect of the unsystematic concentration on her was not so great as might at first sight be expected. In this period a total of 12 hits at most, was claimed and the actual figure was probably less. All firing by the British battleships at a disabled cruiser has been taken as at the *Wiesbaden*, and though the *Colossus*, *Revenge*, *Hercules* and *Agincourt* reported that their target had four funnels, only the *Rostock* of German ships had this number, and could not have been the ship fired at. The probable track of the *Warrior* rules her out, and it is unlikely from the little evidence available, that the *Black Prince* was the ship concerned. It must thus be concluded that the reports of 4-funnels were in error.

Unfortunately, detailed information on the firing of the 5th Battle Squadron in this period is lacking. The *Valiant* reported reopening fire at 1815, one minute after the *Barham*, and at 1817 the enemy were bearing 50° on her starboard bow at a range of 19,000yds, the visibility being temporarily very good. Her target appears to have been the *Helgoland* which was first fired on at 1817. The firing was not fast on account of the long range, but the salvos had an exceptionally small spread, and some fell within 50 or 100yds of the ship. It seems likely that the 5th BS were otherwise engaging the 3rd Squadron and according to the *Hercules*, firing continuously, while the *Kaiser* noted at 1815 that heavy shells were constantly falling near the 5th Division. The 5th BS appear to have checked after their northward turn and the *Valiant* reported lulls in the action when smoke from the explosions in the *Defence*, and from fires in the *Warrior*, obscured the range. On forming astern of the *Agincourt*, the *Barham* opened fire at the *Wiesbaden* and then fired three salvos at one of the *Königs*, the second from the right of those visible, but the target was only sighted at intervals, due to funnel and gun smoke of the British ships ahead. It is not certain whether both the *Valiant* and *Malaya* reopened with the *Barham*, though the *Helgoland* was still intermittently under fire, and it is not likely that the 5th BS scored any hits at this time.

The *Warspite* fired with all turrets in local control after her helm jammed, and at first replied rapidly to the German concentration, but appeared to stop after turning about 270°. Her firing was quite ineffective and the *Friedrich der Grosse* reported that the *Warspite* only replied with single shots.

The 3rd Battlecruiser Squadron opened fire from 1820 on the head of the 1st Scouting Group, and with some assistance from Beatty's ships, developed a concentration of fire which was considered in the *Moltke* to come from eight or ten ships of the *Malaya* or *Iron Duke* class. The chief target was the *Lützow*, and from 1826 onwards hit after hit struck this ship. Two 12in shells hit below the water-line in or near the broadside torpedo flat, and together with two other shells that struck below the water-line further forward, caused such damage that practically the whole of the ship forward of 'A' turret and below the armour deck was soon flooded. Hits were also made on the *Derfflinger* at this time and one a few minutes later on the *Seydlitz*, but the two other German battlecruisers escaped further damage. The range was only 8500–11,000yds and at this distance the 12in/45s of the 3rd BCS, which had been re-equipped with four calibre radius head projectiles, proved very effective. The *Invincible*'s firing at the *Lützow* was very good, and she was well supported by the *Inflexible* which claimed a hit with her first salvo, although the latter expended less ammunition than her two sister ships and used very little APC. The *Inflexible* shifted to a target which was probably the *Moltke*, shortly before the *Invincible* blew up, while the *Indomitable* opened fire at *c*1825, and engaged the *Derfflinger* at an initial range of 9500yds, and subsequently fired a few rounds at the *Seydlitz*.

For 10 minutes little or nothing of the 3rd BCS except gun-flashes could be seen from the German ships, but at 1830 the mist and smoke suddenly parted and the *Invincible* stood out clearly against a background of funnel and cordite smoke. The *Lützow* had turned to starboard and the *Invincible* bore 45° aft, so that an extension to the bridge, which formed a platform for the sounding apparatus, interfered with the view from the forward control tower's periscope. Control of the main armament was shifted to the after position, and the *Lützow* fired three salvos opening at 10,900yds. The first was 400yds over, the second straddled, and as the fall of shot indicator sounded for the 3rd, the red flame of a hit was unmistakeably seen, and in a few seconds the *Invincible* blew up. The *Derfflinger* had already fired five salvos at 30 second intervals in the *Invincible*'s direction before she became clearly visible, but all were well short. She then fired three salvos in 1½ minutes at a range of 9600/9800yds and claimed that her target blew up after the third. The *Derfflinger* was somewhat closer to the *Invincible* than the *Lützow*, which accounts in part at least, for the different range, but the German Official History gives the credit for the *Invincible*'s destruction to the *Lützow*. The *Derfflinger* was also firing her 5.9in at the *Invincible*, which cannot have assisted the control of her main armament.

The fatal shell struck 'Q' turret at 1832 and burst inside, blowing the turret roof off. Flash reached the magazines and the resulting explosion blew the *Invincible* in half, her bow and stern remaining above water for some time. There were only six survivors who were picked up by the *Badger* and 1026 were lost. Several hits, causing no great damage, had been made on the *Invincible* before that on 'Q' turret, and both the *Inflexible* and *Indomitable* reported shells falling near them, the former being repeatedly straddled, though neither was hit. The *Derfflinger* fired one salvo, after the *Invincible* had blown up, at the *Inflexible*, and the *Seydlitz* was also engaging one of the 3rd BCS until 1830, but her ammunition records give an expenditure of only 57-11in between 1710 and 1850, of which 30 rounds were from the port wing turret.

The *Inflexible* lost sight of her target when she turned to port to avoid the wreck of the *Invincible*, and though the *Indomitable* reported checking fire at 1842, it is improbable that she continued so long. The *Lützow* was not fired on by the 3rd BCS after 1832, but she was flooding so badly that she had to reduce speed drastically, and was out of action at 1837. It is believed that the 3rd BCS made a total of eight hits on the *Lützow* in this period as well as three on the *Derfflinger* and one on the *Seydlitz*. The *Lützow* had also been hit twice at about 1819 by the *Lion*, and a serious fire was caused by one of the shells.

After altering course to avoid the *Defence* and *Warrior*, the *Lion* began again at 1817 with a two gun salvo, and fired a total of 10 salvos at the *Lützow* in 4½ minutes, before the latter disappeared in the mist and smoke. The *Lion* opened at 10,800yds, and spotted down a total of 3000 in the first four salvos. She reopened fire at 1828 on the head of the 3rd Squadron and expended seven salvos in four minutes, before the target again vanished in the mist and smoke, opening at 8300yds and spotting up a total of 3200. The chain-rammer of the left gun in 'A' turret apparently failed during this firing, and it was probably at this time that the *Lion* fired three torpedoes, the last of them an 'Extreme Range', at the line of the German battle fleet, but as with other torpedoes fired by the *Lion*, no time was reported. The *Princess Royal* reopened just after the *Lion*, but only fired a few salvos at intervals, and her targets are uncertain.

The *Tiger* reported firing a few salvos at her opposite number from 1819 to 1829, but they were not spotted. She fired her 6in at the *Wiesbaden* from 1819 to 1824, and it would seem that her main armament was also firing at this ship. The *New Zealand* engaged what was thought to be the left hand battleship for a short while at 1819, and then appears to have fired at the *Derfflinger* for 6 minutes, before checking at 1827/28. Her times are uncorrected, and may be some minutes fast. Conditions for the above four battlecruisers in this period were not good due to mist and smoke, and no hits can be credited to them apart from the two on the *Lützow* at 1819.

From the 1st Scouting Group Beatty's ships were scarcely visible, but the *Lützow* at least fired at them in the absence of easier targets.

Of lighter British units, the *Falmouth* and *Yarmouth* opened fire on the *Wiesbaden* at about 1815 or a little before, and the *Falmouth* fired a torpedo at 1821 at 4500/5000yds which failed to hit. They then fired for a short time at two of the *Regensburg*'s destroyers and about 1825 engaged the *Lützow* and *Derfflinger* at a reported range of 5200–7000yds, which illustrates how bad visibility was for the 1st Scouting Group. A number of 6in hits were made on the German battlecruisers, and the *Falmouth* fired a torpedo at the *Lützow* at 1825 at 5500yds which was incorrectly claimed to have hit. The *Yarmouth* also fired a torpedo at the *Lützow* 5 minutes later at 7000yds but this too missed. The *Lützow* which took the British ships to be destroyers replied with 5.9in, but the fire-control of these was temporarily interrupted from the shaking of the ship by one or two heavy shells striking the armour amidships, and she only scored one hit on the *Falmouth*'s foremast. Of the other units of the 3rd LCS, the *Birkenhead* fired eight or nine salvos at the *Wiesbaden*, visibility being temporarily good, and then three or four salvos at two of the German battlecruisers, which were very indistinct, while the *Gloucester* briefly engaged the *Wiesbaden*.

The *Ophelia*, of the 3rd Battlecruiser Squadron's screen, a new destroyer which, except for the passage to Scapa from the builder's yard, had never been under way before taking part in the battle, fired a torpedo without success at 1829 at 7500/8000yds at a target on her starboard quarter, taken to be a ship of the 1st Scouting Group, but more probably one of the 3rd Squadron. The *Ophelia* was not hit, but the *Marvel* of the 12th Flotilla and the *Defender* of the 1st, were each struck by a stray 12in shell which failed to explode. The *Marvel* was hit right forward at about 1815 with little damage, but the *Defender* was hit in the forward boiler room at about 1830, and had to drop out as her speed was much reduced.

An attack was begun by the German 3rd Flotilla and 1st Half-Flotilla at 1837 or perhaps a few minutes previously, on Commodore Michelsen's orders, but the destroyers were recalled, mainly because the British line, which was only discernible from the *Rostock* by gun flashes, had almost ceased firing, and was thought to have turned away. However the *G88* and *V73* each fired one torpedo at c6500–7500yds, and the *V48* probably fired one also, while the *S32* fired four at c7500yds. These torpedoes were apparently aimed at Beatty's battlecruisers or at the leading battleships. The *Duke of Edinburgh*, astern of the battlecruisers, had to turn sharply to starboard at 1847 to avoid a torpedo which missed astern by 50yds, and in the *King George*

V a torpedo may have been seen to break surface 400yds short, but the three reported to have passed astern of the *Tiger* at 1837–1839, and the one stated to have passed under the *Princess Royal* at 1840 would seem to have been imaginary, if the times are correctly recorded, and this applies to one sighted ahead of the *Birkenhead*. Only the *Tiger* appears to have engaged the destroyers with 6in for about a minute at a reported time of 1836.

While running up to attack, the *S32* had fired about 40 rounds at *c*4500–2000yds at the disabled *Shark*, and on returning the *S32* briefly engaged her again, while the *V48*, *S54* and *G42* fired for a longer time at *c*6500–2000yds. The *Shark* which was at first firing from two guns, replied most gallantly and scored a hit on the *S32*'s forecastle, and another near the *V48*'s midships gun, and either this or a further hit damaged the latter's machinery, and the *V48* was soon forced to stop. The *S54* fired two torpedoes at the *Shark* at about 4500yds with shallow depth setting, one of which hit abreast the after funnel and sank her at 1902 with only six survivors. The *G42* then attempted to take the *V48* in tow but the fire directed at the *G42* from secondary and then main armament was too heavy, and an attempt to take off the *V48*'s crew had also to be abandoned. The *V48* is believed to have fired four more torpedoes at the British line, the effects of which are later described.

During the last 20 minutes of this phase there was little fighting compared with that between 1815 and 1840. The 180° turn of the German dreadnoughts was not an easy manoeuvre, as the line was bent and partly under fire, but it was practically completed without incident by 1845, when the battleships were steering *c*257° with the *Westfalen* in the lead, though the *König* altered course at 1846 to 223° for 6 minutes to resume her station, as others of the 5th Division had been steering to the south of 257°, so that the ships ahead could increase their distance. At 1848 Scheer ordered course to be altered 23° to starboard by divisions, and at 1855, when the 1st SG were in sight of the *Friedrich der Grosse*, he again signalled for an 'about-turn' to starboard, so that by just after 1900 the *König* was once more leading the line eastward. The *Markgraf* had to stop her port engine at 1844 as a bent propeller shaft caused overheated bearings though unsuccessful attempts were made to run it again at low power. She could however steam 17 or 18kts on two engines, and maintained her position in the line.

Scheer has been much criticised for this 'about-turn', and various reasons for it have been put forward. These cannot be discussed here, but the wish to save the *Wiesbaden*'s crew had considerable weight, and the German fleet had obtained a good measure of success in the last period of fighting. Scheer had apparently received no information as to the exact position of the British forces, except for a report at 1845 from the *Moltke* that the van bore 88°, which actually referred to the *Canterbury*. This report would, however, confirm Scheer's belief that the British forces, still not known to comprise the whole Grand Fleet, bore more to the south and east than was the case, and Scheer's new course may have been intended to pass to the northward of his opponent which would reverse visibility conditions in his favour.

The old battleships of the 2nd Squadron remained generally to the south-westward of the *Westfalen*, and then turned to follow her, while the *Lützow* steamed slowly out of action on a course of about 223°. At 1850 Commodore Michelsen sent the *G39*, *G40* and *G38* to her assistance, and the *G37* and *V45* arrived almost simultaneously. Hipper and his staff were taken off in the *G39* at 1856 with the intention of transferring to the *Seydlitz*, while the other four destroyers together with the *V30*, *S34* and *S33* which arrived shortly afterwards, remained to screen the *Lützow*. Meanwhile the command of the battlecruisers fell to Captain Hartog of the *Derfflinger*, but the foremast signal halliards and all signalling lights were out of action as were her main wireless aerials, while the steering of the *Seydlitz* had had to be transferred temporarily to the steering gear compartment. However, the four battlecruisers followed the battleships, about 2 to 3 miles on the *König*'s port quarter, steering in a westerly direction, but shortly after 1850 the *Derfflinger* had to stop engines for 2 minutes to secure a part of her torpedo nets which had been torn loose and was in danger of becoming entangled in the port wing propeller. This delayed the *Derfflinger*'s turn to starboard to take station ahead of the battleships, and it was not until just after 1905 that the other three battlecruisers had all completed their turn, and were following astern of her. This delay had important consequences in the next phase of the battle.

When the German fleet disappeared from view, Jellicoe rightly considered the risk of destroyer attacks in uncertain visibility to be too great to follow them. He was also apprehensive of torpedoes fired by the German battleships and of the possible use of mines. He therefore decided to place his forces across the German line of retreat to the Heligoland Bight, and at 1844 altered course to 122° by divisions. Nothing could be seen from the *Iron Duke* and there were no reports from the battlecruisers and other ships ahead, and when asked by Jellicoe if he could see any enemy battleships, Burney in the *Marlborough*, gave a negative reply. At 1855 Jellicoe again altered course by divisions to 167°, though Jerram actually turned to this course just before Jellicoe's signal, to conform to the battlecruisers. The *King George V* had also turned temporarily to starboard at 1852, to avoid the 4th LCS which cut across her bows in taking up a position to the westward. It may be noted that the 3rd and 4th Divisions passed one on either side of the *Invincible*'s wreck at about 1857, and that this wreck, located on 3 July 1919 in 57° 03′ 10″N, 6°07′ 45″E, provided the reference point for charts of the battle.

At 1854 a signal came from Beatty, timed 9 minutes earlier, that a submarine was in sight. The submarine was imaginary, as was the periscope fired at by the *Hampshire* at this time, but at 1857 the *Marlborough* wirelessed that she had been struck by a mine or torpedo, and confirmed that it was a torpedo a minute later. At 1900 Jerram warned Jellicoe by searchlight that there was a submarine ahead, and at 1901 the *Duke of Edinburgh*, then about a mile ahead of the *King George V*, signalled by flags that a submarine was 23° on her own port bow. It was at first thought that the *Marlborough* had been torpedoed by a submarine, but this was not so, and the two reported ahead of the fleet which were apparently hunted by the *Castor* and the 11th Flotilla, were also imaginary.

At 1900 a searchlight signal was received from Beatty that the enemy were to the westward, though they had been out of sight from the *Lion* for about 25 minutes. At *c*1845, however, Beatty had asked the 3rd LCS for the bearing of the enemy's battlecruisers, and the reply, if correctly recorded, said that they had been last seen at 1820, and had altered course to 257°, whereas the *Falmouth* had actually lost sight of them at about 1835. No scouting was attempted by the 3rd LCS, but the 2nd LCS, astern of the fleet, turned southwards at 1843 towards the enemy to discover their course, and also to sink a supposed disabled battleship (actually the *Wiesbaden*). In a signal timed at 1900 the *Southampton* reported that the enemy battlefleet were steering 100°, bearing 190°, number unknown, and gave her position as 57°02′N, 6°07′E which was correct to within 4 miles, and in any case the 2nd LCS were visible from the 1st BS and possibly from the *Iron Duke*. In fact, the bearing was that of the *Derfflinger*, and an approximate reciprocal of the 1900 course of most of the German ships, which were then in the middle of their turn, was given. However, the signal did predict the renewed eastward advance of the German fleet, which would very soon be in contact again with the British, as the actual position of the *König* at 1900 was about 12½ miles bearing 246° from the head of the British 1st Division. The guides of the British divisions bore approximately 291° from the *King George V* at this time, except for the 6th Division which was astern of station, due to the *Marlborough* being torpedoed, and having to avoid other torpedoes.

The 5th Battle Squadron, less the *Warspite*, had generally followed the 6th Division, at first on a course of about 106° and then 111°. At 1856 they turned 23° to port in anticipation of a torpedo attack, presumably on sighting the 6th Half-Flotilla then engaging the *Shark*, and at shortly after 1900 altered course to *c*172° and took station on the port quarter of the *Agincourt*. There was some bunching, as the *Valiant* reported being very close to the *Barham* at 1842, and had to haul out on the latter's port quarter and reduce to slow speed which was maintained for 7 minutes.

The *Warspite* rejoined astern of the 5th BS, just before 1900, but it was found that she could not be steered with any precision, and when still over half a mile from the *Malaya*, withdrew out of action to the north-westward.

The *Inflexible* and *Indomitable* returned to a course of approximately 116° after clearing the wreck of the *Invincible*, and at 1844 altered course to 133° and reduced to 15kts. Two or three minutes later they resumed approximately the previous course, but at 1849 turned to *c*172°. Beatty then ordered them to prolong the line astern, and at 1854 they accordingly turned about 180° to starboard together so that the *Indomitable* was from now on ahead of the *Inflexible*, and proceeded to join astern of the *New Zealand*.

Beatty altered course to 122° at *c*1842 5 minutes later to 145°, and at 1852 to 167° reducing to 18kts. A controversial incident then occurred. As related by Chatfield, Beatty told him to alter course 180° to starboard, as the battlecruisers were now some distance ahead of the main fleet and the visibility was too low to justify closing in on the High Seas Fleet unsupported. Chatfield was anxious to go below and inspect the ship, as a considerable fire was apparently raging on the main deck (actually that in the Navigator's cabin on the upper deck). He thus asked Beatty's Chief of Staff, Captain RW Bentinck to take command for 10 minutes. The turn was begun at about 1854, and owing to the failure of the *Lion*'s gyro-compasses, was continued through *c*360° with the other battlecruisers following, so that it was *c*1904 before the *Lion* again headed 167°. The *Indomitable* and *Inflexible* were steering to take station astern of the *New Zealand* or had already done so, while the 3rd LCS, now joined by the *Canterbury*, had also turned back, and the result of these manoeuvres was that the British battlecruisers made no advance on 167° for the 13 or 14 minutes which it took the *Lion* to reach the

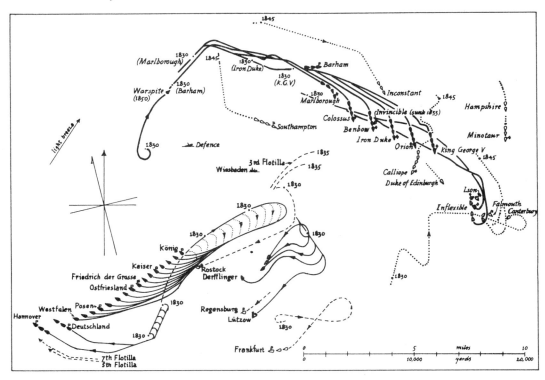

Chart VI: Position at 1900

position where the 3rd BCS had turned back at 1854. It is impossible to say how far this prevented the British battlecruisers from playing a greater part in the next phase of the battle, but Beatty's wish to close the battlefleet in poor visibility was reasonable. At 1854 the *Lion* was $c4\frac{1}{2}$ miles from the *King George V* and the *Inflexible* a mile further ahead, and there had been a third violent and unmistakeable demonstration of the vulnerability of the battlecruisers 20 minutes previously. As events turned out, the British Fleet might well have obtained a greater measure of success after 2000, if Beatty had continued to remain close to the *King George V* from 1930 onwards.

Any firing between 1840 and 1900 has already been noted in the earlier part of this phase. The German battle charts show a hit on the *Lützow* at 1845, but no British ship was firing at her at this time, and also a hit on the *Markgraf* at 1852. Examination of her control room record shows that this hit is based on an entry which refers to the hit at 1835.

Although there was little gun-fire in the last 20 minutes of this phase, an important torpedo attack was made on the rear of the British line, which was, in the contemporary Torpedo School analysis, attributed to two submarines, but was due at first to the *Wiesbaden* disabled between the lines, and subsequently to the crippled *V48*. The *Wiesbaden* was about 10,000yds, 74° on the *Marlborough*'s starboard bow at 1845, before the latter altered course. The *V48* probably had five torpedoes still available, and the *Wiesbaden*'s initial outfit was eight, but it is unlikely that her above water torpedo tubes were still useable, and flooding of her submerged flat from damage is thought to have restricted the number fired to two.

At 1840 the *St Vincent* sighted a torpedo which stopped 200yds short on the starboard bow. This was considered a doubtful report at the time and can be disregarded, but at 1845 the *Marlborough* altered course to port to avoid one which passed astern. She then steered 122°, conforming to Jellicoe's signal, and at 1854 was struck abreast the starboard Diesel generator room by a torpedo, of which the track was not seen. The *Wiesbaden* was still about 10,000yds away so that the torpedo had run this distance. The *Marlborough* listed 7 or 8° to starboard and water entered the forward boiler-room so that fires had to be drawn, but she was able to continue at revolutions for 17kts which gave a speed over the ground of a little under 16kts.

The *Marlborough* altered course to 167° at 1858 and 2 minutes later the *St Vincent* turned away on sighting a supposed torpedo which stopped 100yds short on her starboard quarter. At the same time the *Marlborough* turned to starboard to avoid a torpedo track which passed under her stern, and at 1901 turned to port to avoid two more which passed ahead, one of them close under her bow.

In both the *Marlborough* and *Agincourt* it was thought that a periscope had been seen, and a heavy shock was felt in the *Revenge* and it was believed that she had collided with the submarine which had torpedoed the *Marlborough*. However, no submarine was present, and the two reported, one 3 miles away on the surface, and the other 2 miles off in diving trim, thought to have been seen some time later from the *Neptune*'s fore-top, were also imaginary. The torpedo sighted at 1845 and the one that hit the *Marlborough*, came from the *Wiesbaden*, but the later torpedoes, apart from that sighted by the *St Vincent* at 1900 which is thought to have been imaginary, were from the *V48*.

The damage to the *Lützow* which was the main cause of her later sinking, makes it impossible to say that the Germans had the better of this phase, as her loss was far more serious to them, than was that of the *Invincible*, *Defence* and *Warrior* combined, to the British, but they nevertheless had some considerable success.

CHAPTER 9

Damage to capital ships and armoured cruisers 1815–1900

AMONG THE SURVIVORS from the *Invincible* was her Gunnery Officer, Commander Dannreuther, and he stated that the hit by the shell which struck 'Q' turret, and burst inside blowing the turret roof off, was observed from the Fore Control Top. A tremendous explosion amidships followed almost immediately, indicating that 'Q' magazine had blown up, and the *Invincible* broke in half and sank in 10 or 15 seconds. There was one severely burnt survivor from 'Q' turret, who had been at the range-finder. A photograph in *The Fighting at Jutland* shows flame from 'A' magazine venting through the forecastle and by the foremast, and indicates that an explosion had occurred there, presumably as a result of that in 'Q' magazine. The latter would certainly have involved 'P' magazine which was immediately adjacent to 'Q'.

The *Indomitable* reported that wreckage was thrown 400ft in the air, and when the smoke cleared, the *Invincible*'s bow and stern were each standing about 70ft out of the water, and 50yds apart. The stern was seen by the *Galatea* to sink an hour later, but the bows were still above water at 1430 on 1 June. From the *Derfflinger* it was noted that, as in the *Queen Mary*, a dense black smoke cloud rose several hundred yards in the air without a considerable development of flame. There can be no doubt that flash of ignited cordite from turret to magazine was responsible for the *Invincible*'s loss, which should be credited to the *Lützow*.

There is little information on previous hits. Dannreuther reported that she had been hit several times by heavy shell with no appreciable damage, and the *Indomitable* noted that she was straddled by a salvo and hit in the after part, one minute before blowing up. There is no reason to

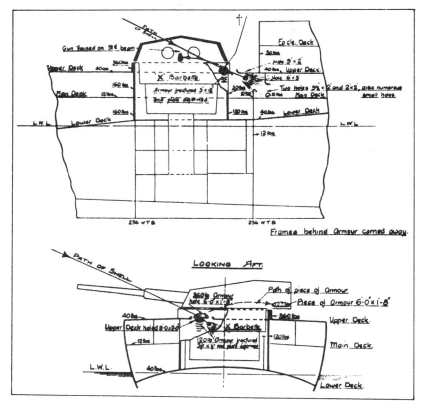

Princess Royal: *hit on 'X' barbette at c1822.*

differ from the German estimate of a total of five heavy hits, all of which
were probably 12in.

There were no hits on the *Inflexible* or *Indomitable*, but in the
former, the inner 'A' tube of 'Q' right gun had been previously cracked
for a length of 30ft during calibration, and the crack extended during
firing.

Of the 2–12in shells coming from abaft the beam, which struck the
Princess Royal at about 1822, one hit the 9in armour of 'X' barbette
obliquely on the forward side about 2ft above the upper deck, glanced
downwards through the 1in plating of the latter and burst just below it,
about 8ft from impact. A large fragment of the 9in armour measuring
6ft × 20in, was broken off with concentric cracks in the plate, and the
fragment was driven through the turntable into the gun-house at the left
side of the left gun, coming to rest on the platform at the rear, after

hitting an unfused shrapnel shell in the shell-bin. All the crew of the left gun were killed, the breech mechanism damaged and pressure pipes destroyed on the left side, but the gun could still be worked. The turret, however, was out of action, as it was jammed in training by the displacement and distortion of the 9in barbette armour. In addition to breaking a large piece off the 9in plate, the impact of the shell had sheared the armour fastenings to the upper deck and completely broken the key to the plate, which was lifted 9in at one end and 5½in at the other. The frames behind the armour were carried away, and the 8in plate adjoining the 9in above the upper deck was cracked at the lower and chipped at the upper corner, while the 3in plate which extended up to the upper deck was deformed below the 9in plate and a piece 3ft × 1in fractured.

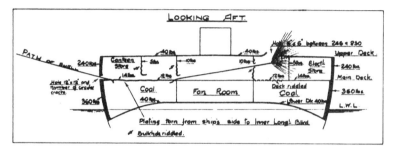

Princess Royal: *second hit at c1822.*

The shell tore a 9ft × 2ft hole in the upper deck, and the burst badly damaged two ¼in bulkheads, and caused considerable damage to light structures, as well as cutting trunks and breathing pipes from the ventilation and cooling plant of 'X' magazine.

The other shell pierced the 6in side armour just above the main deck, and a little forward of 'X' barbette. The angle of impact is given as 15–20° to the plate normal, and the hole as 12in × 12in with a number of concentric cracks. The shell tore the ⅜in–⁵⁄₁₆in main deck over the starboard after reserve bunker for 17ft from the ship's side to the fan-room bulkhead, was deflected upwards, badly damaged the casings of both condenser rooms and burst 52ft from impact on the port side below the 1in upper deck, in which a hole 6ft × 6ft was blown, while the main deck over the port after reserve bunker was riddled. Many casualties were caused among the after 4in crews and salvage party, and

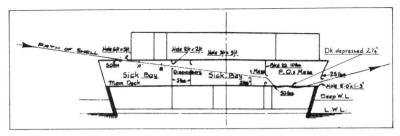

Warspite: hit No 1.

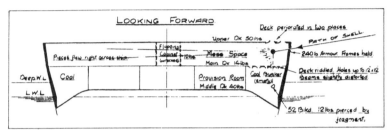

Warspite: hit No 3.

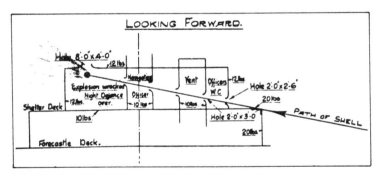

Warspite: hit No 4.

the flash of the burst ignited some cordite on the main deck. Both after engine-rooms filled with dense smoke and some penetrated to the starboard forward engine-room, but dispersed after the fires were subdued.

These two shells, which together killed 11 and wounded 31, were from one salvo from the *Markgraf* at a range of about 13,000yds.

It does not appear that the *Lion, Tiger* and *New Zealand* were hit by heavy shells in this phase though the *Tiger* was hit by a 5.9in which holed the hull plating on the starboard side abaft 'X' barbette, and the only important gunnery breakdown seems to have been the failure of the *Lion*'s 'A' left gun's chain-rammer, as previously noted.

The sole surviving details of the gyro-compass failure in the *Lion* are in the 1916 Torpedo School Report. At the date of Jutland this ship had two Sperry master gyro-compasses, in a compartment adjacent to the lower conning tower. An explosion occurred nearby which put both gyro-compasses out of action. All lights failed, but accumulators had been provided for standby lighting of the lower conning tower magnetic compass, and the ship was only without means to steer by for a few minutes. One gyro-compass was got ready for use next day.

Nothing seems to have survived on the cause of the above explosion.

Of the 28 British battleships only the *Warspite* was hit by heavy shells at this time.

The 13 hits were, in order from forward to aft:

1 Coming from aft, port side. Angle of descent 5–10°. This shell entered through the 1¼in upper deck, in the embrasure near the forward edge of 'A' barbette. It made a hole 6ft × 5ft in the upper deck over the sick bay and passed across the ship being deflected down on to the 1¼in main deck and up again, and went out through the 5/8in starboard hull plating without exploding. Considerable damage was caused in passing through, and chemicals in the sick bay caused a fire.

2 There are no details of this shell which entered through the upper deck in the starboard embrasure.

3 From starboard side. Angle of descent 5–10°. This shell struck the 6in side armour, a little below the upper deck and just forward of the foremost 6in gun, at an angle of 10–12° to the plate normal. It pierced the armour, making a clean hole of *c*12in diameter, though the framing held, and burst 6ft from impact with considerable damage to light structure. The 1¼in upper deck was holed in two places, and the ⅜in main deck riddled below the burst. One large fragment was driven down through the main deck, and another came to rest in the magazine flooding cabinet 30ft from the explosion. The effect of the burst and fragments went right across an athwartships gangway to the port side of the ship, wrecking the foremost magazine flooding cabinet (¼in sides) and all ventilation trunks in the vicinity, as well as cutting voice pipes and fire-control cables.

4 Coming from aft, starboard side. Either a ricochet or deflected upwards off the edge of the shelter deck. This shell passed through plating totalling 1⁵⁄₁₆in in the forward superstructure, and burst 40ft from impact in the night defence officer's station which was wrecked, and a hole 8ft × 4ft blown in the ⁵⁄₁₆in deck above the shelter deck. Considerable damage was caused to light structure all along the path of

this shell as well as near the burst, and a fire started, in which molten lead from lead covered wiring caused some trouble.

5 Probably coming from aft, port side. Angle of descent 10–15°. This shell struck a ¼in door in a store on the forecastle deck by the base of the after funnel, passed through a 1½in screen and two thicknesses of funnel plating, was deflected upwards off the armour gratings, and burst 32ft from impact near the far walls of the funnel. Two of the gratings were knocked down, but the remainder stood a large amount of deformation without fracture, and though part of the funnel was blown away, the draught was not affected. Holes were also blown in the 1in forecastle deck and 1½in funnel screen by the burst, and fragments passing below the forecastle deck pierced the continuation of the funnel screen and entered the 6in battery through the ¼in rear bulkhead.

6 Coming from aft, starboard side. Angle of descent 5–10°. This shell first holed the ¼in plating of a store on the forecastle deck, and then passed through a 1½in screen, four thicknesses of the after funnel plating, and a second 1½in screen. It then struck the 1in forecastle deck which was dented, passed through a boiler-room ventilator on the port side of the ship, being deflected up by the armour gratings, and then through the ¼in vertical plating between the forecastle and shelter decks and finally out through the ½in shelter deck, in which a hole 8ft × 3ft was torn, without exploding after passing through about 5in of plating.

7 From port side. Angle of descent 15–20°. This shell hit the main derrick, holed the pinnace and burst on the starboard side of the 1in forecastle deck inboard of the forecastle deck 6in gun. Most of the fragments went overboard, riddling and pitting the gun shield and gun. The burst blew a hole in the 1in forecastle deck, and there was a hole 4ft ×× 3ft in the ½in side plating abaft the battery bulkhead, and the armour door to the battery was jammed. The most serious effect was due to flash and probably hot fragments from the burst entering the after part of the 6in battery through a small hole in the deck, and igniting a number of cordite charges, but the fire did not spread along the battery as in the *Malaya*.

It appears that a shell fragment ignited a 6in charge which was being taken from its case for loading, and the other three charges in the case also ignited, as did those in four more cases. All the crew of the after starboard 6in-gun were very badly burnt and also some of the crew of the next gun.

8 From port side. Angle of descent 5–10°. This shell pierced the upper tapered part of the belt just below the main deck and about 23ft, forward of the mainmast. The hit was at the top after corner of a plate, the angle being 5–10° to the plate normal, and a piece 2ft × 1½ft was broken off, and a large chip taken out of the next plate. The actual thickness was 6in at the top of the hole and 9in at the bottom. The shell burst 12ft from impact in the upper part of the port feed-water tank, and a large hole was blown in the ⅜in main deck above, while the light floor of the feed tank was shattered, and the 1in middle deck badly distorted at and near the top of the slope above the port side of the wing engine-room and adjacent oil fuel tank. The ⁵⁄₁₆in bulkhead forming the outer side of the feed tank was wrecked, and the forward and inboard bulkheads of the feed tank were holed, and the latter let the sea into the port wing engine-room fan flat and from there it poured into the port wing engine-room

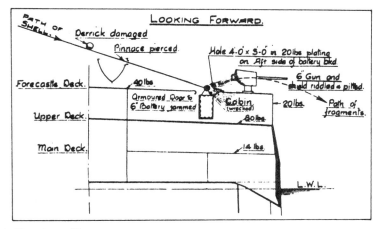

Warspite: *hit No 7.*

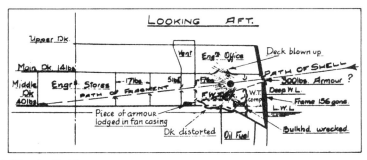

Warspite: *hit No 8.*

through holes in the ventilating trunk, which were later plugged. The flow of water into the feed tank was eventually stopped by putting 400 hammocks into the tank, and shoring them down until they plugged the hole in the armour belt. Most of the fragments from this shell were large, and one passed through the $\frac{7}{16}$in inner bulkhead of the feed tank, and also $1\text{-}\frac{1}{8}$in and 2 other $\frac{7}{16}$in thicknesses of plating before coming to rest 40ft from the burst on the middle deck. The broken piece of the belt also went through the inner bulkhead of the feed tank, and lodged in the engine-room fan casing.

The results of this hit were a good illustration of the error in not carrying the 13in belt armour to the main deck in the *Queen Elizabeth* class.

9 Coming from starboard aft. Full details of this hit have not survived, but the shell went through the end of the after superstructure and then hit the after side of the

communication tube (4in walls) to the torpedo control tower, half severed it and turned it through 30 or 60° before bursting. The starboard side of the after superstructure was holed in many places by fragments.

10 Probably coming from forward, port side. Angle of descent 5–10°. This shell struck the 6in side armour at an angle of 15–20° to the plate normal, 4ft below the upper deck and about 5ft forward of 'X' barbette. It pierced the armour making a 12in diameter hole and broke into two pieces without exploding. The larger part passed through 2–¼in bulkheads and the ventilation trunk from the middle engine room and struck the 4in armour of 'X' barbette, flaking off the surface to a maximum depth of 2¼in. It then holed the ⅜in main deck and came to rest well on the starboard side of the midships line in the engineer's workshop. The other piece passed through the 2–¼in bulkheads and then through the main deck over the ventilation fan flat, also finishing in the engineers' workshop, where a disk of armour, supposed to be from the 6in side, was found. The main deck was badly damaged and as it was by then awash, the large hole over the ventilation fan flat allowed water to enter the flat and thence the middle engine-room.

Much damage was caused by this unexploded shell, which is sometimes considered to have caused the steering gear to jam, as the bulkhead to which the steering engines were attached is said to have been damaged, but the direction of the shell shows that it hit after the steering failure.

11 From port side. Angle of descent given as 15–20°. This shell struck the 1¼in upper deck on a line midway between 'X' and 'Y' barbettes, and about 20ft from the upper deck edge. It tore a hole 7ft6in × 1ft 8in and burst 10ft from impact between the upper and main decks, causing severe damage to light steel work up to 16ft from the burst. This occurred near the ¼in wall of the after main deck magazine flooding cabinet which was wrecked, and a 2in thick door was blown off its hinges in the 2in longitudinal bulkhead which formed the far wall of the flooding cabinet. The explosion riddled the ⅝in main deck, and the base plug of the shell was driven through this and the 1in middle deck and brought to a stop by 'X' magazine cooler c20ft from the burst and c3½ft below the middle deck. The hydraulic exhaust main was holed in 'X' cooler space, which was practically turned into part of the hydraulic tanks.

A large number of ventilation trunks were holed by this shell on the main deck and the fire-main broken. The fire-main pumps continued to pump water onto the main deck, and this found its way into 'Y' cooler space until it rose high enough to burn out the pump starter. 'X' fire-main pump starter was also burnt out by water from the hydraulic system.

12 Coming from forward, port side. Angle of descent 5–10°. This shell struck the ½in side plating just below the upper deck and in line with the after part of 'Y' barbette. It entered the Captain's sleeping cabin, passed through 3–¼in bulkheads, and a 7in midships pillar, and burst 40ft from impact on the 1¼in main deck, in which a hole 4ft6in × 3ft was blown. Severe damage was caused to light structure to 30ft or more from the burst, a ¼in bulkhead beyond the burst being blown away, and in the Captain of the Fleet's day cabin on the starboard side, a ⅜in bulkhead was riddled and the ½in side plating blown out for c7ft × 3ft with the frames twisted and smashed. The escape trunk to the steering compartment was badly damaged,

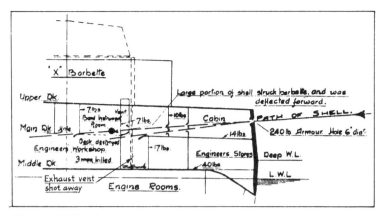

Warspite: hit No 10.

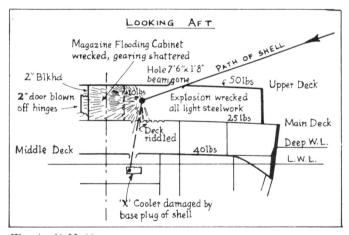

Warspite: hit No 11.

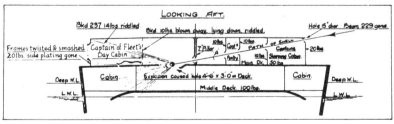

Warspite: hit No 12.

admitting water to the trunk, and this leaked past the sliding door at the bottom of the trunk so that the steering compartment flooded to a depth of 4ft.

13 From starboard side. This shell struck the ¾in hull plating near the stern between the main and middle decks at about the deep load water line and below the Admiral's day cabin. It probably burst in the hull plating in which a hole 4ft × 3ft was blown, while considerable damage was caused to light structure and fittings. The plate edge was opened for a length of *c*20ft to the sternpost and compartments above, including the Admiral's cabin, partly flooded, while the ⁵⁄₁₆in main deck was distorted over the burst. The nose of the shell apparently still capped, was found in an adjacent cabin having pierced 4–³⁄₁₆in bulkheads, and it was considered that the shoulder of the shell had struck the ship's side.

One of the early reports on the damage to the *Warspite*, given in Jellicoe's memorandum of 16 June 1916, says that there were five or six hits abaft 'Y' turret which admitted water from 'Y' turret to the stern between the main and middle decks, the waterline aft being by then about 3ft above the main deck. The only hits that can be identified abaft 'Y' turret are Nos 12 and 13 above and one hit in the previous phase of the battle. It is impossible to say whether there were actually two or three other hits, and if so, whether they were from heavy shells or 5.9in; initial estimates of the number of hits in a badly damaged part of a ship are often reduced on further examination. After noting a number of hits elsewhere in the ship, the above report also says that there were 'a good many other hits of no particular interest.' These last include the hit through the fore funnel during the previous phase of the battle, and Nos 6 and 7 above, as well as three and perhaps more – 5.9in hits, and it is again impossible to say if there were any others from heavy shells, but the probability is against.

The 13 definite heavy hits in this phase cannot be arranged in chronological order, but according to the account of the *Warspite*'s Executive Officer, Commander Walwyn, the *The Fighting at Jutland*, Nos 3 and 13 were before the rest. It is also impossible to credit them to particular ships though the *Ostfriesland*, which reported hits from her third and fourth salvos, probably obtained several. It is unlikely that the *Nassau* made any hits, and all 13 are considered to be from 12in shells.

There are few records of 5.9in hits on the *Warspite*. The most important struck the left gun of 'Y' turret 6ft from the muzzle, and caused a bulge in the gun, reducing the diameter to 14.75in and putting it out of action, though the gun was eventually repaired after removal from the ship. Another, which was at first thought to be an 8in, hit the 11in left side armour of 'X' turret, but nothing was felt inside. Walwyn mentions three more, respectively, aft of the port 6in control hood, through the mainmast, and through the wardroom, and there may have been others.

The water inboard was estimated to have reduced the *Warspite*'s metacentric height from about 6½ft to about 4½ft and until some temporary repairs had been made and bulkheads shored, it was inadvisable to exceed 16kts, owing to the risk of flooding the engine-rooms, the principal danger being from hit No 8.

It was, however, the failure of the *Warspite*'s steering, which caused her withdrawal from the action at about 1900. When the steering gear first gave trouble, the port steering engine was in use, and this slowed down due to the thrust shaft heating at the thrust bearings, and also where the free end of the thrust and worm shaft revolved in the bushed clutch of the starboard steering engine, which was not in use. When the *Warspite* did not respond to the helm, increased helm was given, but the slowing down of the engine prevented the differential valve gear responding to the movement of the steering wheel and the latter was thus hard to move. Very great force must have been used on the wheels in the upper and lower conning towers, and this led to the steering gear jamming temporarily, and also twisted the controlling shaft between the wheels in the upper and lower CTs, and bent the lever connecting the telemotor gear to the differential valve. A very moderate extemporised water supply cooled the steering engine thrust shaft, and the port engine then worked satisfactorily, but control from the steering wheels in the upper and lower conning towers was no longer possible, and as the steering compartment was partially flooded, the position at the steering engine was adopted after the *Warspite* withdrew from action.

The overheating of the steering engine was thought to be due to its continued use under heavy loads from the high speed maintained, combined with distortion of the bulkhead to which it was attached by Hit No 10, but as noted above, this hit could not have played any part, though near-misses might have shaken the hull badly and caused some distortion. Somewhat similar trouble had occurred in the *Valiant* on 4 May 1916 when her steering gear jammed for 3 minutes with 30° port helm.

The *Marlborough* was hit by a torpedo about 25ft below the deep-draught water-line and abreast the starboard Diesel generator room, located outboard of the 6in magazine which was immediately aft of 'B' turret magazine. The hull plating which was ¾in at the point of the explosion, with ⅝in above and ⅞in below, was destroyed for a length of about 28ft, as were all longitudinal and transverse frames, the bilge keel and wing bulkhead in wake of the explosion centre. The hull side and bottom were deeply indented and distorted from the lower edge of the belt to the flat keel plate over a length of about 70ft. The Diesel generator room was wrecked and filled at once, as did the hydraulic engine-room above. The starboard longitudinal bulkhead of the forward boiler-room was distorted, and water entered the boiler-room, particularly between the framing of the water-tight door, leading to the after lower bunker, and the bulkhead, from which the door framing had parted. The forward athwartships bulkhead of the boiler-room was also distorted.

The water quickly rose in the forward boiler-room at first, so that the fires were put out in four boilers within 10 minutes, and as the water continued to rise, fires were drawn in the other two. There was no escape of steam, and with the suctions of the fire and bilge pump, steam ejector and ash expeller pump which were working on the bilge, kept clear of ashes and dirt, the water was lowered to the level of the floor plates by about 1930 and kept there by the ash expeller pump (425 tons/hour).*

The list to starboard was never greater than 7–8° and no compartments were flooded for trimming, though all coal and oil fuel for the other boilers was taken from the starboard side, coal was trimmed from the starboard upper outer bunkers to lower bunkers and oil fuel was pumped from starboard tanks to port emergency tanks. Due to the list and to the lack of stop and non-return valves in the hydraulic exhaust system all firing generators in the turrets (driven by hydraulic turbines) flooded, and difficulty was experienced from 13.5in shells slipping forward as they rolled out of the main cage into the waiting position.

The 1in torpedo bulkhead protecting 'B' and 6in magazines, contributed very largely to localising the damage, and there was no leakage into 'B' space, magazine or shell-room, though slight leakage occurred in the 6in magazine and shell-room. Due to the greater depth of the explosion and the larger charge, (c25ft and 440lb Hexanite-TNT against 12ft and 280lb wet gun-cotton), much greater damage was caused than in the experiments with the old pre-dreadnought *Hood* in the first half of 1914, and no fewer than 40 water-tight compartments

---

*The *Iron Duke* class had the most powerful boiler-room pumps of any of the Grand Fleet capital ships. In the *Benbow* and *Emperor of India* the capacity per boiler room was 1100 tons per hour as two ash-expeller pumps had been fitted, and in the *Iron Duke* and *Marlborough*, 675 tons at the date of Jutland. In no other ship was the figure more than 520 tons.

were involved when the *Marlborough* was repaired. In spite of this she was able to maintain revolutions for 17kts until after midnight, with bulkheads and decks shored where necessary.

As noted previously, this torpedo came from the *Wiesbaden*.

The right gun in the *Marlborough*'s 'A' turret was put out of action at about the fifth round fired by the gun, by what was thought to be a premature, though the damage to the rifling was comparatively small. APC was being fired at the time. The inner 'A' tube was cracked all round, about half-way along the gun, and a large piece of the jacket broken off, with a crack extending 15ft along the jacket.

The loss of the *Defence* was clearly seen by Commander Usborne in the *Colossus*. She was heavily hit aft and an explosion occurred in the after 9.2in magazine. The flame spread at once via the ammunition passages to each 7.5in and thence to the forward 9.2in magazine where an explosion also occurred, and the *Defence* completely blew up and disappeared. Her sinking is usually credited to the *Lützow*, though it was also claimed by the *Markgraf* and *Kaiser*, and less plausibly by the *Kronprinz*. The *Grosser Kurfürst* noted that both her own 12in salvos at the *Defence* hit at short range, but did not claim credit for her destruction. The tables in the German Official History give half the number of hits on the *Warrior* — seven heavy and three medium — but the latter figure cannot be estimated with any certainty.

According to her report, the *Warrior* was hit by at least 15 heavy shells, and about 6 smaller. The worst hit was on the water-line just forward of the engine-room after bulkhead and the shell, after piercing the 6in side armour, passed through the port after reserve bunker, the 2in longitudinal bulkhead protecting the upper part of the engine room, and then through the ¾in armour deck into the port engine-room. It apparently burst in passing through the centre-line bulkhead, wrecking a steam-pipe, and a large fragment of the shell was deflected down and tore a hole through the wings or double-bottom at the after end of the starboard engine-room, so that both engine-rooms flooded. The engine-room forward bulkhead only leaked slightly, but the after bulkhead was damaged and strained and compartments immediately abaft it, below the armour deck, including 9.2in and 7.5in magazines and both dynamo rooms gradually filled, but there was no flooding below the armour deck further aft. Another shell hit near this point but about 6ft above the water-line, and after making a 12in diameter hole in the 6in armour, passed right across the ship without exploding, went through the support of the after starboard 9.2in turret, struck and indented the starboard side armour and fell back into the turret support still unexploded. This shell caused a serious fire from fuzing electrical circuits. A third shell passed through the superstructure and burst against the above turret which was jammed by debris but later cleared. The other turrets could all be worked by hand, though hydraulic power failed.

There were three large holes in the upper deck from other heavy shells. One of these hit forward of the after starboard 9.2in turret and made a hole in the 1in upper deck 6ft across with a long tear 5ft–2ft wide, and also badly damaged the main deck and sent fragments into No 4 boiler room. The second made a hole 15ft × 10ft in the upper deck below the after part of the starboard after 3pdr battery, and the third made a large hole in the after screen bulkhead, as well as one *c* 10ft × 4ft × 2ft in the upper deck, and also holed the 1in main deck. These 3 hits were not an immediate danger, but they allowed large amounts of water to enter when the sea increased in the early morning of 1 June, and thus contributed to the *Warrior*'s eventual loss.

As far as can be deduced from the *Warrior*'s reports, the remaining 9–12in hits were: 1 On 6in armour abreast port feed tank. 2 On starboard forward 4in armour. 3, 4, 5, 6 On hull plating forward. 7 Apparently burst on forecastle deck and damaged starboard side of bridge. 8 Through port side of bridge. 9 Through foremost funnel.

The 6–5.9in hits were apparently: 1, 2, 3, 4. On hull plating forward. 5 Hit fore turret with little effect. 6 Went through 1in upper deck forward of starboard after 9.2in turret, and burst on main deck. The last two hits were from the 2nd SG during the previous phase of the battle.

The number of hits by heavy shells on British capital ships from 1815 to 1900 is estimated as:

	12in	11in	Total
Invincible	5	—	5
Princess Royal	2	—	2
Warspite	13	—	13
Total	20	—	20

Of these 5 were from the 1st Scouting Group, 2 from the *Markgraf* and 13 from the 1st Division and the *Friedrich der Grosse*.

In addition 24 hits, all 12in, are estimated to have been made on other ships – *Defence* 7, *Warrior* 15, *Marvel* 1, *Defender* 1.

Of the German battlecruisers, the *Lützow* was probably hit by 10 heavy shells in this phase of the action, of which 2 were at about 1819 and 8 between 1826 and 1834. The 2 hits at *c*1819 were from the *Lion*, and the remaining 8 from the *Invincible* and *Inflexible*. One of the shells at *c*1819 appears to have been far forward above the side armour or perhaps at the edge of the upper deck, and the other went through the 1in battery roof deck and the port forward armour door of the space between the 5.9in casemates, and then burst just abaft 'B' barbette. A serious fire was started amongst damage control material which was stowed here, and for a time this filled the space between the port and starboard 5.9in casemates with smoke, but neither the gunnery control tower nor the forward 5.9in casemates were seriously affected by this hit.

Of the hits between 1826 and 1834, the most important were by 2–12in shells which struck below the water-line and apparently burst in or near the broadside torpedo flat. One shell seems to have been below the side armour, and the other on the lower part of the $4\frac{3}{4}$in forward belt. As in all German capital ships at Jutland, the torpedo bulkhead did not extend forward of 'A' barbette, and the *Lützow*'s broadside flat was larger than usual as she had 23.6in torpedoes, and was of sufficient volume to take 354 tons of water. It must have been filled instantly and water very quickly spread to other compartments forward and aft of the torpedo flat through strained or damaged bulkheads, ventilation trunks and voice-pipes. From the *Lützow*'s leakage report, it appears that the ventilation trunks from some compartments had no cut-off valves, and in other cases the valves were dangerously sited away from bulkheads, while the door in the forward bulkhead of the broadside torpedo flat was of an entirely inadequate pattern. The water spread most rapidly forward of the broadside torpedo flat, and the *Lützow* must have taken in *c*1000 tons of water almost at once.

Two other shells appear to have hit below the water-line near the bow torpedo flat, and all the compartments below the armour deck in this area also flooded, so that a further 500 tons or so of water entered the ship, but it is not certain how much of this was due to these two hits, and how much to the two by the broadside torpedo flat. It seems likely that the whole torpedo installation in the forward part of the ship, with a total capacity, including the broadside flat, of 740 tons of water, flooded as a result of the two hits by the broadside flat.

In a short time a total of at least 2000 tons of water, including that from the hit at 1713, was in the *Lützow*, and her draught forward had increased by nearly 8ft, so that she had to reduce speed for a time to as

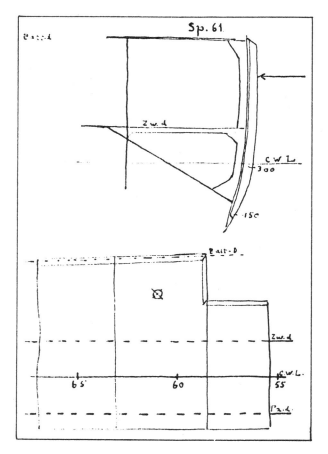

Derfflinger: *second hit at c1830*.

little as 3kts to lessen the pressure on the 1.2in after bulkhead of the broadside torpedo flat which still held though leaking badly. Even so the water continued to spread into other compartments abaft the broadside torpedo flat. Neither of the *Lützow*'s forward main leak pumps could be used as the operating rods were jammed and immovable, and in addition the forward starboard leak pump room soon flooded.

The midships pumps were working but it would seem that the drainage system, that should have allowed the water which leaked from the badly damaged compartments to reach these pumps, was not functioning with full efficiency, and it was impossible to prevent the flooding of further compartments.

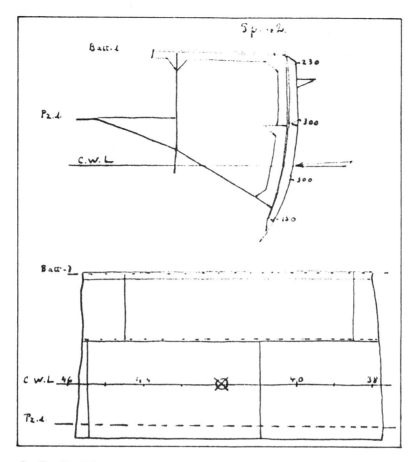

Seydlitz: *hit c1834.*

Of the other hits at this time, one struck the forecastle forward of the 1600 hits, making a large hole in the upper deck, which would permit much water to enter the *Lützow* above the armour deck as her draught increased forward, and three were amidships. One pierced the belt near its 6in lower edge below No 4–5.9in and lodged unexploded in the wings. Another struck the side armour above the water-line near No 3 or No 4–5.9in and burst. Some armour was driven in and jammed No 4 gun permanently, and it appears that the shock of this hit caused the temporary failure of the port 5.9in fire control. The third hit burst on the net-shelf below No 5 – 5.9in.

There appear to have been three hits on the *Derfflinger* in this phase by 12in shells from the *Indomitable*. One hit was probably at 1826 and

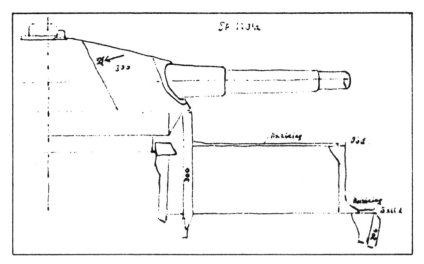

König: *hits c1835, No 2.*

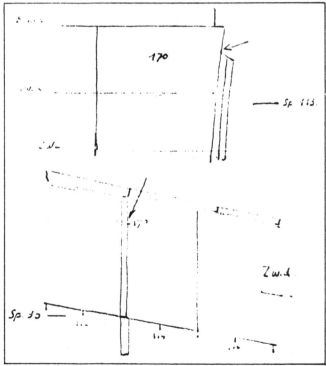

König: *hits c1835, No 3.*

186

the other two at about 1830. The first shell burst in the water near the hull in line with No 1 – port 5.9in. The plating was bulged in for a length of *c*40ft below, and to a lesser extent at, the armour shelf, and some leakage gradually occurred in wing compartments and a protective bunker for 48ft, while the side armour was struck by splinters above the water-line.

Of the other two shells, both of which are believed to have been APC, one struck the 12in side armour on a vertical joint between two plates at main deck level, 3½ft above the legend water-line and *c*8ft forward of the half-way point between the two after barbettes. The shell burst on impact, forcing in the plates by 1½in where hit, and flaking the surface for an area of 25in × 12in. Both plates were also slightly bowed, and the 1.2in armour deck and the main deck were buckled, though this may have been partly due to a subsequent hit on the next armour plate joint aft. The torpedo net fittings were destroyed for over 30ft, and the hull plating bulged in by up to 2½in for a length of 6½ft, and to a depth of 5ft below the armour, which caused the port wings to flood for 25ft.

The other shell burst on striking the side armour where 10¼in thick, 45in below the upper deck and just abaft the sternmost barbette. The plate was bulged in by less than ½in where hit, and the upper edge forced 1½in inwards. The main deck was buckled and below the armour, the hull plating was slightly bulged inwards at the port outer shaft tunnel, and the transverse and longitudinal stiffening angles forced in, but only a little water entered. The torpedo net and net stowage were damaged for 40ft so that part of the net trailed in the water above the port wing propeller and the engines had to be stopped for 2 minutes to secure the net.

The *Seydlitz* was hit at about 1834 by a shell which was most probably a 12in APC from the *Indomitable*. This came from the port quarter, and struck the 12in main belt in line with the after end of the superfiring barbette and on the lwl. The shell, which apparently broke up, forced in the armour by 2in where hit, and the plate was displaced by up to *c*1in, so that some water entered an outer bunker for a length of about 14ft, but otherwise only unimportant damage to the torpedo net and its fittings was directly caused by this shell, which struck the armour obliquely. The *Seydlitz* was however severely shaken, so that the coupling at the upper steering engine flew out, and she had to be steered temporarily from the steering gear compartment.

There were no major calibre hits on the other battlecruisers, and of the battleships only the *König* was frequently hit, being struck by eight

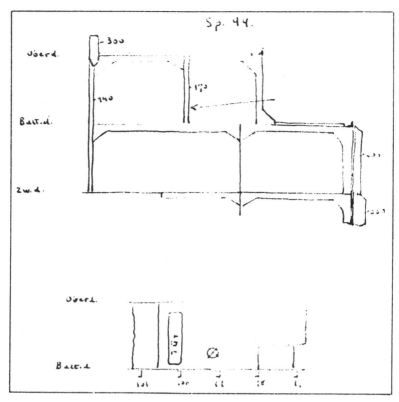

König: *hits c1835, No 4.*

Opposite. König: *hits c1835, No 5.*

heavy shells, seven of which were 13.5in CPC from the *Iron Duke*, and the other a 13.5in APC from the *Monarch*.

All were within a very few minutes of 1835 according to the *König's* times which were a little fast on the *Iron Duke's*.

The individual hits are described below in order from forward to aft. Their chronological sequence is not entirely known, but Nos 4, 6, 5 and probably 1, followed in quick succession. All were estimated to have come from 0–20° forward of the port beam, and are credited to the *Iron Duke*, with the exception of No 6 to the *Monarch*.

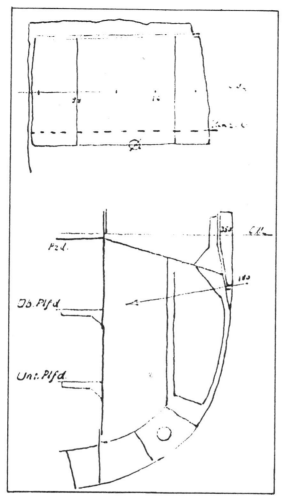

1 Went through the port capstan and towing capstan, and burst on or near the forecastle deck, a little forward of 'A' barbette and near the centre-line. The forecastle deck was holed for an area of about 30sq ft and splinters put the starboard capstan out of action, and did much damage to cabins and fittings on the starboard side of the upper deck, as well as piercing this deck in places and causing small fires.

2 Struck near the right edge of the right face plate of 'A' turret, which was trained on the port beam, and glanced off, bursting over the starboard side of the forecastle deck which was holed by splinters, the largest hole measuring $3\frac{1}{4}$ft × 2ft. The 12in turret armour was very slightly displaced and dented, in both cases by less than $\frac{1}{4}$in.

3 Entered through the side plating $2\frac{1}{2}$ft below the upper deck, and just forward of

the upper belt, in line with the fore part of 'A' barbette. The shell then struck the 6¾in upper belt transverse armour bulkhead near the outer end, was deflected and burst on the main deck *c*3ft from the port side. The fastenings at the outer end of the armour bulkhead gave way, and the latter was driven 4¼ft aft. A piece measuring 47in × 13in × 2in was broken off the armour surface, and there were also cracks in the plate. The main deck was thrown downwards over an area of about 180sq ft between the port longitudinal bulkhead and the deck stringer plate, and also holed for *c*10sq ft further inboard. The upper deck forward of the transverse armour bulkhead, was bowed upwards to a maximum of 12in over a large distance and the 1.2in armour deck sprung in one place immediately abaft this bulkhead. The port longitudinal bulkhead on the main deck was holed for an area of *c*40sq ft, and splinters were driven right across the ship, on and below the main deck, the capstan engine room being holed several times and the anchor-weighing engine put out of action. Damage was caused to compartments and fittings on the main deck, small fires started and some flooding occurred through the hole in the side which was 10½ft above lwl.

4 Went through the side plating just forward of the 5.9in battery and about 2ft above the upper deck, and struck the 6¾in forward diagonal battery bulkhead 8-14in from its lower edge, and at an angle of *c*45° to the plate normal. The shell pierced the armour, making a hole measuring *c*40in × 28in on the outside and 55in × 35in on the inside, and burst on the upper deck. The 0.8in-1.2in upper deck was holed for *c*60sq ft inside No 1 port casemate and also driven downwards. The main deck was forced down over a length of nearly 30ft, and the 1.2in forecastle deck bowed upwards for *c*55ft to respective maxima of 22in and 15in.

In No 1 port casemate two or three charges were ignited and some of the charges in the hoist to No 12 magazine on the upper platform deck also caught fire. The hoist was wrecked and the base of the shell found in the hoist-machinery, while there were many causalties from propellant gases. The 5.9in gun itself was only slightly damaged, but the sights, and all cables were destroyed, and the whole gun crew were killed. Two or three 5.9in shells fell on the main deck but were undamaged. The ⅝in casemate longitudinal splinter bulkhead was holed, and armour fragments entered the galley and chart-room.

5 This was the most damaging hit. The shell struck the extreme lower edge of the armour belt 5½ft below lwl, so that only half the 14½in diameter hole was in the 7in armour and half in the armour shelf. The position of the hit was in line with the after part of 'B' barbette. The shell then traversed a wing-compartment and burst while passing through the wing longitudinal bulkhead 6½ft inboard of the hit. A hole of 25sq ft was made in this bulkhead, and a transverse wing bulkhead 5ft away destroyed. The explosive effect of the shell with many fragments, went through a 6½ft wide protective bunker, which was full of coal, and struck the 2in torpedo bulkhead, 13ft from the ship's side between the upper and lower platform decks. The torpedo bulkhead was holed for an area of 27sq ft with three large cracks running upwards from the hole, and was also bowed inwards by up to 9in above the hole. No 14 magazine on the lower platform deck, immediately inboard of the torpedo bulkhead, was completely destroyed. As usual with the secondary armament in German ships, there were no separate shell rooms, and magazine cases,

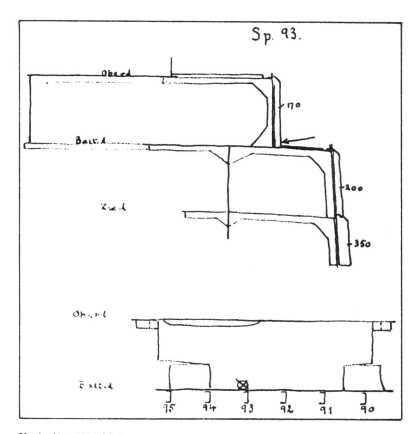

König: *hits c1835, No 6.*

5.9in shells and charges were buried under coal hurled into the magazine from the protective bunker, and some cases were smashed by splinters and fragments of the torpedo bulkhead, and though shells were not damaged, it was afterwards found that the fuze of one 5.9in HE had become armed. About 15 charges ignited, but sea-water flooding rapidly in from the hole in the ship's side prevented a worse disaster. The base-plate and some pieces of the shell were found among the coal in the magazine, close to the torpedo bulkhead, with the head about 5–6ft further inboard. No 12 magazine on the upper platform deck was also damaged, and was quickly flooded by sea-water entering through the cracks in the torpedo bulkhead, while some shell and torpedo bulkhead fragments also entered a 12in magazine.

In addition, the wing compartments and protective bunkers were flooded for a length of 60ft, and it was calculated that 494 tons of water had entered the ship which would give a list to port of 3° 47′. This was corrected by counter-flooding some of the starboard wings with 362 tons of water, but further flooding also occurred. In view of the magazine fire caused by this hit or perhaps on account of the fires caused by hits No 4 and 6, orders were given to flood the whole forward magazine group. Flash and gas which came through the flooding pipes, prevented the flooding system of the other magazines of the group being promptly isolated from that of Nos 12 and 14, with the result that some of 'B' turret magazines flooded, though except for one magazine in which the water was 20in deep, those of 'A' turret remained dry. Apart from Nos 12 and 14, five magazine compartments filled completely, and two more – apparently 'B' shell rooms – were half full. Most of the affected magazine compartments were not drained until after the action was over, while 'B' turret's repeater compass was put out of action and cables leading to 'A' and 'B' were under water, though apparently unaffected.

In addition, leaks through cable glands, and ventilation trunks caused flooding in some store compartments and passages, and a certain amount of water from leaks and fire-hoses entered the ship's control room and transmitting station, which were also affected by gas from burning propellant. The *König*'s draught before the battle was 30ft2in (forw.) 29ft2in (aft) and after the battle 32ft10in (forw.) 29ft1in (aft), with a list to port of 3°, in agreement with the 1630 tons of water reported in the ship at 2351 31 May, of which by far the greatest amount was as a result of this hit.

Pieces of this 13.5in CPC shell were analysed and gave figures of 0.78% carbon and 4.16% chromium with only 0.06% nickel and no molybdenum or tungsten. The 2in torpedo bulkhead plating of low alloy nickel steel was brittle and defective where hit.

6 Struck the 6¾in casemate side armour at the after end of No 1 port 5.9in casemate, just above the upper deck and burst. The hole in the armour was approximately rectangular and measured 28in × 16in on the outside, and 38in × 26in inside. The effect of the burst was mostly downwards, and the 1.2in upper deck was holed outside the armour for *c*10sq ft and was driven downwards over the whole area of the casemate from the combined effects of Hits Nos 4 and 6. The 1.2in longitudinal splinter bulkhead, running below the upper deck 5¼ft inboard of the hit, was bowed by up to 11in from the upper to the main deck, but was not holed, while the main deck, outside this bulkhead, was holed in many places by splinters, bowed by up to 2ft and torn for a length of 23ft at the splinter bulkhead. The 1.2in forecastle deck was slightly bowed upwards, and armour fragments pierced the ⅝in longitudinal casemate bulkhead protecting the fore-funnel uptakes, and damage to the air supply and danger from gas, put all three oil-fired boilers out of action. The starboard and midships boilers were brought into use again, though not at full power at 2035 and 2050 respectively, but the port boiler remained out.

The effects of this hit and of Hit No 4 cannot be entirely distinguished but this shell caused damage in both No 1 and No 2 port casemates. Armour fragments holed the 0.8in transverse bulkhead between casemates Nos 1 and 2, and in the latter two or three 5.9in charges were ignited as were others in the hoist to No 14 Magazine on the lower platform deck, but shells in the casemate were undamaged. The 5.9in gun itself was only slightly damaged, but the sights and cables were destroyed, and the hoist which entered No 2 casemate near the bulkhead between Nos 1 and 2, was damaged and useless. The gun-crew however escaped, as they had just vacated No 2 casemate because of gas danger from Hit No 4, when Hit No 6 occurred.

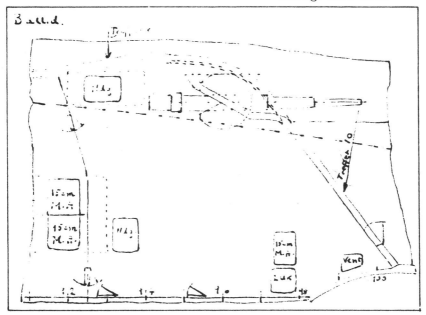

König: *hits c1835, No 6 (plan).*

In addition fires were started in the PO's bathroom and in the fore dressing station, and some flooding on the armour deck resulted from cut fire-mains in the dressing station. The port battle signal station was also put out of action temporarily by smoke and gas. Thirty-six fatal casualties were caused by Hits Nos 4 and 6, of which three-quarters were assigned to Hit No 4, while there were only four killed by Hit No 5.

7 Struck the far (starboard) side of the CT roof near the edge, glanced off and burst *c*40yds from the ship. The 6¾in roof was dented to a depth of 0.6in, and there was also a very narrow crack 20in long. The starboard torpedo periscope was destroyed and splinters cut the cables for the night signal gear and night recognition signal position. A fragment of the rain gutter on the CT slightly wounded Rear Admiral Behncke, who was on the upper bridge.

8 This shell, which was apparently a ricochet, struck the after funnel *c*13ft from the top, and passed through without exploding. The starboard after upper SL was put out of action.

The *Markgraf* was hit once at 1835. The shell which was probably from the *Orion*, struck and burst on the 6¾in armour of No 6 port 5.9in casemate, 9–10ft forward of the gun axis and 5ft above the upper deck.

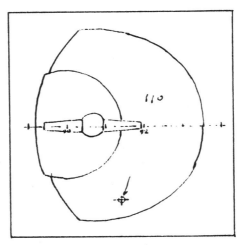

König: *hits c1835, No 7.*

Markgraf: *hit at 1835.*

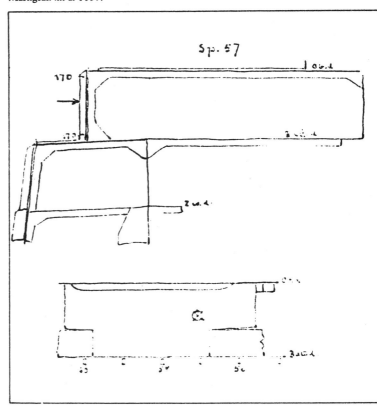

The effect of the burst was outside the casemate, but the armour was holed, and the plate forced 1¼in inwards. The 1.2in upper deck was torn open for a length of 8ft close outside the casemate, and the main deck for a length of 5ft. Armour fragments did much damage, putting the gun out of action, and also the battle signal station, while four of them pierced the 0.6in port and starboard casemate longitudinal bulkheads, one also holing the 0.4in starboard skin plating. The ammunition hoist in No 6 starboard casemate was put out of action, and one man killed in this casemate, while the crew of the No 6 port gun were all killed except for 2 severely wounded.

The *Markgraf* also appears to have been heavily shaken aft by a 'near-miss' at 1833, and this may have been the cause of her port propeller shaft being bent so that the bearings overheated and the port engine had to be stopped.

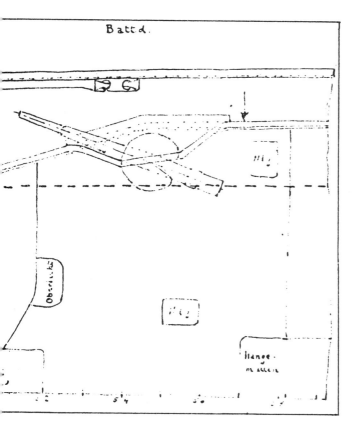

None of the other battleships appears to have been hit in this phase of the action.

The *Falmouth* and *Yarmouth* scored a number of 6in hits on the *Lützow* but details are lacking. They were probably responsible for 2–6in shells which hit the *Derfflinger*, one piercing the anti-rolling tank on the superstructure deck between the funnels and bursting in the warrant officers' mess and the other going through the top of the after funnel, and the 3rd LCS may also have made one hit on the *Seydlitz* which burst on the upper belt.

It remains to make a very approximate estimate of the number of heavy shells that hit the *Wiesbaden* between about 1820 and 1845. At least 300 rounds of 12in to 15in were fired at her in this period, for the most part at 10,000–11,000yds, and 10 to 12 hits claimed – *Royal Oak* 1, *Superb* 2, *Temeraire* 2–3, *Vanguard* 1 and several more, say 5–6 total. Too many ships were each firing a few salvos at her in an unsystematic manner, for any great accuracy, and it seems likely that some of the hits were claimed by more than one ship, though there may have been one or two hits that were not seen. No fatal damage was inflicted on the *Wiesbaden* and she was able to fire a torpedo at *c*1843, while she had already been hit by the 3rd BCS and 1st CS, and torpedoed by the *Onslow*. It is thus thought best to allow only 10 hits from heavy shells in the 1820/1845 period.

The estimates for hits by heavy shells on the German capital ships are:

	13.5in/1400lb	13.5in/1250lb	12in	Total
Lützow	—	2	8	10
Derfflinger	—	—	3	3
Seydlitz	—	—	1	1
König	7	1	—	8
Markgräf	—	1	—	1
Total	7	4	12	23

Of the above 9 were due to battleships, 2 to Beatty's battlecruisers and 12 to the 3rd BCS.

CHAPTER 10

Action between capital ships
Fourth phase 1900–1945

F OR A LIMITED period the ships of the Grand Fleet were able to fire with considerable effect, if only for a few minutes, and for the first time in the battle, very little damage was done in reply to any ship. Destroyer attacks, however, caused the British to turn away, and the Germans were able to withdraw with the aid of effective smoke screens, so that contact was lost.

Jellicoe has often been criticised for turning away, but the manoeuvre was usual in both fleets when threatened by torpedo attack, and the loss of the *Audacious* from a mine of very moderate power had shown that serious under-water damage to British dreadnoughts should not be risked. In any event the German withdrawal under cover of smoke would have broken off the action, unless Jellicoe's divisions had chased directly after them. The evidence available to him was inadequate to justify such a manoeuvre, however attractive it may appear in the light of after-knowledge, particularly if the vulnerability of British ships to under-water damage and their liability to blow up if a turret or barbette were holed, are overlooked.

The eastward advance of the German fleet, initiated by Scheer's signal at 1855, was soon in trouble, due in the first instance to the 1st SG drawing across the head of the line as they took station in the van, and causing the leading battleships to reduce speed. Hipper was in the destroyer *G39* for the whole of this phase as firing restarted before he could board the *Moltke*, finally chosen as the most effective of the German battlecruisers, and the 1st SG were led by Captain Hartog in the *Derfflinger*. The latter's funnel halliards and action signal station spars were serviceable, and a signal was made at 1905 for all battlecruisers to follow in the *Derfflinger*'s wake, and another at 1910 to

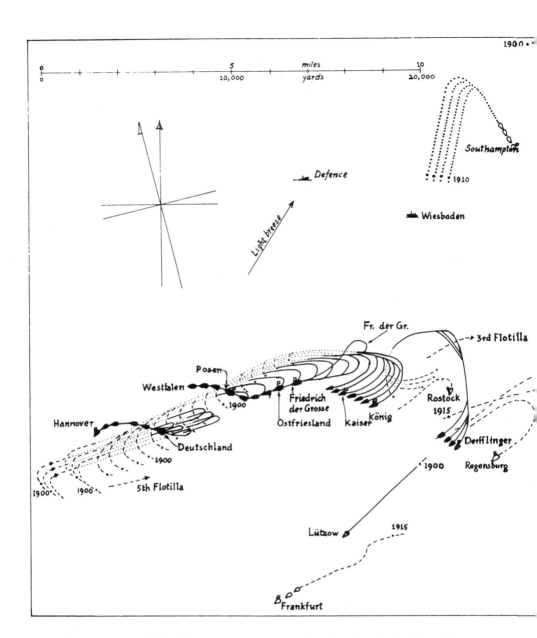

increase speed. By this time they were in line ahead with the *Derfflinger* and *Seydlitz* steering about 83°, and the *Moltke* and *von der Tann* turning to this course.

On completing their turn, the German dreadnoughts were at first

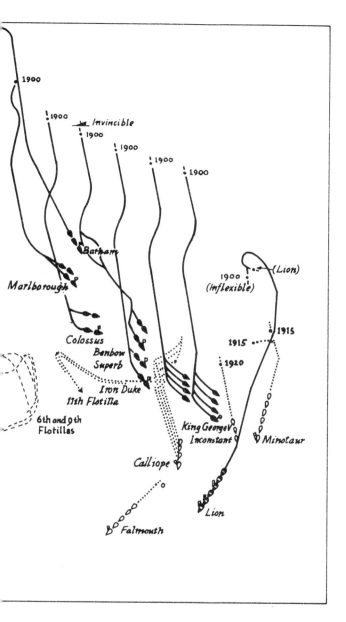

1900

1900 — *Invincible*

1900

1900

1900

1900

Batham

Marlborough

(*Lion*)

1900
(*Inflexible*)

Colossus

1915

Benbow

1915

Superb

1920

Iron Duke

11th Flotilla

6th and 9th
Flotillas

King GeorgeV

Inconstant

Minotaur

Calliope

Lion

Falmouth

Chart VII: Position at 1925

steering c63° but by 1905 the *König* had turned to about 88° and at 1910 the 5th Division were all on this course, with the *Kaiser* beginning to follow. Scheer had signalled for speed to be reduced at 1902, so that the rear of the line could close up and the battlecruisers take station ahead,

199

but the latter did not get clear soon enough and eventually some ships of the 5th and 6th Divisions had to stop their engines and even go astern. For a time the 3rd Squadron lay bunched together and almost stopped. From about 1910 the British fire was increasing while nothing but gun-flashes could be seen from the German ships, and to make room for another about-turn, Scheer at 1913 ordered the 1st SG to attack, literally – 'Turn together towards the enemy. Attack, bring about decision with all means' – though this was followed by another signal at 1914 directing the battlecruisers – 'To operate against the enemy van'. This second signal left the method of operation dependent on the tactical conditions of the battle, but it still meant that the attack was to be pushed home, as tactical orders, dated 10 May 1916, for the 2nd Squadron, for which a sacrificial role was envisaged in certain circumstances, gave this latter signal as the one to initiate an attack regardless of consequences. According to the *Derfflinger*'s signal log these two orders from Scheer were received by wireless (auxiliary – 'Z' station) at 1915 and 1918, apparently in reverse order, and were immediately repeated by flags to the other battlecruisers, but it appears certain that she had begun to turn to starboard as early as 1913, and at 1915 when a speed of 23kts was signalled by the *Derfflinger*, she was steering 167°. At 1920 the *Derfflinger* turned away to starboard and by 1930 she was steering 246° with the other three battlecruisers which had turned somewhat short, disposed approximately on a line of bearing 21°. The *Derfflinger* had suffered severely, but the 1st SG had attracted the greater part of the British fire, which might otherwise have been directed at the battleships as they turned.

It would appear that the *Friedrich der Grosse* and the ships of the 1st Squadron had turned 11–23° to starboard together at 1912, and at 1914 the *König* turned to 122° to bring her broadside to bear. The ships of the 3rd Squadron were too close together and were under a considerable fire from four or five battleships, so that the 'about-turn' to starboard, for which Scheer made the signal at *c*1917, was carried out under very difficult circumstances.

The German second in command, Vice Admiral Schmidt in the *Ostfriesland*, at once began to turn without waiting for the ships astern, in order to hasten matters, and at the same time Scheer had the *Friedrich der Grosse* turned to port to give the 3rd Squadron more room, but even so, some ships were in considerable difficulties. The *Kaiserin* had closed the *Prinzregent Luitpold* before the turn and had to sheer out to starboard. After turning, and while the *Kaiserin* was trying to let the *Ostfriesland* increase distance to leave room for the *Friedrich der Grosse*, the *Prinzregent Luitpold* came up at high speed on the *Kaiserin*'s starboard side, which forced her to remain outside the line for a considerable time, before she could rejoin between the *Prinzregent Luitpold* and the *Kaiser*.

On account of one engine being disabled, the *Markgraf* began to turn before the *Kronprinz* next astern, and kept away to the south-westward for some time to avoid the heaviest of the fire, but this forced the *Grosser Kurfürst* also to head south-westward parallel to her, until the *Markgraf* was able to rejoin the line between the *Kaiser* and the *Kronprinz*, and the *Grosser Kurfürst* between the latter and the *König*.

For several minutes the ships of the 3rd Squadron were thus in a highly dangerous position, very close to one another and proceeding at slow speed, almost in line abreast. The *König* hauled out 400 or 500yds to windward (212°) at 1925 and laid a smoke screen, and at 1928 the *Kaiser* also began to make as much smoke as possible, but by then the British fire had largely died away.

Scheer had signalled for speed to be increased again at 1920, and 2 minutes later ordered Course 257°, and at 1927 212° at 17kts, as far as the 1st Squadron was concerned. The *Westfalen* accordingly led this squadron and the *Friedrich der Grosse* in line ahead on these courses, though they had to turn temporarily to starboard to let the 2nd Squadron get clear. The 3rd Squadron steered 257° on a line of bearing *c*285° from the *König* and at 1930 the *Prinzregent Luitpold*, now leading the squadron, was about 2 miles bearing 100° from the *Friedrich der Grosse*.

The *Lützow* steered about 225°, except for a brief period when she was fired at by some of the 2nd BS and turned temporarily to starboard. The flooding appears to have been partially brought under control, and the *Lützow* was at times steaming at a moderate speed, and at 1930 was 3–3½ miles *c*225° from the *Derfflinger* and about 4½ miles bearing 170° from the *Prinzregent Luitpold*.

Of the other German units, the 2nd Squadron were astern of the *Westfalen* during the eastward advance and turned at the same time as the dreadnoughts, being at 1930 on the *Westfalen*'s starboard bow. The 2nd SG were about 3 miles ahead of the *Lützow* at 1930 while the 4th SG were near the 2nd Squadron. In the 2nd SG the *Elbing*'s port engine was out of action at 1915 from a leaky condenser, which limited her speed to 20kts, for nearly 4 hours, but three of the *Pillau*'s six coal fired boilers were again in operation at 1930 allowing 26kts.

The German destroyer attacks are described on a later page, but in order to understand Jellicoe's movements between 1900 and 1930 they are briefly noted here. At 1900 Scheer ordered Commodore Michelsen to rescue the *Wiesbaden*'s crew, and an unsuccessful attempt was made by four destroyers of the 3rd Flotilla, torpedoes being fired at the rear of the British line at about 1910. At 1915 the real attack was begun by part of the 6th and 9th Flotillas, and the first torpedoes were fired at about 1922. Subsequent attacks were made too far to the northward and had very little if any effect.

The battleship divisions of the Grand Fleet were steering 167° at 1900, with the divisional guides bearing approximately 291° from the *King George V*, except that the 6th Division were astern of station. At 1905 Jellicoe signalled for the battleships to turn together to 201° to close the enemy, but 4 minutes later altered course back to 167°, as he had received the reports of supposed submarines ahead. The 6th Division had to avoid torpedoes from the *V48*, but otherwise conformed to the courses signalled.

As the action developed, the 1st BS at the rear of the British line were for the most part engaged before the ships ahead, and Jellicoe was apprehensive of this squadron, which contained the greatest proportion of older dreadnoughts, being too much exposed, so that at 1912 he signalled the 1st BS to take station astern of the 4th BS. The 6th Division altered course to about 133° at 1918, but the 5th Division continued on 167°, the *Neptune* having to turn out of line to avoid torpedoes fired by the 3rd DF.

From 1909 several ships of the 4th BS opened fire on these destroyers. The 3rd Division did not alter course but the 4th Division turned away by sub-divisions at about 1912. This turn was signalled as 23°, but it appears that the sub-divisions altered course to near 122°, and about 3 minutes later came back into single line ahead, and the 4th Division then steered to take station astern of the 3rd Division. Jellicoe wished to complete his line of battle on course 167°, which appeared to cross the 'T' of the German advance, and accordingly at 1916 signalled the 2nd BS to take station ahead, and 2 minutes later to proceed at utmost speed. The 1st Division altered course at 1918 to 196°, but the 2nd Division continued on 167° so that the squadron could form line ahead before taking station on the 4th BS. The *Thunderer* was only about 200yds from the *Iron Duke* at 1918, and 2 minutes later Jellicoe called for a speed of 15kts to make it easier for the 2nd BS, which were making 19 or 20kts, to take station ahead. The attack of the 6th DF had now begun and at 1921 Jellicoe signalled the 2nd BS to turn together 45° to port, to give room for the 3rd Division to make a 23° turn away by sub-divisions, which was ordered immediately afterwards for the

4th and 1st BS. It was then determined by use of the Bunbury Enemy Torpedo Calculator, a simple speed and course resolver supplied to the *Iron Duke* and to some other ships, that a 23° turn away was not enough, and at 1925 a further 23° turn by sub-divisions was ordered.

The actual courses of the various divisions between 1920 and 1930 were, however, more complicated. The 1st Division turned away together to near 133° at 1922 and at about 1928 returned to line ahead steering 167° and reduced to 15kts, though the *King George V*'s average speed between 1900 and 2000 was 18.6kts. Just previously to turning to 167° the *King George V* had to turn sharply to starboard to avoid the 1st LCS; the 2nd CS were also in the way. The 2nd Division turned together to 122°, and then returned to line ahead, course 167° and reduced speed as the 1st Division.

The 3rd Division turned 145° by subdivisions at 1922, and turned again at 1925 to *c*130°. The 4th Division altered course to 184° at 1920, and first turned by subdivisions to about 150° and then to near 133°.

The 5th Division which was the most exposed, altered course by subdivisions at 1922 to about 100° and at 1926 reformed line ahead and steered 145°, while the 6th Division altered course by subdivisions to 122° at 1924 and 3 minutes later returned to line ahead, course 145°.

The actual position at 1930 was thus that the 1st and 2nd Divisions were steering 167°, the 3rd and 4th Divisions near 133° by subdivisions, and the 5th and 6th Divisions 145°.

Astern of the other battleships, the 5th BS, less the *Warspite*, had steered about 173° from just after 1900 until 1913 when they turned to 156°. At about 1924 they altered course to *c*128°, and at 1927 turned to 105° for 2 or 3 minutes. According to the *Valiant*, speed was reduced from 18 to 10kts at 1922 and then increased to 13, and to 20kts at 1930.

In the van, the *Lion* followed by the other battlecruisers, was back on course 167° at *c*1904, and then turned until she was steering 201° at 1909. At 1915 the battlecruisers increased from 18 to 22kts and turned slightly away, but soon altered course to 212°, and at 1922 increased to 24kts, the *Lion* being about 3 miles on the *King George V*'s starboard bow at 1930.

Of the British cruiser and light cruiser squadrons, the 2nd CS with the *Chester* were at first on the port beam of the 1st Division, but by 1930 the *Minotaur* and *Cochrane* had cut across the leading battleships and were on the battlecruisers' port quarter, while the rest, which had been joined by the *Duke of Edinburgh*, were on the *King George V*'s port bow. The 1st LCS, less the *Galatea*, had been on the disengaged side of the battlefleet making for the head of the line and at 1930 were fine on the battlecruisers' starboard quarter.

The 2nd LCS had engaged the *Wiesbaden* at 4000yds from about 1900 to 1905 but they were then driven off by the fire of some of the German heavy ships, and retired northwards to take station astern of the battlefleet. At about 1930 they passed the *V48*, and the *Southampton* and *Dublin* fired at her at *c*6400yds.

The 3rd LCS with the *Canterbury* were ahead of the *Lion* and then on her starboard bow, while the 4th LCS after crossing ahead of the 2nd BS were to starboard of the 1st Division at 1922 when Jellicoe ordered them to attack the German destroyers.

During this period visibility was much in favour of the British, and to the eastward the Germans could only make out the gun-flashes of their opponents, though to the northward conditions were better. In contrast to this some of the leading British battleships, as well as the battlecruisers, were able to fire at over 9 miles, though from the *Superb* visibility was never much more than 6 miles. The German smoke and artificial fog screens laid by the *König* and *Kaiser*, the 2nd SG, the destroyers with the *Lützow*, and other destroyers on their return from attack, were highly effective in concealing their fleet. Chlorsulphonic acid and sulphur trioxide artificial fog-apparatus was carried by German light cruisers and destroyers, though the latter seem mostly to have employed oil fuel smoke.

The British battleships suffered less from interference by their own ships than in the previous phase, but the *King George V* again complained of the *Duke of Edinburgh*'s smoke, the *Ajax* was masked by the 4th LCS after only one salvo, the *Vanguard* was on at least one occasion masked by the *Colossus*, and the *Thunderer* by the *Iron Duke*.

The first target engaged by the German capital ships in this phase was the 2nd LCS. The *Seydlitz* opened at 1903, followed by the *Markgraf* at 1905, the *Derfflinger*, *König* and *Grosser Kurfürst* at 1907, and the *Kaiser* and *Prinzregent Luitpold* at 1910. The 2nd LCS were under fire from one or more of the above ships for about 12 minutes, at ranges of 10–18,000yds, though the *Grosser Kurfürst* and *Markgraf* mainly fired 5.9in. The *Derfflinger* and *Prinzregent Luitpold* each fired three 12in salvos and the *Kaiser* two, while the *König* was firing for 3 minutes. The *Southampton* reported salvos falling all around her but, as earlier in the battle, the 2nd LCS escaped without loss. With visibility as it was to the eastward, the British battleships could not be engaged effectively, and only two hits were made on the *Colossus* at 1916 from the *Seydlitz* at about 8000yds. A total of four salvos fell close and caused some splinter damage forward in addition.

The *Agincourt* was straddled at 1917 and several shells fell near some other ships at about this time, but that was all. The *Derfflinger, Seydlitz* and *Moltke*, the *Lützow*, and some of the 3rd Squadron were firing, but not the other battleships. The *Kronprinz* attempted without success to range on the British gun-flashes, but neither she nor the *Kaiserin* opened fire, and the *Prinzregent Luitpold* only fired at the 2nd LCS. By about 1925 all the German ships had ceased, and the *Kaiser* which fired three salvos at the British battleships, reported firing her last salvo at 1925 at 17,500yds, the target bearing 29° abaft the starboard beam which indicates the 6th Division. The *Lützow* endeavoured to reply to the ships engaging her, but they were so difficult to make out that she was only able to fire occasionally and without effect.

The *Derfflinger* fired a torpedo at *c*1914 at 8700yds, but this cannot be identified.

Of the British battleships and battlecruisers, the *Erin* did not fire her main armament, and the *Conqueror, Vanguard, New Zealand* and *Inflexible* did not engage capital ships. The *Wiesbaden* still served as a target for some ships, and the *Colossus* opened on her at 1900 at 9700yds and fired three salvos, shifting at 1905 to the *G42* and firing 12in and 4in at only 4000yds. The *G42* which was then endeavouring to take the *V48* in tow or rescue her crew, and had previously been under fire from the *Collingwood*'s 4in, was not hit though heavily shaken so that she developed condenser leakages which gradually reduced her speed to 21kts or less on the following morning. The *Marlborough* fired four salvos at the *Wiesbaden* from 1903 at 9800–9500yds, and hit with the 3rd and 4th which seem to have finally wrecked the *Wiesbaden*, though she remained afloat for several hours. The *Agincourt* also fired briefly at her with 12in and perhaps 6in guns, and the *Revenge* with 6in only. In addition, the *Neptune* fired one 12in salvo, and the *Collingwood* also opened on the *Wiesbaden* with 12in HE, while the *St Vincent* took the *Wiesbaden* as her target at 1854.

Torpedoes, which were probably imaginary, but otherwise must have come from the *V48*, were sighted by two ships of the 6th Division. The *Agincourt* altered course at 1908 to avoid a torpedo which just missed astern, and the *Revenge* turned away at 1909 to avoid one that passed astern.

Apart from the firing described above, and that at the attacking destroyers, the British capital ships engaged the German battleships, the 1st SG and the *Lützow*. As in the previous phase, there was no systematic distribution of fire.

Of the British ships seven fired at the German battleships, 18 at the

1st Scouting Group and three at the *Lützow*. Taking the battleships first, the 5th Division were under a very heavy fire while turning and for a short time afterwards. The *Grosser Kurfürst* was hit seven times, the *König* and *Markgraf* each once, and the *Kronprinz* was violently shaken by several shells exploding near. The hit on the *König* and four of those on the *Grosser Kurfürst* were at 1918/19. Of the other battleships, the *Helgoland* was hit once at 1915; the *Kaiser* was hit at 1923 and again at 1926.

The *Agincourt* reported that four enemy battleships appeared out of the mist at 1906, and fire was opened on one of two which showed clearly against the mist at 11,000yds. With some interruptions the *Agincourt* continued firing until 1926 and claimed at least four straddling salvos and effective hits. It is probable that she scored once on the *Markgraf* at 1914, and the two hits on the *Kaiser* at 1923/26 were certainly due to her. TNT filled CPC was fired throughout.

Unfortunately the *Barham*'s range plot did not give definite times after 1832. At least three hits were claimed on a ship of the *Kaiser* class. The *Valiant* reported firing from 1910 to 1923 though her target is not indicated. One or perhaps both of them engaged the *Grosser Kurfürst*, which was hit by 4–15in shells, while the hit on the *Helgoland* at 1915 should probably be credited to the *Valiant*.

The *Marlborough* opened fire at 1912 on the left hand ship of three *König*s and fired fourteen salvos in 6 minutes at 10,200–10,750yds before her target turned to starboard and disappeared in the smoke. She was firing at the *Grosser Kurfürst*, and claimed hits with her sixth, twelfth, thirteenth and fourteenth salvos, though only three can be credited.

The *Iron Duke* opened at 1913 at 15,400yds on her former target, the *König*, but although very good ranges were obtained, the inclination was at first estimated incorrectly so that her shots fell far to the right, and at 1918, when four salvos of CPC had been fired, the *König* was lost to sight in smoke. One hit was obtained. The *Thunderer* expended three salvos of CPC from *c*1915 to 1918 at the leading battleship of two, visible between the *Iron Duke* and *Royal Oak*. The last salvo was fired over the *Iron Duke*, and the *Thunderer* was then masked by the flagship. At least four hits were claimed, but the *Thunderer* would have been well short at her range of 13,400–12,500yds.

Lastly, the *Canada* opened fire at 1920 at a ship seen very indistinctly on the starboard beam. Five salvos of APC were fired, of which the first, fourth and fifth were corrected 'Up 1000'. Gun range was not recorded, but the range-finder range increased from 10,000 to

12,800yds while firing. The *Canada* made no hits, and it is not known which ship she was engaging.

The 1st Scouting Group came under a heavier fire than the 3rd Squadron, and though the *Moltke* was not hit, and the *von der Tann* only once at 1919 by a 15in, the *Seydlitz* was hit four times in the next 6 minutes from 1914, and again by a 15in at 1927. This last put one gun of the port wing turret out of action, and one of the other hits holed the previously disabled superfiring turret and caused a further propellant fire. The *Derfflinger* suffered worst, and was struck by as many as 14 shells, of which 11 hit between 1914 and 1920 and the others shortly after. Of the total, seven were 15in. The two after turrets were each hit by 15in shells from the *Revenge* and put completely out of action with serious propellant fires, the sternmost at 1914 and the other at 1916 or 1917.

The first ship to open fire on the 1st SG was probably the *Ajax*, which reported firing one salvo of CPC at shortly after 1900 at 18,700yds. This fell short and a spotting correction of 'Up 1000' was given, but the 4th LCS then obscured the range. The *Neptune* was next, though it is believed that her reported time of about 1904 should be 1910 or 1911. She fired four salvos at the *Derfflinger* of which the first at 10,200yds was spotted as over, and claimed hits from the 3rd and 4th at 9800/10,000yds, though none can be credited to her.

The *Revenge* opened fire shortly after the *Neptune*, and also took the *Derfflinger* as her target. Her first salvo at 11,000yds was over, but she came down 800 and straddled with her second. The *Revenge* made five hits, and then shifted to the *von der Tann*, as other ships ahead were firing at the *Derfflinger*. She hit her new target at 1919 but had no further success. The *Revenge*'s least range was c8000yds and her final shots were fired at 9500. She expended sixteen salvos of APC in this period.

The *Hercules* reported opening fire on the *Seydlitz* at 1912, though it is believed that the time was just before this, and claimed hits with HE from her fifth and sixth salvos at about 9000yds. It is probable that she obtained two hits.

Two battleships reported opening fire at 1915, the *Royal Oak* and the *Colossus*. The former sighted three battlecruisers on the starboard beam, and engaged the *Derfflinger*. Visibility was much improved for a few moments, and at 1916 several hits were observed aft. The *Royal Oak*'s opening range was however 14,000yds, and she must have been going far over. Two unimportant hits were made on the *Derfflinger* shortly after 1920, but the target was then lost in the mist, and fire shifted to the *Seydlitz*, only a few rounds being fired before this ship was also lost to sight, though the 15in hit at 1927 must be credited to the *Royal Oak*. She expended far fewer shells than the *Revenge* and only fired about six salvos in this period. The *Colossus* fired five salvos of APC at the *Derfflinger* from 1915 to 1920, or perhaps a little earlier. The range was only 8/9000yds and a total of four hits was claimed from the 4th and 5th salvos, and it is believed that five were made.

The *Collingwood* opened fire on the *Derfflinger* at just after 1915. Hits were claimed from two salvos of HE fired at about 8000yds, but the target was lost in smoke before APC could arrive at the guns. It appears that one hit was obtained.

The *St Vincent* expended 98 rounds of 12in in the battle, of which only a few salvos were fired prior to 1854, and it is believed that she first fired at the *Wiesbaden*, and did not open on the 1st SG until about 1915. The *Seydlitz* was engaged before the *Moltke* and the former was hit by 2-12in APC shells at 9500-10,000yds. The *St Vincent*'s range plot showed that her firing was checked at approximate times of 1910 to 1912 and 1918 to 1920 before ceasing at 1926.

Five battleships reported opening fire at 1917, the target in each case being the *Derfflinger*. The *King George V* fired a salvo at 12,800yds which was spotted as short, and only expended a total of nine rounds of CPC. The *Benbow* began with a 2-gun salvo from her forward turrets, and then spotted down 1600yds and fired five salvos of APC (4–5 gun and 1–4 gun) before ceasing at 1924/25. A hit was incorrectly claimed at 1920 near the *Derfflinger*'s after turret at 12,200yds. The *Superb*, which got off seven salvos in 4½ minutes, opened at 11,000yds. The first salvo was spotted as short, but hits were claimed from the third and fourth fired with 12,200 on the Director sight, though it is unlikely that any were obtained. The *Bellerophon* also opened at 11,000yds, and reported straddling more than once. She obtained one hit, but the *Temeraire* which fired seven salvos of HE, reported a range of about 12,500yds and was going over initially.

Lastly the *Malaya* reported opening at 1920, and fired briefly at the *von der Tann* at a reported range of 10,400yds.

The 1st Scouting Group were also engaged by the British battlecruisers. The *Lion* opened fire at about 1914, and fired four salvos, at 16,100 to 18,000yds. The leading ship, presumably the *Derfflinger* was engaged but the target was soon lost in the smoke, and this also applies to the *Princess Royal* which reported firing for 3 minutes from 1914 at the same ship at 18,000yds. Neither scored a hit.

The *Tiger* reported engaging the 3rd ship from 1916 to 1920 at

19,750 to 20,200yds, the last figure being corrected, 'Down 2000'. These ranges were well over the 1st SG, and near the *Rostock*, which was between them and the 3rd Squadron and not far from the latter. Of the 12in battlecruisers only the *Indomitable* fired at this time, and her range of 13,800yds, indicates that her target may have been the *Regensburg*.

There were five hits on the *Lützow* in a few minutes from 1915.

The *Monarch* opened on the *Lützow* at 1914 and fired five salvos of APC before the target was lost in spray and smoke at about 1918. The first salvo was at 17,300yds and was corrected 'Up 1000', but the 4th and 5th were thought to have straddled at 18,450yds. The *Orion* opened at 1915 and fired six salvos of APC, ceasing at 1920 as the target became indistinct. The *Orion*'s report gives the range as 19,800yds, and says that the last two salvos were seen to straddle, while her track chart shows an opening range of 18,700yds increasing to 19,700 at 1920.

The *Centurion* also fired at the *Lützow* and opened at 1916, expending 19 rounds of APC. The first three salvos were short and the fourth said to be over, and the *Centurion* then had to cease as the *Orion* was in the line of fire, while one of the *Lützow*'s escorting destroyers, probably the *G40*, laid a smoke screen. The reported range of 17,500yds must refer to one of the short salvos, though according to the *Centurion*'s range plot, the initial gun range was *c*1000yds less.

The *Lützow*'s seven escorting destroyers all began to make smoke when the first salvos fell near and soon hid her completely from the British ships. The *G38* went ahead at full speed while making smoke, and came under heavy fire, one salvo straddling her with three shells *c*50yds short and two the same distance over. The *Orion*'s firing at 19,700/19,800yds was at the *G38*, and the five hits on the *Lützow*, from the *Monarch* and/or the *Orion*'s earlier salvos. The *G42* which joined the screening destroyers shortly afterwards also made smoke, and the *S33* proceeded to the southwards of the *Lützow* to mislead the British ships.

During this period only three torpedoes were fired at the German ships, two by the *Marlborough* and one by the *Revenge*. The *Marlborough* fired one at the *Wiesbaden* at 1910, and a hit was thought to have been seen, but as the torpedo was fired for a target making 15kts, it missed. Her second torpedo was fired at 1925 with 'Extreme Range' setting at the 5th battleship from the left in a column of eight, which was the *Kaiser*. It was not realised that the target was steering away, and this also missed. The *Revenge*'s torpedo was fired at about 1915 at a ship stated to be the *von der Tann*, and likewise failed to hit.

What was thought to be the first German destroyer attack, was the attempt to rescue the *Wiesbaden's* crew, ordered by Scheer at 1900, and made by the *S53, V71, V73* and *G88* of the 3rd Flotilla. They passed through the German line between the 5th and 6th Divisions, but abandoned the rescue attempt as the *Wiesbaden* was under heavy fire, and some of the British battleships opened on the destroyers, while it was thought that they might interfere with the fire of their own line. However, the *V73* fired one torpedo and the *G88* three, at *c*6500–8000yds at the second and third ships of the 1st BS. The torpedoes were probably fired at about 1910, and 7 minutes or so later, the tracks of three were sighted by the *Neptune*. She turned away and then towards them and they passed near the port quarter, one being very close.

The *Royal Oak* and *Benbow* opened fire with 6in at 1909, the latter at 8000yds, and the *Bellerophon* also fired at the destroyers from her fore turret and 4in guns, as did the *Colossus*. The *Iron Duke* joined in the firing with 6in at 1911 at 10,000–9000yds, the *Conqueror* with 13.5in at 1912, and the *Canada* with 6in shortly afterwards. The *Neptune* also reported firing on destroyers with 12in and 4in from 1910, but her gunnery times for this period are several minutes slow, and she was firing at the 6th and 9th Flotillas. The *Iron Duke* claimed to have sunk one destroyer and hit another, while the *Bellerophon* reported a possible 12in hit, but no hits were made, and it is possible that some of the above ships were firing at the *G42*, returning from her attempt to aid the *V48*.

The actual attack by part of the 6th and part of the 9th Flotilla, was begun on Commodore Heinrich's initiative at 1915, and it was not until 6 minutes later that Scheer gave the order. He had, in fact, just previously told Heinrich in a signal timed at 1916, that the 2nd, 6th and 9th Flotillas were to launch an attack during the night. None of the 12th Half-Flotilla took part, the *V69, V46* and *S50* being astern of the *Regensburg* and *V45* and *G37* with the *Lützow* as were the *V30, S34* and *S33* of the 18th Half-Flotilla. Thus only ten destroyers attacked and they had already expended 21 of their 60 torpedoes. Those taking part were as follows, the number of torpedoes available being given in brackets after each destroyer:

Leader 6th Flotilla: the *G41* (3), 11th Half-Flotilla, the *V44* (4), *G87* (4), the *G86* (5).

Leader 9th Flotilla: the *V28* (2), 17th Half-Flotilla, the *V26* (4), the *S36* (5), *S51* (3), *S52* (3). 18th Half-Flotilla, *S35* (Probably 6).

Although the 9th Flotilla were ordered to attack immediately before the 6th, the latter were the first to advance against the British line, as the *G41* led the other three destroyers on 100° at utmost speed under an increasing fire from 6in and also heavy guns. When the *G41* had closed to *c*7500yds she was hit by a 6in shell which burst on the forecastle, and turning to starboard fired two torpedoes (the 3rd had apparently been damaged). The *V44*, *G87* and *G86* followed, each firing three torpedoes at *c*8500-9000yds. The target conditions were favourable and the British line was clear and distinctly seen. The *G87* was then hit by a 6in shell which passed through the ship below the bridge without exploding, and a heavy shell burst very near the *G86* to starboard, the splinters causing damage forward, including one torpedo out of action and the forward oil bunker holed, so that one boiler was temporarily cut out. The *G41* and *G86* were reduced to 25kts, or less, but all four returned without further damage under cover of oil fuel smoke and artificial fog.

The eleven torpedoes from the 6th Flotilla were probably fired between 1922 and 1924, but the parts of the British line aimed at are not recorded.

The 9th Flotilla attacked to port of the 6th, and were at first hidden by their smoke, but then ran into a heavy fire from the secondary and main armaments of a number of ships. The *V28* was hit by a 6in shell on the water-line forward which made a large hole, and turned away to starboard at *c*7500yds, but only fired one torpedo, as the other misfired and remained in the tube. The order had been given for each destroyer to fire four torpedoes if available, which was amended by the 17th Half-Flotilla to all torpedoes, but this was not done. Thus the *V26* fired two torpedoes at *c*7000yds but the target was then hidden by smoke, and the *S52* was near the line of fire, the *S36* only fired one torpedo as the signal to fire four was not seen, and the *S51* also fired one at *c*7500yds. The *S52* fired three at this range, and the *S35* was thought to have fired two. The latter was hit amidships by a heavy salvo and broke in two and sank immediately with all her crew and the survivors of the *V29*. Splinters from heavy shells caused unimportant damage to the *S52*, and the *S51* was hit by a 6in shell which flooded the forward stokehold, put the forward steering engine out of action and reduced her speed to 21kts, but she returned safely, as did the *V28*, whose speed was limited to 17-19kts, and the rest of the 17th Half-Flotilla, under cover of smoke and fog.

Visibility conditions were not so good as for the 6th Flotilla, though the 9th approached closer. Their first torpedoes were probably fired at about 1926, and the *S51* reported firing at the centre of the British line and the *S52* at the van.

The first ship to open fire on the attackers with 6in was the *Royal*

Oak at about 1916, followed by the *Agincourt* at 1918 and then by the *Marlborough* and *Revenge*. The *Iron Duke* opened at 1924, and reported ranges between 7600 and 12,000yds during firing. The *Benbow* and *Canada* also joined in the action, while the *Tiger* reported opening at 1927 and the *Valiant* at 1928. The *Malaya* fired her two remaining starboard 6in, and the *Barham* probably fired briefly. The first four ships mentioned were initially firing at the 6th Flotilla, but it is not otherwise possible to give targets or to credit the 4–6in hits to particular ships. Nor is the quantity of 6in ammunition fired at the 6th and 9th Flotillas known, but it was considerable, as in the whole battle the *Agincourt* and *Canada* each fired over 100 rounds, the *Valiant*, *Revenge* and *Royal Oak* over 80, and the *Marlborough*, *Benbow* and *Iron Duke* 50 to 60. The uselessness of 4in batteries in daylight compared to 6in, is well illustrated, as only the *Temeraire* and *Neptune* fired more than a few rounds at this time, and neither expended more than 50 rounds in the whole battle.

The German destroyers were also engaged by the main armament of several ships. The *Vanguard* fired two salvos at 1920 at the 6th Flotilla, the range being 8300yds, and at 1925 shifted to the 9th Flotilla, and fired about three salvos. At 1930 she reported firing another three salvos or so at a disabled light cruiser, distant 9/10,000yds, which was presumably one of the damaged destroyers.

The *Neptune* and *Marlborough* each fired one salvo at about 1920, and at 1925 the *Conqueror* opened at 11,000yds from her after turrets. The *Barham* may have fired her 15in, the *Malaya* expended 2–15in salvos at 8000yds, and the *Bellerophon* also used her 12in. The *Iron Duke* fired one 5-gun salvo at 9600yds at 1927, and 3 minutes later the *Canada* opened, firing three salvos, while the *Temeraire* also expended three salvos, and the *Hercules* fired a few salvos of 12in at only 6000yds according to her account. The *Collingwood* fired her 12in for a few minutes at a damaged destroyer on her quarter, and from about 1925 the 12in battlecruisers also opened, the *New Zealand* firing two salvos, the *Indomitable* about six and the *Inflexible* two. The only precise range given for these last three ships is 8200yds by the *Indomitable*, and the *New Zealand*'s figure of 17,800 is clearly in error.

It is estimated that about 150 rounds of 12in to 15in were fired at the 6th and 9th Flotillas, and counting the 'near-miss' on the *G86*, three hits made. It is thought that the *S35* was sunk by two shells of the *Iron Duke*'s salvo, but it is impossible to credit the 'near-miss' to a particular ship. The German Official History says of the British main and secondary armament firing at the destroyers, that some salvos fell right among them, but the shooting was hampered by smoke and alterations of course, and was not very effective.

A counter-attack on the German destroyers was made by the 4th LCS on Jellicoe's orders at 1922, and the *Castor* and some of the 11th Flotilla also took part. Jellicoe warned the 4th LCS not to get in the way of the battlecruisers' firing, and not to go too near the German battlefleet, and they broke off at 1936, though the *Castor* did not turn back for another 10 minutes or so. The 4th LCS only expended a total of 22-6in and 108-4in in the whole battle, and no damage was caused to the German destroyers. It is impossible to assign the various torpedoes reported by British ships, as a result of the 6th and 9th Flotillas' attack, to individual destroyers or even to one or other of the two flotillas, and it is also uncertain how many of those reported were imaginary. Most of the torpedoes were aimed at the rear of the British line and reached the 1st BS, and some the 5th BS, while those aimed at the leading divisions were only sighted by the 4th LCS. The torpedo reported by the *Inflexible* passing 150yds astern at 1925 or 1945, and that reported by the *Oak* passing about 200yds ahead of the *Iron Duke* at *c*1935, are believed to have been imaginary.

No fewer than nine torpedoes were reported by the 4th LCS, but it is very doubtful if there were actually as many. The *Calliope*, then making 27½kts, reported sighting four which were all running well and leaving tracks resembling those of non-heater torpedoes. One track was seen 100yds off and passed 5yds or less ahead; a second seen 150yds away, passed 5-15yds astern, and two others sighted well ahead, passed 100-150 and 400 -500yds ahead.

The *Caroline* reported two torpedoes close at 1934/35. One passed down the port side, and the other which was only avoided with difficulty, came down the starboard side, surfacing at the end of its run when abeam, and passing close to the stern. At about this time the *Comus* also reported a torpedo passing ahead, and another close astern, while the *Constance* signalled at 1939 that a torpedo was passing from starboard to port.

It is thought that the tracks reported by the *Comus* and *Constance* may have been the same as some of those seen by the *Calliope* and *Caroline*, but it is impossible to say if all the six torpedoes noted by the two latter ships were real.

Eleven torpedoes, most, if not all of which are thought to have been real, were avoided by the 1st BS between about 1933 and 1937. Some were highly dangerous, and but for the sharp look-out kept, skilful use of the helm and a measure of good luck, might have scored several hits.

The *Colossus* turned to port at 1935 to avoid a torpedo reported as running slowly and erratically, and signalled its approach. The *Collingwood* immediately afterwards sighted another coming straight at the ship. She was probably already under helm, and a large amount of helm was then put on, and the track passed 10yds astern as the *Collingwood* turned away. At the same time a second track which was probably that sighted by the *Colossus*, and which was running level with the first, about 200yds apart, passed 30yds ahead.

The *Marlborough* sighted two torpedoes on the starboard bow at 1933. She turned to port, and then back to starboard, and one track passed ahead, and the other close under her stern. A third torpedo sighted on the starboard beam could not be avoided, but was running too deep and the track passed under 'Y' turret.

The *Revenge* turned to port at about 1935 to avoid two torpedoes which were near the end of their run. One broke surface 25/30yds on the starboard beam after she had altered course, and the other passed 30yds astern at about the same time.

The *Hercules* sighted a torpedo 800yds on the starboard quarter after turning to port. She continued turning away and the track passed 40yds ahead, but the track of a second torpedo seen 700yds off 10° abaft the starboard beam, was lost to sight when avoiding the first torpedo, and though the turn to port was checked to prevent the stern swinging into this torpedo, it was believed to have passed very close. This second torpedo was probably identical with one avoided by the *Agincourt*, the track passing 100yds ahead of her. At the same time another torpedo track passed 50yds ahead, and the *Agincourt* then avoided a third torpedo which was running slowly and just missed her stern. At least four torpedoes were reported to have passed through the line of the 5th BS close to the *Barham*, and were avoided by a turn away of about 65–70° at *c*1937, but further details are lacking.

The next attack was begun by the 3rd Flotilla at 1923. The *S53, V71, V73* and *G88* took part while the *S54*, which had not been able to rejoin after sinking the *Shark*, followed *c*700yds astern, and the *S32* also joined the attack. The 3rd Flotilla broke through between the 2nd and 3rd ships of the 5th Division, and made for the northern end of the other destroyers' smoke screen. On clearing this, no large ships were seen, and the flotilla turned southwards towards what were thought to be five or six destroyers chasing a damaged boat of the 6th or 9th Flotilla. These destroyers which belonged to the British 12th Flotilla, had already opened fire, and a brief action took place at *c*6500yds. The *G88* fired a torpedo at this range at the second vessel from the right, though she was not made out distinctly, but the *S32* obtained a clear glimpse of the British line shortly after the *S53* turned southward, and fired one torpedo at *c*10,000yds.

The *S54* alone kept on to the eastward, and also sighted the British battleships, firing one torpedo at about 10,000yds. She sighted the *Wiesbaden* a long way off on the port beam, and the *V71* had previously seen the latter about 4 miles away. A final attempt by the 3rd Flotilla to reach the *Wiesbaden* on their return, failed as they lost sight of her. The *Revenge* reported altering course to port at 1943 to avoid two torpedoes which passed astern, and the *Moresby* noted one ahead and one astern at 1948. The *St Vincent* also reported that a torpedo passed between herself and the *Neptune* at a time given as 2000 to 2010, but it is thought that all these were imaginary, though it is possible that one of the first four may have been from the *S32*, and the last from the *S54*.

The 2nd Flotilla's attack was cancelled in course of preparation, and the 7th Flotilla remained near the 2nd Squadron so that some destroyers were at the head of the German line after the 'about-turn'. The 5th Flotilla began an attack at 1938 and proceeded on *c*100° but they did not get clear of the increasing smoke and fog until 1950, saw no battleships, and turned back under fire from destroyers of the British 12th Flotilla, to which an ineffective reply was made.

Meanwhile the *Faulknor*, leader of the latter flotilla, had opened fire on the disabled *V48*, which was also under fire from some of the 2nd LCS, and from the *Valiant*'s 6in which shifted to this target at 1935. A division of the 12th Flotilla – the *Obedient, Mindful, Marvel, Onslaught* – then attacked and sank the *V48* by gunfire. Three survivors were apparently picked up by a Swedish steamer 8 hours later.

The passage of the German torpedoes through the British line did not affect the movements of the four leading divisions although the approach of the German destroyers had resulted in an irregular formation of the fleet at 1930. At 1935 Jellicoe signalled for the Divisions to alter course to 178°, and then ordered the battlefleet to form single line ahead. At 1940 Jellicoe informed the 2nd BS that his course was 212°, and 2 minutes later signalled the 3rd and 4th Divisions to form single line ahead on this course.

As a result of these orders the 1st Division turned to starboard until at 1942 they were steering 235° and had increased to 18/19kts. The 2nd Division were steering 241° at 1945 and the 3rd Division came back into single line ahead, and at 1942 turned to 212°, while the 4th Division conformed to these movements.

The 1st BS were in the middle of avoiding torpedoes by large turns to port at 1935, and it was not until 1940 that the 5th Division were steering 190° and increased to 20kts. The 6th Division steadied on course 178° at about this time, but turned sharply to port again at about 1942 to avoid supposed torpedoes, and an imaginary submarine, returning to near their previous course at 1945.

The 5th BS generally bore a little aft of the 6th Division's port beam. They were steering 128° at 1930, and then turned to 139°, reducing to 18kts at 1935. A turn of about 65–70° was made to port to avoid torpedoes, and after this the 5th BS were steering 190° turning to 152° at 1944.

The battlecruisers continued on 212° at 24kts until 1940, and then on 209° at 18kts. By 1945 the *Lion* was nearly 6 miles 223° from the *King George V*, and the *Lützow*, the nearest German capital ship, was about 10½ miles away to the north-westward of the *Lion*. In a signal timed 15 minutes earlier, Beatty had reported the enemy as bearing 291°, distant 10 to 11 miles. This indicated the bearing of the 1st SG accurately, but the distance was about 2 miles too great. The *König* was actually 11 miles from the *Lion* but was hidden from view by the 1st SG. The *Lion*'s own position was given incorrectly, but her location relative to the *Iron Duke* was approximately known. Apart from this, no reports of the Germans were made until 1945.

As usual imaginary submarines were sighted. The *Calliope* signalled the presence of one to the 4th LCS at 1939, and the *Inflexible* reported a submarine a minute later. Others were thought to have been seen by the *Centurion* and *Agincourt*.

The *Westfalen* continued to lead the 1st Squadron and the *Friedrich der Grosse* on 212° until *c*1950 when Scheer signalled course 167°. The 3rd Squadron at first steered westward, but by 1940 the *Prinzregent Luitpold* was heading 212°, with the others beginning to form in a line of bearing approximately 21°. The 1st Scouting Group continued in line of bearing and steered 246° until 1935 when course was altered to 257°. Both the 1st SG and the 3rd Squadron were directed by Scheer to close in from the eastward.

The *Lützow* also altered course to 257° at just after 1930 and seems to have reduced speed. At 1945 she was about a mile and a half to the southward of the *Derfflinger*, while the 2nd Squadron was on the 2nd Division's starboard bow and beam.

Important information concerning the British fleet had now reached Scheer. At 1932 a searchlight signal from the *V30* was taken in by the *Regensburg* as stating that large enemy vessels were in *c*122°, though the *V30*'s war diary states more correctly that they were sighted in *c*32° on course *c*122°, and it was not until the signal had been passed to him by the *Regensburg*, that Scheer was certain the whole of the Grand Fleet was present. A signal from the *Frankfurt* received in the *Friedrich der Grosse* at 1942 but timed 20 minutes earlier, and also passed visually to the *Posen*, reported that the *Lützow* was under fire from strong hostile forces, bearing 32°, and a signal from the *V28* to the *Regensburg*, for passing to Scheer and Hipper, timed at 1940 and received at 1948, reported more than 20 large enemy vessels.

There was very little firing at either side's capital ships in the last 15 minutes of this phase. The *Lützow* fired her last shots at 1945, and the *Royal Oak* reported that shells were seen falling fairly close to the *Benbow* at this time, though the German battle charts show the *Lützow* as 13 miles away.

CHAPTER 11

Damage to capital ships 1900–1945

T HE *COLOSSUS* WAS the only British ship hit during this phase of the battle. Of the two shells from the 1st SG which struck at 1916, one hit the sounding machine platform on the port signal deck and passed overboard, but the other which entered the foremost superstructure on the starboard side, just abaft the fore-funnel, did some damage. This shell burst on the port side of the lower gun deck, about 24ft from impact, but the explosion was very local in effect.

Four – 'R' cases each containing 6–4in charges, were ignited by splinters, but the lids, which were intended to vent easily, blew off gently at very low gas pressures, and there was no sign of any cordite explosion. The fire was extinguished in a few minutes and did not ignite any cases stowed near, the minimum distance between cases being 8ft.

Fragments struck 4–4in HE shells, two of which were cut in half, the lyddite in one smouldering. A fifth 4in fell undamaged into the stokehold fan-flat. Slight damage was caused to one port 4in gun, the range-finder of 'P' turret and in 'A' boiler-room, the downtake being just under the burst.

Both shells were from the same salvo, and are credited to the *Seydlitz*.

The only serious breakdown was apparently in the *Lion* at about 1930 or possibly earlier, when the right main cage of 'X' turret was put out of action by a projectile falling back on top of the cage in a mistaken attempt to double-load the waiting position. The damage was cleared but the cage could only be used for shells, charges being passed by auxiliary hoist.

Of the German ships, the *Lützow* was hit five times between 1915 and 1918 by the *Monarch* and/or the *Orion* at *c*18,500yds. Of these hits

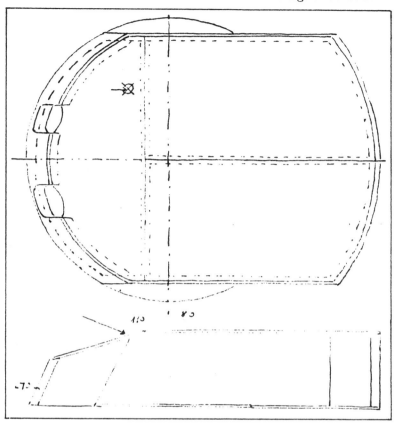

Derfflinger: *hit at 1914.*

two were from the port side and three from starboard. One shell coming from the port side struck the right gun of 'A' turret just outside the gun port. The whole of the upper part of the jacket outside the turret was torn away but the shell was deflected by the $10\frac{3}{4}$in turret face armour and the gun port shield, and only small splinters entered the turret destroying the right sight and wounding two men. The elevating gear was not affected, but the gun was completely disabled.

The other shell coming from the port side apparently entered through the battery roof deck just abaft the third barbette and burst on or below the 1in upper deck, causing heavy casualties in the after dressing station, and cutting power cables for the sternmost turret which were here led above the armour deck. The sternmost turret was thus reduced to hand-working which meant that it was virtually out of action, but power was restored before the *Lützow* sank. The 1.2in armour deck was apparently torn up by this shell but without damage to the ammunition spaces below.

After these two hits the *Lützow* turned to starboard and the three remaining hits were from this side. One shell struck the starboard side armour somewhere below 'B' barbette, and as a result No 1 starboard 5.9in magazine filled and had to be abandoned, while it appears that other flooding also occurred as a direct or indirect result of this hit.

Another shell struck low down on the after part of the 8¾in right side wall of 'B' turret and made a hole of $c2\frac{1}{2}$sq ft in area though no shell splinters entered the turret. Fragments of armour, however, were driven in, and part of the armour plate was found on the right cartridge loading tray. The right upper hoists and the loading gear and elevating pump belonging to the right gun were wrecked so that this gun was put out of action. A 12in fore charge (76lb) laying in the right upper cartridge hoist, which was in the upper position, caught fire, but the main charge (201lb) immediately above it did not, as it was protected by flash-doors which had been fitted to the *Lützow*, and flash-doors also prevented flames reaching the working chamber.

The officer of the turret was killed by propellant gas, which also penetrated to the transmitting station through voice-pipes, and those of the crew who were standing behind the right gun were killed, but some of this gun's crew managed to escape. The whole turret was temporarily out of action, and filled with smoke, but the left gun was in use again after about ½ hour, with sea-water in the elevating pump as the glycerine had leaked away through damaged pipes. In the *Lützow* the turrets had a 1in longitudinal splinter bulkhead, which would protect the left side of the turret in this instance.

The third shell from starboard struck the 6in casemate armour of No 4 starboard 5.9in and apparently burst, but the gun was not put out of action, though the armour was bulged in to some extent, and dark coloured smoke penetrated to the 5.9in transmitting station via the voice pipe which had to be plugged.

The *Derfflinger* was hit by fourteen shells in this phase. The first hit at 1914 was one of five by 15in APC shells from the *Revenge*. This struck the roof of the aftermost turret 3ft to the right of the right gun axis, and close below the join between the 4.3in sloping and 3.15in horizontal roof plates. The sloping plate inclined at $c15°$ to the horizontal, was heavily depressed and scooped where struck for a

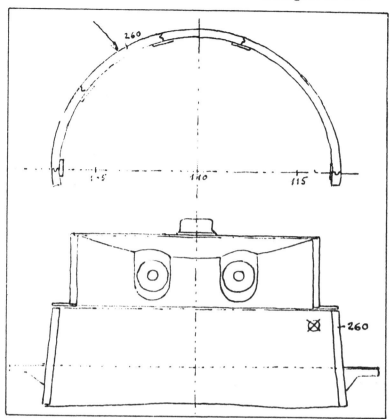

Derfflinger: *hit at 1916/17.*

length of 55in with two long cracks, and most of the calibre size hole was in this plate, though the edge of the flat roof was also broken away, for 18in × 26½in. The turret, trained about 37° abaft the port beam, was jerked round to the limit of its port bow training by the impact. The shell burst on the right cartridge hoist about 4ft from impact, and ignited one main and one fore charge on the right cartridge loading tray, and also one main and one fore charge in the cage of the right upper cartridge hoist which was down in the working chamber. The flash spread to the magazine handing room immediately below the working chamber, and ignited one main and one fore charge in the loading tray of each of the two lower cartridge hoists, as well as three main charges being transported to the hoists, and nine fore charges which were still in opened magazine cases. A total of seven main and thirteen fore charges were thus ignited, but in the gun-house which had a splinter bulkhead as in the *Lützow*, two main and two fore charges at the left gun were not burnt, though the outer coat of the double silk bags of the fore charges was singed. In the magazine handing room two fore charges in an opened case were also unburnt though similarly singed. No charges in unopened magazine cases were burnt.

The flames and gas killed all the turret crew of 75, except two who escaped through one of the holes for throwing out used cartridge cases, but one of them later died. Large amounts of gas spread through voice pipes to the starboard transmitting station which had to be abandoned for 8 minutes, and gas also affected some of the steering compartments. The magazines and shell rooms were flooded, though if the *Derfflinger*'s damage control record is correct, this was not done until some time after those of the after superfiring turret, hit 2 or 3 minutes later, had been flooded.

The explosive effect of the shell was considered to be relatively small. In the gun-house, the right cartridge hoist shaft was destroyed, as was the range-finder, while all fittings belonging to the right gun were badly damaged by splinters, but the right gun itself received only trifling damage, as did the left gun, and the 1in splinter bulkhead was not pierced nor was the armouring of the rear of the turret damaged. In the working chamber and handing room all hoists, except the left upper cartridge hoist, were much distorted and torn, but apart from splinter damage all cables and electrical equipment appeared to be usable. The wood of the magazines was slightly scorched.

The next hit from the *Revenge* was at 1916 or 1917. This shell coming from 41° abaft the port beam, struck the after superfiring barbette 18in below the upper edge of the fixed armour, and on a line between the two guns, but nearer to the right gun, the position of impact, measured radially from the barbette centre, being 33° aft of the transverse diameter. It pierced the 10¼in armour and burst in the upper part of the turn-table between the two guns and below the Captain of turret's platform. One main and one fore charge on the right cartridge loading tray were ignited, and also one main and one fore charge in the cages of both upper cartridge hoists, which were down in the working chamber, as well as one main and one fore charge on both the right and left transfer conveyors in the working chamber. The flash spread to the magazine handing room, which in this turret was below the switch room and the shell handing room, and ignited one main and one fore

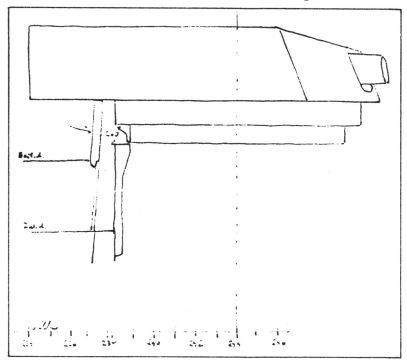

Derfflinger: *No 1 of six hits prior to 1920.*

charge in the cages of both lower hoists which were down. In all, seven main and seven fore charges were ignited, but in the gun-house which had a longitudinal splinter bulkhead, one main and one fore charge at the left gun remained unburnt, as did two main charges which were out of their magazine cases in the handing room, and two fore charges in an opened case.

Of the turret crew six men managed to escape through the left entrance port or through the left hole for used cartridge cases. Gas affected all four main engine rooms, both turbo-dynamo rooms and a number of other compartments, but gas-masks enabled the crews to continue working, except that some compartments on the main deck had to be evacuated for a few minutes, and on this deck flash caused a fire to port. The magazines and shell rooms were flooded, and about an hour later, leaking water caused a switchboard short-circuit that put one turbo-dynamo out for some time.

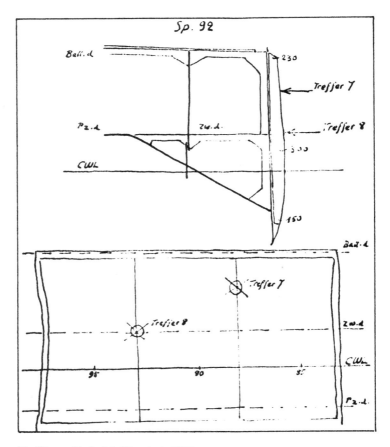

Derfflinger: *No 3 of six hits prior to 1920.*

This was the only occasion in the battle when a British shell actually pierced heavy armour and burst inside. The hole had an external diameter of 17–18in, with cracks extending to a similar distance from the circumference, and pieces of plate broken away up to 13½in from the edge of the hole, the hard surface being much cracked or spalled. The armour plate was not displaced, and its fastenings only slightly slackened. In the turret the side plates of the cradle carriers were perforated by the shell bursting between them, the training gear pinions and the cartridge slide and cartridge waiting tray for the right gun were destroyed, and all fittings received numerous damage from splinters. In the working chamber both cartridge hoists and transfer conveyors were largely destroyed, and cables and electrical equipment much damaged,

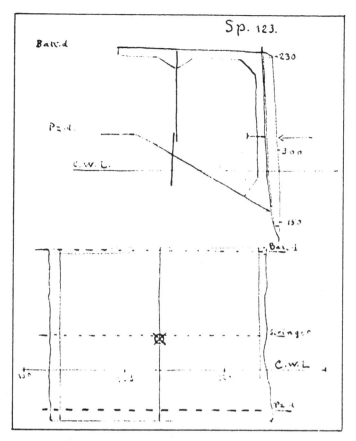

Derfflinger: *No 4 of six hits prior to 1920.*

while in the handing room the hoists were badly distorted and torn, and wood slightly scorched.

It will be noted that in both turrets there were too many charges in transit between magazine and gun.

Two more shells from the *Revenge* hit aft. One apparently burst or broke up before going through the hull plating close under the quarter deck and 48ft from the stern. The port longitudinal bulkhead was holed, and some cabins damaged while the shell cap was found in the Captain's sideboard amidships. The other shell struck the hull plating 10ft further forward immediately below the quarter deck, and burst just inboard. It caused great damage tearing holes over 16ft diameter in the main and quarter decks, and partly destroying the port side longitudinal bulkhead. The shell base pierced three longitudinal bulkheads, a transverse bulkhead (these four of up to 0.4in), about ten light cabin bulkheads and the ⅝in starboard skin plating, and finally struck the inside of the 4in starboard side armour, 44ft forward of where the shell hit, and just above the main deck. The armour plate was forced 1½in outwards, and bulged 1in with long cracks in the hard surface.

The remaining hit from the *Revenge* passed through the upper part of the fore funnel without exploding.

Of the other six hits prior to 1920, five are believed to have been by 12in APC from the *Colossus*, and one by a 12in HE from the *Collingwood*. All came from a direction approximately on the *Derfflinger*'s port beam, and hit between 1916 and 1920, and probably within a shorter interval. In order from forward to aft, the hits by the *Colossus* were:

1 Grazed the after part of 'A' barbette (10¼in armour), just beyond the longitudinal centre line and 3ft above the upper deck. The plate was scarred to a depth of less than ½in, and the shell deflected on to the 1in upper deck, 13ft away to starboard, and then overboard. The upper deck was only bulged in by up to 4½in for 8ft × 5ft, but a violent blow was felt in 'A' turret when the barbette was hit, and some of the crew were thrown off their feet. A heavy shock was also experienced far below 'A' turret on the hold deck, which put the starboard Diesel dynamo out of action for 4 minutes, and very briefly interrupted the power supply to 'A' turret training motor, enabling the time of the hit to be fixed at 1918. The port Diesel dynamo was apparently already out of action as a result of the ship being heavily shaken, but the time of this is not clear, and it may possibly have also occurred as a result of this hit.

2 Struck No 3 – port 5.9in (loaded), and burst on the port shield, completely wrecking the gun, which was cut off *c*7½ft short and bent upwards. The 3in port shield, which was hit just to the right of the gun, was displaced and badly cracked but not pierced. A plate of the 6in casemate armour was cracked to a depth of 1¼in, the armour fastenings torn or slackened in the embrasure to the right of the gun, and the inside of the casemate and the battle signal position damaged. The torpedo-net was also damaged, as were the upper deck and battery roof deck by splinters, and a splinter holed the shield of the 3.5in AA gun above. As with some other lyddite filled shells, a thin yellowish gas-cloud was produced by the burst.

Nos 1, 2 and 4 – port 5.9in were also apparently out of action at about this time, but it is not clear exactly how this occurred. No 4 gun was damaged by splinters from this hit, and the muzzle blown out by a premature, but Nos 1 and 2 were not disabled permanently, and a photograph shows no apparent damage to the barrels outboard of the ship, apart from what may be splinter marks on No 1, which may have come from the underwater hit at 1825.

3 Struck the 12in side armour 3¼ft above the legend, and probably just below the actual water-line, on a vertical joint between two plates under No 6–5.9in. The shell

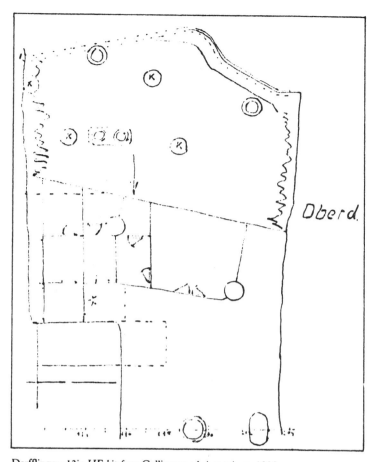

Derfflinger: *12in HE hit from* Collingwood, *just prior to 1920.*

broke up or possibly burst, but the armour was holed, though the plates were apparently not displaced. The 'D' shaped hole, measuring 45in × 18in, was entirely in the after plate, which had otherwise only a few slight cracks, while the surface of the forward plate was spalled with extensive concentric cracks to 4¾in deep. The torpedo net fittings were destroyed for a length of 16ft, and an armour fragment damaged the joint between the longitudinal splinter bulkhead and the armour deck slope, 10ft inboard of the hit. Water entered an outer bunker through the hole in the side, and the hull plating was buckled by 1½in below the armour so that some water leaked into the wing compartments for a length of 20ft.

4 This shell hit and broke up on a vertical joint between two plates of the side armour, where 10½in thick, about 4ft below the upper deck and c4ft aft of the half-way point between the two after barbettes. The plate on the forward side of the

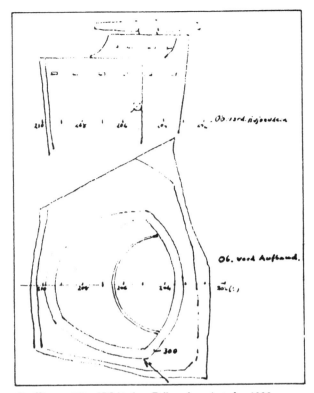

Derfflinger: 12in APC hit from Bellerophon, *just after 1920.*

Opposite. Seydlitz: *second hit from* Hercules *c1914-1920.*

joint had already been hit at about 1830 on its other vertical joint (the *Derfflinger*'s side armour plates here ran without horizontal joints from the belt lower edge to the upper deck) and was now holed for 16in × 24in (internal dimensions), with a piece 11in × 10in hurled into the ship, and concentric cracks 2in to 4¾in deep. The plate was forced in 2in where hit and 1¼in at the upper edge. A piece 11in × 6in was also broken off the plate on the after side of the joint.

The 11in × 10in piece of armour hurled into the ship made a large hole in the 1.2in longitudinal splinter bulkhead, 9ft inboard the hit, passed through the workshop and fell down the ventilation shaft of the port after engine room on to the armour deck, after travelling a total distance of 30ft and piercing 2¼in of plating.

5 Went through a skylight amidships on the quarter deck, about 80ft from the stern, and after ploughing a narrow furrow across the deck, burst on its starboard side

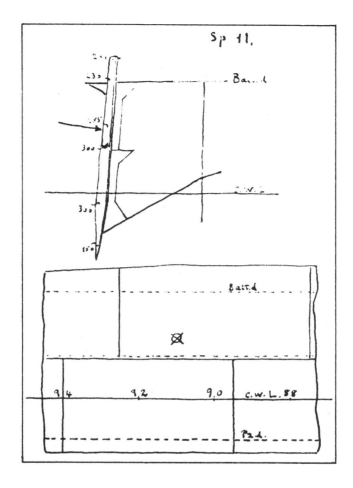

tearing a hole of *c*10ft diameter. The main deck was driven down 16in and holed by splinters, and other splinters pierced the side longitudinal bulkhead which was bulged 8in inwards. Considerable damage was caused to cabins on the main deck by this hit.

The 12in HE from the *Collingwood* hit the superstructure side above the battery roof deck, in line with the bridge. It burst in the sick-bay, blowing a hole *c*18ft × 7½ft in the superstructure side, while inboard of the port casemates, the 1in battery roof deck was holed for *c*5ft× 2¼ft, and bulged to a maximum of 6in for a length of 30ft and from the longitudinal casemate bulkhead to the side of the funnel. The 5/16in

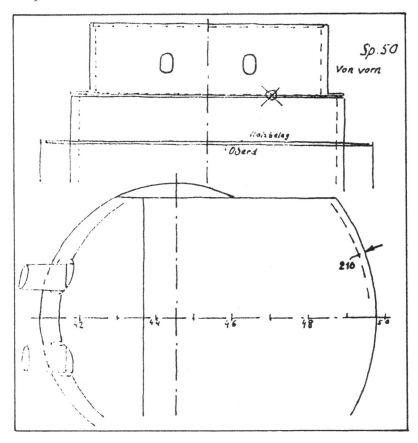

upper deck was slightly bowed below the hole in the battery roof deck and had a *c*14in diameter hole from a fragment. Above the shell burst, a hole *c*15ft × 12ft was blown in the superstructure deck, which was also holed by numerous splinters, and damaged for a length of *c*50ft and across to the starboard side of the deck. The upper superstructure deck was also holed for *c*8ft × 8ft and slightly bowed for 20ft, while among other damage, splinters and fragments cut the cables for the night recognition signals and other signalling lights, damaged three searchlights, and tore out a section of the armour grating in the fore funnel. Some damage was also caused to No 1 port and starboard 3.5in gun positions, though the guns were not put out of action.

Of the three hits shortly after 1920, two were by 15in shells from

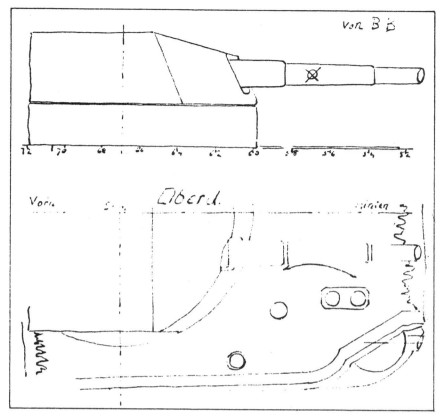

Opposite. Seydlitz: *second hit from* St Vincent c*1914–1920*.

Seydlitz: *hit at 1927.*

the *Royal Oak*. One passed through the after funnel at the level of the searchlights, and the other through the under structure of the same funnel at the height of the boat-deck, in both cases without exploding.

The third hit was by a 12in APC from the *Bellerophon*, which struck the conning tower obliquely, coming from abaft the beam. The hit was on the port side of the CT 8in forward of the vertical joint between the curved side and rear plates, and about 1½ft above the upper superstructure deck. The shell broke up, or perhaps burst, and the 12in armour was not holed, pieces up to 2in thick being broken out of the hard surface, and the armour joint somewhat slackened. The upper superstructure deck was holed for about 6ft × 3ft below the hit, and the lower superstructure deck for 20in × 8in. The CT vibrated severely,

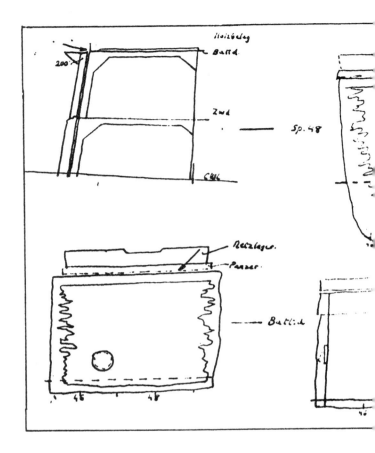

Köni*g: hit at 1918.*

but neither the fire-control nor the conning of the ship were interfered with, though gas entered the CT and GCT through sighting slits, and a splinter destroyed the range-finder in 'B' turret.

In addition to the damage from the above hits, it appears that the Director-pointer gear in 'B' turret failed during this period, so that only 'A' turret remained at full efficiency.

The *Seydlitz* was hit by 4 – 12in shells between 1914 and 1920, and by a 15in at 1927. Of the 12in shells, two were HE from the *Hercules* and two APC from the *St Vincent*. One shell from the *Hercules* went through the after upper searchlight platform and the starboard upper edge of the adjoining centre-line ventilation trunk, and then overboard. The starboard upper searchlight was wrecked, and twelve small shell

232

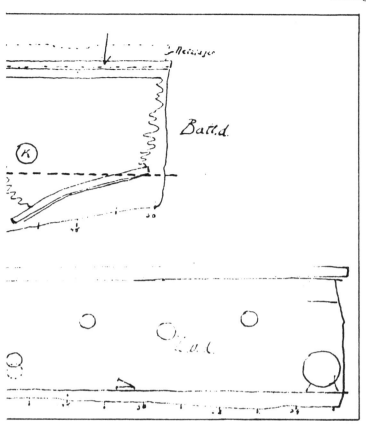

splinters were found in the main-top, which indicate that the shell burst near the ship.

The other shell from the *Hercules*, burst on a net boom close to the upper belt, and just abaft No 3 port – 5.9in. The hit was 5ft below the battery deck, and the upper belt armour, here 11¼in, was undamaged, but the torpedo net fittings were destroyed over a large area, and the hull plating below water was bulged in for a length of 30ft and for a maximum depth of 11½ft below the belt lower edge. Frames were bent and the port wing compartments flooded for a distance of 40ft.

The first hit from the *St Vincent* was probably a ricochet, and pierced the hull plating and upper deck at the waterway abreast of the bridge, exploding on entry. The 1in battery deck was badly bulged under the point of explosion and holed by splinters. The sick-bay was wrecked, but the port longitudinal bulkhead was only bulged in a few places. A few splinters entered the CT through the slits and wounded one man. This hit later allowed water to spread to the port forward outer bunker for a length of 63ft, and thence gradually to the protective bunker below and to the stokers' bathroom.

The second hit from the *St Vincent* came from about 30° abaft the port beam and struck the 8¼in rear armour of the previously disabled superfiring turret which was still trained 5° forward of the starboard beam. The hit was on the lower edge of the rear armour, 7ft to the right of the turret centre-line, the angle of impact being within 15° of the normal to the plate. The shell burst in penetrating, most of the explosive effect being inside the turret, and the hole in the armour measured 20in × 16in with many concentric cracks, while the 2in turret floor plate was bent outwards at the edge. A large piece of armour flew into the turret, and armour and shell fragments wrecked or damaged the range-finder, the shell and cartridge loading trays, both upper shell hoists, both hand rammers and the right cartridge slide, as well as igniting two main and two fore charges still laying in the cartridge loading trays. Shells in the ready position racks were thrown about but not smashed. Mats and other gear in the turret continued burning, but the fire was put out during a pause in the action. Splinters, deflected down outside the turret, wrecked a ventilation trunk, and holed the 1in battery deck, cutting the main and exciter cables for the main training gear of the sternmost turret, which were led round the superfiring turret just below the battery deck. The sternmost turret had no hand training gear, but it appears that the auxiliary training motor remained in operation.

The 15in hit from the *Royal Oak* at 1927 struck the right gun of the port wing turret, on the right side, about 7ft from the turret face. The gun was badly dented and flattened, and thrown violently to one side with damage to the cradle and distortion of the cradle carrier. It was completely out of action, and the turret training gear was temporarily disabled due to a fuze in the exciter circuit burning out.

The left gun was undamaged but the Director-pointer gear was put out of action and the turret could no longer fire with the others. The shell which came from the port quarter, burst about 8ft above the upper deck, and splinters damaged the port casemate range-finder, and entered the aftermost 5.9in casemate through the 1.4in upper deck. Splinters also indented the muzzle of No 5 – port 5.9in and this gun was out of action, though not permanently disabled.

The *von der Tann* was hit once at 1919 by a 15in shell from the

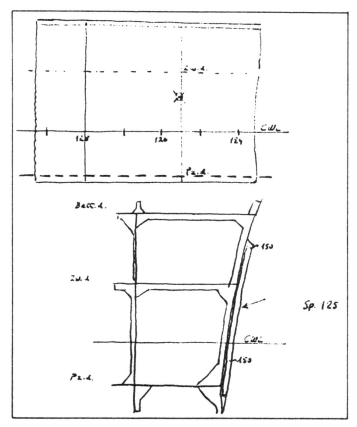

Grosser Kurfürst: *hit No 2.*

Revenge. This struck and burst on the ventilation shaft abaft the after CT, just to starboard of the centre line and $8\frac{1}{2}$ft above the upper deck, a little below the lower edge of the CT. The ventilation shaft and nearby superstructure were destroyed, the CT support, which held firm, was holed by numerous splinters and bulged in, and the upper deck and 1in main deck pierced in several places. Splinters drove through the sighting slits into the after CT, killing four and wounding all the others inside, but the 8in armour was only scarred by splinters and damaged over an area of 18in × 8in to a depth of $1\frac{1}{4}$in. The effect of the explosion spread along the upper and main decks, and through ventilation trunks to the starboard engine room, where splinters and debris came to rest on the condenser, though some were stopped by the armour gratings, and there was also danger from smoke and gas in the engine-room.

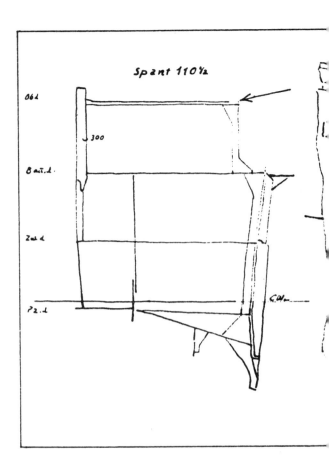

Grosser Kurfürst: *hit No 3.*

The *König* was hit once at 1918 by a 13.5in shell from the *Iron Duke*. This came from about 45° on the *König*'s port bow and struck below No 7 – 5.9in, passing through the rolled-up torpedo-nets, the chamfer at the upper edge of the side armour and the upper deck, before bursting in the POs mess, short of the longitudinal splinter bulkhead. The shell made a dent 18in wide and 4¾in deep in the chamfer of the 8in side armour, and the upper deck (1.2in and 1in joint plate) was holed for 6½ft × 2¼ft and bulged 6in upwards. The 1.2in longitudinal splinter bulkhead, *c*13ft inboard from the ship's side, was bowed by up to 4¾in but not pierced, while the main deck was driven downwards for a considerable length to a maximum of 28in, and torn away at the longitudinal splinter bulkhead, and partly at the deck stringer plate. Much damage was caused to light structures on the main deck, and

236

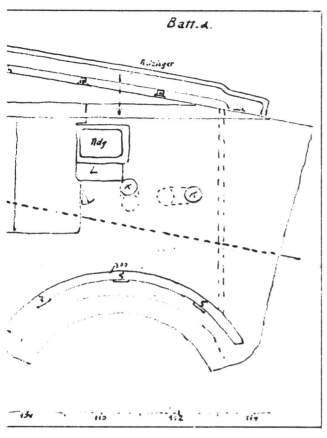

Batt. A.

splinters pierced two ventilation trunks on the upper deck and also struck the after superfiring turret.

The *Grosser Kurfürst* was hit seven times in this phase, four of the hits, including at least 2 – 15in, being at 1918/19. The chronological order is not known, and they are given below from forward to aft. Nos 3, 4, 5 and 6 were from the *Barham* and/or *Valiant*, and Nos 1, 2 and 7 from the *Marlborough*. All were from the port side.

1 13.5in ricochet struck the upper edge of the 6in forward side armour 73ft from the bows, apparently with little effect. The plate hit was the next one forward to that hit at 1709.

2 13.5in APC struck and burst on the after edge of the same plate as hit by No 1,

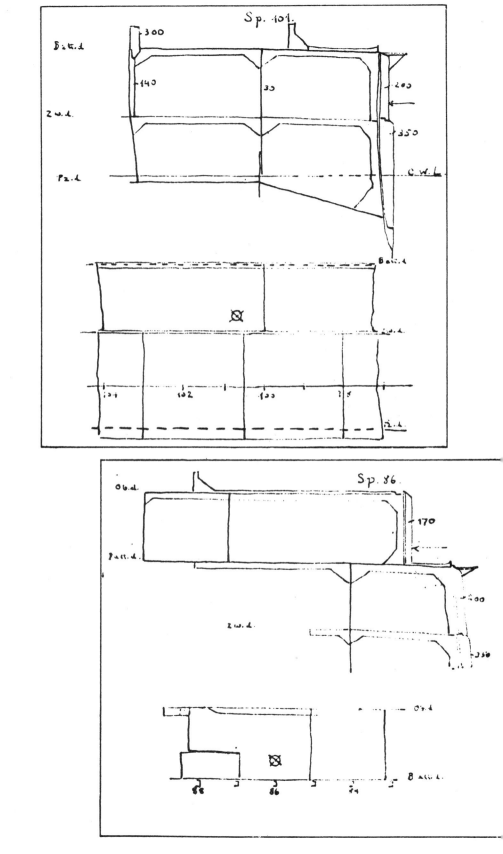

about 5ft abaft that hit, and 3½ft above the legend, and probably just below the actual, water-line. The effect of the burst was outside the ship, but the 6in armour was holed for 51in × 35in, and bent inwards by up to 8in, while the upper armour support 32in below the upper deck was forced in by 1½in. Armour fragments driven into the ship made a hole of 51in × 43in in the 0.4in longitudinal bulkhead, *c*10ft–11ft inboard of the hit, and remained laying behind the bulkhead.

Below water, the hull plating was bulged in by up to 4¾in for a length of 30ft and to 8ft below the legend water-line. The rivetting leaked, the ½in transverse docking bulkhead was buckled for 6ft from the hull side and six frames were broken at the longitudinal frame. The armour deck, here flat and 4¾ft below lwl, was undamaged but the angle plates below it were bent and torn. As a result of this hit, compartments on the main and armour decks were flooded, and water spread to compartments below the armour deck. Almost the whole fore-part of the ship, except for the submerged torpedo flats and trimming tanks, gradually filled up to the main deck.

3 15in APC hit and pierced the forecastle deck edge abeam of 'A' barbette, and burst close to the barbette opposite an armour joint, and about 6ft above the upper deck. The surface of the 12in barbette armour was flaked, and the 1.2in upper deck holed and bowed downwards, but relatively little damaged. The forecastle deck, 0.3in at the edge, then 0.6in, and 1.2in close to the barbette, was ploughed up from the hull side, and the 1.2in part holed from below and bulged upwards for a length of 45ft by up to 12in. All fittings were destroyed over a large area in the upper part of

Opposite. Grosser Kurfürst: *hit No 4.*

Grosser Kurfürst: *hit No 5.*

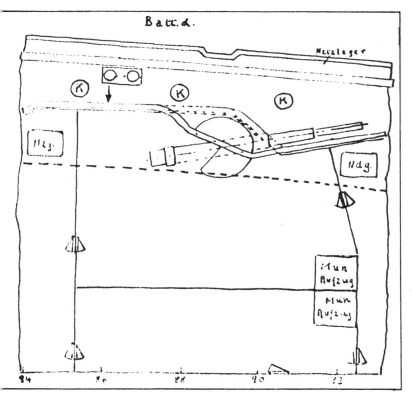

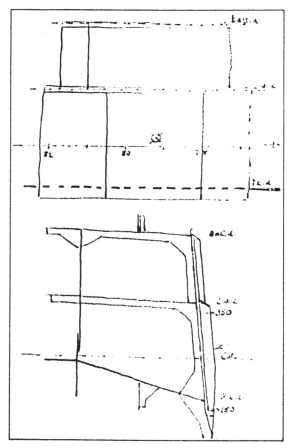

Grosser Kurfürst: *hit No 6.*

the ship forward, and everything inflammable burnt forward of the barbette with development of heavy smoke. Both forward capstans were out of action from the destruction of steam pipes.

4 15in APC struck and burst on the 8in upper belt, abeam of 'B' barbette. The hit was about 1½ft above the lower edge of a plate, which was at main deck level, and 3ft forward of the after edge. The effect of the burst was kept out by the armour, but a large hole measuring 55in × 43in was made in the plate, though the latter was little driven in, being held by the rabbeted armour joints. The skin plating behind the armour was destroyed for a length of c6ft, extending in part from the upper to the main deck, and armour fragments made a hole of c6ft × 3ft in the 1.2in longitudinal splinter bulkhead, 13ft inboard, and largely destroyed the reserve dressing station. Otherwise relatively little destruction was caused by this shell, and there were apparently no casualties. The ¼in main deck was only slightly damaged, and had two small holes inboard of the splinter bulkhead. The torpedo net stowage was

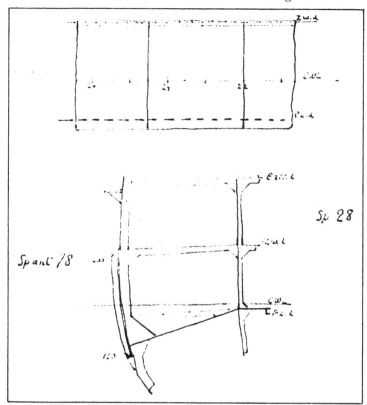

Grosser Kurfürst: *hit No 7.*

destroyed for *c*10ft, and some flooding occurred on the main deck from water entering through the hole in the side armour.

5 15in APC struck the 6¾in casemate armour of No 2 port – 5.9in gun, 2ft above the upper deck and 12ft aft of the gun mounting axis, and burst in penetrating, the explosive effect being both inside and outside the armour. A hole of 26in diameter was made in the armour, and the plate bowed in by 2in locally, and driven in 1¼in at the lower edge. The 5.9in gun was put out of action, but the nearest ammunition 26ft–30ft from the hit was not ignited. The 0.8in casemate transverse bulkhead, 3ft from the line of the hit, was little damaged, but the 0.6in longitudinal bulkhead, 19ft from the hit, had two large holes, which together reached from the upper to the forecastle deck, as well as three other fairly large holes. Some of the armour and shell splinters, which caused the above damage to the longitudinal bulkhead, went through a second 0.6in longitudinal bulkhead, inboard of the battle signal station, and then pierced the air supply trunk to the forward stoke-hold and also the fore

241

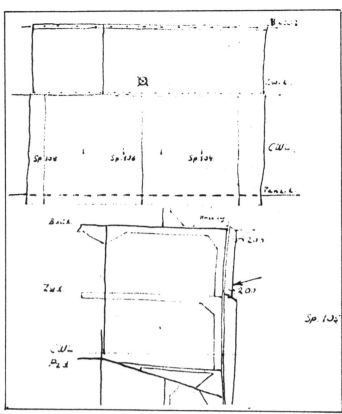

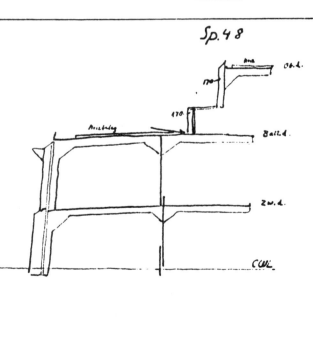

242

funnel uptakes. The upper deck was much bowed down, but had only two small holes, inside the casemate where 0.8in, but outside over an outer bunker, where 1.2in, it was holed for *c*4½ft × 1¼ft near the casemate armour, though not bowed. The torpedo net was damaged, and there was some danger from smoke and gas, which were drawn off through splinter holes to the stoke-hold.

6 This 15in shell hit and burst on the 14in belt armour, just abaft the fore funnel and 8in above the legend, but below the actual water-line. The hit was approximately in the middle of a plate, which was crushed in at the position of impact by up to 4in in an 18in diameter circle. The plate was bowed 1½in vertically and half as much horizontally, and forced inwards 1½in at the upper, and 3¼in at the lower edge where 7in thick. Inboard of the armour the hull plating was torn, and the armour deck buckled in two places by 3in, and its slope distorted downwards at the ship's side. Transverse bulkheads were also buckled, and the main deck slightly bulged for a length of 30ft. Considerable damage was done to the hull plating below water, as it was forced in by up to 13in for a length of 23ft and for a depth of 28in below the armour. As a result a wing compartment and a protective bunker were flooded, and water apparently also entered an outer bunker.

7 13.5in burst short of the ship about 18ft abaft the sternmost barbette. The surface of the after side armour (8in with 6in lower edge) was slightly scarred by splinters, and a plate forced inwards by up to 1¾in, so that two wing compartments made

Opposite. Markgraf: *hit at 1914.*

Kaiser: *hit from* Agincourt *at c1923-26.*

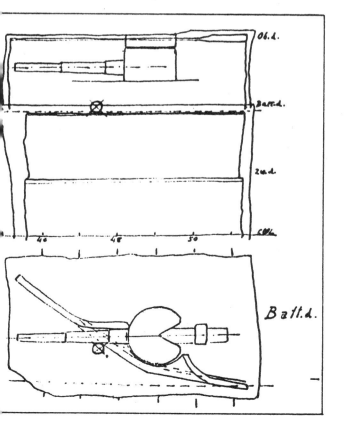

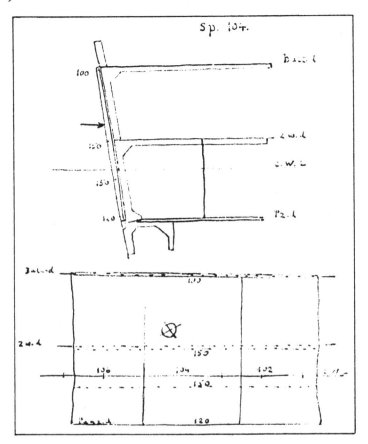

Helgoland: *hit at 1915.*

some water, though the hull plating was undamaged below the armour. The main deck was severely buckled at the ship's side, the torpedo net and its stowage damaged, and above the armour the hull plating was riddled by splinters with considerable damage to cabins.

The water which entered as a result of these hits caused a list of 4° to port which was reduced to ¾–1° by counter-flooding. About 800 tons of water remained in the ship after the leaks had been stopped, but large quantities of water subsequently entered the forward part of the ship from Hit No 2, so that the *Grosser Kurfürst* had to slow down when near Heligoland on 1 June. Draught before the battle was 29ft6in (fore)

28ft6in (aft), and after the battle 34ft 1in (fore), 29ft 2in (aft), indicating that over 3000 tons of water were eventually present in the ship.

The *Markgraf* was hit once at 1914 by a shell coming from well forward of the port beam. This struck the 8in upper belt armour between the two forward barbettes, 16in from the lower edge of a plate, which was at main deck level and directly above the vertical joint between two 14in plates of the main belt. The shell shattered on the armour, which was undamaged, and the greatest movement was that of the 2 – 14in plates which took up the pressure through the rabbeted joints and were displaced by up to 1in. Some damage was caused to the torpedo-net, booms and stowage, the main deck was slightly buckled, and a compartment flooded between the slope of the armour deck and the water-line.

The shell is believed to have come from the *Agincourt* and was thus a 12in TNT filled CPC.

The *Kaiser* was hit twice by similar shells from the *Agincourt* between 1923 and 1926, both coming from the starboard quarter. Little data has survived on one hit, but it appears to have been by a shell which burst short of the ship, and caused some unimportant damage to hull plating, net-booms and cabins aft.

The other shell pierced the 1in upper deck just forward of the lower edge of the casemate armour of No 7 starboard 5.9in and broke up in the hammock stowage below. The head of the shell was found there, broken into a few large pieces, but the body remained in one piece 20 – 24in long, and after making a hole of 43in × 20in in the support of No 7 – 5.9in, made another of 43in × 32in in the main deck, and came to rest in the inner bunker below. The TNT filling burnt quietly without explosion. The hole in the 1in upper deck measured *c*8ft × 3ft and extended under the 6¾in casemate armour, the lower edge of which was grazed with slight bulging in and concentric cracks. Little damage seems to have been done to the support of No 7 – 5.9in, which remained firm, and a fire which broke out in the hammock stowage was easily put out, though water from hoses partly flooded the telephone exchange.

The *Helgoland* was hit once at 1915 by a 15in AP shell, which came from *c*30° on the port bow, and was from the *Barham* or *Valiant*, probably the latter. This struck the forward side armour where 6in thick, 32in above lwl, and directly in line with the forward broadside TT. The shell broke up and the filling scattered in a yellow-green cloud, but the armour was holed, and part of the base of the shell found in the ship. The hole in the plate was large, measuring 4½ft in width, and on average 21in high with a maximum of 34in, and the plate was hit *c*32in from its forward edge, so that the plate ahead was displaced by up to *c*7in and the one aft by under 1in. The 0.3in battery and main decks were bulged or buckled by up to 4in inboard of the hit, and the port capstan damaged, while No 1 port – 5.9in was slightly damaged by splinters but could still be fired. About 80 tons of water entered the ship.

In addition to these hits on capital ships, the *Wiesbaden* was hit by the *Marlborough*, and though as previously, no accurate estimate can be made, a figure of three – 13.5in hits is given here. The *S35* was probably struck by 2–13.5in shells from the *Iron Duke* and a 'near-miss' on the *G86* can be counted as a hit, but it is not known which ship was responsible.

	15in	13.5in/1400lb	13.5in/1250lb	12in	Total
Lützow	—	—	5	—	5
Derfflinger	7	—	—	7	14
Seydlitz	1	—	—	4	5
von der Tann	1	—	—	—	1
König	—	1	—	—	1
Grosser Kurfürst	4	3	—	—	7
Markgraf	—	—	—	1	1
Kaiser	—	—	—	2	2
Helgoland	1	—	—	—	1
Total	14	4	5	14	37

All were due to battleships, the 5th BS making five, and the above figures, if contrasted with the total of two obtained by the Germans, show how much conditions favoured the British in this phase of the battle.

CHAPTER 12

Last daylight contacts 1945—2130
Action between capital ships
Fifth phase 2019—2039

Sunset was at 2014/5, but the last of the daylight did not vanish until about 2130, and further contacts occurred between the two fleets, one resulting in an engagement between heavy ships. With full knowledge of the relative positions of the combatants, it would seem that some favourable opportunities were missed by the British, but such information was not available at the time.

Scheer had ordered the 1st Squadron to steer 167° at c1950 and for the next 30 minutes the *Westfalen* led them and the *Friedrich der Grosse* on 173°. The 3rd Squadron returned to line ahead at 2000, and about 8 minutes later turned in succession to follow astern of the other dreadnoughts. The 1st Scouting Group came into line ahead at 1951, course 190°, and at 2000 turned in succession to about 173°, and at 2015 the *Derrflinger* was about 2½ miles on the *Westfalen*'s port beam while the *Hannover* was about 2 miles on the *Westfalen*'s starboard bow.

The *Lützow* steered 257° and increased speed to about 11 kts. She was about 1¼ miles on the *König*'s port quarter at 2015, and about to cross the latter's track. The *G40, G38, V45* and *G37* remained in company, while the *V5* made artificial fog for 10 minutes in passing with the 5th Flotilla. Hipper was still in the *G39*, and intending to board the *Moltke*, though as the 1st SG were shortly to be in action again, it was some time before he could do this.

The movements of the German destroyer flotillas are described subsequently, and the 2nd SG were 2½ – 3 miles ahead of the *Westfalen* at 2015, and the 4th SG a similar distance ahead of the *Hannover*.

At 1949 the *Lützow* had signalled the *Seydlitz* that six British battlecruisers bore 100°, but both the *Lützow* and *Seydlitz* had their main wireless out of action, while the former's auxiliary wireless was

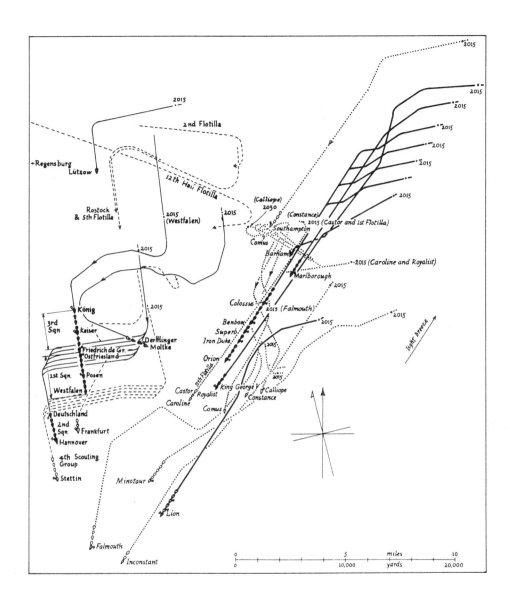

also disabled, and though the signal was recorded by the *Frankfurt* and
Regensburg at 2001/2, neither informed Scheer, though the *Regensburg*
notified the 2nd Flotilla. The signal as recorded by the two light cruisers
adds that the battlecruisers were drawing past to port of the *Lützow*, and

the *Regensburg* gives the bearing as 145° which was much nearer the actual direction.

The five airships that had gone up at about 1130, had been ordered to return because of uncertain weather. The *L14* turned back at 1930 when about 50 miles from Lindesnes, and must have flown over the area of the battle, but saw and heard nothing. She reported visibility of one mile at 2000 when her signalled position was about 15 miles to the north-westward of the *Barham*. The *Falmouth* may have sighted the *L14* at 2019 on the port beam.

In the Grand Fleet the 3rd and 4th Divisions steered 212° from 1942 to 2000, but the others had first to take station ahead or astern. By 2000 all the Divisions except the 6th were steering within 5° of 212°, and the 6th 201° with the 5th BS 180°.

The battlecruisers steered 209° then 235° and by 2000 223°, when the *Lion* was about 5½ miles ahead of the *King George V*. At 1945 Beatty had signalled the *Minotaur* by searchlight for passing to the *King George V* that the leading enemy battleship bore 291°, course *c*212°, and this information reached the *Iron Duke* at 1959. The bearing given was correct for the *Westfalen* but she was 15 or 16 miles away, and the report presumably referred to the *Lützow*, which bore about 6° more to the north and was about 5 miles nearer.

On receiving this signal Jellicoe ordered his divisions at 2000 to alter course to 257° increasing to 17kts, and notified Beatty of the Fleet's course. The 1st Division steered 246° for 4 minutes to increase their distance from the 2nd Division, and the 6th Division steered 263° for a time. The 5th BS altered course to 268° at 2004, and the battlecruisers after turning to *c*232° at 2006, altered course to 257° at 2015 and reduced to 17kts.

Other reports referring to units of the German fleet were also made between 1945 and 2015, and Jellicoe afterwards considered that he should have ordered the 4th LCS to search for the enemy when he turned to 212° at 1942. The *Southampton* in a signal timed at 1945, reported that the enemy had detached an unknown number of ships of unknown type, which were steering 302° at 1915, and this signal, if the correct text has survived, refers to Scheer's 180° turn, and particularly to the *Friedrich der Grosse*.

In a wireless signal timed at 1950, Beatty submitted to Jellicoe that the van of the battleships follow the battlecruisers, and that the whole of the enemy's battlefleet could then be cut off. The battlecruisers's position, course and speed were not given. Jellicoe accordingly ordered the 2nd BS in a searchlight signal, timed at 2010, to follow the battlecruisers. Their exact position was not known to Jerram as they were out of sight, but at 2015 the 1st Division altered course to 241°, while the other Divisions continued on 257°. It is very doubtful if Beatty had seen any German battleships, as distinct from battlecruisers, for over an hour and the 1st Scouting Group were also out of sight at 1950, though the *Lützow* was presumably still detectable, and the *King George V* had been following the *Lion* until 2000, with their mean courses between 1945 and 2000, converging by 2°.

At 2000 Beatty ordered his light cruisers to sweep to the westward and locate the head of the German line before dark, and as the *King George V* was out of sight from the *Lion* by 2010, the *Minotaur, c*3½ miles on the *Lion*'s port quarter, was asked to give her bearing which was 10°, 5 miles, but the *King George V* soon disappeared from the 2nd CS.

On receiving Beatty's 2000 signal, the 3rd LCS formed on a line of bearing 167°, and steered 257°. At 2010 the *Falmouth* signalled to Beatty that ships bore 336°. This was near the bearing of the 1st SG, but the 4th SG were actually sighted and the signal should have read 268° as given in the *Falmouth*'s report of sighting five enemy cruisers. The 3rd LCS increased speed and were soon in action with the 4th SG.

At *c*2007 the *Castor* sighted enemy destroyers to the north-westward, and the *Calliope, Constance* and *Comus* made to attack them, followed by the *Castor* and eight destroyers of the 11th Flotilla. The vessels sighted were the 5th Flotilla returning from their abortive attack at 1950. The *Castor* reported them by flags to the *King George V* at 2014, but this was apparently not passed to the *Iron Duke* until 12 minutes later, and the *Castor* and her destroyers presently returned to their station ahead of the battlefleet, as the 5th Flotilla made no attack, though the three light cruisers continued to chase after them.

In addition to these two contacts, which both resulted in minor actions, the British battlecruisers would soon be engaging their old opponents of the 1st SG, as at 2015 the *Lion* and *Derfflinger* were 7 miles apart and after the former's turn to 257° were on courses which converged at nearly 90°.

There were the usual sightings of imaginary submarines between 1945 and 2015, the *Hampshire, Shannon* and *Duke of Edinburgh* firing at one of these supposed targets. At 2018 the *Calliope* opened fire on the 5th Flotilla which was steering southward. The German destroyers turned away, and following the *Rostock* and other destroyers with her, broke through between the ships of the 3rd Squadron. The three light cruisers pursued them to the north-westward and at 2026 sighted

German battleships about 8000yds away in *c*300°. These were thought to be two or three *Pommerns* or *Helgolands* and four *Kaisers*, but were actually the 3rd Squadron. The *Prinzregent Luitpold, Kaiser* and *Markgraf* made out first one and then a second light cruiser, as well as some destroyers, and the *Markgraf* opened fire with 5.9in at 2027/8 followed by the *Prinzregent Luitpold* and *Kaiser* with 12in at 6300–7000yds, though the two latter only fired one and two salvos respectively.

The destroyers which belonged to the 11th Flotilla, turned away at once, as the *Castor* signalled the eight destroyers with her to reform at 2022. The *Calliope* was hit five times by the *Markgraf's* 5.9in and had 2 – 4in guns disabled, but she fired one torpedo at 6500–7000yds at what was thought to be the leading *Kaiser* at *c*2030 before zig-zagging away at full speed. The Germans ceased firing at 2035, and a supposed explosion was seen on one of the *Kaisers* 3 minutes later, but the torpedo failed to hit.

The *Agincourt* reported sighting a torpedo at 2025 and shortly afterwards another was reported by the *Benbow*, but both were imaginary.

Although the *Falmouth* had sighted German ships at 2010, it was not until 2017 that the 2nd and 4th Scouting Groups made out any British light cruisers. While reporting two ships of the *Chatham* class to Scheer by wireless at 2019, the *Frankfurt* sighted British battlecruisers beyond them, apparently steering 212°, and this was added to Boedicker's signal. At 2021 the *Stettin* also wirelessed Scheer that four enemy light cruisers were in sight. None of the reported positions was correct, the battlecruisers being placed too far to the west, and the 3rd LCS too far north, particularly by the *Frankfurt*, which also placed them too much to the west.

The 2nd SG turned away as some salvos from the British battlecruisers were directed at the *Pillau*, but the 4th SG steered southward, while the *Falmouth* first turned to 167°, and then led the 3rd LCS south-westward at full speed. She opened fire at 2018 at 9600yds, and though the 4th SG were very indistinct, and few salvos fell close to them, the *München* was hit by 2–6in shells. The second burst in the upper part of the 3rd funnel, and severely damaged the casings round the four after boilers so that steam was maintained with difficulty. The *Falmouth* wirelessed to Jellicoe and Beatty at 2028 that she was engaging enemy cruisers, but gave her position at least 6 miles too far to the north.

Visibility was worse for the 4th SG, and only the *Stettin* and *München*, the latter expending 63 rounds, continued firing for long. No hits were made though the range fell to 6000yds, and at about 2031 the 4th SG turned together 90° away. The 3rd LCS turned to follow them 3 or 4 minutes later, but at 2038 they were lost in the mist, and the 3rd LCS broke off and made for their station ahead of the *Lion*.

The action between the battlecruisers was about to begin as Boedicker made his sighting report, and Beatty's presence so far to the south was unsuspected by the 1st SG. Hipper was on the point of transferring from the *G39* to the *Moltke* when fire was opened. Of the six British ships, the *Lion*, *Princess Royal* and *Tiger* had all been frequently hit, but their hulls had escaped serious injury. In the *Lion* 2 – 13.5in were disabled, a third was on hand loading and the main cordite supply to a fourth not in use. The *Princess Royal* had 2 – 13.5in out of action from a hit, and another from a breakdown, while in the *Tiger* 1 – 13.5in was out of action from a defect, two were restricted in their speed of firing, and two more were on individual laying and director training. The *New Zealand*, *Indomitable*, and *Inflexible* were virtually unscathed, with 1– 12in defective in the *Inflexible*, but capable of being fired.

Of the four German ships, the *Derfflinger* and *Seydlitz* had been heavily hit and their hulls badly damaged. In the former 4–12in were disabled and another two without Director-pointer gear, while the *Seydlitz* had 4–11in out of action, a fifth without Director-pointer gear, and two more with auxiliary training only. The *Moltke* and *von der Tann* had been damaged to some extent in their hulls, and though the *Moltke* had all her 11in guns, the *von der Tann* had two out of action, two on handworking, and the remaining four liable to give trouble again.

The odds were thus far more in favour of the British than when Beatty's original six ships first faced Hipper's five, and in addition visibility was much against the Germans, while the 1st Squadron provided only limited support. The British battlecruisers steered *c*230° from 2020 to 2029 and then turned to *c*201° and to 212° at 2035. The 1st Scouting Group were initially steering near 173°, and at 2024 the *Derfflinger* turned away to *c*201° and then to 257°, and continuing in the same general direction until 2041. The three battlecruisers astern of the *Derfflinger* turned away earlier and more sharply during the action and did not follow her exact course.

The *Princess Royal* opened fire at 2019 at 12,000yds, but her initial target was the head of the 1st Squadron, seen to the left of the 1st Scouting Group. She then shifted to the *Seydlitz* and engaged at *c*9500yds until 2028, when the target appeared to drop astern on fire and to be hidden by a smoke screen. Her report notes that her target could now be seen without any interference from the *Lion*'s smoke, and good ranges obtained for the first time. Repeated hits were claimed and two scored on the *Seydlitz* at 2024 and 2028.

The *Lion* fired one salvo at the light cruiser *Pillau* at 2020 which fell short, and reopened on the *Derfflinger* at 2023. She expended fourteen salvos in 6 minutes at gun-ranges varying from 10,850 to 8700yds before her target disappeared in the mist. One hit was obtained at 2028 which temporarily jammed the *Derfflinger's* fore turret. The *Tiger* opened on the *Pillau* at 2021, and it would seem also fired at the 1st Squadron before checking at 2028. The *Pillau's* report notes that the shooting was bad.

The *New Zealand* opened fire at 2021 on the 1st Squadron at a range given as 11,500 or 13,000yds. She shifted to the *Seydlitz*, and made three hits shortly before checking at 2031, when the target appeared to be on fire forward, and to be hauling out of the line listing heavily. Her range to the *Seydlitz* was 9100 to 9600yds.

The *Indomitable* also opened fire at 2021, and her target which was obscured in rapidly failing light by the ship ahead appearing to drop back, seems to have been the *Seydlitz*. The opening range was 8800yds, and the ship engaged was thought to be on fire, and not replying to the *Indomitable*. No hits are credited to the latter. Conditions were very difficult for the *Inflexible* due to funnel and cordite smoke of the ships ahead, and no ranges were obtained. Her target cannot be identified, but was perhaps the *Moltke*, and the *Inflexible's* expenditure of only 88 rounds in the whole battle indicates that she fired little at this time.

The 1st Scouting Group's reply was not effective as the British ships could only be seen distinctly on rare occasions and spotting was impossible, so that firing had to be interrupted frequently. As well as the remaining heavy guns, 5.9in were used. The *Seydlitz* opened fire at 2020 but expended very few rounds of 11in, while the *Moltke* which opened at the same time only fired intermittently. The *Derfflinger* got off eight 2-gun 12in salvos between 2022 and 2031 at ranges varying from 6600 to 11,400yds, the target for the salvo at 2031 being described as a smoke cloud, and the *von der Tann* opened at 2024, and fired a total of 9-11in shells at 9600 to 12,000yds from the 4 guns employed.

No heavy calibre hits were made by the 1st SG in this phase, but there was a 5.9in hit on the *Lion*. Both the 1st Destroyer Flotilla, which was screening the British battlecruisers, and the 2nd CS on their port quarter, noted that the German shells were going over Beatty's ships, and at 2029 the 2nd CS turned together 23° away to avoid steaming into the German salvos, one from the *Moltke* having just fallen about 1000yds short.

The van of the 1st Squadron was under fire from some of the British battlecruisers, which could only be discerned by their gun-flashes, and the *Westfalen* was closely straddled and struck by splinters, while other salvos fell near the *Nassau*. At 2022 two imaginary torpedo tracks were seen to starboard from the *Westfalen* and one from the *Rheinland*. These were thought to have come from a supposed submarine at which the 2nd SG opened fire, and the *Westfalen* had now to reduce speed and lead the dreadnoughts westward to keep clear of the 1st SG crossing ahead. The *Posen*, fourth in the line, was the only ship of the 1st Squadron to fire at this time. No more than gun-flashes could be made out, but the *Posen* opened at 2028 at 10,900yds when near the turning point, and engaged the British battlecruisers with her 11in until 2035. She obtained one hit on the *Princess Royal* at 2032, and also fired at the *Indomitable* which appears to have been repeatedly straddled.

The *Westfalen* continued to lead to the westward until 2043 when she turned to *c*173°. The British salvos were reported as well placed by the *Westfalen*, but the *Helgoland* noted that the spread was greater than that of the *Valiant* firing at a much longer range at *c*1817, and the *Oldenburg* reported extremely wild firing from one ship. It is not clear to what extent 'overs' at the 1st SG were confused with salvos fired at the 1st Squadron.

Some of the British battlecruisers engaged the 2nd Squadron which had crossed ahead of the 1st SG as the latter turned away. The pre-dreadnoughts had continued on *c*173° until *c*2030 when they turned to 212° in sucession. At 2035 they turned together to 263°, as they were under an accurate fire, and the visibility was too bad to reply.

Neither the *Lion* nor the *Inflexible* opened fire again, and in the other battlecruisers it could not be determined whether their 3-funnelled targets were pre-dreadnoughts or the *Helgoland* class. The *Princess Royal* reopened at 2030 and fired at the *Hannover* at 9500–9850yds until 2034 when the latter was obscured by smoke. The 3rd and 4th salvos straddled, the *Hannover* being struck by fragments of 13.5in AP shell.

The *Tiger* also reopened at 2030 and fired for 6½ minutes at 11,200 to 7600yds. Her target, for at least some of the time, appears to have been the *Hessen* which was not hit. The *New Zealand* shifted from the *Seydlitz* to the *Schleswig-Holstein* at 2031 and scored one hit a minute later. She then fired at the *Schlesien*, which was struck by many splinters from a short salvo close ahead, and continued until the target became obscured at a time given as 2039. The *Indomitable* fired at the *Pommern*, and also scored a hit, but ceased at 2033 as the fall of shot could no longer be seen.

According to the German Official History 23 rounds of 11in were fired by the 2nd Squadron – *Hannover* eight, *Hessen* five, *Schlesien* nine, *Deutschland* one – but the ships' reports make it clear that they did not open fire, and thus expended their 11in against imaginary submarines next morning. Apart from a brief glimpse from the *Hannover* and *Hessen*, only muzzle flashes of the British ships could be made out.

The *Princess Royal* fired a torpedo with 'Extreme Range' setting at 2030 or 2032, the target being the centre ship of three 3-funnelled battleships, distant 10,000yds. The torpedo left correctly, but the track was not observed from the *Princess Royal*, and it possibly misran badly and was the torpedo seen to cross the *Inflexible*'s bows at 2035. An imaginary submarine breaking surface was sighted by the 1st LCS then on the battlecruisers' port bow, at 2029, but the position given in the wireless report was many miles out. A heavy shock was felt in all the British battlecruisers, in some of the 2nd CS and in the *Cordelia*, at a time variously given between 2034 and 2044. In the *New Zealand* what appeared to be a burst of air under water, was seen about 50yds on the starboard beam, and the *Inflexible* noted a large swirl of oil about 100yds away, also on the starboard beam. In the *Indomitable* it was at first thought that the ship had been torpedoed, and speed was temporarily reduced to 14kts. The foregoing may have been caused by an explosion in the *Nestor*'s wreck, which was the nearest to the battlecruisers' track of the ships sunk earlier in the action, though it is not shown as less than 3 miles astern of the *Inflexible*'s 2040 position on charts of the battle. Shortly after 2050, the *Indomitable* and *Inflexible* turned away on sighting an imaginary submarine to port, and the *Indomitable*'s track chart shows a turn of *c*130° to starboard at 2054, the previous course being resumed at 2102.

Of the German heavy units not engaged in these actions, the 3rd Squadron followed the 1st, and the *Lützow*, which had crossed to the westward astern of the German Fleet, altered course to near 173° at 2035. At 2021 Jellicoe signalled his divisions to alter course to 235°, and informed Beatty of the Fleet's course. At 2025 he altered course to 257° and at 2028 to 212°, notifying Beatty of this last alteration. This brought the 3rd, 4th and 5th Divisions into single line ahead astern of the 2nd Division, while the 1st Division which had continued on 241° until 2028, was on the *Orion*'s port bow, and the 6th Division which had complied with the 2021 signal, was on the *St Vincent*'s port quarter. Both these divisions steered 212° from 2028, but the 5th BS after turning to 235° altered course to 196° at 2031 and at 2040 to 218°, increasing to 20kts.

Gunfire could be heard to the south-westward, but Jellicoe had no precise information of the German battlefleet. From the *Iron Duke* the *Calliope* was seen to be hit amidships, the flash lighting up the whole of her upper deck, but it was impossible to tell which German ships were engaging her, and in a signal which is recorded as being made at 2038, Jellicoe asked the *Comus* at whom she was firing. The reply 'Enemy's battlefleet bearing 257°' at least indicated that Jellicoe's 212° course was not unsuitable, though he afterwards thought that he should have closed, and might then have been able to fire a few rounds.

From the British point of view it was unfortunate that none of their battleships could take part in these actions. Jerram asked for Beatty's position, course and speed in a signal timed at 2021, but not sent until 2040, and the reply was delayed until 2101, as the *Lion*'s main wireless was out of action, and then gave her 2040 position about 6 miles too far to the north-eastward. In fact, even if the *King George V* had steered straight for the *Lion*'s 2028 position at 20kts from 2000, she would still have been nearly 5 miles away at 2018, instead of her actual distance of 7 miles, and would have been no nearer the German battlecruisers which were also 7 miles away, and well in range had the visibility been better.

The westward movement of the German fleet was not in accordance with Scheer's intention, and at 2036 and again at 2052 he signalled Course 167°. The *Westfalen* led the dreadnoughts on *c*173° at 2043, and 5 minutes later the 2nd Squadron returned to line ahead steering 167°, the *Hannover* being about 2½ miles on the *Westfalen*'s starboard bow. The movements of the 1st SG at this time are not clear, but they appear to have altered course to *c*235° at 2041, and by 2047/48 were steering *c*167°. They were very close on the 1st Squadron's port beam, and by 2050 had altered course to near 111°. They were then heading straight for the British battlefleet, but at 2100 when, according to German charts, they were less than 4 miles from the *Orion* and just forward of her beam, the 1st SG turned to 257°.

The British battleship divisions continued on 212° until 2101, but the 5th BS altered course to about 246° at 2054, to keep clear of the 6th Division limited to 15¾kts by the *Marlborough*'s torpedo damage, but at 2058 they turned to 212°, as they had crossed astern of the 6th Division, and were on their starboard quarter. The battlecruisers also steered 212°, and at 2045 Jerram informed Jellicoe by wireless that they were not in sight. They had not been seen from the *King George V* for at least half an hour, though their gun flashes had indicated their position. Ten minutes later Beatty asked the *Minotaur* for the position of the 2nd BS. The reply that they had last been seen at 2010, was not true as far as the other ships of the 2nd CS were concerned, as the *King George V* had been in sight 5 miles away to the north-north-eastward from the *Shannon* at 2045.

The situation was not clear to Jellicoe, and at 2046 he asked Beatty for the enemy's bearing. This information did not arrive until after 2100, but at 2046 the *Falmouth* wirelessed that enemy battlecruisers bore 347°, course 235°, giving her own position as 56° 42′N, 5° 37′E which was at least 5 miles too far to the northward. The 1st SG's bearing and course were however given correctly, though it is not certain that these were the ships sighted. Although maximum visibility was still about 5 miles at 2100, and it would not be quite dark for half an hour, Jellicoe decided not to seek a further engagement until the next day. He was between the German fleet and its bases, and did not intend to risk a night action, without doubt correctly, as the British night-fighting technique was very inferior to the German, and indeed virtually non-existent. Accordingly at 2101 he signalled the battleship divisions to alter course to 167°, and 4 minutes later the 5th BS conformed and followed between the 5th and 6th Divisions. All Squadrons and Flotillas were notified that the Fleet's course was 167° by wireless at 2110.

Meanwhile, contact had again been made with the German fleet. The *Caroline* and *Royalist* were on the *King George V*'s starboard bow, and ahead of the *Castor* and her destroyers, when at shortly before 2100, three German ships, thought to be pre-dreadnoughts, were sighted closing slowly from 302°. The *Caroline* reported them to Jerram as distant 8000yds, and warned that they might be making a torpedo attack, but this signal made by flashing-lamp was apparently not taken in by the *King George V*.

The ships sighted were actually the leading German dreadnoughts. At shortly after 2100 several vessels were made out on the *Westfalen*'s port bow in the uncertain twilight, but their identity was in doubt, as the whereabouts of the 4th SG was not definitely known. A searchlight challenge was unanswered, and as seven destroyers led by a cruiser could then be distinguished, the *Westfalen* turned 68° to starboard at 2105 to avoid any torpedoes already fired, and was followed in succession by the *Nassau* and *Rheinland*, though the other ships of the 1st Squadron turned 90° to starboard together. The *Westfalen* and *Nassau* opened fire at 8100–7700yds on the *Caroline* and *Royalist*, now visible ahead of the *Castor*, but the rest of the 1st Squadron apparently saw nothing of the attackers. The *Caroline* and *Royalist* also turned away, as did the *Comus* which had made to join them, and they soon disappeared.

The *Westfalen* only expended 7–11in shells in 2 minutes 24 seconds, and at 2110 turned to 167°.

Both the *Caroline* and *Royalist* attacked, the former firing two torpedoes at 7600yds and the latter one at 8000, the times being given respectively as 2105/06 and 2110. All were fired at the centre ship of three, thought to be *Deutschlands* by the *Caroline* and *Nassaus* by the *Royalist*. The *Caroline*'s two were well directed as the tracks were sighted by the *Nassau*, one passing close to her bows, and the other under her fore-turret. Unfortunately the *Caroline* could fire no more as, in attempting to reload the two starboard tubes, one of the torpedoes jammed.

The *Castor* sighted on her starboard quarter what appeared to be the German battlecruisers, closing the British fleet. The *King George V* also sighted these ships and, in a wireless signal timed at 2105, reported them to Jellicoe as the British battlecruisers bearing 280°, steering 212°. The *Caroline*'s signal to attack had been seen and at 2106 Jerram negatived this by searchlight, believing the ships to be Beatty's, but the attack had already been made. Jerram's signal, however, was intercepted by the *Castor*, and the 11th Flotilla fired no torpedoes. Meanwhile, fire was opened on the two light cruisers ahead of the *Castor* and she turned her flotilla away, expecting the British fleet to open fire. At about 2114 the *Nassau* fired a starshell, which positively identified her as German, the British fleet having none. However, fire was still not opened on the German ships, while the *Castor* did not attack for the curious reason that it was not dark enough to do so, unsupported by fire from the Fleet, and the enemy were soon lost to sight.

The powerful 11th Flotilla missed a fine opportunity on this occasion, and in the prevailing conditions had a much better chance of inflicting serious damage than the 2nd BS. The ships seen by the *Castor* to open fire were the *Westfalen* and *Nassau*, but those first sighted by her and also those reported by Jerram appear to have been the German battlecruisers.

At the rear of the British line, the 2nd LCS had engaged three destroyers of the German 12th Half-Flotilla, and this encounter was reported by the *Southampton* in a searchlight signal which was apparently not taken in, and then in a wireless message timed at 2055, while it was also reported by the *Marlborough*, and the *Southampton* further reported, in a signal timed at 2112, that the previously mentioned enemy had been driven towards *c*300°.

By about 2115 Jellicoe had also received information on the German Fleet from Beatty. In a wireless signal timed at 2040, but not received in the *Iron Duke* until 2105, the German battlecruisers and pre-dreadnoughts were reported to bear 313°, distant 10–11 miles, from the *Lion* and to be steering 212°. The *Lion*'s position was given as 56° 40′N, 5° 50′E. Course 212°. Speed 17kts. At 2040 only the pre-dreadnoughts could have been seen from the *Lion* and they were 6–7 miles away and bore *c*300°, while the bearing and distance given happened to be near those of the 1st Squadron. The *Lion*'s own position was also in error, and placed her about 6 miles too far to the north-eastward.

The location of the German Fleet was clearly still to the westward of the British, and Jellicoe continued on 167°. At 2117 he ordered the Fleet to assume night cruising order with the 2nd, 4th and 1st BS forming three columns each of eight ships in single line ahead, and the columns disposed abeam to port one mile apart, the 5th BS being on the port flank. This formation was never completed, owing to the *Marlborough*'s reduced speed, and by 2130 only the 4th BS had formed a single column, while the 5th BS were between the 5th and 6th Divisions. At this time the 4th LCS were about 4 miles on the *King George V*'s port bow, and the 2nd LCS about 9 miles astern of the latter, while the destroyers, except for the 1st Flotilla and six others with the battlecruisers or 2nd CS, had been ordered to take station 5 miles astern of the battlefleet at 2127.

Beatty continued on 212° until 2130, when the *Lion* was *c*10½ miles bearing 240° from the *King George V*, and then turned to 167°. The battlecruisers' speed was 17kts as was the battlefleet's, and by 2135 the 2nd CS were following astern of the *Inflexible*, while the 1st and 3rd LCS were steering 212° for their station wide on the *Lion*'s starboard bow. The *Lion* was no more than 6 miles ahead of the *Westfalen* at 2130, and when Beatty turned to 167°, his forces' position was as if they were acting as vanguard to the German Fleet. This was unknown to either side, though some of the 2nd CS were sighted by the *Hannover*.

Of the ships that had fallen out during the day, the *Warspite* was 30 miles or more to the northward of the *Barham* at 2030. Twenty minutes later she wirelessed the latter, requesting the battlefleet's position, and stating that there were two big holes abreast the engine-room, the wing-engine room had not yet flooded, and that she could steam 16kts. Evan-Thomas's reply, sent at 2107, ordered her to Rosyth. At about 2130 she met the *Defender* towing the *Onslow* but soon outdistanced the two damaged destroyers. The *Acasta* was still stopped carrying out emergency repairs. The *Warrior* was being towed by the *Engadine* at about 8kts.

Scheer had never intended to fight a battle with the whole Grand Fleet, and unless he could get to the eastward of the British and make for home, it was virtually certain that he would have to do so next day. The *Westfalen*'s turn to starboard at 2105 was thus most unwelcome, and in a signal timed at 2114 Scheer ordered the Battle Fleet to maintain course 142° (which led to Horns Reef). Speed was to be 16kts, and the 2nd Squadron were to take station at the rear of the line, and the battlecruisers prolong the line astern.

The references to the 2nd Squadron and the battlecruisers are omitted in the British Admiralty's intercept, but this includes information that the German main body was to proceed in, which seems to be otherwise unrecorded.

Very few ships appear to have taken in the first transmission of this signal at *c*2116, but a repeat was received at 2125, and a further signal from Scheer timed at 2129, and received at 2135, gave the night cruising formation. The 2nd Squadron were to take station astern of the 3rd, the battlecruisers take station at the rear of the line, the 2nd SG ahead and the 4th SG to starboard. The *Westfalen* meanwhile proceeded on 167° with the 2nd Squadron on her port bow until 2135 when she turned to 201°, to clear the 4th SG crossing ahead, and did not alter course to 142° until 2143.

The 2nd Squadron were also steering 167°, and at shortly before 2130 the *Hannover* made out the smoke of four large ships ahead, and also a high masthead light. The ships which the *Hannover* immediately reported by wireless, were the 2nd CS, the light belonging to the *Shannon*, and they were then on the British battlecruisers' starboard quarter, and crossed the *Hannover*'s bows about 2½ or 3 miles ahead. British destroyers, presumably the 2nd Cruiser Squadron's screen, were briefly sighted at 2135, ahead to starboard and steaming at full speed, but this was apparently not reported. On receiving Scheer's night formation signal Rear Admiral Mauve ordered the 2nd Squadron to reduce to half speed but he did not begin to take station astern until 2155, when the situation ahead had become clearer.

Hipper boarded the *Moltke* at 2057 (also at 2105) and decided that the 1st SG would proceed towards the head of the line at 20kts. Only the *Moltke* and *Seydlitz* could comply as the *Derfflinger* and *von der Tann* were limited to 18kts, the former by the amount of water that entered forward at higher speed, and the latter by dirty fires which had to be cleaned. Hipper's increase of speed could be justified for the *Moltke* but not for the *Seydlitz* and it would have been better to have limited her speed to 18kts or less, for similar reasons to the *Derfflinger*'s.

The 1st SG turned to 235° at *c*2113, and at about 2125 to 167°. They were then astern of the *König*, but from about 2135 the *Moltke* and *Seydlitz* proceeded to pass up the port side of the 3rd and 1st Squadrons and reach the van.

The *Lützow* was still steering *c*175° at 11kts with her four destroyers, and in a signal timed at 2105 the *König* reported that she had lost sight of her. It was still hoped that the *Lützow* might get home, but it was impossible to limit the Fleet's speed to hers. The *Frankfurt* and *Pillau* were on the *Hannover's* port bow at 2130, with the 4th SG which had been joined by the *Elbing*, on the *Westfalen's* starboard bow, and just turning to cross ahead of her, as the *Hannover* had requested them to take station ahead of the 2nd Squadron.

Scheer called for morning airship reconnaissance off Horns Reef in a signal timed at 2106, which was not received by the Naval Airship Division, and at 1950 Captain Bauer, the Leader of Submarines, who was in the *Hamburg*, had ordered available boats from the 3rd Submarine Half-Flotilla at Borkum Roads, the *U53* at Heligoland if ready, and the *U67* cruising off Terschelling, to proceed northwards at once, reporting their 0400 positions.

The German destroyer flotillas were to carry out night attacks, but fortunately for the British the position of their battlefleet was not known, so that the flotillas had to be spread between 55° and 190°. There were defects in the plan adopted, and no success was obtained. Scheer had told Commodore Heinrich in the *Regensburg* as early as 1916 that his three flotillas were to attack during the night, and at 2000 both Heinrich and the Senior Leader of Destroyers, Commodore Michelsen, in the *Rostock*, were ordered by Scheer to direct all flotillas to attack.

Heinrich had available the ten destroyers of the 2nd Flotilla which had only fired one torpedo with two damaged, so that they had 57 left, and three destroyers of the 12th Half-Flotilla with 15 torpedoes. In order to obtain a view, less obscured by haze and smoke, the *Regensburg* turned back with these destroyers at *c*2010 and made for a position northward of the German rear, and not far from where the *Indefatigable* had sunk, wreckage being noted by the *B97* and *G103*. The 2nd Flotilla were to attack in the sector 55° to 100° and, if it appeared inadvisable to return via the German Bight, were to make for Kiel round the Skaw. The next sector, 100° to 122°, was allotted to the 12th Half-Flotilla. Just after the destroyers had been given their orders, and 14 minutes before they were finally detached at 2030, a signal was received from Scheer, that the *Rostock* was to conduct all attacks. Heinrich had foreseen this, and had therefore confined his flotillas to the tactically less favourable northern sectors to avoid obstructing Michelsen. This meant that the most promising sectors would be given to the coal-fired destroyers of the 5th and 7th Flotillas. Heinrich notified Scheer and Michelsen of the orders issued, and Michelsen then informed Scheer that Heinrich would direct the attacks of his flotillas independently.

Both the 2nd Flotilla and 12th Half-Flotilla encountered British forces earlier than intended and at 2052 the 2nd LCS opened fire on the latter at 3500–5500yds. The destroyers turned away, and the *S50* was hit by a 6in shell which did not explode but put one boiler out of action amongst other damage, so that she had to reduce to 25kts and return to the German Fleet. The destroyers made smoke and artificial fog, and the *V69* and *V46* resumed their course at 2110. In addition to the 2nd LCS, the *Benbow* fired one salvo of 6in, and a round from 'B' turret, while the *Valiant* believed that the 2nd LCS were firing at a submarine on her starboard bow, for which she altered course. The *Barham* fired some rounds of 6in at a supposed submarine during the battle, possibly at this time.

The 2nd Flotilla sighted the British 2nd LCS and 12th Flotilla at 2045–2050, and also turned away, gradually describing a large circle to starboard, so that they did not resume their eastward course until 2130 or 2140. This delay caused the 2nd Flotilla to pass far astern of any British battleships, though the *V69* and *V46* approached much nearer. Of the other oil-fired destroyers, the *G41* and the 11th Half-Flotilla had only three torpedoes left between them, and were sent to take station at the head of the line. The 9th Flotilla had lost three destroyers, and of the remainder the *V28* and *S52* had no torpedoes left, while the *V28* was also damaged, as was the *S51* which had two torpedoes, and these three took station on the 1st Squadron.

The other five destroyers of this flotilla had a total of 21 torpedoes available and, in company with the *G42* of the 3rd Flotilla which still had six torpedoes but was reduced in speed, joined the *Rostock*, and at 2130 were steaming towards the head of the line. The other five surviving destroyers of the 3rd Flotilla had 20 torpedoes left, though the *G88* had only one. They did not regain touch with the German Fleet for some time after their final attempt to reach the *Wiesbaden*, but by 2045 had joined the *Regensburg* and, for the time being, were retained as a reserve. Lastly the *G38, G40, V45* and *G37* with a total of 20 torpedoes were accompanying the *Lützow*, the *G39* with six torpedoes, the 1st SG and then the *Moltke*; the *S32*, which had only one torpedo left, was with the *Rostock*.

The destroyers of the 5th and 7th Flotillas had each one oil-fired and three coal-fired boilers, and the fires in the latter were very dirty, so that in order to prepare them to some extent for smokeless steaming during the coming attacks, speed had to be held to 17–18 or at the most 21kts, and even at 15kts sparks and funnel smoke were visible at a considerable distance. As the British fleet speed during the night was 17kts, this was a serious handicap, and in addition the position where they were detached by the *Rostock* at *c*2110, was near the rear of the German line, whose alterations of course hampered these flotillas. Neither had yet fired any torpedoes, so that the 5th had 44 and the 7th 36 available.

Michelsen thought that the British would probably steam southward under the Jutland coast during the night and assigned the sector 122° to 156° to the 7th Flotilla, and 156° to 190° to the 5th. Owing to Michelsen's and Heinrich's flotillas being detached from different positions, there was however a gap between the 122° boundaries of the sectors of the 12th Half-Flotilla and 7th Flotilla. The 5th Flotilla proceeded generally 173° after they were detached, and should have begun to search their sector at 2230, but they were delayed 30 minutes by having to pass twice through the German line, and also by smoke interfering with visual signals. The 7th Flotilla which were steering 139° passed through the line of the 3rd Squadron at about 2125, and 3 minutes or so later the *S23* was briefly lit up by SL and fired at. Recognition signals stopped further firing, and the 7th Flotilla altered course to 122° to get further away from the German Fleet, and proceeded in close order at 17kts.

There were thus no German destroyers in the sector between 122° and 173°, where the British battleships were to be found.

CHAPTER 13

Damage to capital ships
and pre-dreadnoughts 2019–2039
Condition of *Seydlitz* and *Lützow*

Two hits were recorded on British ships, the time being given as about 2032, and the *Lion* and *Princess Royal* the ships concerned. The hit on the *Lion* was by a 5.9in from the 1st SG, which holed a steam pinnace and burst on the upper part of an engine-room uptake, causing some splinter damage and a small fire.

The hit on the *Princess Royal* was by an 11in shell from the *Posen* which struck the starboard strut of the foremast about 20ft above the forecastle. The strut was nearly half severed, and the shell then passed through the fore-funnel and more than half severed the port strut. The shell did not explode, and the hit was not noticed aloft, while the Director tested correctly afterwards. All voice-pipes in both struts and the auxiliary Director circuit were cut, and the base of the fore-funnel was reported as seriously damaged, presumably by this hit.

Of the German ships, the *Derfflinger* was hit at 2028 by a shell from the *Lion* coming from some way abaft the port beam. This struck the port side of 'A' barbette, just forward of the transverse diameter and c3ft below the upper edge of the barbette, and glanced off, bursting close to the barbette and about 2½ft above the upper deck. The surface of the 10¼in barbette armour was spalled for 17in × 11in to a depth of 0.3in with concentric cracks, while the 1in upper deck was holed between the barbette and the side longitudinal bulkhead for 11½ft × 4ft. The ¼in upper main deck was also holed for 4ft × 2¼ft, and fittings destroyed in the vicinity. The water excluding packing was partly torn away and jammed the turret, but this was quickly put right by the gun crews. The turret was also heavily shaken, which temporarily interrupted the power supply to the training motor, and some small splinters entered through a sighting slit.

There were five hits on the *Seydlitz*, the first at 2024 from the *Princess Royal*. The shell came from *c*10° abaft the port beam, and struck the 6in armour of No 4 port – 5.9in casemate, 12ft aft of the gun mounting axis and 5ft above the battery deck. It burst in penetrating, the explosive effect being inside the casemate, and a hole of 30½in × 29½in was made in the armour with many cracks below the hole. The gun was badly dented and put out of action, and one ready cartridge burnt, but the magazine was not affected, though the magazine party felt the pressure, and placed a wooden cover on the lower opening of the hoist trunk. Fragments of armour and splinters pierced the 0.8in casemate longitudinal bulkhead, 18ft from the hit, in about 10 places, wrecked most of the port – 5.9in fire-control cables and the engineer's workshop inboard of the casemate, and cut the cables to the main W/T transmitter. The after funnel casing and stokehold ventilation trunks were also pierced, and two fans put temporarily out of action, so that the stoking positions concerned had to be vacated for a short time from smoke and gas.

The casemate longitudinal bulkhead was also bowed by up to 8in, but the 0.8in transverse bulkhead, only 2ft from the line of the hit, was undamaged. There were large holes in the battery deck, and splinters entered coal-bunkers, in one of which a short-circuit caused a fire, and penetrated the main deck. The port forward power supply to the 5.9in and 3.5in hoists was also wrecked, and after the battle, when the casemates were partially under water, the damage caused by this hit allowed water to enter the port inner bunker of No 2 boiler-room.

The second hit from the *Princess Royal* at 2028 came from about 20° abaft the port beam, and hit the Admiral's chart-house, bursting about 5ft above the bridge and 3ft from the conning tower. Splinters swept the starboard bridge and a few entered the CT through the sighting slits. A good deal of damage was done to the forward searchlights, two being put out of action, and the casualties were four killed and five wounded, three of the latter, including the Navigating Officer, being in the CT. The gunnery control tower vibrated violently but the sighting slits had been closed, and the Director-pointer gear escaped serious damage, though the range-finder showed a large elevation error.

Of the three hits by the *New Zealand* on the *Seydlitz*, the first at 2028 struck the 2¾in roof of the aftermost turret about 8ft from the rear and 5ft from the right edge. The shell was deflected and burst about 3ft from impact. There were two impact marks, several scars and slight cracks less than ½in deep in the roof armour, which was bowed to a

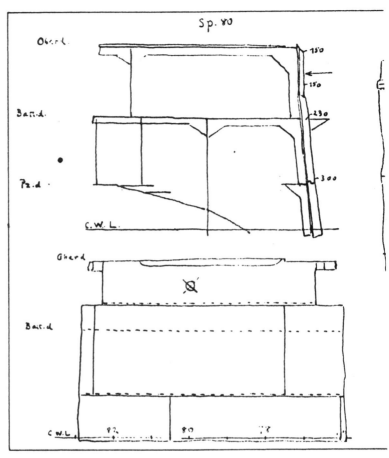

Seydlitz: *hit at 2024.*

maximum of 5½in over an area of 16ft × 10ft, and a roof girder and supports were bent. Both upper shell hoists were put out of action by the cables of the operating switch being cut, the right hand ventilation trunk of the smoke expulsion motor was torn away, and the wiring from the motor starter cut, the damage in each instance being due to the bent roof girder. Splinters from the shell burst struck the superfiring turret, and made a few scars on the right gun. The main training gear of the aftermost turret was already out of action.

The other two hits from the *New Zealand* were both by shells

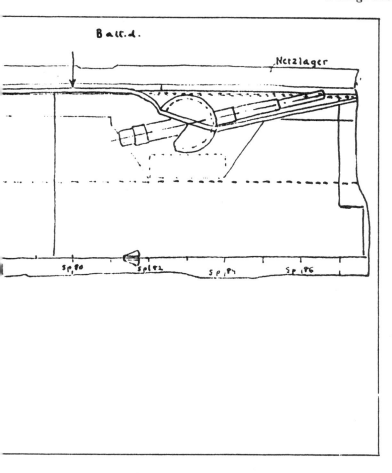

apparently coming from about 40° abaft the port beam, and occurred at
c2030. One shell struck a plate of the 12in armour belt just forward of a
vertical joint, and about 1½ft below the horizontal joint between the
main and upper belt armour, the hit being below and just abaft No 6
port – 5.9in. The shell broke up or burst, and most of it was deflected
outside the armour, but a 'D' shaped hole, measuring 16in × 24in and
much broken away on the inside, was made in the plate forward of the
joint, while the plate aft of the joint was only chipped at the edge. There
was no displacement of the armour plates. Fragments of armour and

267

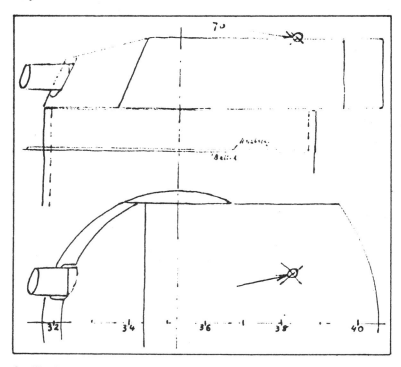

Seydlitz: *hit at 2028.*

Opposite. Seydlitz: *first hit from* New Zealand *at c2030.*

shell splinters entered an outer bunker which became flooded for a length of *c*35ft.

The other shell struck a plate of the upper belt, where it was 12in thick, just above the horizontal joint with the main belt, and below and a few feet aft of the 2024 hit. It burst after penetrating a small distance into the plate, making a hole with overall dimensions of 4ft × 2ft and much broken away on the upper inside, though it appears that no shell splinters entered the ship. The 12in main belt plate was slightly driven in, and the surface and edge broken away in a semi-circle on the outside, with numerous cracks.

Water entering through this hole slowly filled the port outer bunker of No 2 boiler-room, and spread into the protective bunker

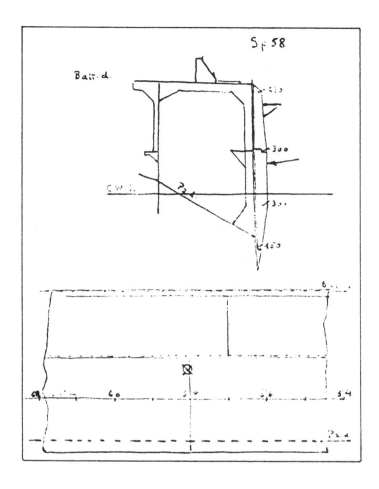

below via an armoured manhole door which had been distorted by the hit. It also spread from the above outer bunker into the port stoking position of No 2 boiler-room through a damaged ejector pump pipe, but was pumped or drained from the stokehold. In addition water entered the port outer bunker of No 1 boiler-room through a damaged bulkhead, and leaked into the port outer bunker of No 3 boiler-room. Later on, as the *Seydlitz*'s draught increased, further flooding of this last bunker occurred from water which had entered the casemates and spread gradually to No 3 boiler-room protective bunker, whence it was drained into the stokehold and pumped out.

No details are known of the hit by the *Indomitable* on the *Pommern* but the shell from the *New Zealand* that hit the *Schleswig-Holstein* at

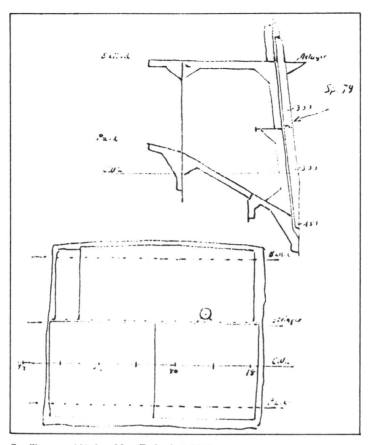

Seydlitz: *second hit from* New Zealand *at c2030.*

2032, went through an air-intake shaft at the level of the superstructure deck, making holes of *c*16in diameter, and burst against the inner 4¾in armour of the starboard after upper deck 6.7in casemate, 5½ft above the upper deck and 3½ft from the after end of the casemate. The explosive effect of this shell, which came from about 20° forward of the port beam, and which was thought to be an HE, was in front of the armour, but a plate of the latter, hit 2ft below the upper edge, was holed for 21in × 17in and driven inwards by up to 5ft at the after edge. The superstructure deck was torn up for a length of 15ft, and bowed upwards over the displaced armour plate where 1.2in thick, while the 1.4in upper deck was driven downwards. Light structures were damaged near the burst, and inside the casemate, the 6.7in gun was put

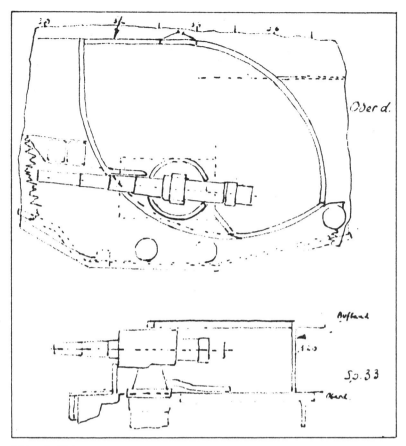

Schleswig-Holstein: *hit at 2032.*

out of action from damage to the training gear and right run-out spring. Two exposed cartridges, in rear of the gun, were ignited, and one of them was thought to have exploded, a rare occurrence with German charges. Much smoke was produced by smouldering debris and casualties were three killed and nine wounded.

In addition to these hits, a splinter from one of the *New Zealand*'s shells which burst short of the *Schlesien*, pierced her foretop high on the mast and killed one man.

The estimated hits on German heavy ships in this phase given in the table overleaf.

	13.5in/1250lb	12in	Total
Derfflinger	1	—	1
Seydlitz	2	3	5
Schleswig-Holstein	—	1	1
Pommern	—	1	1
	3	5	8

The *Seydlitz* followed the *Moltke*, after Hipper had boarded the latter at about 2100, at a higher speed than was wise in view of the amount of water present in the forward part of the ship. At 2100 the total quantity of water in the *Seydlitz* was calculated to be 2636 tons with an increase in draught forward of 8ft 4in, a decrease of 3ft 3in aft, and a list of 2° 5′ to starboard. This was in itself no very serious danger to the ship, and among other compartments the forward 11in and 5.9in ammunition spaces and the broadside and bow torpedo flats were still unflooded. The large hole in the starboard side caused by the 15in shell at 1706, was however not far above the 2100 waterline, and the faster the *Seydlitz* steamed the greater would be the intake of water.

In the *Lützow* further troubles arose from the flooding of the ammunition spaces of the forward turrets. This was thought to have occurred through leakage from an emergency exit of the broadside torpedo flat, and also through local lack of water-tightness at the port torpedo bulkhead and side longitudinal bulkhead. It appears that 'A' magazines first began gradually to fill at about 2000 and 'A' shell room was next affected, and then apparently 'B' magazines. Drainage attempts were not successful as there was already too much flooding in the vicinity, but it seems to have been possible to keep the water down in 'B' at least for a time, though 'A' magazines and shell room had to be abandoned after sending up as much ammunition as possible to the working chamber.

There was no fire-control communication with 'A', as the cables of the order-transmission equipment were shorting under water, and voice-pipes were flooded. The ship's control-room was also leaking, but the water could be kept down and it remained in operation.

The total weight of water that had entered the *Lützow* by 2130 is not known, but her draught forward was still increasing, and water entering above the armour deck would soon become a very serious problem.

CHAPTER 14

Events during the night
2130 31 May – 0300 1 June

THE NEXT PHASE covers the moonless night and the 1¼ hours of dawn twilight on 1 June. Of the rival Commanders in Chief Jellicoe had the more difficult problems to solve. Scheer had to reach the swept channels through the minefields in the German Bight in time to avoid being brought to battle by the entire Grand Fleet next day, whereas Jellicoe had first to prevent his battleships becoming involved in night fighting, and then be in a position to intercept the High Seas Fleet in daylight before it could attain the mined area. Scheer decided to return via Horns Reef, the shortest route, and detached most of his destroyers to attack the British, relying on the night-fighting abilities of his dreadnoughts to brush aside any opposition.

Unless accurate information on the German course could be obtained, Jellicoe could only guess Scheer's route from the four that were possible. Three of these led to swept channels in the German Bight, one via Horns Reef, a second to the west of Heligoland, and a third further west and then past Borkum and along the German coast. The fourth route, round the Skaw to the Kattegat and then to Kiel was not likely to be used by a fleet with damaged ships as it was much longer. Jellicoe's knowledge of the swept channels is not certain, but he knew of those via Borkum and Horns Reef and also that there was possibly another route to the west of Heligoland. Of these Jellicoe thought that the route past Borkum was the most likely. He knew that the German fleet was to the west of the British at nightfall, and he continued on 167° at 17kts through the night, with Beatty steering a similar course a dozen miles to the westward.

This course was well suited for intercepting Scheer next morning if he used the Borkum route, and was likely to keep the British capital ships away from the German fleet during the night. Jellicoe's intended formation of three columns of eight battleships with the columns disposed abeam a mile apart, might make it easier for the ships to maintain station, and lessen the risk of mistaking one another for the enemy, as well as that of the German destroyers finding them, but it was highly dangerous if they had to fight a night action or meet a destroyer attack. The stationing of the British destroyers, other than those with Beatty, 5 miles astern of the battlefleet, was intended to screen the latter from attacks by the German flotillas, and to decrease the chance of the British flotillas' mistaking their own heavy ships for the enemy. It might also serve to bar the way if Scheer crossed astern of the British fleet making for Horns Reef. Jellicoe at 2132 ordered the *Abdiel* to lay her 80 mines 158° to 201° from a position 15 miles bearing 215° from the Vyl Lightship, which was c9 miles to the WSW of the similar minefield which she had laid on 4 May. These mines were laid between 0124 and 0204 on 1 June, but did not cause any damage to the German fleet though the *Abdiel's* previous field did so.

The German fleet did encounter some of the British destroyers, but the latter could not stop Scheer's progress towards Horns Reef though they were able to delay it. The fighting between these forces was the principal feature of this phase, but it did not begin until 2330. Previously, other actions took place between some of the light cruisers and destroyers.

The 4th BS had taken up their night formation by 2130, and the 2nd BS began to do so at 2135 but of the 1st BS only the 5th Division were able to take station on the port beam of the 4th BS, while the *Marlborough* and her Division gradually fell astern on the 5th Division's port quarter. The *Iron Duke's* actual course appears to have been c166°, and diverged very slightly from that of the battlecruisers, while the *Marlborough* at first steered more to the west and from c2215 slightly more to the east than the *Iron Duke*. The 5th BS either followed the 5th Division, or were between them and the *Marlborough*. At 2203 they turned through 180° and continued for 5 minutes before turning to 167°. This was to reduce their distance from the *Marlborough*, but a turn to starboard begun at 2241 and eventually continued through 360° was due to a report of imaginary destroyers crossing their bows some distance ahead.

The 4th LCS continued ahead and the 2nd LCS took up a position on the starboard quarter of the fleet. Of the British destroyer flotillas, the *Castor* and the 11th were the most westward, with the 4th, 13th, 9th and 12th in order to the eastward. The 11th Flotilla got out of position, after an action with German light cruisers, so that most of the fighting with the German battlefleet fell on the much weaker 4th Flotilla.

The 11th Flotilla was at its initial strength with the *Castor*, *Kempenfelt* and 14 'M' class destroyers, but in the 4th Flotilla, two destroyers had been sunk or disabled and five were with Beatty so that the *Tipperary* and *Broke* were left with 10 of the 'K' class. The 13th Flotilla had lost three destroyers sunk or disabled, and thus comprised the *Champion*, seven 'M' class destroyers and the *Termagant* and *Turbulent* of the 10th Flotilla. The 9th Flotilla consisted of four 'L' class with the *Morris* of the 10th Flotilla, as the *Moorsom*, with no torpedoes left and short of oil, was ordered home at about 2200. The 12th Flotilla had one destroyer with Beatty, and thus had the *Faulknor* and *Marksman* with 13 of the 'M' class. All flotilla leaders and destroyers present had their full number of torpedoes except in the 13th Flotilla where the *Petard* had none, the *Nicator* one, *Nerissa* two, *Moresby* three and *Turbulent* probably one. The *Castor* and *Champion* each had two submerged TT and seven torpedoes.

The vessels with Beatty were not involved in the night's fighting.

Scheer's order that course 142° was to be maintained, was generally received at 2125, but it was not until 2143 that the *Westfalen* turned to it, and at 2146 Scheer gave a new course 137° to compensate for the delay in turning. This signal was received incorrectly by the *Westfalen*, the course being read as 156° instead of 137°, and she therefore turned to 156° at about 2208, and it was not until about 2245 that the *Westfalen* altered course to 133° in accordance with a further signal from Scheer, timed at 2232. In a subsequent signal timed at 2302, Scheer gave the course as 130° for Horns Reef lightship, and the *Westfalen* turned accordingly at about 2320.

The pre-dreadnoughts of the 2nd Squadron began an 'about-turn' to port at 2155 and headed back to take station astern of the *König*. The *von der Tann* and *Derfflinger* began to steam up the port side of the dreadnoughts, and when abeam of the *Friedrich der Grosse* were again ordered to take station at the rear of the line and joined astern of the 2nd Squadron.

The night formation of the German battlefleet was completed by about 2230 with 24 ships in single line ahead, the order being: *Westfalen, Nassau, Rheinland, Posen, Oldenburg, Helgoland, Thüringen, Ostfriesland, Friedrich der Grosse, Prinzregent Luitpold, Kaiserin, Kaiser, Markgraf, Kronprinz, Grosser Kurfürst, König, Deutschland, Pommern, Schlesien, Schleswig-Holstein, Hessen, Hannover, von der Tann, Derfflinger.*

The courses steered by the *Moltke* and *Seydlitz* are not certain, but for the first hour their mean course diverged to some extent from that of the *Westfalen* to starboard. At about 2220 they were steaming up to starboard of the 4th SG, and then crossed ahead, forcing the *Stettin* to slow down. At 2230 the *Moltke* suddenly sighted four large British ships forward of the port beam. These were the four *Orion*s and the *Moltke* turned away without having time to fire torpedoes. The *Thunderer* saw the *Moltke* challenge three times, but did not open fire as it was considered inadvisable to indicate the battlefleet's position unless an obvious attack was intended. The *Boadicea*, 500yds astern of the *Thunderer*, saw the *Moltke* approaching about 23° abaft the starboard beam at high speed. The German ship challenged when turning away, and was estimated to be in sight for 30 seconds. Directions were given for firing the *Boadicea*'s starboard TT (18in), but the *Moltke* disappeared.

The *Seydlitz* apparently lost touch with the *Moltke* at this time, and probably crossed from port to starboard ahead of the action now beginning between the 4th SG and 2nd LCS, but the *Moltke* cut across the *Hamburg*'s bows from port to starboard in the middle of the fighting, forcing her to turn hard to starboard to avoid a collision, and then once more steamed up to starboard of the 4th SG.

The *Seydlitz* had now reduced speed, and her proceedings during the next hour are not clear, though she appears to have been latterly steering south-eastwards at revolutions for 19 or 20kts, and must have penetrated the British formation astern of the 2nd and 4th BS, but no contacts were made.

The *Moltke* again sighted the four *Orion*s about 34° forward of the port beam at *c*2255, once more turning away temporarily, and sighted them for the third time to port ahead at about 2320. She was not seen by the British ships and gave up the attempt to pass to the eastward, heading 212° and then 167° at increased speed. Her main wireless was out of action, and no report could be sent to Scheer at the time.

The *Lützow* was able to continue southward for the first two hours of the night, though her speed was reduced to 7kts, and there was some hope of bringing her into port. Both the 2nd SG (*Frankfurt* and *Pillau*) and the 4th SG with the *Elbing* and *Rostock* were to eastward of the battleships, and not as ordered in Scheer's 2129 signal, while the *Regensburg* was astern of the *Derfflinger*.

The disposition of the German destroyers at 2130 has been recorded, and relatively little occurred during the next two hours. Michelsen ordered the five effective destroyers of the 9th Flotilla and the *G42* to attack the enemy reported at shortly before 2130 by the *Hannover*, but they were allocated a sector between 190° and 212° so that nothing was seen. In a signal timed at 2232 Michelsen ordered that by 0200 all flotillas were to be reformed and in company with the battlefleet off Horns Reef, or on the way round the Skaw. The 2nd Flotilla drew blank and of the 12th Half-Flotilla, the *V69* and *V46* saw the flashes of the action between the 4th SG and 2nd LCS far off to starboard but met no British ships, while the damaged *S50* joined the *Regensburg* at 2225 and was subsequently attached to the 3rd Squadron. The 5th Flotilla did not begin their search until 2300 and, with speed kept down to 18kts to reduce smoke, were still near their own fleet at this time. The 7th Flotilla also kept their speed down to 17–18kts. They had a brush with the British 4th Flotilla and altered course to 167°, briefly to 122°, and after a second contact with the 4th Flotilla to 139° without splitting into groups. Of the other destroyers the *G41* and the 11th Half-Flotilla took station in the gaps in the 3rd Squadron, and two from the *V28, S51* and *S52* then in company with the *Friedrich der Grosse* were ordered by Scheer at 2215 to go to the *Lützow*, but only the *S52* was in a condition to do so, and she failed to find her.

Although the distance from the *Westfalen* to the *Lion* increased from about 6 miles at 2130 to *c*12 at 2300, that to the *King George V* fell from about 9 miles to perhaps 6½ miles in the same period and by 2330 the head of the German line had entered the space between the British battlefleet and the 4th Flotilla without anyone on either side being previously aware of it, though the 5th BS may have been 2 miles and the 6th Division *c*4 miles from the *Westfalen* at 2330. The *Moltke* could not report her encounters with the 2nd BS, and though the *Boadicea* recognised her as a large ship, no report was made except a flash-lamp signal to the *Thunderer* that hostile ships were on the starboard beam.

Scheer could see the actions to the eastward in which his light cruisers took part, and received reports of British cruisers and destroyers, the latter steering 167°. He did not, however, receive any reports of capital ships in the first two hours of the night. One valuable item was obtained, the *Elbing* reporting in a signal timed at 2219 that the British recognition signal from 2200 onwards was 'Ü' which was amended to 'UA' by the *Frankfurt* in a further signal timed 14 minutes later. The *Princess Royal*'s reply to a flash-lamp signal from the *Lion* at 2132, requesting the challenge and reply then in force as her own record had been lost, is usually considered to have been the source of this information though only the first two letters were obtained. The Germans who alternatively used a system of coloured lights, had a poor opinion of British recognition signals, as a Tactical Order dated 25 June 1915 recommended that if deception was intended, British ships were to be called with badly manipulated searchlights, and a two-letter challenge given, in the hope that special care would not be taken to see that the exact challenge was made.

No fresh information regarding the position of the German battlefleet reached Jellicoe from any of his ships between 2130 and 2330, as Beatty's signal, timed at 2100 and received in the *Iron Duke* at 2141, stating that the enemy bore 336° and were steering 235°, only repeated the information in the *Falmouth*'s 2046 signal, with some adjustment to the enemy's bearing. The *Castor* signalled at 2250, via the *Kempenfelt*, that she had been engaged by enemy cruisers, and both this action and that of the 2nd LCS were seen from the British battleships, but gave no indication of the German heavy ships' proceedings. More data on German movements was forthcoming from intercepted wireless signals deciphered by Room 40 at the Admiralty and passed to the Operations Division who forwarded a selection to Jellicoe. The first to reach Jellicoe during the present period was in a signal timed at 2105 and received in the *Iron Duke* at 2139, stating that three destroyer flotillas had been ordered to attack during the night. This was based on Scheer's 1916 signal to the *Regensburg*, ordering the 2nd, 6th and 9th Flotillas to attack in the night, and the deciphered text had been passed to the Operations Division as long ago as 1940.

This was followed by a signal timed at 2158 and received in the *Iron Duke* at 2223, that at 2100 the rear ship of the enemy battlefleet was in 56° 33'N, 5° 30'E course *c*167°. This was based on a signal by the *Regensburg* to the 2nd and 6th Flotillas timed at 2103, which was passed to the Operations Division at 2125. The *König*'s true position at 2100 was 56° 39'N, 5° 33'E, and the position quoted in the Admiralty signal was very near that of the *Hannover* leading the 2nd Squadron, while the *Iron Duke* was at that time in 56° 38'N, 5° 47'E. Jellicoe however believed the *Iron Duke* to have been in 56° 39'N, 5° 42'E at 2100, and Beatty to have borne 280° from the *King George V* in accordance with Jerram's mistaken sighting signal timed at 2105. From Beatty's signals timed at 2040 and 2100, the German battlecruisers, presumably at or near the head of the line, were thus thought by Jellicoe to have been in about 56° 47'N, 5° 24'E at 2100 steering 235°, and he had further apparent reason for distrusting information from the Admiralty, who had made a serious error in placing the *Friedrich der Grosse* in the Jade at 1110.

The third Admiralty signal was timed at 2241 and received in the

Iron Duke at 2248. This stated that the German battlefleet had been ordered home at 2114, with the battlecruisers in rear, course 137°, speed 16kts. This was based on Scheer's course and formation signals of 2114, 2129 and 2146, of which the deciphered texts had been passed to the Operations Division at 2155–2210. The text of Scheer's 2106 signal calling for early airship reconnaissance at Horns Reef was also passed to the Operations Division at 2210, but never forwarded to Jellicoe. Had this been sent it would, together with the German course reported in the 2241 signal, have provided Jellicoe with a strong indication of Scheer's whereabouts next morning, though some weight might still have been given to the reasoning from British ships' signals. The Operations Division also had the texts of signals from the *Regensburg* and *Rostock* reporting the sectors assigned to the German flotillas, but this was again not passed to Jellicoe.

The first of the night's actions was a brush between the British 4th and German 7th Flotillas. Shortly before 2200, the *S24* made out a line of destroyers ahead, but they were mistaken for the 2nd Flotilla, and it was not until the *S24* challenged at about 500yds that it was realised that they were British. The *S24, S15, S16* and *S18* each fired one torpedo, and the *Garland, Contest* and *Fortune* fired a few 4in shells. The *S16*'s torpedo partially misfired and fell overboard, but two torpedoes running on the surface passed close astern of the *Garland*, one mising by 10ft, and a third torpedo was sighted by the *Fortune*. The 4th Flotilla were completing their turn to 167° after taking station astern of the battlefleet, and both sides quickly lost contact, as the 7th Flotilla turned away before also proceeding on 167°. They were again in contact at 2242 when the *S24* fired one torpedo which passed close astern of the *Unity*, but their courses then diverged.

The *Frankfurt* accompanied by the *Pillau*, sighted the *Castor* and some of the 11th Flotilla, and took them to be five cruisers, reporting them at 2158 steering 55°. They were then recognised as a light cruiser and destroyers, and as the German 2nd Flotilla was known to be further north, the *Frankfurt* and *Pillau* each fired a torpedo at about 1100yds, and turned away without firing or using searchlights, to avoid drawing the destroyers towards the German battlefleet. They were not detected by the *Castor* or her flotilla, which turned away and steered southward.

The 4th SG were also proceeding in this direction with the *Hamburg, Elbing* and *Rostock* on the port quarter, and these three ships were sighted by the *Castor* on her starboard bow. They made the first two letters of the British challenge correctly, followed by two other letters, and then switched on their searchlights and opened rapid fire to which the *Castor* at once replied. The action began at *c*2213 and lasted for at most 5 minutes before both sides turned away. The range was reported at *c*1100–2700yds. The *Castor* only expended 26–6in and 32–4in during the whole battle, but she made 3–6in hits on the *Hamburg*, though no great damage was caused. The *Castor* was straddled by the first German salvo, and was hit by a total of about ten shells, but as with other British light cruisers, her side armour prevented serious damage. One shell set her motor-boat on fire which lit up the ship, and three struck the bridge cutting all electric circuits. Otherwise only the *Marne* was hit by a 4.1in which caused little damage. The *Castor*, and *Magic* each fired a torpedo, and the track of the *Castor*'s passed under the *Elbing* as she turned away. The other destroyers took no part, apparently because they were blinded by the flash of the *Castor*'s guns and/or believed that they were being fired on by British ships.

The 11th Flotilla's courses for 2 hours after this action are not clear, but they encountered the 2nd SG on more than one occasion before 2330. The 2nd SG did not open fire but at *c*2240 the *Magic* fired a torpedo at what were taken to be three large cruisers 2500–3000yds away, while the *Marne* also fired one at a light cruiser at 3/4000yds. At 2257 the *Frankfurt* sighted a light cruiser and five destroyers passing to port on a northward course, while the *Mystic* saw a 3-funnelled cruiser passing close to port, steering in the opposite direction, but no torpedoes were fired.

The *Moltke* and *Seydlitz* had forced the *Stettin* to slow down when they crossed ahead, and this reduction in speed was not observed by the rest of the 4th SG so that they closed up in irregular formation. The 2nd LCS, in which the *Dublin* had changed station to second ship, (it is not known when or why) came into sight *c*3000/3500yds away and somewhat abaft the port beam on a converging course, and they sighted the German ships at about the same time, and were the first to challenge. The *Southampton* switched on her searchlights and opened fire, and at the same moment the German ships replied, their searchlights being trained on the target before switching on. In addition to the four light cruisers of the 4th SG, the *Hamburg*, *Elbing* and *Rostock* took part and a violent action ensued at ranges which are given as from 800 to 2500yds, though the *Rostock* reported over 3000. The time of opening fire was probably 2235, and the fighting only lasted about 3½ minutes, the *München* expending 92–4.1in. The first salvos started fires in the *Southampton*, the *Stettin*, *München* and *Rostock* firing at her, the *Stuttgart* at the *Dublin*, and the *Elbing* at both, while data is lacking for the *Frauenlob* and *Hamburg*. The *Stettin* was hit by two shells at the beginning and a splinter damaged the steam pipe to the siren, escaping steam seriously impairing visibility and a turn to port for a torpedo shot was given up. Of the 2nd LCS only the *Southampton* switched on her searchlights and the other three used the German lights as their point of aim. A fire started on the *Dublin*'s mess decks over the forward magazines and she hauled out 34° to port so that the enemy shells fell short. The *Southampton*'s guns had probably opened at two ships and it was not long before her searchlights went out and most of her guns ceased firing. Three cordite fires broke out, and in one the flame passed down the midships hoist leading to the ammunition passage, but it got no further and the fires were soon extinguished. Although worsted in the gunnery action, the *Southampton* fired a torpedo with high-speed setting, and this hit the *Frauenlob* in the port auxiliary engine room. The old light cruiser quickly heeled to port, and also turned to port at slow-speed, while shells hitting aft started a fire involving the after magazine, but one gun continued firing until she capsized with only nine survivors. The *München* turned to port and then hard to starboard to avoid a collision, but she fired an 18in torpedo, which failed to hit, at the *Southampton*, while the *Stuttgart* turned hard to starboard and lost touch with the rest of the 4th SG, presently joining the 2nd Division. The *Hamburg* also turned hard to starboard to avoid the *Moltke*, and was passed by the *Elbing*, while both light cruisers were later overtaken by the *Rostock*, and only the *München* remained with the *Stettin*. The 2nd LCS meanwhile turned together to the eastward, and the action was broken off. The *Dublin*, whose Navigating Officer had been killed, lost touch and did not rejoin until next day, while the rest took station near the 5th BS. The *Southampton* was hit by 2–5.9in and about 18–4.1in and extensively damaged though no serious injuries were caused. Only one 6in was disabled, and her starboard midship guns were silenced by casualties to their crews and to those of the port guns. A second torpedo could not be fired as most of the torpedo tube crews were manning the searchlights. The *Dublin* had 5 – 5.9in and 8 – 4.1in hits and was also considerably damaged without vital injury, while the *Nottingham* and *Birmingham* were not hit. Only the *Elbing* of the German cruisers engaged had 5.9in and her shooting was good. Apart from the *Frauenlob* only seven hits were made on the German ships, two on the *Stettin*, three, of which two burst in the water alongside, on the *München*, one on the *Hamburg* and one on the *Elbing*. In the *Stettin* No 4 port gun was put out of action by a direct hit on the face of the shield. The shell which hit the *Hamburg* burst on a fore-funnel signal yard and caused numerous casualties. The *München*'s helm became almost immovable at the end of the action, and she was steered from the steering gear compartment for *c*2½ hours until the trouble was traced to a bent wheel shaft.

The *Moltke* and *Seydlitz* took no part in this action apart from the incident involving the *Moltke* and *Hamburg*, while the *Valiant* noted that several shots fell close and that at 2249 a light cruiser of the *Southampton* class passed on the port side. In the *Vanguard* it was thought that a torpedo attack on the 2nd BS was taking place and her report states that she could have fired without using searchlights but considered it better not to reveal the 4th BS.

In the next 1½ hours from 2330 the German battlefleet passed to the eastward astern of the British squadrons. Of the destroyer flotillas, the 4th alone offered opposition while the only larger ship to give support was the *Black Prince* with tragic result. Scheer had ordered the German main body to resume course 133° in a signal timed at 2330 and this, or initially 130°, was generally maintained by the *Westfalen* except during the actions with destroyers, so that her mean course between 2330 and 0100 was about 6° to the south of that ordered.

The *Moltke* steered approximately 167° between the tracks of Jellicoe's and Beatty's forces, at times at 24kts. By *c*0100 she was on the *King George V*'s starboard bow and probably not more than 6 miles away, steering near 145° and was thus again closing the British battlefleet. The *Seydlitz*, which had become separated from the *Moltke* at about 2230, temporarily reduced speed at 2340 to 7kts, and altered course to 212° to help extinguishing a fire under the forecastle. At 2345 she again headed 122°, and just afterwards sighted three or four large ships steering 167° and just afterwards sighted three or four large ships steering 167° and only *c*1600yds on the port beam. The *Seydlitz* turned to starboard until she was steering 347°, and made the British day-time recognition signal ('PL'), and at the same time the light at her mainmast head lit up. The British ships were lost to view in the *Seydlitz*'s smoke, and at 2358 three large destroyers, at first taken to belong to the German 2nd Flotilla, were sighted *c*2200yds on the port beam. The *Seydlitz*, which was still steering 347°, turned away 90° to starboard, and at 0012 headed 122° for Horns Reef at revolutions for 21kts. She was now to the eastward of both fleets and apparently maintained revolutions for 20kts which gave a speed over the ground of about 18kts. At *c*0008 she reported the large ships to Scheer as four battlecruisers steering 167°, though the position given was much in error to the south-eastward, but it was later thought that they were the 5th BS. The *Frankfurt*, which was not far away, also reported four battlecruisers steering 145° at about this time, and gave the same incorrect position as the *Seydlitz*, but she was apparently repeating the latter's signal which was made on auxiliary wireless.

The large ships seen were the 6th Division about 2½ miles to the eastward of the 5th BS, and British reports place the encounter at about midnight. The *Marlborough* sighted smoke ahead which crossed from starboard to port and back again, before coming down the starboard side. The *Revenge* saw what was at first taken for destroyers approaching, and had given the order to fire her 6in when it was seen to be a large ship. An incorrect reply was given to the *Revenge*'s challenge and the ship, which appeared to resemble a British battlecruiser, disappeared rapidly astern. The *Agincourt* also saw an unidentified ship closing at high speed, but did not challenge, to avoid indicating the Division's position. The *Fearless* astern of the *Agincourt* sighted what appeared to be a German battleship passing down the starboard side. As her course led to the destroyers following the battlefleet and the 6th Division had not opened fire, the *Fearless* did nothing and in any event the ship was said to be too far abaft the beam when identified, for the *Fearless* to fire a torpedo. None of these four ships made any report to Jellicoe. The three destroyers sighted may have been the *Broke*, *Sparrowhawk* and *Contest* and the *Spitfire*, while recovering from the effects of a bow to bow collision with the *Nassau*, saw the *Seydlitz* pass close astern at high speed steering c300°.

The *Seydlitz* steamed faster than was advisable in view of her damage forward, but the *Lützow* was in a far worse state. Until 0045 she was able to continue southward at 7kts or less, but her draught forward then started to increase again, and it was clear that she could not be kept afloat much longer.

Of the German Flotillas, the 2nd began their return via the Skaw at 0008. This decision which was signalled to Scheer, Michelsen and Heinrich, was a bad one, as it deprived Scheer of his best flotilla which had 57 torpedoes available, although permission had been given by Heinrich to use this route if a return to the German Bight seemed inadvisable, and Scheer's operational orders allowed for cut off German forces doing the same.

The five destroyers of the 9th Flotilla and the *G42*, sent after the ships sighted by the *Hannover*, turned for Horns Reef at 2300, while the *V69* and *V46* of the 12th Half-Flotilla arrived there at 0100. Three of the four groups of the 5th Flotilla altered course to join the German fleet or to make for Horns Reef in accordance with Michelsen's 2232 order, within 30 minutes of beginning their search at 2300, though the *G8*, *G7* and *V5* continued southwards until 0030. Shortly after midnight the *G9* and *G10* reported a 4-funnelled light cruiser steaming on 167° at high speed, but neither destroyer attacked, as the cruiser disappeared before it was certain that she was not the *Rostock*. The *G11*, *V1* and *V3* were taken briefly under fire at 0020 by the *Stettin* or *München*. In the 7th Flotilla, the *S19*, *S23* and *V189* proceeded 111° (in error for 128°) at 2355 to enlarge the area searched, but the rest kept together and continued on 139° to avoid getting between the combatants in the destroyer attacks on the German line to the southward.

Both Jellicoe and Beatty continued on 167° at 17kts during this period, and though it was clear that serious fighting was taking place astern of the battleships, Jellicoe believed it to involve light cruisers and destroyers only and seems to have thought that Scheer's heavy ships would be forced westward or delayed on their supposed southerly course, as a result of the fighting between the British and German light units. With full knowledge of the proceedings of the German fleet, it might seem that the gradual eastward movement of the glare from the gunflashes mentioned in several ships' reports, including that of the *Superb* only two astern of the *Iron Duke*, might have given a clue to the German battleships' whereabouts if combined with their course as given in the 2241 signal from the Admiralty, but it was not so interpreted at the time.

More definite information was available but was never passed to Jellicoe. None of the ships that sighted the *Seydlitz* at about midnight made any report. The *Malaya* saw the *Westfalen* at *c*2340 in the flash and glare of the burning *Tipperary* and correctly identified her class by the conspicuous crane. The *Valiant* at about the same time made out two ships with at least 2 funnels and a crane amidships but thought they were cruisers. (Both the *Roon* and *Prinz Heinrich*, which might have been present, had cranes of a type similar to the *Westfalen*'s). No report of these sightings was made to Jellicoe.

The *Birmingham* then near the *Malaya* signalled to Jellicoe and Beatty at 2330 that battlecruisers, unknown number, probably hostile, were in sight 32°, course 167°, but the position given was 30 miles astern of the *Iron Duke*. A position relative to the *Malaya* would have been more useful and the German ships' course reached Beatty as 235° which added to the confusion. It is not certain what the *Birmingham* actually sighted. Her action report indicates that it was the leading German battleships, which had temporarily turned to the southward during their action with the 4th Flotilla, but if the *Birmingham* was on the *Malaya*'s starboard quarter as usually supposed, the bearing given does not agree with this, and it may have been the 2nd SG or possibly the *Seydlitz*.

This was the only signal concerning German heavy ships that Jellicoe received during the actions with the 4th Flotilla. It was at first believed in this flotilla that they were engaged with cruisers, but it was later realised in some of the destroyers that battleships were present, yet no report was made, though among the latter destroyers were the *Ambuscade* and *Garland* which were undamaged or virtually so. As earlier in the night, much information was obtained from intercepted and deciphered German signals, but this was not passed to Jellicoe. Thus at 2315 the Operations Division had the text of Scheer's 2232 signal giving the German fleet's course as 133°, and a partial text of Michelsen's, to the effect that all destroyer flotillas were to be assembled by 0200 at Horns Reef or on course round the Skaw. At 2350 the text of a repeat of Scheer's 2302 signal was available, giving the fleet's course as 114° (misread for 130°) and also their 2300 position as 56° 15′N, 5° 42′E which placed the centre of the German battlefleet with an error of about 3 miles only. Two other signals passed to the Operations Division at midnight or shortly afterwards confirmed the German course as 133° or 130°.

There was no question of Jellicoe intervening in the fighting astern, even if he had known that the enemy battlefleet were engaged. The above information, however, would have indicated quite clearly where it would be found at daylight and there is no doubt that he would have made for Horns Reef if he had known that Scheer was so doing.

According to the intended disposition of the British flotillas, the 11th would have been the first to be engaged but it was not in station and its whereabouts are not certain. Groos thought that it was probably following the German fleet in mistake for the British, and it would seem that it passed astern of the German line at about the time that the leading battleships became engaged with the 4th Flotilla. Apart from the damaged *Castor*, the 11th Flotilla still had 57 torpedoes while the 'broadside' of the 4th Flotilla was only 24. The 13th Flotilla, next to the 4th, gave no support and when numerous overs fell near, the *Champion* altered course to the eastward and increased to high speed, losing touch with most of her destroyers and forcing the 12th Flotilla to turn off course and slow down. The reason given for this curious conduct was that none of her flotilla could attack, as British forces were between them and the enemy. Of larger ships the *Black Prince*, to port of the 4th Flotilla, opened fire, but neither the 5th BS and 6th Division nor the *Fearless* and 2nd LCS intervened. The distance between the 5th BS and the *Westfalen* probably increased from about 2 miles at 2330 to 5-6 miles at 0020, while the 6th Division remained about 4 miles away.

On the German side the fighting was at first confined to the four leading battleships - the *Westfalen, Nassau, Rheinland, Posen* - and to the *Rostock*, the *S32, Stuttgart, Elbing* and *Hamburg* which were on the battleships' port beam, though Schmidt turned the rest of the 1st Squadron together to 246° to keep out of the way of possible torpedoes during the first action.

The Germans were sighted shortly before 2330, but were at first taken for the 11th Flotilla and it was not until 2330 or perhaps 2329, that the *Tipperary* challenged and the *Westfalen* at once switched on her searchlights and opened fire with 5.9in and 3.5in. The Germans were on a converging course, the *Tipperary* bearing 30° forward of the *Westfalen*'s port beam and barely 2000yds away. The first salvo swept away the *Tipperary*'s fore bridge and bow gun, and the *Nassau, Rostock, Elbing, Hamburg* and the *S32* joined in at the *Tipperary* and the destroyers astern of her while the *Rheinland* opened fire with 5.9in at the *Black Prince*, to port of the 4th Flotilla, at 2335, at 2400-2800yds. The *Westfalen*, which did most of the firing, expended 92 rounds of 5.9in and 45 of 3.5in in 5 minutes at 2000-1500yds, turning away 90° to starboard and increasing to utmost speed as she opened fire to avoid torpedoes. The *Nassau* and *Rheinland* also turned away as did the *Rostock* and the *S32* between these two battleships, but the *Elbing* tried to pass through the line ahead of the *Posen* and was rammed at an acute angle on the starboard side aft. Both the *Elbing*'s engine rooms filled, her steering engines and dynamos were out of action, and she drifted down to starboard of the German line. The *Posen* was unharmed.

The *Tipperary* was the main German target, and her whole forepart was quickly wrecked and set on fire, but her after guns opened and both starboard torpedoes were fired. Escaping steam then obscured her gunners' view, and she drifted astern, badly on fire with the cartridge boxes for her forward guns exploding. The *Spitfire* next astern, fired her two torpedoes with long range setting, at a target reported as less than 1000yds away, which was apparently the *Rostock*, and also opened fire with her guns at the searchlights of the ships firing at the *Tipperary*, while the *Garland* and possibly other destroyers, also used their guns. The *Spitfire* then turned away to load her spare torpedo, though this was not done as the davit had been hit, and circled round the head of the German line to discover too late that the three leading battleships, thought by the *Spitfire* to be two cruisers, had resumed their original course and then that the *Nassau* 450yds away was coming straight for her. The *Spitfire* managed to turn to meet the *Nassau*, still believed to be a cruiser, port bow to port bow, and the latter heeled 5–10° to starboard with the shock of the collision, so that the two 11in shells fired from her fore turret at maximum depression only passed through the *Spitfire*'s bridge screens and the bottom of her second funnel. The combined effects of the collision and gunblast seriously damaged the *Spitfire* forward, but the 3rd bulkhead held and she was able to reach the Tyne. The *Nassau* left 20ft of her upper side plating on the *Spitfire*, the resultant hole limiting her speed for the time being to 15kts.

The *Sparrowhawk*, *Garland*, *Contest* and *Broke* which were originally following the *Spitfire* in that order, each fired a torpedo and turned away to port, but of the destroyers astern of the *Broke* – *Achates*, *Ambuscade*, *Ardent*, *Fortune*, *Porpoise*, *Unity* – only the *Ambuscade* fired one, and the *Unity* lost touch with the rest of the flotilla. It is not certain whether the targets were the battleships or light cruisers, but none of the nine torpedoes fired in this first action hit. Except for the *Spitfire*'s and for the *Tipperary*'s where the details are not known, all were fired with high speed setting, and at reported ranges of 800–1200yds.

Some success was obtained by the British 4in gunfire. The *S32* was hit by two shells, one of which cut the main steam pipe in the after boiler room, and the other hit below the bridge, but she was able to get going again after an hour with sea water in her boilers, and managed to reach the Danish coast near Lyngvig. The *Westfalen* was hit once and the *Nassau* twice with damage to searchlights and casualties to bridge and searchlight personnel, while Captain Redlich of the *Westfalen* was slightly wounded, but the two hits at 2336 on the *Rheinland* were by 6in from the *Black Prince*. Here again damage and casualties were caused to searchlights and their crews by one of the shells.

The *Broke* then led the remaining destroyers of the 4th Flotilla to the southward, except for the *Garland* which had become temporarily detached, while the German battleships, apart from the *Nassau* to port of the line, reformed and resumed their previous course with the *Rostock* 1100yds on the *Westfalen*'s port beam. This had scarcely been done when the *Broke* sighted a large ship a little before the starboard beam, and her challenge immediately brought searchlights on to her and a rain of shells from the *Rostock* at 1700–1500yds. The latter turned to starboard to pass between the *Westfalen* and *Rheinland* to leave them a clear field of fire, and was hit on the port side just abaft the bulkhead between the two foremost of the five boiler rooms, by a torpedo running on the surface. Both boiler rooms filled, and the main turbines, steering engine and dynamos temporarily stopped. The *Rostock* drifted astern and passed through the line of the 2nd Squadron between the *Deutschland* and *Pommern*, causing considerable disorganisation so that the *Schlesien* and *Schleswig-Holstein* had to sheer out of the line, but the *Rostock* presently got under way again and limped after the fleet having to stop more than once from salt in the remaining boilers, and listing 5° to port with 930 tons of water in her.

The *Westfalen* sighted the *Broke* 35° on the port quarter, and 1500yds away at 2350. She turned away as previously, but only fired for 45 seconds, expending 13 – 5.9in and 13 – 3.5in shells. The *König* at the rear of the 3rd Squadron opened fire on destroyers to starboard and turned to port at shortly after 2340. These are believed to have been units of the 11th Flotilla. The latter were then steering northward, and the *Minion*'s log records that at 2345 fire was opened on the flotilla from the starboard beam, and course was altered to 257°, and speed increased to 22kts. A wonderful opportunity seems to have been lost for an attack on the rear of the German line when the van was heavily involved.

The *Broke* was badly hit forward by the *Rostock* almost at once, and her helm jammed and engine room telegraphs put out of action. As a result she rammed the *Sparrowhawk* just forward of the bridge, cutting halfway through the ship. While the two vessels were locked together, the *Contest* rammed the *Sparrowhawk* aft, cutting 5ft off her stern and jamming her rudder. The *Contest* had to reduce to 20kts, losing touch with the rest of the flotilla, but the *Sparrowhawk* was completely crippled and eventually had to be scuttled. The *Broke* had been hit at least seven times, and had three boilers out of action as well as heavy casualties but, in spite of a further encounter with the enemy, managed to reach the Tyne on 3 June.

The *Contest* and *Ambuscade* each fired one torpedo with high speed setting at a reported range of 1000yds, but it is impossible to say which hit the *Rostock*. The latter was also hit by 3–4in, which may have come from the *Broke*.

After this action the *Achates* led the 4th Flotilla, in order: *Ambuscade, Ardent, Fortune, Porpoise* and *Garland*, about 3 miles to the eastward and then turned southward. The *Nassau* was still to port of the German line, as were the *Schlesien* and *Schleswig-Holstein* towards the rear. At midnight the *Westfalen*, which had resumed her previous course, exchanged recognition signals with the *Stuttgart* and *Hamburg* and turned away to let them pass from starboard to port. Shortly afterwards at about 0010, the *Westfalen* sighted the *Fortune* approaching 10° abaft the port beam, and the leading Germans were seen by the 4th Flotilla. The *Westfalen* challenged, lit up the target with her searchlights and opened fire, turning away at utmost speed. The first salvo struck the *Fortune*'s bridge, and apparently brought down her mast, and after firing 7 – 5.9in and 8 – 3.5in shells in 28 seconds, the *Westfalen* ceased fire, as the *Fortune*, already ablaze, had become the target for other ships. The *Rheinland* opened fire with her 5.9in at a destroyer, probably the *Ardent* 1500yds away on the port beam, but had to cease as either the *Stuttgart* or *Hamburg* came too near the line of fire. The *Rheinland* turned away with the *Westfalen*, and a torpedo passed about 50yds from her side. A 3-funnelled destroyer, presumably the *Fortune*, lit up by the *Westfalen*'s searchlights, was engaged, and two hits claimed, but the target turned away at high speed and disappeared. The *Rheinland* only expended 26 – 5.9in and no 3.5in in the whole battle so she cannot have fired for long, but the *Posen, Oldenburg* and *Helgoland* also took part. The *Posen* saw three destroyers, apparently the *Fortune, Porpoise* and *Garland* approaching on a similar course, and opened fire in succession on the first two at 1700–900yds. According to the *Posen*'s account the *Fortune* was badly hit, and dropped astern sinking, and the *Porpoise* was also damaged, while the *Garland* escaped. The *Fortune* was seen to fire two torpedoes which the *Posen* avoided, by turning away as did the ships immediately astern of her. The *Oldenburg* also fired on the *Fortune* and *Porpoise*, while the *Helgoland* expended 6 – 5.9in salvos at the *Fortune* at 2600yds.

Although the above firing was soon to dispose of the *Fortune*, she replied with her 4in, a shell striking one of the *Oldenburg*'s forward searchlights, and among numerous casualties killed the officer in command of the 3.5in guns and three other officers, disabled the helmsman, and also wounded Captain Höpfner and two more officers. With her helm unmanned, the *Oldenburg* was in danger of colliding with the *Posen* or *Helgoland*, but Höpfner reached the wheel and steadied her on course. The *Ambuscade, Ardent* and *Garland* each fired a torpedo with high speed setting at reported ranges of 700–1500yds without success. The *Porpoise*, screened to some extent by the *Fortune*, was hit by at least two shells and her steering damaged, while the air-chamber of her spare torpedo exploded and holed the main steam pipe. She was, however, able to get under way with two boilers out of action, and returned home safely.

The 4th Flotilla were now reduced to four destroyers. The *Achates* turned away to the eastward in the erroneous belief that cruisers were chasing her. She still had three torpedoes but the *Ambuscade*, which followed for a time, had none. The *Ardent* with two left turned back to the southward, while in the *Garland* with one, it was believed that she was being chased to the north-eastward. Except for the last-named with a boat struck by a 5.9in shell at some time during the night, none of the four had yet been hit.

Meanwhile the *Black Prince* had approached too near the German fleet, and the *Thüringen*, sighted a ship approaching on a converging course *c*40° on the port bow. No reply was made to the *Thüringen*'s challenge, and the ship turned away. The *Thüringen*'s searchlights showed a British armoured cruiser of the *Black Prince* class, and fire was immediately opened. The first salvo struck near the after turret, which appeared to be blown overboard, and set the *Black Prince* on fire, while the following salvos all hit, raking the *Black Prince* from aft as she tried to get away. After the last salvo but one, a violent explosion marked the unfortunate cruiser's end. Altogether the *Thüringen* fired 10–12in, 27–5.9in and 24 – 3.5in shells at 750–1100yds. The *Ostfriesland* also opened fire, but only with 5.9in, and it is not clear whether the *Nassau*, to port of the German line, used her 11in, though it is probable. The latter sighted a 4-funnelled cruiser to port ahead that appeared to turn for a torpedo shot, and fired for 2 minutes at 1500–900yds, while the *Friedrich der Grosse* which sighted the *Black Prince* 40° on the port bow, fired both 12in and 5.9in at 1300 to 900yds, and noted that after 46 seconds there were two heavy explosions forward and aft, and the ship sank. According to the *Ostfriesland* the *Black Prince* managed to fire one or two salvos which fell astern. There were no survivors and 857 were lost. The exact time of this action is uncertain but it was near 0010.

The *Nassau* turned to starboard to avoid the *Black Prince*'s wreck, and forced the *Kaiserin* to haul out of the line, and a collision was only averted by the *Nassau*'s going full speed astern. After this, the latter sought to join the 2nd Squadron, and took station between the *Hessen* and *Hannover* an hour later.

The *Ardent* had again turned southward, and smoke, thought to come from the *Ambuscade*, was sighted ahead, so that the *Ardent* closed, to discover too late that she had again encountered the leading German ships. She fired a torpedo, but the *Westfalen* had already sighted the *Ardent* 40° forward of the port beam, and her searchlights were on the latter at 900 yards. The *Westfalen* opened fire at 0025, and turned away 90°. She expended 22–5.9in and 18–3.5in shells in 4 minutes 10 seconds, and it was noted that the *Ardent* was first wrecked forward and sank after a boiler and steam-pipe explosion. The *Posen* also fired at the *Ardent* at 1100–1300yds, and reported that her salvos found the target at once. According to some accounts the *Rheinland* and *Oldenburg* took part as well, and at about this time the *Helgoland* fired 5–5.9in salvos at an unidentifiable 3-funnelled destroyer (the *Ardent* was 2-funnelled), 2200yds or less away.

The 4th Flotilla was now completely dispersed, largely due to the *Westfalen* whose firing had been conducted with great skill although she was not fitted with Director-pointer equipment. The Germans had employed searchlights most effectively in combination with their guns, though on one occasion a light cruiser to starboard accidentally lit up her own line, and only a very limited use had been made of star shells. Grand Fleet Battle Orders emphasised that the primary duty of British destroyers was to engage enemy destroyers with gunfire, and though great bravery and dash were shown by the 4th Flotilla, both Captain Redlich of the *Westfalen*, and Commodore Michelsen considered that there was also a great lack of training in torpedo attack. The destroyers came in separately and fired their torpedoes while still closing, always approaching too near, while the German turns-away resulted in the torpedoes passing at very acute angles of intersection, and of the 17 fired, only one hit. No attacks from ahead were noticed by Michelsen. Several torpedoes were observed to have come to the surface near the *Rostock* after running only about 1600yds, and this indicates that they had been fired cold to reduce the initial dive. Although the sky was fully overcast and visibility low, the night was not completely dark, and according to the *Rheinland*, the British destroyers were badly blacked-out.

At 0012 the *Regensburg*, stationed last in the German line, sent the *S53*, *S54* and *G88* to investigate a burning ship seen to port. This was the wreck of the *Tipperary*, still afloat though the *S32* had counted eight heavy explosions, while laying stopped nearby. The *S54* was hailed by the *Rostock* and remained by her. The *S53* rescued nine of the *Tipperary*'s survivors from a raft, and then sighted a ship on the port bow which did not reply when challenged, but immediately afterwards flashed that she was the *Elbing*, and requested the *S53* to come alongside. In turning to do so the *S53* sighted the *Broke*, lit up the target with her searchlight, and fired a torpedo with shallow depth setting, at *c*650yds which ran under the *Broke*. The *G88* fired a similar torpedo at *c*350yds which also missed, and both destroyers fired a few shells at the *Broke*, scoring two hits amidships. The latter replied to the *G88* with her one available gun, but the Germans did not continue the action, as the *Broke* was thought to be sinking and also to allow the *S53* to go to the *Elbing*. The *Sparrowhawk*, was then sighted by the *S53*, but she proceeded to the *Elbing* and lost touch with the *G88* which turned southwards, encountered some of the 11th Flotilla, and with no torpedoes left and her speed reduced by the failure of a feed pump, made off. The *S52* after unsuccessfully searching for the *Lützow* on the starboard quarter of the German fleet, had also encountered the 11th Flotilla at 0017. The *Castor* turned to ram and fired at very short range, but the *S52*, which had no torpedoes left, avoided her, and was not hit though the *Castor* believed her to be sunk. The *S52* then got away at full speed, making oil-fuel smoke, and after reporting the British destroyers to Scheer, steered for the Skaw and then for the Danish coast, a split boiler tube causing a reduction in speed to 21kts for 1½ hours. The *Tipperary* did not sink until some time after the *S53* and *G88* had left her, and the remaining survivors then abandoned ship and most of those eventually rescued were picked up by the *Sparrowhawk*.

Further east, the *Frankfurt* had encountered two of the rear destroyers of the 12th Flotilla, and opened fire at 2350. The *Menace* had to turn very sharply to avoid being rammed, and the *Nonsuch* after trying to get into position to fire a torpedo, made off to the eastward at full speed and lost touch with her flotilla.

During the first action between the German battleships and the 4th Flotilla, overs had fallen near the 9th Flotilla to port of the 13th, but these were taken in the leading destroyer *Lydiard*, to come from large British ships. Course was altered to 122° at 20kts and then to 212° at 25kts to cross ahead. Initially there were only four destroyers following the *Lydiard*: *Liberty, Landrail, Morris* and *Laurel*, but they were then joined by the *Unity* of the 4th Flotilla, and when the *Champion* increased speed and made off to the eastward, only the *Obdurate* and *Moresby* followed and the remaining seven destroyers of the 13th Flotilla – *Nerissa, Termagant, Nicator, Narborough, Pelican, Petard* and *Turbulent* – joined astern of the *Unity* without the *Lydiard* being aware of it. When the augmented 9th Flotilla crossed ahead of the supposed British ships, the rear destroyers were thus very close to the head of the German line.

The latter had resumed course after the destruction of the *Ardent*, but at *c*0035 the *Westfalen* sighted a suspicious smoke cloud to starboard and two large destroyers 20° on the port bow and about 1100yds away. As she was apparently attacked on both sides the *Westfalen* made straight for the two destroyers, which were the *Petard* and *Turbulent*. The *Petard* sighted the leading German ship about 65–70° on the starboard bow and 400 or 500yds away. She had no torpedoes left, and increased to full speed, turning slightly to port to avoid being rammed, and clearing the *Westfalen*, thought to be one of the old *Wittelsbach* class, by about 200yds. The *Petard* was then caught in the *Westfalen*'s searchlights and four shells of the 13 – 5.9in and 6 – 3.5in fired in three salvos by the latter's starboard battery hit but no vital damage was done, though a considerable oil fuel fire occurred in No 2 stokehold, and speed was reduced to 28kts, while it was thought in the *Westfalen* that she had been sunk in 80 seconds.

The *Westfalen*'s attention was now concentrated to port on the *Turbulent* which had turned to a parallel course to avoid being rammed, and had run on close ahead. The *Westfalen* turned 11° to starboard to allow her port battery to fire salvos, and right at the outset a shell struck the *Turbulent* in the stern and hurled the after gun overboard. A total of 29 – 5.9in and 16 – 3.5in shells were fired at her and according to the *Westfalen*'s account, the *Turbulent* sank after 5 minutes from a boiler exposion, but she remained afloat for some time.

Both the *Narborough* and *Pelican* sighted the leading German ship, and the latter saw the next astern also, but they were at first taken for British light or armoured cruisers, and though the action took place about 1000yds away, neither of these destroyers, which still had all their torpedoes, intervened.

The *Turbulent* on fire aft, but still capable of steaming, was now sighted to port by the *Thüringen* and *Ostfriesland*. The latter took no action, but the *Thüringen* fired a 3.5in star shell and opened fire at 0047 on what was thought to be a light cruiser of the *Birkenhead* class. The first salvo hit, and caused a large fire forward, and after the expenditure of 18 (also as 28) – 5.9in and 6 – 3.5in shells at 2600–2400yds, a second star shell showed the target apparently capsized to starboard. The *Turbulent*, however, was still afloat, and was sighted on fire at about 0100 by the *V71* and *V73* astern of the line with the *Regensburg*. The two destroyers closed, and picked up thirteen survivors from the water, and the *V71* fired a torpedo which ran under the target. A second torpedo from the *V71* may have hit but the explosion seen on the *Turbulent* may have been due to her ammunition. The *V71* and *V73* then steamed off as British forces were thought to be in the immediate vicinity, and the *Turbulent* finally sank soon afterwards. Ten explosions were seen in her at short intervals, from a time given as 0058, by the *G86* to starboard of the 3rd Squadron.

Captain Redlich, of the *Westfalen*, had now led the German line past all the British units except the 12th Flotilla which was well out of station, and the *Champion*'s fragment of the 13th, and the attack of the 12th Flotilla on the German 3rd and 2nd Squadrons forms the principal feature between 0100 and 0300. The 1st Squadron was not attacked and maintained course 133° at 16kts, as did the rest of the fleet apart from such turns-away as were made in consequence of destroyer attacks, and at 0300 the *Westfalen* was about 13 miles 240° from Horns Reef lightship. Visibility was poor and it had begun to rain shortly after dawn, while the SSW wind freshened so that great smoke clouds drifted away from the fleet and obscured the eastern horizon. The German line remained unchanged in this period, apart from the 2nd Squadron whose order was: *Deutschland, Pommern* (until sunk), *Hessen, Hannover* with the *Nassau* joining the line between the last two at 0120. The *Schlesien* and *Schleswig-Holstein* joined astern of the *von der Tann* and *Derfflinger* at 0040, and 20 minutes later took station ahead of the two battlecruisers, and then steamed up to port of the line, but their progress was very slow, and at 0210 they were still abaft the *Hannover*'s port beam, resuming station astern of her at 0225.

The *Moltke* had again closed the British battlefleet and at about 0120 crossed not far ahead without either side being aware of it. She then steered to join the High Seas Fleet and at just after 0300 was in visual touch with the van of the 1st Squadron. The *Seydlitz*, to the eastward of the German line, steered for Horns Reef and apparently still maintained revolutions for 20kts, but her navigational equipment had been seriously damaged or put out of action, while the flooding forward made it very difficult to estimate her actual speed over the ground. The most experienced helmsmen had been wounded and only hand soundings could be made, and as a reduction in speed was necessary each time, further errors were introduced in the reckoning. As a result the *Seydlitz*'s course lay to the northward of that intended, and at about 0240 Horns Reef North Buoy was sighted *c*2 miles on the starboard bow. She then twice lightly touched ground forward, but got off by going astern, and after the buoy had been identified with certainty, steered for Horns Reef lightship which was passed at 0400.

In the *Lützow* a last attempt to go astern failed as she could not be steered against the wind and rising sea, while her forecastle was already partly submerged and her propellers coming out of the water. Destroyers were called alongside at 0055 and the crew were taken off by the four escorting her, the *G40, G38, V45* and *G37*, and at 0145 the *G38* was ordered to torpedo her. The first torpedo passed under the after part of the ship which was considerably reduced in draught by the weight of water forward, but the second hit amidships. The *Lützow* heeled over to starboard and disappeared in 2 minutes about 45 miles astern of the *Westfalen*. The position of her wreck is given as 56° 15'N, 5° 53'E.

The wreck of the light cruiser *Wiesbaden* also sank at about this time or perhaps an hour or so later. There was only one survivor, picked

up by a Norwegian steamer late on 2 June. The *Elbing* had remained
stopped since her collision with the *Posen* as it was impossible to get her
turbines going again. The *S53* came alongside at 0105 and took off her
crew except for Captain Madlung and a small party, and then steered for
Horns Reef at full speed. A sail was rigged in the *Elbing* to try and take
her nearer the coast, but at about 0200 British destroyers were sighted
to the southward, and orders were given to scuttle her. The
Sparrowhawk, laying disabled nearby, saw her go down, bows first. The
Elbing's cutter rescued one of the *Tipperary*'s survivors and lit a flare to
attract attention to others, and 5 hours later the party in the cutter were
picked up by a Dutch trawler.

The *Rostock* was taken in tow by the *S54* and for a short time made
as much as 10kts, steering a southerly course which was thought likely
to avoid British forces, but it was impossible to overcome the salting of
the boilers, the cause of which was never discovered. At 0225 the *V71*
and *V73*, which had been ordered to go to her by the *Regensburg* nearly
an hour before, arrived and screened the tow. The *Frankfurt* and *Pillau*
which had lost touch with each other for 1¼ hours from 2330, crossed
from port to starboard of the High Seas Fleet at *c*0130. The *Stettin* and
München remained to port, and by 0300 the *Regensburg*, which had
steamed up to starboard of the line, and the *Stuttgart* were ahead of the
Westfalen, while the *Hamburg* was to starboard of the line, but rejoined
the *Stettin* *c*2 hours later.

Shortly before 0200, the *Regensburg* signalled all flotillas to
assemble at the head of the 1st Squadron. Their actual strength was very
weak apart from the coal-burners of the 5th and 7th Flotillas as, with the
2nd Flotilla returning home via the Skaw, and other oil-burning
destroyers escorting the *Rostock* or laden with survivors of the *Lützow*
and *Elbing*, there were only 11 modern destroyers with more than one
torpedo, and three of these were limited to 25kts or less.

Jellicoe decided to continue on 167° until 0230 when both he and
Beatty would turn 180°, and the battlecruisers close. An imaginary
torpedo track was sighted by the *St Vincent* at 0215, but otherwise there
were no incidents. It was very misty at daylight with visibility of only
2-4 miles, though the *Shannon* noted a figure of 6 miles to the south and
west at 0245, and Jellicoe decided to form line of battle on turning to
347° and to ignore the submarine danger to a long line. The *Westfalen*
was about 27 miles to the north-eastward at 0230 but this was unknown
to Jellicoe. The turn was delayed, as the *Galatea* appeared ahead and did
not reply when signalled, so that the *Iron Duke* fired a 6in across her stern
and it was not until 0239 that the *King George V* began her turn,

followed in succession by the rest of the 2nd BS, and then by the 4th BS and 5th Division. The 5th BS were about 4 miles astern and began their turn at 0244, altering course at *c*0300 to 324° to take station ahead of the *King George V*. The *Lion*, about 14 miles away to the south-westward, turned to 347° at 0243 and to 10° at 0257, to close the battlefleet.

Jellicoe's battle line thus consisted of 23 dreadnoughts, but the 6th Division were not in touch and had fallen at least 12 miles astern. The bulkheads of the *Marlborough*'s forward boiler room had begun to give at revolutions for 17kts, and at 0156 Burney wirelessed that the *Marlborough* would have to ease to 12kts, and that the rest of the division were continuing at 17kts. Jellicoe ordered the *Marlborough* to proceed to the Tyne or to Rosyth by 'M' channel to the southward of the Dogger Bank. Meanwhile Burney signalled the *Fearless* to transfer him to the *Revenge*. This was accomplished at shortly after 0300, and the *Revenge*, which had turned to 347° at 0253, resumed station ahead of the *Hercules* and *Agincourt* at 0330, but it was not until 16 hours later that they rejoined the battlefleet. The *Marlborough* turned northwards after transferring Burney, and did not receive the order to make for the Tyne or Rosyth until after 0400.

Jellicoe had the 4th LCS in company and three of the 2nd LCS were near the 5th BS, but none of the destroyer flotillas was present, though Beatty, not engaged during the night, formed a submarine screen with his destroyers, and the light cruisers in company with him at nightfall were all present, except the *Chester* ordered to the Humber at 0230.

No information on the German battlefleet reached Jellicoe, and Scheer was similarly ignorant about the British capital ships. The *Faulknor* made a full report before the 12th flotilla attacked, stating that the enemy battlefleet were steering 122°, bore approximately 212°, and that the *Faulknor* was 10 miles astern of the 1st BS. This was timed at 0152, and was followed by a signal that the *Faulknor* was attacking and by another timed at 0212, that the enemy's course was 190°, but none of the signals got through, possibly due to German jamming. The *Faulknor* was apparently about 25 miles north-eastwards of the *Iron Duke* at 0200.

As previously the Operations Division at the Admiralty had information that was never passed to Jellicoe. The deciphered texts of two intercepted signals giving the 0030 position of the German battlefleet as 55° 57′N, 6° 15′E and the 0100 position of the van as 55° 50′N, 6° 25′E were passed to the Operations Division at 0120 and 0125. The first position was probably accurate to within 5 miles and the second to within 3½ and, taken in conjunction with previous deciphered signals that had never been passed on, indicated what the High Seas Fleet was doing. A signal was sent to Jellicoe by the Admiralty timed at 0148 and received in the *Iron Duke* at 0155, stating that at midnight the *Lützow* was in 56° 26′N, 5° 41′E, steering 167° at 7kts in a damaged condition, and also that all U-boats were being hurried from German ports to attack, and that one flotilla was returning round the Skaw. This was based on four more intercepted signals but made no mention of undamaged capital ships.

The German deciphering of signals was far behind the British at this date, and Scheer obtained no information on Jellicoe's fleet from this source, during the battle, though Neumünster deciphered Jellicoe's order to his destroyers to take station 5 miles astern of the battlefleet and transmitted this at *c*2240, but it does not appear to have reached Scheer until after his return to harbour. A signal from the *Moltke* via the *G39*, stated that at 0030 she was in *c*55° 33′N, 5° 55′E steering 167° at 24kts, and was being driven off by four large enemy vessels. This was not received in the *Friedrich der Grosse* until 0127, and was in any event misleading as the *Moltke*'s sightings of the 2nd BS had occurred earlier and further north.

Scheer's signal requesting airship reconnaissance off Horns Reef was never received, but Commander Strasser took the initiative and five airships were sent up during the night. The *L24* and *L22* were to scout northward, the *L17* to the west of Horns Reef, the *L11* north-west of Heligoland, and the *L13* to the north and west of Terschelling. Visibility was in general very low, and up to 0300 only two reports of hostile forces had been received, both from the *L24*. The first was located about 50 miles westward of Bovbjerg, and the second about 20 miles nearer the Danish coast. Both forces were entirely imaginary.

The 12th Flotilla's attack on the 3rd and 2nd Squadrons was the last major action in the battle. The *Nonsuch* had lost touch and the *Mischief* was with the 2nd CS, so that the flotilla's strength was 14, each with four torpedoes though the *Faulknor* could only fire two a side. The last named was leading with the 1st Division – *Obedient, Mindful, Marvel, Onslaught* – on her starboard quarter, and the 2nd Division – *Maenad, Narwhal, Nessus, Noble* – similarly to port, while the *Marksman* with the 2nd Half-Flotilla – *Opal, Menace, Munster, Mary Rose* – followed astern. They were proceeding on 167° at 17kts, when at 0143 the *Obedient* and then the *Faulknor* sighted strange ships on the starboard bow steering 122° (actually 133°). These were quickly identified as the *Kaiser* class, and the *Faulknor* turned to a parallel course, and increasing to 25kts, ordered the 1st Division to attack. At 0150 the German ships were lost to sight in the mist, and the 1st Division were ordered to take station astern of the *Faulknor*, while the latter led round to starboard through 180° to attack on a 302° course, and ordered the rest of the flotilla to follow round and attack the enemy. It was now just before 0200 and the German ships were almost immediately sighted again, still on the same course.

The *Faulknor's* 180° turn led her and the 1st Division towards the 2nd Half-Flotilla, and in avoiding the former, the *Marksman* lost touch with her four destroyers, and none of the 2nd Half-Flotilla was able to attack. The *Mindful* had only two boilers in working order, and her speed was therefore reduced, so that she attempted to attack on a southward course and did not follow the *Obedient*. The intended plan of attack was thus partially disrupted from the start.

The German units involved comprised the 5th Division and the 2nd Squadron with the *Nassau*. Their order was – *Markgraf, Kronprinz, Grosser Kurfürst, König, Deutschland, Pommern, Hessen, Nassau, Hannover, Schlesien, Schleswig-Holstein* – the last two being to port of the others. Except perhaps for the *Deutschland*, the 2nd Squadron appear to have been well astern of station. The *Grosser Kurfürst* had developed a leaky condenser, so that her centre turbines had to be stopped from 0003 to 0147. The destroyer *S50* was seen from the *Faulknor* to be close on the *Grosser Kurfürst's* port quarter. Conditions favoured the attackers as it was sufficiently light to hamper the use of searchlights, but dark and misty enough to make the flotilla a difficult target. German destroyers were also expected to be closing the battlefleet from port and starboard, and the leading German ships were exchanging recognition signals with units of the 9th and 5th Flotillas to starboard of the line. The *Hamburg* was also near and apparently on the 5th Division's starboard beam.

The *König* had momentarily sighted British destroyers 30° forward of the port beam at 0147 and had opened fire, but they quickly disappeared, and when the *Markgraf* made out destroyers 20° abaft the port beam at 0202, fire was withheld as their identity was in doubt, and whatever destroyers were seen, they were not the leading units of the 12th Flotilla. From the *Kronprinz* destroyers of uncertain nationality were also made out, but the *Grosser Kurfürst* at 0204 sighted about six apparently 4-funnelled destroyers, 10 or 20° forward of the port beam and only 1500–1700yds away, which were attacking at high speed in single line ahead and in very close order. The *Grosser Kurfürst*, whose Director-pointer installation was destroyed, turned away 68° and opened fire with 5.9in and 3.5in on the *Faulknor, Obedient*, and *Nessus*, scoring a hit on the last named at *c*2200yds. The *König* also opened fire with 5.9in and turned away, but the *Kronprinz*, which had likewise turned away, did not fire, though the *Markgraf*, which turned away on sighting two torpedo tracks, did so. All four dreadnoughts had begun to turn away by 0206, and the *Deutschland* followed, and also opened fire, but only expended a few 3.5in shells, possibly because great clouds of smoke from the *König*'s damaged fore-funnel uptakes and ventilation shaft obscured the range. The *S50* turned towards the British destroyers and came under fire from a ship of her own line, one shell passing through a ventilator.

The *Faulknor* fired her first torpedo at 0202 and her second at 0203, the *Obedient* fired one at just before 0204 and another at 0209, the *Marvel* fired two at just after 0204 and two at 0207/08, while the *Onslaught* fired two at 0208/09 and two at 0211/12. The *Marvel*'s four and the *Onslaught*'s last two were fired with high speed settings and the others with long range. The reported ranges were 3000yds for the *Faulknor* and *Onslaught*, 3500 for the *Obedient* and 1800–1700 for the *Marvel*, while the torpedo director settings were, *Faulknor*, enemy's speed 18kts, inclination 120° to torpedo track: *Obedient* 18kts, 130°: *Marvel*; 18kts, 90°: *Onslaught*; 20kts, 130° (probably first two only). The German course was estimated at 122° by *Faulknor*, 100° *Obedient*, *Marvel* and probably 122° for *Onslaught*'s first two. The *Faulknor* fired her first torpedo, which was thought to have missed ahead, at the second ship, and her other torpedo, which was believed incorrectly to have hit, at the third ship, while the *Obedient* fired her first at one of the dreadnoughts and her second at the 2nd Squadron. The *Marvel* fired her first two torpedoes at the dreadnoughts, and her last two probably ran between the 2nd and 3rd Squadrons or perhaps between the *Deutschland* and *Pommern*, while the *Onslaught* fired all four at the 2nd Squadron. The *Obedient* thought that her first torpedo hit, and the *Onslaught* claimed correctly that a big explosion resulted from her first. The *Mindful* had meanwhile sighted the German ships on her starboard bow, and turned to fire, but she was twice masked by other destroyers and on both occasions had to turn away to avoid being rammed.

In the German line the *Faulknor*'s first torpedo was not seen, but the *Grosser Kurfürst* saw the track of her second pass close ahead and the *Obedient*'s first exploded in the *Kronprinz*'s wake about 100yds astern, and gave rise to the hit claimed by the *Faulknor* and *Obedient*. In the *Markgraf* the tracks of the *Marvel*'s first two torpedoes were seen in the director telescope and she turned away, but one passed parallel to the ship about 30 yards off and the other track, which was travelling on a line towards the bridge, ran under her. The *Marvel's* last two torpedoes were not sighted from the German line, but at 0210 the *Onslaught's* first hit the *Pommern*, and after a series of explosions in rapid succession, her hull broke in two, the stern capsizing as the *Hannover* passed *c*1000yds away after hauling out to starboard. All 844 of the *Pommern's* crew were lost. The *Onslaught's* third torpedo then passed close astern of the *Hannover* and she turned away at utmost speed. A violent repeated shock was felt in her a minute or two later from explosions in the *Pommern's* wreck, though it was thought at the time that she had probably run over a submarine. In the *Hessen* it was also thought that a submarine was responsible for the loss of the *Pommern*, and at *c*0212 the *Hessen* opened fire at an imaginary submarine diving to starboard. The *Nassau* and then the *Schlesien* and *Schleswig-Holstein* sighted the indistinct outlines of three or four destroyers in the smoke and mist to port. The *Nassau* turned to port and fired for a minute at 5500 to 4400yds before turning away 90°, but the second torpedoes from the *Obedient* and *Onslaught* ran by, the one track close ahead and the other astern. The *Schlesien* turned away and took two destroyers under fire, the *Onslaught's* last torpedo passing ahead shortly afterwards, while the *Schleswig-Holstein* also turned away, and opened fire with 6.7in HE at 0212 as she returned to her previous course. Her first salvo was fired at 1600yds, and a shell from the second at 1100yds struck the *Onslaught's* bridge and mortally wounded her captain as well as causing other casualties and starting a fire, and the destroyers then disappeared.

The *Faulknor* had altered course to 325° after firing her torpedoes, and passed down the German line engaging with her 4in guns though no hits were made. The ships at the rear of the German line, erroneously thought to be three *Rostock* type light cruisers, then opened a heavy fire, and the *Faulknor* altered course to 358° and increased to full speed. She then turned back to keep in touch, but believed that a German cruiser was approaching, and turned to 257° losing sight of the enemy. By then only the *Obedient* and *Marvel* were in company, as the *Mindful* and *Onslaught* joined the *Opal* of the 2nd Half-Flotilla after the attack.

The 2nd Division of the 12th Flotilla should have attacked immediately after the 1st, but the *Maenad* had her tubes trained to starboard expecting to attack on a southward course, and did not turn until about 5 minutes after the *Faulknor*, firing one torpedo with long range setting at a reported 4000yds, while the *Narwhal* fired two at 3000yds. The *Maenad* again turned southward on her own and fired two more torpedoes at 4000yds. A hit was claimed with the first of these two, and the *Narwhal* also thought that her first torpedo had hit, but all missed and it does not appear that any of these five were sighted by the Germans. The *Maenad* opened fire with her after 4in but made no hits and, though straddled, was not herself struck.

Neither the *Nessus*, which was hit by a 5.9in shell from the *Grosser Kurfürst* earlier in the attack, and had a boiler out of action, nor the *Noble* fired any torpedoes, and their movements and those of the 2nd Half-Flotilla at this time are not known, though the 2nd Division less the *Maenad* later joined the *Opal* and the destroyers of the 2nd Half-Flotilla, while the *Marksman* and *Maenad* joined the *Champion*.

From the British point of view this action was more skilfully fought than those of the 4th Flotilla, and no destroyers were lost as against four (including the *Sparrowhawk*). In each action however, only one hit was made from 17 torpedoes fired.

Near the head of the German line some of the 5th Flotilla had closed from the westward and the *V2*, *V4* and *V6* were to starboard of the 1st Squadron steaming up towards the van. At 0215 they were about 200yds or less on the beam of the *Westfalen* and *Rheinland* when a violent explosion blew the forecastle off the *V4*. The other two destroyers went alongside and rescued the survivors, and the *V6* then sank the wreck by a torpedo after 35 rounds of 3.5in had little apparent effect, and the *Deutschland* had disregarded a request to ram. It is probable that the *V4* struck a drifting mine, but the cause of the explosion cannot be determined with certainty.

The *Champion*, *Obdurate* and *Moresby* to eastward of the 12th Flotilla, heard firing and at 0215 turned towards it. The *Marksman* then joined, and at 0225 the *Champion* led round to the southward. Judging from signals between the *Champion* and *Marksman*, suspicious ships glimpsed in *c*167° were thought to be German, but for some unknown reason the *Champion*, which had now been joined by the *Maenad*, turned away to the eastward at 0234 followed by the others. As the *Moresby* which was furthest astern turned, she sighted four ships of the *Deutschland* class bearing 257° 4000yds off and apparently steering 122° at full speed. The *Moresby* hauled out to port and turned to attack, but of her three remaining torpedoes only one could be fired immediately, and the target then disappeared in mist and smoke. The torpedo was fired with high speed setting at 3700yds and was aimed at the third ship seen. It was thought to have hit but passed ahead of the *von der Tann* which turned away at 0242 to avoid it.

A short engagement took place between the *Garland* and *Contest* and the *G40*, *G38*, *V45* and *G37*. These four destroyers had been with the *Lützow* and had her survivors to the total of *c*1250 aboard, 700 being in the *G37*, while the *Contest* was limited to 20kts by her damaged bow. The British destroyers were sighted at about 0225 and a brief action developed on opposite courses at 1300–4500yds. No hits were scored on either side, and a torpedo fired by the *V45* at 0230 at 3300yds passed 500yds astern of the *Garland* running on the surface.

CHAPTER 15

Damage to capital ships, pre-dreadnoughts and armoured cruisers 2130 31 May – 0300 1 June

THE ONLY BRITISH armoured ship engaged in this phase was the *Black Prince*. It would seem that events took a similar course to those in the *Defence*, though the latter blew up more quickly after being seriously hit. The German Official History gives the same number of hits as on the *Warrior* – fifteen heavy and six smaller – but an accurate estimate is impossible, though twelve might be a better figure for hits by heavy shells, and many more smaller shells than six must have hit. Steel flash covers for the tops of the 6in dredger hoists had been approved for the *Black Prince*, but it is not certain that they had been fitted.

Damage was caused by the 4in guns of the British destroyers and by the 6in of the *Black Prince*. The *Westfalen* was hit by a 4in shell from the *Tipperary* which exploded in her fore-funnel, completely destroying the port forward upper searchlight, and smashing the mirror of the starboard forward lower one. The *Rheinland* was hit by 2-6in from the *Black Prince*. One shell burst on the support of the port forward upper searchlight pedestal, and cut the cables to all four forward searchlights, as well as damaging the lower two and the fore-funnel. The other shell struck the hull plating and burst on the forward transverse armour bulkhead where it was 6½in thick, 4ft from the ship's side and about 1ft below the battery deck. The bulkhead was apparently bulged in where struck, and the fastenings to the battery deck burst loose, while this unarmoured deck was bowed upwards over a large area. The starboard hull plating, 52ft away, was dented by a shell fragment, light structures and fittings in the vicinity of the hit entirely destroyed, and the steam capstan put out of action.

In the *Oldenburg* a 4in shell fired by the *Fortune* from almost dead astern exploded in the port forward upper searchlight, and splinters and

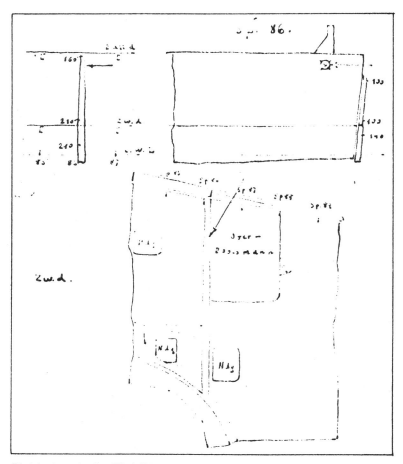

Rheinland: *6in hit from* Black Prince.

fragments struck the bridge. There was also a premature in No 4 port 5.9in gun at the 11th round fired, which disabled the gun and cradle. The *Nassau* was hit by a 4in shell from the *Spitfire* which burst on the support of the port forward searchlights and put both out of action. A second 4in shell probably burst on the water just short of the ship in line with the after turret, and splinters disabled the port after upper searchlight. A good deal of damage was caused by the collision with the *Spitfire*. The two ships' courses converged by about 1° at impact, the *Nassau* making 16kts, and the *Spitfire* perhaps 25, and the latter's bow was lifted up, and she drove along the *Nassau's* side, striking No 1 port

5.9in gun which was wrenched aft, while the gun mounting was torn up from the battery deck and both gun and mounting wrecked. Most of the hull damage was high up, near the forecastle deck, and the port side plating was torn for a length of *c*50ft and to a maximum depth of 11½ft. The forecastle deck was also bent in and upwards for *c*20ft × 16ft. Owing to the calm sea no water entered, but the *Nassau* was limited to 15kts until the hole could be temporarily patched.

Numerous casualties were caused in these four ships by the 1–6in and 3–4in shells which struck the forward searchlights or fore-funnel. The total was 28 killed and 56 wounded.

According to the *Hessen*, in the ship next astern of the *Pommern* when the latter was torpedoed, a succession of brief detonations, each accompanied by smoke columns of different colours, white, black or whitish yellow, first occurred, followed by dark red flames starting from starboard and spreading over the whole ship. In the *Schlesien* some distance away on the *Pommern*'s port quarter, it was noted that there were two columns of flame close together and reaching over the mastheads. A large explosion then broke the *Pommern* in two, and countless fragments fell near the *Deutschland*, including one which made a very heavy splash, and was perhaps a turret roof or a portion of the upper deck. As the *Hannover* passed 3–4 minutes later, the *Pommern*'s stern capsized so that the rudder and propellers were seen. Part of the wreck was still visible from the *Schlesien* when she passed *c*10 minutes after the *Pommern* had been torpedoed, and also from the *von der Tann*, a further 10 minutes or so later. It would appear that the explosion of the *Onslaught*'s torpedo set off some of the *Pommern*'s 6.7in shells, and that the explosion of these spread to other shells and charges, and then to the ammunition spaces on the far side of the ship which were still unaffected by water flooding into the hull from the torpedo damage on the port side. As was customary for the secondary armament in German ships, there were no separate shell rooms, and shells and charges were stowed together in the 6.7in magazines. In the *Pommern* class the 11in shell rooms and magazines were also combined, or closely adjacent on the same deck, with common handing rooms, an arrangement not followed in later ships.

The *Schlesien* bent a propeller shaft slightly in passing over a wreck during the night, and some British ships also reported striking wreckage, among them the *Colossus* at 2330 with some damage to her starboard propellers.

Of the ships torpedoed in the daylight battle, the *Marlborough* maintained revolutions for 17kts without serious trouble until about

0100 when it was noticed that the starboard longitudinal bulkhead of 'A' boiler room and also the starboard corner of the forward transverse bulkhead were gradually coming in. Additional shores were placed, but it was thought unsafe to continue at the present speed, and although the boilers in the other two rooms were being fed with fuel from the starboard side only, this merely maintained the *Marlborough*'s list at 7–8°, so that further flooding was taking place in inaccessible compartments. It was also thought that the fire of 'A' and 'B' turrets would probably bring down the shores, and it was unlikely that the bulkheads would hold if this occurred. Speed was thus reduced to 12kts shortly before 0200 according to Burney's signal to Jellicoe, though the *Marlborough*'s captain's report says 15 and then 13kts. After stopping engines for Burney to board the *Fearless*, the *Marlborough* appears to have proceeded at 11kts.

The *Seydlitz*'s condition did not become dangerous until after she reached Horns Reef, and as previously noted, revolutions for 22 and then for 20kts were maintained. This was too high a speed for a ship with so much damage forward, and had soon to be considerably reduced.

In the *Lützow*, whose damage was solely due to gunfire, the water below the armour deck gradually spread until nearly all compartments forward of the conning tower and below the armour deck were flooded. All electric light forward seems to have failed by midnight, though it appears that the port switchboard room on the upper platform deck remained unflooded, and according to some accounts a number of men were trapped there. Above the armour deck water reached the upper and lower main decks through the large shell holes in the forecastle, and spread through ventilation ducts to compartments on the armour deck so that most of the ship above this deck and forward of 'A' barbette was also flooded. Three attempts were made to stop these shell holes but the continually increasing draught forward allowed the sea to break over the forecastle, and prevented any success. Water also entered the foremost 5.9in casemates and found its way below, and eventually the remaining pumps could no longer keep the water down in the ship's control room or in the foremost oil-fired boiler-rooms, and these had to be vacated.

The last figures from the *Lützow*'s damage control indicate that 4209 tons of water were present below the armour deck and 4142 tons above, and the total of 8351 tons was calculated to increase the draught forward by 28½ft and reduce that aft by 15ft. These figures do not however include the water in the ship's control room and foremost boiler rooms, and there was certainly much other flood water in the *Lützow* before she was scuttled, as the water line was then at the upper edge of 'B' barbette, which indicates that the draught had increased by about 40ft from its original figure at the forward end of the keel line about 90ft abaft the stem and about 115ft forward of the leading edge of 'B' barbette.

The *Lützow's* report states that her draught forward was 56ft shortly before it was decided to abandon her, and that her propellers were coming out of the water, and this is in reasonable agreement with her damage control's calculated figures above. A very large additional amount of water must have flooded in between then and 0145 to increase her draught forward to approximately 70ft, and it is clear that her torpedoing at this time did not much hasten her sinking.

CHAPTER 16

Events on the morning of 1 June, and return to base

AFTER 0300 ON 1 June there were two brief contacts between surface units, but the return of the fleets was not without incident, though neither side achieved any success with their submarines, and the only damage was caused by a British minefield laid four weeks previously.

Jellicoe continued on 347° at 17kts in single line ahead until 0342, with the 5th BS 2 miles ahead of the 2nd BS. There was, however, only one destroyer, the *Oak*, in company and the most recent information concerning the enemy was the Admiralty's 0148 signal to the effect that the damaged *Lützow* had been in 56° 26'N, 5° 41'E at midnight, steering 167° at 7kts, that all submarines were being hurried from German ports to attack, and that one flotilla was returning round the Skaw. This probably reached Jellicoe at about 0300 and in a searchlight signal timed at 0330, Jerram was warned to look out for damaged battlecruisers ahead or on either bow, and probably with a large number of destroyers.

Meanwhile to the westward the Zeppelin *L11* had approached Beatty's ships, and their brief firing at her was heard in the battlefleet just before 0320, and more continuous firing from the 3rd LCS at 0335. The reason for this was not immediately known to Jellicoe, and at 0342 he ordered his divisions to alter course separately to 257°, but 10 minutes later resumed his previous course in line ahead. The 5th BS conformed generally to these movements a few minutes after the other battleships, while some of the latter fired briefly at the *L11*.

Jellicoe's intention on the evening of 31 May had apparently been to close Horns Reef if the German fleet were not encountered at daylight, but the absence of destroyers prevented this, though it was increasingly doubtful if the enemy were in his vicinity. Definite information on the High Seas Fleet reached Jellicoe at about 0410 in a signal from the Admiralty timed at 0329. This gave the deciphered text of Scheer's 0230 position signal, which had been passed to the Operations division at 0300, and stated that at 0230 the German main fleet had been in 55° 33′N, 6° 50′E, steering 133° at 16kts. It was now certain that Scheer had taken the Horns Reef route and that there was no chance of resuming the action with the German battlefleet.

Accordingly at 0413 Jellicoe signalled his ships to form divisions in line ahead, disposed abeam to port of the 5th division, and at 0430 to resume course 347°. Visibility was still only 2½ miles at this time, and the 5th BS kept about this distance ahead of the *Iron Duke* until 0503, when Jellicoe signalled them to take station 2200yds to starboard of the *Colossus*.

There was still, as far as Jellicoe was aware, the possibility of meeting disabled German ships. An Admiralty signal, timed at 0312, and based on a signal of the *S53* to the *Regensburg*, referring to the *Elbing*, stated that the crew had been taken off a damaged light cruiser in 55° 45′N, 6° 25′E, and that destroyers were standing by at 0300. This time should have been 0200 but the Admiralty passed it on incorrectly, while the position was actually the *S53*'s 0200 reckoning and far to the south-eastward of where the *Elbing* was scuttled. The chance of finding the *Lützow*, which for all Jellicoe knew was still afloat, was incomparably more important than a damaged light cruiser, and in a searchlight signal timed at 0430 Jellicoe warned the leading ships of his divisions to look out for the *Lützow*, damaged, ahead.

The next information regarding possible German stragglers came from the *Dublin* in a wireless message timed at 0430, stating that a cruiser and two destroyers, probably hostile, were in sight, bearing 77°, course 167°. The *Dublin* had lost touch with the British fleet and her position given as 55° 30′N, 6° 33′E was too far to the south-eastward, and the time of sighting half an hour late. The ships seen were the *Rostock* shortly before she was scuttled, and her attached destroyers but the former's crippled condition escaped notice.

Another signal from the Admiralty timed at 0530, was probably received by Jellicoe soon after 0600. This stated that the *Elbing* was still afloat at 0347 without her crew, and gave her supposed 0300 position as in the 0312 signal. It is not clear on what intercepted but misunderstood German signal, this totally erroneous information was based, though it may have been a further signal from the *S53* to the *Regensburg*, but at 0603 Jellicoe altered course, leading ships together and the rest in succession to 122°, and steered towards the *Elbing*'s reported position, instead of the *Lützow*'s.

The three undamaged ships of the 6th Division were not far away during this period but did not rejoin Jellicoe. The *Faulknor*, *Obedient* and *Marvel* joined them shortly after 0330, and all three battleships briefly fired at the *L11*, while wreckage from the *Rostock* was passed at *c*0515 and thought to be from a capital ship, as fog canisters were mistaken for large propellant cases.

The *Marlborough* was joined by the *Fearless* soon after 0400, and both ships briefly fired at the *L11*. They steered 351° until about 0430, and then altered course to 205° to make for 'M' channel. The *Marlborough* was able to maintain revolutions for 14kts giving about 12½kts over the ground.

Beatty increased speed to 20kts at 0305 and steered 10° or 353° until 0404 when course was altered to 325°. Some of his ships fired at the *L11* and about 0320 both the *Falmouth* and *Canterbury* sighted an imaginary torpedo. Beatty had little if any knowledge of the night's events and the Admiralty signal of 0148 regarding the *Lützow* was not received in the *Lion* until 0340 via the *Iron Duke*. In a signal timed at 0350 and despatched 14 minutes later, Beatty pointed out that when last seen the enemy were to the west, steering 212° proceeding slowly, and that a Zeppelin had passed astern steering 257°. He requested permission to sweep on 212° to locate the enemy, and ordered his light cruisers, to spread well to the westward. Shortly after this Beatty may have received the Admiralty 0329 signal giving the German fleet's 0230 position, and at 0423 course was altered back to *c*353° and by 0510 Beatty joined astern of the battlefleet. In a wireless signal timed at 0440, Jellicoe informed Beatty that the enemy fleet had returned to harbour and instructed him to try and locate the *Lützow*. At 0520 he increased to 20kts altering course, as Jellicoe asked him where he was going, and pointed out that the fleet's course was 347° at 17kts. Beatty's replies indicated that he wanted to sweep southward and eastward in search of the cruiser reported by the *Dublin* at 0430, which he now apparently believed to be the *Lützow*, before again turning to 347°. Accordingly at just after 0540 the battlecruisers turned to 122° and proceeded on this course at 20kts until 0616 when they turned to 167°.

The 2nd LCS, less the *Dublin*, regained touch with Beatty at 0430 and the *Galatea*, now limited to 24kts, about 15 minutes later. As the *Canterbury* was with the 3rd LCS, Beatty had then twelve light cruisers, while Jellicoe had the 4th LCS and four light cruisers attached to the battle squadrons and fleet flagship, giving a total of nine, and the five remaining armoured cruisers stayed with the battlefleet after Beatty rejoined. There was still a serious lack of destroyers in contact with the battlefleet at 0600. Of the original total of seventy-eight flotilla leaders and destroyers, seven had been sunk, one was completely disabled, and thirteen were returning home, either short of fuel, damaged, or escorting those that were. Of the remaining fifty-seven, three were with the 6th division and one with the battlefleet, while the 2nd CS still retained their original four, and eight of the 1st Flotilla plus the *Christopher* and *Ophelia* of the 4th, were with the battlecruisers. The other thirty-nine, as well as the *Castor* and *Champion*, were not in touch with any heavy ships, and the greater part, comprising the whole of the 11th Flotilla, the *Ambuscade* of the 4th and the *Opal, Mindful, Narwhal, Nessus, Noble, Menace, Munster* and *Mary Rose* of the 12th, were with the *Castor*. The 11th Flotilla had proceeded on 167° from midnight to 0230 astern of, and between, Jellicoe and Beatty, and had then turned northward. They were joined by the above destroyers of the 12th Flotilla at shortly after 0400, and were then not far from the battlefleet, and would probably have made contact in better visibility. The *Lydiard*, however, had led the augmented 9th Flotilla far to the westward after crossing ahead of the *Westfalen*, steering 212° until 0115 and then 277° until 0535. The *Liberty, Landrail, Morris, Unity, Nerissa, Termagant, Nicator, Narborough, Pelican* and *Petard* were still in company with the *Lydiard* at 0535, and nearly 80 miles to the westward of the battlefleet.

The Harwich Force received orders at 0309 to join Jellicoe and replace units short of fuel. This was far too late, and though Tyrwhitt sailed at 0350 the only service he could perform was to provide screening destroyers for the *Marlborough*.

The *Westfalen* was about 13 miles bearing 240° from Horns Reef Lightship at 0300, and apart from some temporary alterations of course due to imaginary submarines, steered 133° until about 0400, and then *c*125° until shortly before 0600 when the Lister Deep was reached, and the *Westfalen* headed southwards to pass to the east of the Amrum Bank. A speed of *c*15kts was maintained though the need to take soundings when approaching the coast in low visibility at *c*0500 caused some reduction.

The *Stuttgart* looked out for navigation marks ahead of the 1st Squadron, and later performed a similar service for the *Friedrich der Grosse* and 3rd Squadron. The *Moltke* had joined up with the 1st Squadron at just after 0300 and Scheer ordered the 1st Scouting Group to return to harbour in a signal timed at 0324. The *von der Tann* increased to 22kts for a time, and at 0540 rejoined the *Moltke*, but the two battlecruisers did not steam on ahead of the battleships, and the *Derfflinger* remained at the rear of the line for the present.

In a further signal timed at 0338, Scheer ordered the 2nd SG to take station astern, the 4th SG to take station ahead, destroyers (of which only thirteen had yet joined the line) to screen the fleet against submarines, and the 2nd Squadron to proceed into harbour. The latter, however, remained astern of the dreadnoughts as Scheer ordered the fleet to proceed into harbour eastward of the Amrum Bank in a signal timed at 0354, which also gave the fleet's course at 122°. There had been no news of the *Lützow* since 0047 when her midnight position, course and speed, as intercepted by the British Admiralty, had been received from the *G40*. At 0315 when she would have been about 60 miles north-westward of Horns Reef Lightship, assuming that she had continued on 167° at 7kts, Scheer asked for her position, but it was not until 0424 that a reply was received that she had been sunk at 0145.

For news of the British fleet Scheer depended on his airships, but visibility conditions, which were no better at sea-level off Horns Reef than further west, were also difficult for them. The *L24* had already made two reports of imaginary forces and in a signal timed at 0300 and received at 0319, she reported that numerous enemy vessels, at least 12 units, were at 0300 15–20 miles to the north-westward of Hanstholm in northern Denmark, and Scheer considered that the *L24* had sighted the British battlefleet, which he now believed had withdrawn to this area at nightfall. This sighting again appears to have been entirely imaginary. The German 2nd Flotilla were about 30–35 miles north-eastward of the reported position at 0300 but it does not seem that this was the force concerned. Apart from imaginary submarines and a supposed torpedo from the second of them, the 2nd Flotilla's return was uneventful, and there is no mention of an airship in any of their reports. Further signals from the *L24* received at 0333 and at 0520 referred to non-existent ships.

Meanwhile the *L11* had located part of the British fleet, but Scheer seems to have considered that her first report might refer to the Harwich force, and though her later reports indicated that much stronger forces than had at first been thought were to the north-westward of Heligoland, it was not realised that the whole Grand Fleet was in this area.

The *L11* had seen nothing of Heligoland which was hidden in low lying fog, when she passed over the island, and mist at greater heights limited visibility to 2–4 miles. However, at 0300 smoke was seen to the northward and the *L11* made out what were thought to be six British battleships with 2 tripod masts and 2 funnels, of the *Bellerophon, St Vincent* or *Neptune* class, six other battleships of unidentified class and numerous smaller vessels. These were reported in a signal timed at 0310 and received at 0330, as twelve British battleships and many smaller vessels in sight in *c*54° 45′N, 5° 25′E steering 10° at high speed. It was actually the British battlecruisers and 2nd CS that the *L11* had taken for battleships, and their position was at least twenty-five miles to the north-eastward of that given.

The *L11* took station astern of the force sighted at 3600–3900ft but she was fired at, and had to make several circles to the eastward. While thus engaged at 0340, she sighted a second group of six battleships with two tripod masts and two funnels, with light forces in company, steering 347° and then altering course to 257°. These were duly reported as six more enemy dreadnought-type ships in *c*55° 03′N, 5° 35′E in a signal timed at 0340, but not apparently received until 0435. This signal also gave their alteration of course and added that the *L11* was being driven off by gunfire and was in touch with the enemy battlefleet. This time the *L11* had sighted the rear ships of Jellicoe's battle line and correctly identified them, but the position given was similarly in error to that in her previous signal.

While keeping in touch, the *L11* sighted a further group at 0350 which approached from the north-eastward, altered course astern of her and came between her and the British battlefleet. These were thought to be three battlecruisers with tripod masts and three funnels of the *Australia* or *Invincible* class, accompanied by four smaller vessels. The *L11*'s signal timed at 0400 and received at 0433, reported them as three enemy battlecruisers, steering 257° in *c*55° 15′N, 5° 25′E, and stated that it was very misty and difficult to maintain touch. The ships sighted were Burney's three battleships and the three destroyers with them, and their position was at least 30 miles to the eastward of that given by the *L11*.

Several ships of the last two forces sighted, now engaged the *L11* which presented a good target at 3600ft – 6200ft. She was not hit though badly shaken by near-misses, and eventually had to run before the wind to the north-eastward and at 0420 lost sight of all British ships. It had rarely been possible to make out more than one squadron at a time in the mist and fog over the sea, though others were disclosed by their gun-flashes. The *L11*'s fourth signal, timed at 0410 and received at 0447, stated that the reported enemy vessels were steering 347° and that several in *c*55° 27′N, 5° 45′E were now out of sight in the haze; the *L11*'s position was uncertain and visibility low. At 0435 she came down to 1600ft but visibility was no better, and no further contact with British ships was obtained.

In spite of mistakes in identification and incorrect positions, the *L11* had performed well in difficult conditions, and Scheer now knew that the British forces to the north-westward of Heligoland were not seeking battle near Horns Reef, and as he believed the rest of the British fleet had been located by the *L24*, informed the Naval Airship Division at 0608 that airship reconnaissance was no longer necessary.

A number of imaginary submarine alarms disturbed the High Seas Fleet's return. The *Hannover* had opened fire on a supposed submarine at 0253, and 10 minutes later the *Oldenburg* signalled that a submerged enemy submarine was in sight to starboard and Scheer ordered a 45° turn together to port. It was thought that the explosion in the *V4* might have occurred through ramming a submarine, and several ships at the rear of the line believed themselves to be attacked in the area to the south-westwards of Horns Reef. At 0406 imaginary submarines to starboard were fired on by the *Schleswig-Holstein*, *Schlesien*, *Hannover* and *Hessen*, while the *Markgraf* also fired a shot, and the fleet turned away to port for a short time. In the *Hessen* a supposed torpedo track was sighted from the fore-top, while the *Hannover* fired rapid salvos, not at the usual imagined periscope, but at an alleged submarine, 10° forward of the starboard beam that was said to have dived with her conning tower above water 700–900yds away! At 0413 the *Hannover* and *Hessen* opened fire on an imaginary submarine to port, and their violent shooting threatened to damage the *Stettin* and *München* closing in from the eastward, so that Scheer had to order cease fire.

In the *Nassau* an imaginary torpedo track, sighted 40° abaft the port beam, appeared to pass 50yds astern, and at about this time the *Nassau* joined the *Derfflinger*, and in the 2nd Squadron the *Schlesien* and *Schleswig-Holstein* passed the *Hannover* which had sheered out of line, and took station astern of the *Hessen*.

At 0520 there was an explosion on the starboard side of the *Ostfriesland*, at first thought to be from a submarine's torpedo, but the *Ostfriesland* soon signalled that bits of a mine had been found on her quarter deck. She had in fact struck one of those laid by the *Abdiel* on 4 May. No very great damage was done, and the *Ostfriesland*, after sheering out of line, proceeded ahead again at 0524 at slow speed, and screened by the *V3*, *V5* and for a time the *G11*, followed astern of the 3rd, and presently of the 2nd Squadron. Her speed gradually increased to 15kts at 0940.

The ships of the 3rd Squadron turned sharply to port when it was realised that the *Ostfriesland* had struck a mine and this caused the 2nd Squadron to close up, so that some of the pre-dreadnoughts had to stop, but Scheer ordered the 3rd Squadron to maintain the present course, and in a signal to the fleet timed at 0533, further ordered that ships were to keep straight on in the event of danger from mines.

Meanwhile the 3rd Squadron had entered the minefield and most of the ships reported mines. The *Kaiser* dropped a mine-buoy, and this was mistaken for a periscope by the *Hessen* and *Schlesien*, which both opened fire at about 0555. The firing was described as violent or heavy by other ships, and in these actions with imaginary submarines, the *Hessen*, *Schlesien* and *Hannover* fired a few rounds from their 11in. The *Regensburg* at the rear of the fleet signalled at 0603 that a torpedo track had been sighted to port, and 3 minutes later the *Frankfurt* signalled that a submarine had been sighted to starboard, but neither was real.

The *Seydlitz* passed Horns Reef Lightship at 0400, and steered for the Lister Deep, screened against submarines by six destroyers (the *S24* and 13th Half-Flotilla) that had sighted her at 0345. The *S24* and *S18* were detached at 0515 and at 0540 the *Seydlitz* joined the fleet, and took station astern of the 2nd Squadron at 0605, while the *Derfflinger* and *Nassau* went ahead. It was no longer possible to maintain the fleet's speed of 15kts, as the *Seydlitz* was now so low forward that her bow-wave broke over the forecastle and the planing action of the inclined decks increased the danger so that she had to reduce to 10 and then to 7kts.

In a wireless signal timed at 0444, the *Regensburg* had ordered the 7th Flotilla to act as submarine screen for the battlecruisers, the *V28*, the 12th Half-flotilla and the 5th Flotilla for the dreadnoughts, and three of the 6th Flotilla for the 2nd Squadron, while the remaining available destroyers were to close the 3rd Squadron. As noted above some of the 5th and 7th Flotillas were screening the damaged *Ostfriesland* and *Seydlitz*, and at 0600 the other dreadnoughts and battlecruisers were being screened by a total of sixteen destroyers. There was none screening the 2nd Squadron at that time, as the *V44* and the *G86*, which had been by the head of the line, failed to find them until shortly after 0700, and during the search in poor visibility the *V44* had mistaken the 3rd Squadron for British battlecruisers which contributed to the delay. Five destroyers of the 9th Flotilla, *G42*, and the 14th Half-Flotilla had not joined by 0600, and the last named did not do so until about 0850 when they screened the *Derfflinger*, while the other six destroyers were still further astern.

The four destroyers with the *Lützow*'s crew on board – the *G40*,

G38, *V45* and *G37* – sighted the *Champion* with the *Obdurate*, *Moresby*, *Marksman* and *Maenad* at about 0325. A brief action developed on approximately opposite courses at 2400–7400yds. The German destroyers opened a rapid but ineffective fire, and the *G40* fired one and the *V45* two torpedoes at 2400–2700yds. The *Champion* replied, but according to one account only fired a single 6in round, and turned away to avoid two torpedoes, the first track passing under her bows and the other missing close astern. The *Moresby* also sighted two torpedoes, one of which was just avoided, and three were seen from the *Maenad*. The British destroyers opened fire, the *Obdurate*'s forward 4in gun bursting. The Germans soon vanished in the mist and were not pursued.

The *G40* was hit by a 6in shell which damaged her after turbine, but was able to keep going at 26kts for another 10 minutes before stopping from loss of steam, and was taken in tow by the *G37*.

The *Dublin* at 0430 had reported the *Rostock* and her destroyers as a cruiser and two destroyers, probably hostile, bearing 77° and steering 167°. In reply to subsequent signals this was amplified to the armoured cruiser *Roon* apparently steaming fast, with at least two destroyers and possibly another cruiser, all being lost sight of in the fog.

In fact the *Rostock* was proceeding southward in tow of the *S54* and screened by the *V71* and *V73*, when at about 0355, the *Dublin*, taken to be either two light cruisers of the *Birmingham* class, or an armoured cruiser and two destroyers, was sighted approaching four or five miles away to the south-westward. At about this time the *L11*'s report of twelve British battleships steering 10° at high speed came in, and it was incorrectly thought that the *Rostock* might be only about 20 miles away. The *S54*, *V71* and *V73* were called alongside to take off her crew. The *Dublin* did not close, while the *Rostock* and the *S54* continually made the first two letters – 'UA' – of the British challenge, and smoke screens were employed so that the *Dublin* which replied repeatedly to the challenge, was uncertain of the ship's identity.

At about 0405 the *S54* put off and proceeded eastwards and 10mins later the *Dublin*, this time taken to be two further cruisers, was sighted *c*35° to starboard and 3–4 miles away, steering 10°. Once again the *S54* continually flashed 'UA' as well as other disconnected letters, to which the *Dublin* again replied, and made off at full speed. The *Dublin* steamed towards her at high speed, and then turned away to port so that the *S54* could steer for Horns Reef.

Meanwhile the *V71* and *V73* remained near the *Rostock*, and although scuttling charges had been placed, three torpedoes (two by the *V71* and one by the *V73*) were fired to hasten her sinking, which occurred bows first, at *c*0425; the *V71* and *V73* then proceeded at full speed to Horns Reef.

Although the *Dublin* was taken to be at least two ships when sighted, no other vessel was present. The *V71*'s signal reporting the *Rostock*'s sinking, was timed at 0412 and gave a position *c*55° 18′N, 6° 18′E which was over 20 miles too far to the south.

Neither of the above encounters was creditable to the British, and there is farcical element in the proceedings of the three submarines sent to intercept returning German ships, as their orders were those for the operation planned for 2 June, and although their time of leaving Harwich was advanced by 15 hours to 1900 on 30 May, they were not told of any change in the plan, and to save their batteries for 2 June, neither the *E26* nor *E55* kept a continuous watch on the previous day, although the *D1* apparently did so. Under their orders the *E55*, *E26* and *D1* were to spread on a line bearing 270° from the Vyl lightship and 4, 12 and 20 miles from this mark.

The *E26* was the first to sight Horns Reef at 2335 on 31 May. The Vyl lightship was sighted at 0100 and the *E26* settled on the bottom in her position between 0200 and 0300. The High Seas Fleet passed not very far away at about 0400, but the *E26* sighted nothing all day. The *E55* sighted Horns Reef half an hour after the *E26*, and at 0020 a Zeppelin, probably *L24*, approached flying low, and the *E55* went to the bottom to the west of Horns Reef. At 0045 a noise was heard as of a sweep passing very close, and between 0215 and 0530 eleven explosions of varying strength were audible, but nothing was seen during daylight on 1 June except an out of range destroyer at 0825. The *D1* reached her position and dived at 0430 1 June, not long after the High Seas Fleet had passed, and sighted nothing throughout her patrol. All three left after dark on 3 June, and although several German submarines had been sighted, only the *E55* was able to get in a shot at the *U64* at 1813 2 June, but the torpedo narrowly missed and exploded on the sea bed.

The *Talisman* with the *G2*, *G3*, *G4* and *G5* was approaching her station (approximately 54° 30′N, 4° 00′E) when a wireless message from the Admiralty was received, ordering two submarines to be detached towards the Lister Deep, to remain 48 hours and attack damaged German ships. The *G3* and *G5* were accordingly detached at 0400 1 June, and by *c*1130 reached positions near the westward or north-westward edge of the British minefields laid on 10/11 September 1915, but the German route lay to the east of the minefields. On the way *G3* and *G5* sighted the *Marlborough* and *Fearless*, and began an attack before the latter were recognised. The *G5* returned over 12 hours before the *G3*, and in company with the *G2* and *G4*, unsuccessfully attempted to attack a German submarine, probably the *U46*, on the morning of 3 June. The *Talisman* and all four submarines arrived at Blyth during 4 June.

At *c*0400 the *Malaya* struck a submerged object on the starboard side that scraped along under the bottom. This was thought most likely to have been a submarine, but was wreckage not connected with the battle. Some additional damage was caused to the hull plating near and below that from the hit at 1720 on 31 May.

The firing at the *L11* was unsystematic and that from the turret guns was handicapped by the need to expend the projectiles in the guns and cages before shrapnel could be used. Nine battleships, two battlecruisers and four smaller ships opened fire with 15in to 3pdr guns but no hits were made on the *L11* which was at a height of 3600ft – 6200ft and was 536ft 5in long and 61ft 4in diameter, though she was badly shaken by heavy shells passing near and perhaps by bursts of 6in and smaller time fuzed shells.

Jellicoe continued to sweep the area of the night actions for another 5 hours and it was not until 1108 that a signal timed at 1044, was sent to the Admiralty stating that the Harwich force was not required except for destroyers to screen the *Marlborough*, and that Jellicoe was ascertaining that no disabled ships were left and was returning to base. The signal also stated that the whole area had been swept for disabled enemy cruisers without result and that the weather was very misty, and in fact visibility was seldom more than 3 to 4 miles during the forenoon.

The *King George V* passed wreckage from the *Rostock* and, as Burney's ships had done, mistook fog canisters for large propellant cases, and at about 0840 the *Castor* with the *Kempenfelt* and twenty-three destroyers rejoined. Wreckage from the *Turbulent*, *Ardent*, *Fortune* and *Black Prince* was passed, and the *Barham* sighted a supposed submarine, apparently oil from the *Ardent's* wreck, and perhaps her submerged hull. The 2nd CS sighted the bows of the *Sparrowhawk* but nothing further was found. In a signal timed at 0917 and based on intercepted German signals, the Admiralty told Jellicoe that at 0620 submarines had been ordered to close the *Elbing*, whose position was now given as 55° 51'N, 5° 55'E. The fleet had passed through this position shortly before 0600, and was again approaching it, but Jellicoe's 1000 alteration of course to 336° removed his ships from the submarine danger, and he maintained this course without incident until 1108 when it was altered to 302°.

The *Revenge, Hercules* and *Agincourt* still failed to rejoin the battlefleet, and were at least 45 miles to the northward by 1000. They had passed wreckage from the *Black Prince*, possibly the *Elbing* and the *Frauenlob*.

Jellicoe had given Beatty the battlefleet's future position and course in a signal sent at 0700, and ordered him to keep to the eastward, but owing to errors in the *Lion's* reckoning this was not done, and Beatty did not sweep to 32° after 0730 as he had proposed and Jellicoe approved. At 0945 Beatty turned to 235° and contact was made with the 5th BS. He then conformed to Jellicoe's course taking station astern of the battlefleet's starboard column until 1104, when he altered course to 325°, preparatory to sweeping the area of some of the daylight fighting, up to 57° 30'N, 5° 45'E as ordered by Jellicoe in a signal sent at 1007.

Jellicoe did not receive any news of the *Indefatigable* and *Queen Mary* having sunk until a signal from Beatty, sent at 1001, was taken in and this only gave the approximate position of their wrecks. Information on the cause and time of their loss was not given until two further signals from Beatty were sent at 1250 and 1303, and in the interim Jellicoe seems to have thought that they might have been mined.

Of the ships not in company, the *Warrior* had been towed by the *Engadine* for about 100 miles from 2040 31 May making for Kinnaird Head, but a swell got up with an increasing SW wind, and at 0715 the *Engadine* was ordered to take off the *Warrior's* crew. The latter was listing *c*6° to port with every sea washing over the upper deck and her stern 2 or 3ft above water, while the flooding was already 2ft deep on the main deck and increasing. It was thought she would sink in an hour or at most 2 or 3 hours when abandoned at 0825, unless the sea moderated, but all accessible water-tight doors and hatches were closed in case the weather improved.

The *Engadine*, which was unable to pass the news and position of the *Warrior's* abandonment until 1405, made for Rosyth with all 743 survivors, and arrived at 0135 2 June.

The *Dublin* joined the battlefleet shortly before 0800 and transferred to the 2nd LCS when Beatty's force made contact about 2 hours later. Of the thirty-nine flotilla-leaders and destroyers not in touch with any heavy ships at 0600, twenty-four had joined Jellicoe with the *Castor*, while the *Narborough, Nerissa* and *Pelican*, which until 0535 had been proceeding further and further westward with the *Lydiard*, joined the battlecruisers soon after 1000. The *Champion* in company with the *Obdurate, Moresby* and *Maenad* was still not in touch. These three destroyers and the *Marksman* had picked up three survivors from the *Ardent* and seventeen from the *Fortune* at 0430–0530 and at about 0600 the *Marksman* was detached to the totally disabled *Sparrowhawk*. An attempt to tow the latter failed, and Burney, who passed by at 0845, ordered the *Marksman* to sink her, and the *Marksman* then joined the *Faulknor* at about 1000. The *Sparrowhawk*'s bows had previously parted from the rest of her hull, and remained afloat until sunk by the *Laurel* on 3 June. The remaining eight destroyers of the above thirty-nine were returning home by 1100, in most cases from shortage of fuel.

Apart from the *Seydlitz*, the German battleships and battlecruisers passed through the channel to the east of the Amrum Bank without incident, but the *Ostfriesland* encountered further trouble subsequently. The 2nd Squadron was detached to the Elbe, and the rest passed the outer Jade lightship between *c*1200 and 1345, the *Ostfriesland* being the last. The *Grosser Kurfürst* had to reduce speed near Heligoland from the amount of water that had entered forward, and fell astern of the formation, but rejoined off Schillig. The light cruiser *München* sighted an imaginary torpedo coming from port aft at 1040 when off Heligoland, and opened fire on an equally imaginary periscope. On arrival the *Posen, Nassau, Westfalen, Thüringen* and *Helgoland* took up outpost duty in Schillig Roads with the 4th Scouting Group and 5th Flotilla after the latter had refuelled, while the *Kaiser, Kaiserin, Prinzregent Luitpold* and *Kronprinz* anchored in Wilhelmshaven Roads outside the locks in support. The remainder of the heavy ships entered harbour.

The *Ostfriesland*, screened against submarines by a seaplane and the *V3* and *V5*, had taken the route to the west of Heligoland after passing through the Amrum Bank channel, instead of that to the east as the fleet had done. There was no incident until 1120 when the *Ostfriesland* was about 5 miles from Heligoland and the escorting seaplane dropped two bombs on a non-existent British submarine to starboard, and gave the alarm. The *Ostfriesland* turned sharply away, and the torpedo bulkhead, which had been torn in one place by the mine explosion, burst open further, and more water entered so that she had to reduce to slow speed and took a list of $4\frac{3}{4}°$ to starboard. At 1320 the *Ostfriesland* signalled for a pumping steamer to be sent, but 25 minutes later the Outer Jade Lightship was passed and the water was now held, so that she could increase to 9 and then 10kts, and at 1715 entered the North Lock at Wilhemshaven.

Units of the mine sweeping and harbour flotillas had been sent out to provide an additional screen for the fleet against possible submarine attack, and a number of seaplanes were also employed, one of which reported a hostile submarine to the westward of the Amrum Bank, while there was a subsequent report of three bombs having been dropped where a submarine had dived near the Amrum Bank lightship. No British submarines were near these positions, which were well to the eastward of the *G3* and *G5*.

At 0835 the *Regensburg* received a signal from the *V45* stating that the *G40* had been damaged in action and taken in tow, and giving a 0700 position near the Horns Reef lightship, which was nearly 15 miles in error to the southward. A further signal came in at 0903 from the *S32* that she was completely disabled and had anchored 2 miles from Lyngvig lighthouse. The *Regensburg*, which was in the Amrum Bank channel, turned back at 0910 to meet the group with the G40, and was accompanied by the *V30, S34* and *S33*. The *Regensburg* took on 1177 of the *Lützow*'s survivors from the *G40, V45* and *G37*, but the *G38* had gone on ahead, and proceeded home with the *V71*. The *V73* transferred her *Rostock* survivors to the *V71*, and then proceeded to the *S32*, and after taking her in tow, was met by the *G39* and *G88* released from screening the *Moltke*. The *G40*, though at times under her own steam, proved very troublesome to tow, seven lines having broken. The *S32* was also difficult, but both were brought back safely.

The rest of the British battlefleet's return to Scapa Flow was comparatively uneventful. The *Valiant* screened by the *Moon* and *Mounsey* was detached to Rosyth at 1550 1 June and arrived at 0700 next day. The 2nd CS were ordered to search for the *Warrior* at 1615, though the correct position was not given until midnight, and an imaginary submarine was reported by the *Hampshire* at 1720. At 1925 the *Revenge* and *Barham* sighted one another and at last Burney's three battleships rejoined.

Jellicoe's course during this period was 302° until 1315 and then 336°, followed by 298° at 1905, and speed 16 or 17kts. At about 2000 the *Malaya* had to shut off the burners in 'A' boiler room as oil from the damaged bunkers was finding its way into the air space of 'A' stokehold and there were slight oil leaks into the stokehold itself. She could however steam at about 20kts with her remaining boilers.

The three 'K' class destroyers of the 2nd Cruiser Squadron's screen were detached between 1300 and 1400 as they were short of fuel while the *Mischief* eventually joined the battlefleet's screen, and together with all the other destroyers of Jellicoe's or Burney's force, except for the two detached with the *Valiant*, remained in company. It was necessary to reduce the fleet's speed to 14kts at 0300 on 2 June as the sea had risen, and after course was altered to 270° at 0315, there was a further reduction to 13kts from 0420 to 0800. Speed was then gradually increased and the *Iron Duke* arrived at Scapa at 1130 three quarters of an hour after the *Colossus*'s Division which had been sent on ahead unscreened at 0730. At 2145 2 June Jellicoe reported to the Admiralty that the battlefleet was at 4 hours' notice and ready for action. Beatty turned for Rosyth at 1615. The *Sparrowhawk*'s bow, wreckage from the *Wiesbaden*, and a boat marked *V29* had been passed while the wreck of the *Invincible*, whose bow was still above water, was also sighted. The *Birmingham* reported a submarine's periscope in sight at 1548 which was probably imaginary.

There were thirteen destroyers in company with the battlecruisers at 1100, but two of the 1st Flotilla had then to leave as they were short of fuel, followed by two more at 1330 and a further two and the *Pelican* at 1540-1600. At 1930 the last six had to reduce to 13kts and the battlecruisers and light cruisers increased to 21. The *Champion* did not rejoin, and was ordered back to Rosyth at 1630, while two of her three destroyers had already left from shortage of fuel. The *Canterbury* was detached to Harwich at about 2030, and at 0040 2 June the *Southampton* had to turn stern to sea and reduce to 10-15kts to make temporary repairs to damage near the water-line. The *Birmingham* remained by her, and by 0300 she had once more set course for Rosyth, and anchored there at 1145 about 3¼ hours after the battlecruisers, which had been met by six destroyers at about 0515.

The *Chester* had arrived in the Humber at 1600 1 June, and all the destroyers returning from damage or lack of fuel got back safely, and under their own power except for the *Onslow* towed by the *Defender* and the *Acasta* by the *Nonsuch*. The last to arrive was the *Broke* which reached the Tyne at 1800 on 3 June after the *Active* and *Constance* had searched for her on the previous day.

The *Nicator* returning with the *Petard* was attacked by the *U52* off Berwick at 1530 1 June, but the torpedo fired at *c*700yds was seen running on the surface and the *Nicator* turned away so that it passed ahead and then exploded for some unknown reason.

Eight destroyers of the Harwich Force were detached to screen the *Marlborough*, and Tyrwhitt received orders at 1735 1 June from Jellicoe and at 1902 from the Admiralty, to return with the rest of his force. A false report by the *Termagant* of four enemy destroyers 30 miles from May Island – actually units of the Forth local flotilla – delayed Tyrwhitt's return and he did not arrive at Harwich until 1930 2 June.

The 2nd CS continued searching for the *Warrior* until the morning of 3 June without finding any traces of her, and the 3rd LCS with four destroyers left Rosyth on the evening of 2 June and abandoned their search which was also unsuccessful, 48 hours later. The *Minotaur* sighted a submarine at 2135 2 June and claimed to have sunk her by gunfire, but she was actually the *E30* of the Blyth Flotilla and was undamaged. The *Gloucester* reported that a torpedo, which was probably imaginary, passed under her at 0400 3 June, and late that day, in company with the *Laurel*, found the bows of the *Sparrowhawk* and these were sunk by the *Laurel* in a position given as 56° 25′N, 6° 40′E.

To prevent the possible recovery by the Germans of secret documents from the *Invincible*'s wreck, the Blyth Flotilla was ordered to send a submarine as soon as the weather allowed, to sink any part that still showed above water. The *G10* accordingly sailed at 0300 3 June, but found nothing after searching for 48 hours. A desk from the *Invincible* containing cyphers drifted ashore on the Danish coast.

The *Warspite* had made for Rosyth as ordered on the evening of 31 May. She had to be steered from the engine room, but was in no danger from her damage, as the port wing engine room was practically water-tight with bulkheads shored where necessary, and her metacentric height was still about 4½ft. It was difficult to establish wireless communication on the morning of 1 June, but at about 0830 the *Barham* received a signal that the *Warspite*'s 0610 position was 56° 39′N, 1° 43′E course 257° with speed of advance 16kts. This was passed to Jellicoe, and by him to Rosyth at 0902 with instructions to send local destroyers to screen the *Warspite*.

The latter had gradually increased speed and at 0935 was zig-zagging at 19kts when two torpedoes passed close to the ship, one on either side. No track or periscope was seen as the breeze was causing many 'white horses' on the waves, and the *Warspite* increased to 21 and then 22kts, signalling to Rosyth at 1017 that two torpedoes had missed her in 56° 31′N, 0° 40′W and that she was returning with no escort. The submarine was the *U51* which approached to within 650yds, but her periscope then dipped shortly before the first torpedo was to be discharged. Both bow tubes were immediately fired, but only one torpedo left its tube. The *Warspite* was mistaken for a ship of the *Canopus* class, and it would seem that one of the two torpedoes reported was imaginary.

At 1142, just as the first two torpedo-boats of the local flotilla were in sight, a periscope was seen close under the *Warspite*'s bows. Orders were given to increase to full speed and to put the helm over to ram, but it took time to transmit orders to the engine room steering position, and the submarine was missed by a few yards. The *Warspite* then zig-zagged away at full speed, but this made it necessary to reshore bulkheads and after four more torpedo-boats had joined, speed was reduced to 21kts at 1240.

The submarine was the *U63* which had begun an attack on a ship taken to be a cruiser on the starboard beam. The sound of propellers was then heard, and through the periscope a glimpse was seen of the bridge of what was taken to be a 3-funnelled cruiser – actually the *Warspite* – close astern, and clearly about to ram. At that moment the *Warspite* fired a round from a gun on her bridge, and the *U63* immediately dived, struck the bottom at 160ft, and shot up to 23ft. The *Warspite* fired 4–6in rounds at her and she was hunted by patrol vessels and attacked with depth-charges but got away at 90–115ft.

The *Nepean*, *Negro* and *Phoenix* joined the screen at about 1300, and the *Warspite* arrived at Rosyth at *c*1500 without further incident and proceeded into No 1 Dry-dock.

The *Marlborough* was more damaged than the *Warspite*, but not in danger provided the sea remained fairly calm and she was not again torpedoed or mined. It was decided not to counter-flood any of the port wing compartments, as the list of 7–8° was no danger to the ship and it was better to retain buoyancy. There is some doubt as to the *Marlborough*'s exact course as her compasses were in error, but it appears to have been 205° until 0535 and then 223°. Owing to her deep draught it was considered better to go to Rosyth rather than the Tyne. The *Fearless* was in company but there were no destroyers, and at 0415 the Admiralty ordered the Rear Admiral East Coast to send two to the eastern end of 'M' channel. At 0600 Tyrwhitt asked Jellicoe for instructions but did not receive a reply until 0836. This, which was timed at 0700, directed him to send four destroyers to screen the *Marlborough*, proceeding to Rosyth via 'M' channel, and gave her last reported position, 55° 30'N, 6° 03'E at 0430, steering 212° at 14kts. At 0915 Tyrwhitt accordingly ordered the *Laforey*, *Lookout*, *Lawford* and *Laverock* to proceed to escort the *Marlborough* and gave her 0830 position as 54° 41'N, 5° 10'E, extrapolated from her reported 0430 position and considerably in error. In any event the Harwich force was still far away, as its 0830 position was given as 52° 40'N, 3° 02'E.

So far the *Marlborough*'s return had been free from submarines, but at 0930 two bearing 257° about eight miles off, and approaching with their conning towers showing, were observed. These dived 5 minutes later and the *Marlborough* altered course to the southward. As previously mentioned they were the British *G3* and *G5*.

At 1050 the *Marlborough* resumed her previous course, but 2 minutes later an oily patch was seen about two miles astern, and then the track of a torpedo overhauling the ship, but this passed along the port side 400yds off. The torpedo came from the *U46* which had sighted two vessels 11° on the starboard bow and soon identified them as a 4-funnelled destroyer (*Fearless*) and an *Iron Duke* class battleship, listing to starboard and down by the head. The torpedo was fired at 3300yds and the *U46* did not pursue on the surface as she might have done.

The *Marlborough* altered course to the westward soon after 1100 and at about this time a 100-ton submersible pump was lowered into 'A' boiler room, some of the armour gratings having been cut away. At 1135 speed was increased so that the *Marlborough* was making *c*13½kts over the ground, and round about noon the pump was started and worked very well. At about 1350 the Harwich force was sighted, and as the four destroyers sent to the *Marlborough* had not yet found her, the *Lance, Lassoo, Lysander* and *Lark* were detached, and within the next hour, the other four also joined, so that the *Marlborough* had a screen of eight destroyers and all seemed satisfactory though speed had to be reduced again by 1 or 2kts to lessen the pressure on bulkheads.

Between 1600 and 1630 the small destroyers *Ness* and *Albatross*, sent by the Rear Admiral East Coast, joined, and at 1718 course was altered to 290°, and at 2046 to 268°. At 1835 the Admiralty asked the *Marlborough*'s draught of water, and on receiving the reply of an estimated 39ft, directed her at 2125 to proceed to Rosyth for temporary repairs, as she was already doing, and at 2150 course was altered to 323°.

Meanwhile the SW wind had been freshening and by 2200 was force 6 with a rising sea. The ship began to work and though extra shores were placed in 'A' boiler-room, dirt was disturbed by the working of the ship and continually choked the suctions of the ash expeller and submersible pump so that the water level rose. The steam ejector was tried but the canvas hose burst and a spare hose blew away from the joint. By 2300 the weather was too bad for the *Albatross* to keep up and though in a signal timed at 2330 the *Marlborough* informed Rosyth that she would arrive within gun range of Inchkeith at 1330 2 June, her condition suddenly became serious, as at *c*2330 the submersible pump was shifted to clear its suction, and the roll of the ship took it against the shores of the starboard after lower bunker door which were knocked away. This was the site of the largest leak into 'A' boiler room, and as the water was already too deep for the shores to be replaced, the level at midnight was about 4ft below the grating round the tops of the boilers and still rising. If 'A' boiler-room completely flooded it was impossible to predict where such a large amount of water might penetrate, and it was possible that the engines might have to be stopped. Accordingly the *Marlborough* reduced to 10kts and steered to get under the lee of Flamborough Head about 45 miles away. Jellicoe was informed of the situation in a signal timed at midnight, and tugs urgently requested from the SNO Tyne, though this latter signal was apparently not despatched until 0120, just after Jellicoe had ordered tugs to be sent from the Humber.

At 0047 the *Marlborough* warned the *Fearless* and destroyers to be prepared to come alongside and take off the ship's company, but meanwhile a diver had gone down in 'A' boiler-room and kept the pump suctions clear so that the water stopped rising at 1300. The *Fearless* was requested at 0152 to keep station 300yds to windward of the *Marlborough*'s forebridge to reduce the seas breaking on her, and the destroyers of the *Lance*'s division began to lay an oil track ahead and to windward of the *Marlborough* at shortly after 0200. This was most successful and speed was again increased to 12kts, while a signal had been received from the Admiralty directing the *Marlborough* to go to the Humber for temporary repairs.

The *Canterbury* on her way to Harwich was ordered by Jellicoe to proceed to the *Marlborough*'s assistance, but by 0630, when the former was off Flamborough Head, there was no need of further help. The *Marlborough*'s steam ejector was repaired at about 0430, and three quarters of an hour later when she was reported by Flamborough Head, the water in 'A' boiler-room was well below the floor plates. The weather improved near the land and at 0530 the destroyers stopped making their oil track. Piloted by the *Fearless* and drawing 40ft, the *Marlborough* arrived in the Humber at 0800, and 2 hours later secured to No 3 buoy off Immingham.

While in the Humber additional pumps and shoring were provided, 'A', 'B' and 6in magazines and shell-rooms were cleared into lighters, and the sheet anchor and cables landed. As far as possible stores and heavy weights were moved aft from the forward part of the ship, and oil fuel pumped to the port side. The wing compartments abreast the port engine room were flooded, and some stores moved from starboard to port. On the evening of 3 June the starboard longitudinal bulkhead of 'A' boiler-room began to give slightly and was strengthened by additional shores. Next morning the salvage ship *Linnet* arrived from Dover and placed an 8in submersible pump in 'A' boiler-room and by that evening the *Marlborough* was drawing 33ft 6in forward and 31ft 6in aft and was on an even keel. Nothing could be done with divers owing to the strong tide and muddy water. The *Marlborough* left on 6 June escorted by four 'M' class destroyers from Harwich, and proceeded to the Tyne for permanent repairs, standing a heavy swell satisfactorily at 10kts.

The German submarines had no success against the returning British fleet. Neither the *U53* nor *U67* received the order, timed at 1950 31 May, to proceed northwards at once, but the *U19*, *U22* and *U64* left the Ems at 2145 followed by the *U46* at 0400 1 June. In a signal timed at 0554, Scheer, who did not yet know that the *Elbing* had been sunk, ordered a submarine to be sent at once to her in *c*55° 51′N, 5° 55′E, and the *U19* and then the *U64* and *U22* made for this position, as did the *U53* shortly after leaving Heligoland. Jellicoe turned to 336° near the *Elbing*'s supposed position at 1000 about an hour before the *U64*, arrived.

The *U22* and *U19* briefly sighted destroyers but otherwise only sundry wreckage was found.

Meanwhile the German wireless deciphering station at Neumünster had informed Scheer in a signal timed at 0830 that a damaged British ship had been in *c*55° 03′N, 5° 15′E, steering 223° at 0715. This was based on a signal from the *Marlborough* to the *Champion* which actually gave her position as 55° 05′N, 5° 44′E, and in a signal timed at 0943 Scheer ordered a submarine to be sent. The *U46* was best situated and as previously described, sighted and unsuccessfully attacked the *Marlborough* before the *U46* had received any orders based on the ship reported by *Neumünster*, and it was not until shortly after 1300, that orders to chase the ship reported by Neumünster could be passed to her. Though subsequently ordered to proceed as far as Flamborough Head, she was still 25 miles away at 0925 2 June when the *Marlborough* was safely in the Humber, and at 1630 the *U46* turned back. She had sighted five light cruisers and nine destroyers of the Harwich force, at high speed about 11,000yds off.

The *U67* also left her area off Terschelling in search of the ship reported by Neumünster, but saw nothing and turned back at 1830 1 June.

Another important signal was sent out by Neumünster, timed at 0910 1 June. This stated that at 0845 the enemy battlefleet had been in *c*55° 27′N, 6° 45′E steering 347° at 20kts. The signal intercepted was from Beatty to Jellicoe and gave the battlecruisers' 0815 position. It was hoped that it might be possible to attack the British fleet when it altered course to the westward and orders were sent to the *U64*, *U22*, *U19* and *U53*. Bad weather forced all four to abandon operations early on 2 June.

The submarines off the British coast from the Humber northwards were, except for the *U47*, due to leave their stations on the evening of 1 June, and in a signal timed at 0720 on 1 June and sent out repeatedly by the wireless transmitters at Bruges and Nauen, Captain Bauer instructed them to remain another day if at all possible, as damaged ships were expected to be returning from the Skagerrak. The *U24* and *U32* were to patrol off the Tyne, instead of the Forth, during this period. This signal was only taken in by the *U24* initially, and several submarines never received it at all.

Jellicoe's route to Scapa passed to the northward of the *U43* and *U44*. The *U43* heard nothing of the battle, and left on the morning of 2 June. She had unsuccessfully attacked two patrol vessels the previous day, and had been repeatedly hunted. The *U44* learnt from Bruges on the evening of 1 June that British forces and damaged ships were making for the Forth, and concluded from a lively exchange of wireless signals between British units that some squadrons were making for Scapa. She hoped to intercept these in daylight on 2 June but the weather was so rough at dawn that she could not have been held at attacking depth, and proceeded home.

Of the two submarines to the eastward of Peterhead, the *U66* left on the evening of 1 June, and the *U47* a day later.

Off the Forth, the *U63* was returning with her starboard engine disabled, when she encountered the *Warspite* as previously noted, and after escaping, continued homewards. The *U51*'s unsuccessful attack on the *Warspite* has already been described, and she started back during the night of 1/2 June.

The *U32* attacked a destroyer at 0815 1 June but the torpedo missed. The order to proceed to the Tyne was received at 1600 that day, and the *U32* left accordingly. Her sector off the Forth was the one through which the battlecruisers returned, but only a few destroyers were sighted off the Tyne, and the *U32* started for home on the evening of 2 June.

The *U70* was already on her way home, when the signal to remain another day was received at 0630 2 June. On account of the heavy sea she did not return to her station, and after cruising at 90° to the probable British route without sighting anything, resumed her voyage home at 2200 2 June. The *U24* took in Bauer's order and at once made for the Tyne, but she had no more success than the *U32* and left some hours before her.

The *U52* saw two darkened vessels, thought to be light cruisers or destroyers, pass through the mined area off Berwick early on 1 June.

Soon afterwards a partly taken in wireless signal showed that there had been a battle in the North Sea, and the *U52* proceeded northwards to try and get in touch with the *U24* and *U70*. The former was sighted at 0520 but had received no message, and the *U52* returned to her station off Berwick. She was forced down by a destroyer on two occasions, and as previously noted attacked the *Nicator* unsuccessfully. Her rudder then jammed, but it was eventually disconnected, and she started for Horns Reef steering with her propellers.

All six submarines had thus left the vicinity of the Forth when the *Valiant* and the British battlecruisers returned on the morning of 2 June.

The *UB21* and *UB22* had both left their stations off the Humber by the morning of 1 June. The former had fired a torpedo at the old destroyer *Earnest* which passed about 50yds astern.

The *U75*, returning from minelaying off the Orkneys, crossed the scene of part of the daylight action on 1 June. The wreck of the *Invincible* was sighted at 1400 and also a British destroyer in the vicinity, but nothing was seen of the battlecruisers though they were not far away. By the morning of 2 June it was blowing a gale and after three times encountering and avoiding British submarines off Horns Reef, the *U75* arrived at Heligoland on 3 June.

Of the Flanders Flotilla the *UC6* and *UC10* laid their mines to the north of the Inner Gabbard and to the south of the sunk lightship during the night of 31 May – 1 June, and the *UB10* sighted eight destroyers, presumably part of the Harwich force, steering 122° when about 20 miles off Southwold at 0800 1 June. Attempts to keep the *UB* boats out for another 24 hours failed as wireless communication could not be established, and when they started their return home at 1600 2 June, none of them knew of the battle.

CHAPTER 17

Bringing in the *Seydlitz*: damage to the *Ostfriesland*
Repair of the capital ships

IT REMAINS TO take up the story of the *Seydlitz*'s return to Wilhelmshaven. She had taken station astern of the 2nd Squadron at 0605 1 June but could not maintain the fleet's speed of 15kts and had to reduce to 10 and then 7kts. By this time the *Seydlitz* was low enough forward for large amounts of water to enter the compartments above the armour deck between the forward citadel and foremost boiler room bulkheads via the battery deck, which had been badly damaged on the starboard side by the first shell to strike the ship. This shell had done much other damage, and all compartments in this section above the armour deck soon filled. Water then poured into 'A' barbette on the battery and main decks and spread below so that first the shell rooms and then the magazines of 'A' turret flooded. At the same time other water from 'A' barbette entered the broadside torpedo flat through the emergency escape, and though it was possible to keep the water down in the flat, the personnel were evacuated.

Leakage now increased into the torpedo transmitting station and into the ship's control room, neither of which had any effective drainage, and in consequence of the foremost boiler-room bulkhead yielding slightly, the torpedo transmitting station was abandoned at 0605 and the ship's control room at 0710. This made navigation of the *Seydlitz* still more difficult, as orders to the engine rooms had to be passed by a chain of messengers and voice pipes, and the nearby 2nd SG were asked for help. The *Pillau* was detached to pilot the *Seydlitz* at 0830 and at the same time Wilhelmshaven was asked to send out two pumping steamers and leak-stopping material. The *Pillau* took station ahead at 0845 steaming 7kts, but just after 0900 the *Seydlitz* grounded off Hörnum at the southern end of Sylt. Soundings forward gave 43 –

44ft, the first certain indication of the ship's draught. The port and midships after trimming tanks, and the port after wings for a length of 57ft were counter-flooded, and at 0930 the *Seydlitz* came off an hour and 40 minutes before high water.

The 1st Minesweeping Division arrived at this time, and as it appeared doubtful if the channel to the east of the Amrum Bank could be passed owing to the *Seydlitz*'s great draught, it was decided to turn back and make for Heligoland Bight by the route to the west of Amrum Bank and of the big British minefield laid on 10/11 September 1915. One group of the 1st M/S Division led with their sweeps out, and the second group replaced the four destroyers of the 7th Flotilla as an anti-submarine screen. A 10° course was steered for the Lister Deep until 1025, when the *Pillau* passed on Neumünster's 0910 signal, that at 0845 the enemy battlefleet had been in 100 α (c55° 27' N, 6° 45E) only 20 or 25 miles WSW of Horns Reef lightship, and it was evident that the eastward channel would have to be attempted after all.

The 1st M/S Division formed line abreast ahead of the *Pillau* and *Seydlitz*, sounding and signalling the depth of water by flags while the *S36*, which had temporarily joined to screen the *Pillau*, assisted, and the *Seydlitz* felt her way through the deepest channel. Occasionally there was no water quite deep enough, and the *Seydlitz* then drove through with increased engine revolutions, sliding just above the ground. The narrows to the westward of Hörnum at the beginning of the Amrum Bank channel were passed at 1230, and 2 hours later the *Seydlitz* reached the Vortrapp Deep bell-buoy, and completed the passage.

Meanwhile the ship had continued to sink slowly deeper. In the forward part only the broadside torpedo flat had any buoyancy left as the other last remaining unflooded compartments below the armour deck in this part of the ship had filled. This was probably to some extent due to water from above, entering through the inevitable leaks of the torpedo striking-down hatch, while the foremost trimming tanks below the bow torpedo tube had sprung a leak from the groundings. Although the undamaged ship's metacentric height was c10ft, the water plane had considerably diminished, and the reduced stability was evident in the slow heeling over under rudder action at her very low speed.

Water also gradually spread from the port outer bunkers that had been affected by shell hits, into other bunkers through leaky partitions and bunker doors, and water that was now entering the port forward and No 4 casemates flowed down through coal shoots in spite of all efforts to make these and the casemates water-tight. The list to starboard had disappeared through the counter-flooding when aground off Hörnum, and through the gradual equalisation of the flooding forward, and the water entering the port bunkers produced an increasing list to port, which further endangered the port casemates.

At first the water was drained to the stokeholds and pumped out, but the drainage system here was already heavily loaded and in no event could the stokeholds be endangered by flooding, so that the casemates were continuously bailed by bucket gangs. In spite of all efforts the port outer and protective bunkers gradually filled except for the protective bunker of the aftermost boiler room. The three fishes of the bow escutcheon were now in the water and served as a draught mark, while the list to port increased quickly to 8°, and it could not be predicted whether the remaining stability could resist the further slow but persistent increase and whether the caulking of the port casemates could prevent further water breaking in.

Additional signals requesting the urgent despatch of pumping steamers were sent by the *Pillau* at 1100 and at noon Scheer and Hipper were informed of the *Seydlitz's* progress. Just before 1600 a message came from Hipper that if necessary the ship should be beached in a suitable position in the Amrum Bank channel, but she was already in the Schmal Deep some miles to the southward of the Vortrapp Deep buoy. The *Seydlitz* steered south-east for the Hever mouth to come inshore and then southwards along the coast in c50ft of water. Preliminary preparations were made for abandoning the ship, and to provide as much relief as possible, she went astern from now onwards instead of 85revs (slow speed) ahead. An attempt to tow the *Seydlitz* was made by one of the minesweepers but the latter was not powerful enough. Several attempts by the *Pillau* all failed because the line parted owing to the lack of suitable gear on the *Seydlitz's* stern for the load to be taken gradually.

The *Seydlitz* therefore continued astern under her own power, and fortunately the weather remained calm. At 1700 the starboard after wings were counter-flooded for a length of 57ft to combat the list to port, and at this time the *Seydlitz's* condition was probably at its worst with a calculated 5329 tons water aboard, giving a draught of 46ft 1in forward and 24ft 4in aft. as against the pre-battle figures of 30ft 6in forward and 29ft 8in aft. The forward end of the keel line, where the draught was taken, was c65ft abaft the stem. The theoretical list to port was 2° 56′, but the actual list was 8°.

At 1730 the pumping steamers *Boreas* and *Kraft* arrived and made fast to starboard and port. The *Boreas* pumped out the compartments above the armour deck between the forward citadel and foremost boiler room bulkheads, while the *Kraft* should have drained 'A' turret magazines and shell rooms, but her centrifugal pump failed to produce suction, and the *Kraft* was thus useless to the *Seydlitz* except that both steamers now and then helped her rudder action.

During the night of 1/2 June the *Seydlitz*'s condition remained fairly constant and several tugs and lighters arrived to her aid, so that her progress was given some assistance by towing over the stern. Her course led towards the peace-time position of the Weser lightship, and owing to her draught of *c*46ft, the *Seydlitz* again grounded temporarily to the eastward of the Steingrund.

At daybreak on 2 June the weather deteriorated, with a north-west wind force 8, and an unpleasant sea began to rise. This particularly endangered the water-tightness of the port 5.9in casemates, and efforts were concentrated on caulking and draining them. The *Pillau* made a lee, while the *Boreas* pumped out the port forward casemates, and the *Kraft* went ahead to windward to lay an oil track. These measures proved successful.

The possibility of submarine attack to the southward of Heligoland was feared, and against this the *Seydlitz* was virtually defenceless as only one AA gun was usable on each side, and counter-manoeuvring impossible with the ship steaming astern at 3–5kts, so that anti-submarine protection lay entirely with the minesweeper screen and the *Pillau*. The latter piloted the *Seydlitz* towards the Jade by continual signalling, as the battlecruiser's speed was too low and the current from the Jade mouth too strong, for her to steer in the *Pillau*'s wake, but the difficult task of selecting a route with 50ft of water was accomplished, the Outer Jade lightship was passed at 0730 and 20 minutes later the *Seydlitz* anchored off the bar as, to the general surprise, the starboard anchor, cable and cable-holder were still in order amid the wreckage of the forecastle.

The wounded were now taken off the ship, and at the next high water at noon, the *Seydlitz* again proceeded stern first, assisted by the sea-going tug *Albatross*, and crossed the bar. Sufficient water was found inside the bar and it was decided not to beach the *Seydlitz* for patching NW by N of the Minsener Sand lightship as originally intended. All went well until 1420 when the *Seydlitz* grounded outside the boom and her stern swung across in the very strong ebb. At 1930 her stern swung round on the flood tide and at 2000 she came off with her stern towards the boom. The *Albatross* could not bring her stern round, and was holed by the starboard outer propeller in an attempt to make fast alongside. The *Seydlitz* was virtually unmanageable in the strong flood tide, and it was impossible to point either her stern or bow towards the boom gate until about 2300 when she passed the gate going ahead, and at 0325 3 June anchored in the Vareler Deep.

It was now possible for divers to examine the under-water damage, and some patching work was done, while the *Boreas*, various other pumps supplied by the dockyard and the ship's own drainage system, pumped out the bunkers and other gradually filling compartments. The broadside torpedo flat could be kept drained, and endangered bulkheads, particularly that at the forward end of the foremost boiler room, were made secure. As much weight as possible was removed from the forward part of the ship, including both 11in guns, the roof and some of the armour plates of 'A' turret.

Although the *Seydlitz* took the ground temporarily at low water and some of the under-water damage was thus accessible, the patching and draining work was hindered by the strong currents, and also by the *Seydlitz* often having to maintain her position with her engines as the anchor did not hold. It was thus decided to bring the ship into the South Lock of the Third Entrance, which measured 853ft × 114ft 10in with a depth at MHWS of 45ft at the outer sill and 36ft at the inner, and complete the patching in the shelter of the lock, so that the *Seydlitz*'s draught could be reduced sufficiently for her to enter the dockyard.

Accordingly at high water 1430 6 June, the *Seydlitz*, assisted by a powerful tug fore and aft, entered the South Lock stern first, drawing 45ft 11in forward and 23ft 3in aft, and with a list to port of 5–8°. The patching now made rapid progress, and the compartments between the forward citadel and foremost boiler-room bulkheads, the bunkers, and finally the compartments in the forward part of the ship, below and above the armour deck, were gradually drained. The 11in guns were also removed from the port wing turret, and by the morning of 13 June draught figures were 34ft 3in forward and 28ft 1in aft with very little if any list. At 0540 that day the *Seydlitz* was towed out of the lock, and at 0815 was in the large Wilhelmshaven floating dock.

Of capital ships, only the *Ostfriesland* was damaged by enemy weapons during the return to harbour, though the *Malaya* received minor damage below the water-line by striking wreckage. Unfortunately the *Ostfriesland*'s full damage report has not survived, and many details are not known. The mine (charge probably 300lb wet gun-cotton) exploded below the starboard forward wing turret, and according to one account, the hole measured *c*40ft × 16ft, and photographs show that the external effect extended from the lower edge of the armour belt, which was apparently not distorted, to the bilge keel, the greatest damage being rather nearer the belt. The starboard protective bunkers, wings and one series of double-bottom compartments were flooded from a line just forward of the conning tower to the centre line of the middle funnel, a length of *c*115ft. The torpedo bulkhead, which was 1.2in thick and *c*14 – 15ft inboard, was only slightly damaged in one place, where it was bulged inwards and torn, so that water entered one of the magazines. Scheer states that the *Ostfriesland* shipped 400 tons of water. No details appear to have survived on the further damage to the torpedo bulkhead caused by the sudden turn at 1120.

As far as possible the damaged British battleships and battlecruisers were repaired on the north-east coast where the dockyard at Rosyth could now be used, though far from complete. The *Warspite* went straight into No 1 dry-dock at Rosyth on 1 June, and was undocked on 4 July but her repairs were not finished until 20 July, and she left for Scapa two days later to rejoin the 5th BS. The *Tiger* was in No 2 dry-dock at Rosyth from 3 June to 1 July and was ready on the following day. The *Lion* was in the basin at Rosyth from 5 to 26 June, initially at 4 hours' notice, and then at Armstrongs on the Tyne from 27 June to 8 July for 'Q' turret to be removed and her armour repaired. She was in No 1 dock at Rosyth from 8 to 20 July when her repairs were completed as a 3-turret ship, but 'Q'. turret was not replaced until a further visit to Armstrongs from 6 to 23 September. The *Princess Royal* was at Rosyth until 10 June when she went to Portsmouth and was repaired there from 13 June to 15 July, occupying No 14 dry-dock from 15 June to 10 July, and arrived back at Rosyth on 21 July.

The *Malaya* was docked in the floating dock at Invergordon on 4 June and undocked on 24 June when her repairs are said to have been completed, though she did not rejoin the 5th BS until 11 July. The *Marlborough* arrived in the Tyne from Immingham on 6 June, and was repaired by Armstrongs in the Admiralty floating dock at Jarrow. Her repairs were completed on 2 August and she arrived at Cromarty three days later.

The *Barham* was repaired at Devonport in No 8 dry-dock from 5 June to 4 July and left next day. She carried out full speed trials on 6 July in Bute Sound to determine the maximum speed of her class at their Jutland loading, and arrived at Scapa on 8 July.

Neither the *Colossus* nor the *New Zealand* had any special dockyard repairs.

The Germans largely relied on floating docks for the repair of their capital ships as neither Wilhelmshaven nor Kiel possessed a dry-dock that could take the *Derfflinger* or *Seydlitz*, and Kiel did not have one that could take the *Moltke* or *König* class.

The *Seydlitz*, as related above, was docked in the large floating dock at Wilhelmshaven, and her repairs were completed on 16 September. The *Ostfriesland* and *von der Tann* were accommodated in dry-docks at Wilhelmshaven, and their repairs completed on 26 July and 2 August respectively. The *von der Tann* appears to have been delayed by troubles in her fore turret which proved defective when fired.

The *Moltke* was for a short time in dry-dock at Wilhelmshaven and then went to Blohm and Voss at Hamburg where she was docked in a floating dock, and her repairs completed on 30 July. The *Markgraf* and *Grosser Kurfürst* were also accommodated in floating docks at Hamburg, and their repairs, by Blohm and Voss and Vulkan respectively, were completed on 20 and 16 July.

The *König* and *Derfflinger* went to Kiel, where there was only a single floating dock capable of taking ships of this size. The *König* was docked from 4 to 18 June and her repairs were then undertaken by Howaldt and completed on 21 July. The *Derfflinger* had been docked for preliminary repairs in the Wilhelmshaven floating dock, previous to the *Seydlitz*, and was in the Kiel floating dock from 22 June to 15 July, but her repairs in Kiel Dockyard were not completed until 15 October.

The less seriously damaged dreadnoughts, of which only the *Helgoland* required dry-docking, were all repaired at Wilhelmshaven, though in some cases the work was not at once taken in hand. No dates for the completion of repairs are recorded for the *Kaiser* and *Oldenburg*, and for the others the dates are: *Helgoland* 16 June, *Nassau* 10 July, *Rheinland* 10 June, *Westfalen* 17 June.

CHAPTER 18

Summary and discussion

F ROM BRITAIN'S POINT of view Jutland was a thoroughly unsatisfactory battle: her fleet of very considerable numerical superiority suffered far heavier losses than it inflicted, although they were too small relative to its strength to affect the situation at sea.

It must be noted, too, that the High Seas Fleet was in no condition to continue the battle at daybreak on 1 June, as of the battlecruisers only the *Moltke* was in good fighting order, and the speed of three of the four *König*s was appreciably reduced. However, it had never been any part of Scheer's plan to engage the whole of the Grand Fleet, and though he had doubtless hoped for a still more favourable loss ratio, he could at least claim partial success, the most usual result in any operation of war. Scheer was ready to try again on 19 August 1916, but the main fleets did not meet on this occasion, when the *Nottingham* and *Falmouth* were sunk by submarines. However, as stated in his report to the Kaiser of 4 July on the Battle of Jutland, Scheer did not consider that such operations could force Britain to make peace, even if highly successful, and this could only be achieved by the unrestricted submarine campaign against British commerce. Endless speculation is possible as to what might have happened at Jutland if Jellicoe and Scheer, or their subordinate commanders, had acted differently, but for much of the battle lack of visibility had a more dominant influence than any of the Admirals.

The *Lützow* was the most powerful ship lost, while the three British armoured cruisers and the *V4* were no longer first line units; the *Pommern* and *Frauenlob* were obsolescent. According to revised casualty figures the British lost 6094 killed, 674 wounded and 177 made prisoner, a total of 6945, as against the German loss of 2551 killed and

Ships lost at Jutland		
	British	German
Battlecruisers	*Queen Mary, Indefatigable, Invincible*	*Lützow*
Pre-dreadnought Battleships	—	*Pommern*
Armoured Cruisers	*Defence, Warrior, Black Prince*	—
Light Cruisers	—	*Wiesbaden, Elbing, Rostock, Frauenlob*
Flotilla Leaders	*Tipperary*	—
Destroyers	*Nestor, Nomad, Turbulent, Ardent, Fortune, Shark, Sparrowhawk*	*V48, S35, V29, V27, V4*

Casualties in British ships blown up				
	Killed	Wounded	Made prisoner	Total
Queen Mary	1266	6	2	1274
Indefatigable	1017	—	2	1019
Invincible	1026	1	—	1027
Defence	903	—	—	903
Black Prince	857	—	—	857
	5069	7	4	5080

Casualties in the other British ships sunk				
Warrior	71	36	—	107
Tipperary	185	4	8	197
Nestor	6	8	80	94
Nomad	8	4	72	84
Turbulent	96	—	13	109
Ardent	78	1	—	79
Fortune	67	2	—	69
Shark	86	3	—	89
Sparrowhawk	6	—	—	6
	603	58	173	834
Total	5672	65	177	5914

Casualties in German ships blown up			
Pommern	844	—	—	844

Casualties in other ships sunk			
Lützow	115	50	—	165
Wiesbaden	589	—	—	589
Elbing	4	12	—	16
Rostock	14	6	—	20
Frauenlob	320	1	—	321
V48	90	—	—	90
S35	88	—	—	88
V29	33	4	—	37
V27	—	3	—	3
V4	18	4	—	22
	1271	80	—	1351
Total	2115	80	—	2195

507 wounded, for a total of 3058. By far the greater part of the British casualties were incurred in the five large ships which blew up.

The casualties in ships that remained afloat were thus 422 killed, 609 wounded, 1031 total for the British and 436 killed, 427 wounded, 863 total for the German. These are detailed in the table below.

The types of heavy guns tabulated below were mounted in the battleships and battlecruisers present at Jutland, and the German 15in, mounted in the *Bayern*, is included for comparison.

In 1916 British new gun muzzle velocities were determined at a charge temperature of 80°F and German at 59°F. When comparing British and German guns given in this book, about 30fs should therefore be added to the German muzzle velocity.

The propellant weights in the table are for MD Cordite size 45 in British guns, and for RPC/12 in German. The weights of the guns include the breech mechanism. The actual bore of the German 11in guns was 11.14in.

The 13.5in Mark VI was only in the *Erin*.

The 13.5in Mark V guns in the *King George V* and *Iron Duke* classes, and in the *Queen Mary* and *Tiger*, fired 1400lb shells, while those in the *Orion* and *Lion* classes fired 1250lb.

12in Marks XI, XI* and XII were mounted in the *St Vincent* and

Casualties in surviving ships

	Killed	Wounded	Total
Marlborough	2	2	4
Colossus	—	9	9
Barham	26	46	72
Valiant	—	1	1
Warspite	14	32	46
Malaya	63	68	131
Battleships	105	158	263
Lion	99	51	150
Princess Royal	22	81	103
Tiger	24	46	70
Battlecruisers	145	178	323
Southampton	29	60	89
Dublin	3	27	30
Calliope	10	29	39
Caroline	2	—	2
Chester	29	49	78
Castor	13	26	39
Light Cruisers	86	191	277
Defender	1	2	3
Broke	47	36	83
Acasta	6	1	7
Porpoise	2	2	4
Spitfire	6	20	26
Moorsom	—	1	1
Nessus	7	7	14
Onslaught	5	3	8
Obdurate	1	1	2
Onslow	2	3	5
Petard	9	6	15
Flotilla Leader and Destroyers	86	82	168
All surviving British ships	422	609	1031

Ostfriesland	1	10	11
Oldenburg	8	14	22
Rheinland	10	20	30
Nassau	11	16	27
Westfalen	2	8	10
König	45	27	72
Grosser Kurfürst	15	10	25
Markgraf	11	13	24
Kaiser	—	1	1
Prinzregent Luitpold	—	11	11
Schlesien	1	—	1
Schleswig-Holstein	3	9	12
Battleships	107	139	246
Derfflinger	157	26	183
Seydlitz	98	55	153
Moltke	17	23	40
von der Tann	11	35	46
Battlecruisers	283	139	422
Frankfurt	3	18	21
Pillau	4	19	23
Stettin	8	28	36
München	8	20	28
Hamburg	14	25	39
Light Cruisers	37	110	147
G40	1	2	3
S32	3	1	4
B98	2	11	13
G41	—	5	5
G87	1	5	6
G86	1	7	8
S36	—	4	4
S51	—	3	3
S52	1	1	2
Destroyers	9	39	48
All surviving German ships	436	427	863

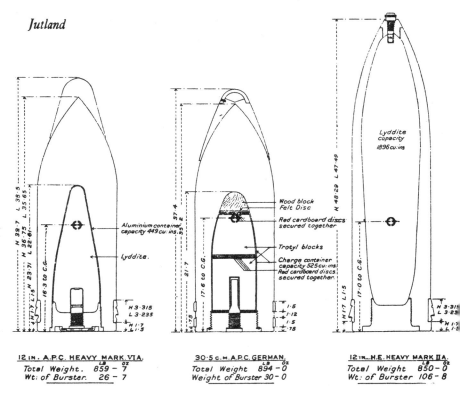

12 IN. A.P.C. HEAVY MARK. VI.A.
Total Weight.   859 – 7
Wt: of Burster.   26 – 7

30·5 c.m. A.P.C. GERMAN.
Total Weight   894 – 0
Weight of Burster 30 – 0

12 IN. H.E. HEAVY MARK II.A.
Total Weight   850 – 0
Wt: of Burster 106 – 8

Comparison of British and German APC and HE shell, and British CPC.

Colossus classes and in the *Neptune*.

12in Mark XIII guns were in the *Agincourt* only, and Mark X in the *Bellerophon* and *Invincible* classes, the *Indefatigable* and *New Zealand*.

The German 12in mountings allowed 16° elevation in the *Prinzregent Luitpold*, and 13½° in other ships.

11in SKL/50 guns were in the *Seydlitz* (16° elevation), and *Moltke* (13½°), while the *Nassau* class and the *von der Tann* had 11in SKL/45s and the pre-dreadnoughts 11in SKL/40s.

German heavy guns were built up from shrunk on tubes and hoops, while British guns were in addition strengthened circumferentially by wire-winding. German heavy guns had the Krupp horizontal wedge breech, and very much smaller chambers than their British equivalents, which also differed in using the Welin stepped-screw breech block. The German propellant was of tubular grain, and at least partly contained in a heavy brass case, while the British propellant

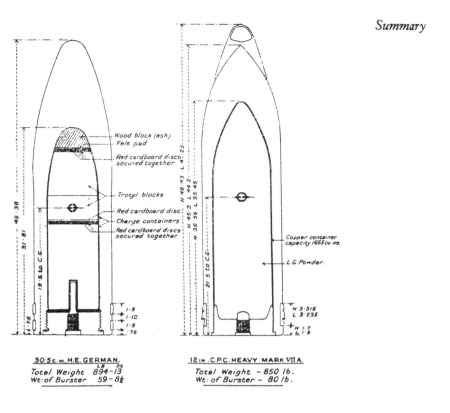

Wood block (ash)
Felt pad
Red cardboard discs
secured together.

Trotyl blocks

Red cardboard disc.
Charge containers
Red cardboard discs
secured together.

Copper container
capacity 1665 cu. ins.

L.G. Powder.

30·5 c.m. H.E. GERMAN.
Total Weight 894-13 LB OZ
Wt: of Burster 59-8½

12 IN. C.P.C. HEAVY MARK VII A.
Total Weight – 850 lb.
Wt: of Burster – 80 lb.

of cord form grain, was in silk bags. Further details on the propellant charges are given subsequently in the section dealing with ammunition fires and explosions. The British 12in were not particularly accurate, but the larger guns could make very good shooting, and were at least equal to German guns in this respect.

At Jutland all heavy guns were mounted in twin turrets, though triples had been introduced in the Italian, Austrian, Russian and United States navies, and ships with quadruple turrets had been laid down in France. In British ships training, elevation and run-out of the guns, hoists, breeches and loading rammers were operated by hydraulic power provided by steam driven pumps and piped to the various turrets. The *Invincible* had originally been fitted with electrically powered turrets but these had been replaced. Except in the *Agincourt*, loading could be carried out at any angle of elevation, as the chain rammer was fitted on the end of the gun slide. However, in many of the

British heavy guns

Gun	Length bore in calibres	Weight of gun incl. B.M. (tons of 2240 lb)	Projectile (lb)	Propellant (lb)	Muzzle Velocity New gun (fs)	Range (yds) at Max. elevation
15in Mark I.	42	100	1920	428	2472	24,400 at 20°
14in Mark I.	45	84.7	1586	344	2507	24,400 at 20°
13.5in Mark VI.	45	76.6	1400	265	2445	23,100 at 20°
13.5in Mark V.	45	76.1	1400	297	2491	23,740 at 20°
			1250	293	2582	23,820 at 20°
12in Mark XI, XI*, XII	50	66.7/67.7	850	307	2852	21,200 at 15°
12in Mark X, XIII.	45	Mark X 57.7	850	258	2725	18,850 at 13½°
		Mark XIII 60.7				

German heavy guns

Gun	Length bore in calibres	Weight of gun incl. B.M. (tons of 2240 lb)	Projectile (lb)	Propellant (lb)	Muzzle Velocity New gun (fs)	Range (yds) at Max. elevation
12in SKL/50	47.4	51	893	277	2805	20,500 at 13½°
						22,400 at 16°
11in SKL/50	47.4	40.8	666	231	2887	19,500 at 13½°
						21,000 at 16°
11in SKL/45	42.4	39.2	666	231	2805	22,000 at 20°
11in SKL/40	36.8	44.6	529	146	2690	20,600 at 30°
15in SKL/45	42.4	76.6	1653	403	2625	22,200 at 16°

earlier British dreadnoughts and battlecruisers there was insufficient hydraulic power available and, as the run-out of the guns took about 11 seconds at maximum elevation, it was quicker to run-out and load with the gun at a small angle of elevation and then re-elevate.

German turrets varied far more in their details than did British, but the guns were always run-out by compressed air, loading was at a small fixed angle of elevation, and in all 11in guns the breeches and loading rammers were hand worked. Otherwise the 11in SKL/40 mountings were hydraulically powered, and the 11in SKL/45 ones electric, but for the 11in SKL/50s elevation was hydraulic with electrically driven pump for each turret, and the same was the case in all 12in mountings, where the breeches and rammers were also hydraulically worked, while in the 15in the hoists were hydraulic in addition.

Details of the ammunition supply are given subsequently when considering ammunition fires and explosions.

The maximum rate of fire in the German 11in and 12in dreadnoughts and battlecruisers approached three rounds per gun per minute, while in the British ships, where the hoists were usually slower, it was nearer two rounds per gun.

Two salvos, or one round per gun per minute, was seldom exceeded by either side in the battle so that the maximum possible rate of fire was of little significance.

British dreadnoughts and battlecruisers generally carried about 100 rounds for each heavy gun, and German ships 80 to 90. The principal types of shell in British ships were capped armour piercing (APC), capped pointed common (CPC) and nose fuzed high explosive (HE). All three were carried in most ships, but the 15in ships had no HE, the *Canada* no CPC, and the *Agincourt* APC and a special TNT filled CPC only. About 60% of the outfit was APC for 13.5in and 15in guns, and rather less for 12in.

The German types of shell were APC and a base fuzed HE, which approximated to an uncapped semi-armour piercing (SAP), and was not carried in 11in dreadnoughts and battlecruisers, while for 12in guns about 70% of the outfit was APC.

The heads of the heavy shells in use at Jutland were of somewhat diverse form, but approximated to a radius of four calibres, except for the 529lb 11in which was nearer two calibres. Armour piercing shell was usually made in both navies from a steel containing about 0.7% Carbon, 3% Nickel and 2.5% Chromium. The shell heads were hardened, a mild steel cap was used, and the bursting charge amounted to $c3\%$ of the total weight in most instances. German shells were not hardened to the same extent as British ones, which proved to be too brittle, and a bursting charge of TNT desensitized by the addition of beeswax was used with a gaine and delay action fuze, while the head of the cavity was filled by a wood block. British shells had a lyddite (picric acid) bursting charge, which did not require a gaine, and did not have a delay action fuze. Their behaviour was far from satisfactory as shown on a later page.

CPC shell had a hardened point with a mild steel cap, and the bursting charge which consisted of a mixture of pebble and fine grain black powder, amounted to about $6\frac{3}{4}$-$9\frac{1}{2}\%$ of the total weight, being least in the 15in. German SAP had a TNT burster of about $6\frac{1}{2}\%$, and British HE a lyddite, or in some a TNT, burster which generally amounted to about 13 or 14% of the total weight. As usual there are slight discrepancies in the figures for expenditure of heavy gun ammunition, but the following table is believed to be as accurate as possible.

British heavy calibre ammunition expenditure					
	15in	14in	13.5in/1400lb	13.5in/1250lb	Total all heavy calibres
King George V	—	—	9	—	—	
Ajax	—	—	6	—	—	
Centurion	—	—	19	—	—	
Erin	—	—	—	—	—	
1st Division	—	—	34	—	—	34
Orion	—	—	—	51	—	
Monarch	—	—	—	53	—	
Conqueror	—	—	—	57	—	
Thunderer	—	—	—	37	—	
2nd Division	—	—	—	198	—	198
Iron Duke	—	—	90	—	—	
Royal Oak	38	—	—	—	—	
Superb	—	—	—	—	54	
Canada	—	42	—	—	—	
3rd Division	38	42	90	—	54	224
Benbow	—	—	40	—	—	
Bellerophon	—	—	—	—	62	
Temeraire	—	—	—	—	72	
Vanguard	—	—	—	—	80	
4th Division	—	—	40	—	214	254
Colossus	—	—	—	—	93	
Collingwood	—	—	—	—	84	
Neptune	—	—	—	—	48	
St Vincent	—	—	—	—	98	
5th Division	—	—	—	—	323	323
Marlborough	—	—	162	—	—	
Revenge	102	—	—	—	—	
Hercules	—	—	—	—	98	
Agincourt	—	—	—	—	144	
6th Division	102	—	162	—	242	506
Total 2nd, 4th, 1st BS	140	42	326	198	833	1539

	15in	14in	13.5in/1400lb	13.5in/1250lb	Total all heavy calibres	
Barham	337	—	—	—	—	
Valiant	288	—	—	—	—	
Warspite	259	—	—	—	—	
Malaya	215	—	—	—	—	
5th BS	1099	—	—	—	—	1099
Lion	—	—	—	326	—	
Princess Royal	—	—	—	230	—	
Queen Mary	—	—	c150	—	—	
Tiger	—	—	303	—	—	
New Zealand	—	—	—	—	420	
Indefatigable	—	—	—	—	c40	
1st and 2nd BCS	—	—	c453	556	c460	c1469
Invincible	—	—	—	—	c110	
Inflexible	—	—	—	—	88	
Indomitable	—	—	—	—	175	
3rd BCS	—	—	—	—	c373	c373
Total British Fleet	1239	42	c779	754	c1666	c4480

The very small expenditure by the 1st Division of the battlefleet should be noted.

The type of shell fired is not known for the *Royal Oak, Warspite, Malaya, Princess Royal, Tiger* and the three lost battlecruisers, though it is believed that the *Queen Mary* fired only APC, and the *Princess Royal* and *Tiger* mainly this type. Figures which in some cases have been slightly adjusted to agree with the total expenditure are given for other ships:

15in – *Revenge* all APC. *Barham* 136 APC, 201 CPC. *Valiant* 278 APC, 10 CPC.

14in – *Canada* all APC.

13.5in/1400 – *King George V* all CPC, *Ajax* all CPC, *Centurion* all APC, *Iron Duke* all CPC, *Benbow* all APC, *Marlborough* 138 APC, 24 CPC.

13.5in/1250 – *Orion* all APC, *Monarch* all APC, *Conqueror* 16 APC, 41 CPC, *Thunderer* all CPC, *Lion* all APC.

German heavy calibre ammunition expenditure

	12in	11in/666lb	11in/529lb	Total all heavy calibres
König	167	—	—	
Grosser Kurfürst	135	—	—	
Markgraf	254	—	—	
Kronprinz	144	—	—	
5th Division	700	—	—	700
Kaiser	224	—	—	
Prinzregent Luitpold	169	—	—	
Kaiserin	160	—	—	
6th Division	553	—	—	553
Friedrich der Grosse	72	—	—	
Ostfriesland	111	—	—	
Thüringen	107	—	—	
Helgoland	63	—	—	
Oldenburg	53	—	—	
Fleet Flag & 1st Division	406	—	—	406
Posen	—	53	—	
Rheinland	—	35	—	
Nassau	—	106	—	
Westfalen	—	51	—	
2nd Division	—	245	—	245
Total Fleet Flag, 3rd & 1st Sq	1659	245	—	1904
Lützow	c380	—	—	
Derfflinger	385	—	—	
Seydlitz	—	376	—	
Moltke	—	359	—	
Von der Tann	—	170	—	
1st Scouting Group	c765	905	—	c1670
Deutschland	—	—	1	
Pommern	—	—	—	
Schlesien	—	—	9	
Schleswig-Holstein	—	—	—	
Hessen	—	—	5	
Hannover	—	—	8	
2nd Squadron	—	—	23	23
Total German Fleet	c2424	1150	23	c3597

12in - *Superb* 16 CPC, 38 HE, *Bellerophon* 41 APC, 21 CPC, *Temeraire* all HE, *Vanguard* 15 CPC, 65 HE, *Colossus* 81 APC, 12 CPC, *Collingwood* 52 APC, 32 HE, *Neptune* 27 CPC, 21 HE, *St Vincent* 90 APC, 8 CPC, *Hercules* 4 APC, 12 CPC, 82 HE, *Agincourt* all TNT filled CPC, *New Zealand* 172 APC, 76 CPC, 172 HE, *Inflexible* 10 APC, 59 CPC, 19 HE, *Indomitable* 99 APC, 10 CPC, 66 HE.

The amount of HE fired by 12in gun ships is noteworthy as this type of shell was of little use against heavily armoured German vessels. HE was also carried in 13.5in ships but it is unlikely that any was fired by the *Princess Royal, Tiger* or *Queen Mary.*

Of the total of *c*3597 heavy shells, 3160 were APC and 437 SAP. Figures giving the individual expenditure of SAP in 12in ships have survived in a few instances, but the *Lützow* probably expended most, if not all, of her outfit of 200, the *Derfflinger* fired 87, *Markgraf* 20, *Prinzregent Luitpold* 10, *Kaiserin* 2, and *Oldenburg* and *Helgoland* none. A fair number were also fired by the *Kronprinz* but no figure appears to be extant.

Hits on British capital ships

	1548-1654	1654-1815	1815-1900	1900-1945	1945-2130	Total	Total by all heavy shells
Lion	9-12in	4-12in	—	—	—	13-12in	13
Princess Royal	6-12in	—	2-12in	—	1-11in H	8-12in	
						1-11in H	9
Queen Mary	est 3-12in	—	—	—	—	est 3-12in	
	4-11in H					4-11in H	est 7
Tiger	14-11in H	1-11in H	—	—	—	15-11in H	15
New Zealand	1-11in H	—	—	—	—	1-11in H	1
Indefatigable	est 5-11in H	—	—	—	—	est 5-11in H	est 5
Invincible	—	—	est 5-12in	—	—	est 5-12in	est 5
Barham	1-12in					5-12in	
	1-11in H	4-12in	—	—	—	1-11in H	6
Warspite	—	2-11in H	13-12in	—	—	13-12in	
						2-11in H	15
Malaya	—	7-12in	—	—	—	7-12in	7
Colossus	—	—	—	2-11in H	—	2-11in H	2
Total	19-12in	15-12in					
	25-11in H	3-11in H	20-12in	2-11in H	1-11in H	54-12in	c85
						31-11in H	

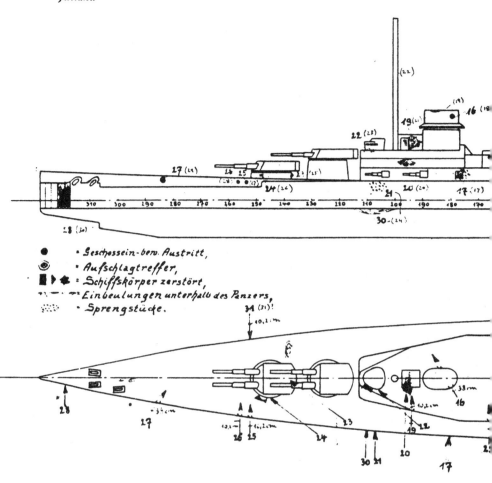

Derfflinger: *plan showing hits suffered at Jutland.*

The number of hits scored by heavy shells in each phase of the battle have been given previously, but for convenience they are repeated below.

It is doubtful if some of the British figures are as high as they would have been if the assessment had been made on German lines. Detailed repair drawings still exist for the *Tiger*, and in this ship, all hits have been enumerated.

350

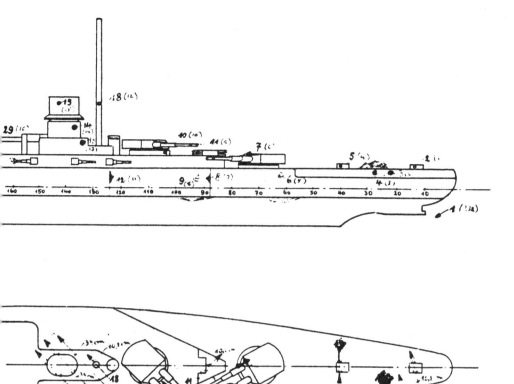

In the *Lützow*, the total number of heavy hits cannot be determined with certainty. The preliminary estimate was 24 hits by heavy and 1 by medium shells. A reconstructed diagram shows thirty-one hits, of which one on the starboard wing propeller shaft housing was from fragments, giving a total of thirty, but such reconstructions are liable to overestimate the number of hits, and some were probably by medium or light projectiles. It is therefore considered better to adhere to the figure

Hits on German capital ships and 2nd Squadron

	1548-1654	1654-1815	1815-1900	1900-1945	1945-2130	Total	Total by all heavy shells
Lützow	4-13.5in L	4-15in 1-13.5in L	2-13.5in L 8-12in	5-13.5in L	—	4-15in 12-13.5in L 8-12in	24
Derfflinger	—	3-15in	3-12in	7-15in 7-12in	1-13.5in L	10-15in 1-13.5in L 10-12in	21
Seydlitz	1-15in 4-13.5in H	6-15in	1-12in	1-15in 4-12in	2-13.5in L 3-12in	8-15in 4-13.5in H 2-13.5in L 8-12in	22
Moltke	4-15in 1-13.5in H	—	—	—	—	4-15in 1-13.5in H	5
Von der Tann	1-15in 2-13.5in H	—	—	1-15in	—	2-15in 2-13.5in H	4
König	—	1-15in	7-13.5in H 1-13.5in L	1-13.5in H	—	1-15in 8-13.5in H 1-13.5in L	10
Grosser Kurfürst	—	1-15in	—	4-15in 3-13.5in H	—	5-15in 3-13.5in H	8
Markgraf	—	3-15in	1-13.5in L	1-12in	—	3-15in 1-13.5in L 1-12in	5
Kaiser	—	—	—	2-12in	—	2-12in	2
Helgoland	—	—	—	1-15in	—	1-15in	1
Pommern	—	—	—	—	1-12in	1-12in	1
Schleswig-Holstein	—	—	—	—	1-12in	1-12in	1
Total	6-15in 7-13.5in H 4-13.5in L	18-15in 1-13.5in L	7-13.5in H 4-13.5in L 12-12in	14-15in 4-13.5in H 5-13.5in L 14-12in	3-13.5in L 5-12in	38-15in 18-13.5in H 17-13.5in L 31-12in	104

Note: In this and previous table H = heavy, L = Light.

The total number of hits by heavy shells, given above for the surviving German ships, is as certain as such matters can ever be.

of twenty-four heavy hits. The six additional hits given by the diagram are listed, with explanations which must be taken as highly speculative:

1 From port side. Battery roof deck by 'B' barbette – ? 6in or additional effect of *c*1819 hit from *Lion* that burst just abaft 'B'.

2 From port side. Near No 2 – 5.9in – ? 6in. Not mentioned in the *Lützow*'s account of 5.9in troubles.

3 From starboard side. Side armour near 'A' and 'B' – May be confused with *c*1915 hit below 'B'.

4 From starboard side. Apparently on upper deck near 'B' – ? 4in.

5 From starboard side. On side near aftermost barbette. May be confused with 1615 hit on armour.

6 From starboard side. Near No 3 – 5.9in. May be confused with *c*1915 hit on armour of No 4 – 5.9in.

To calculate the percentage of hits to rounds fired, it is necessary to deduct the number of heavy shells fired at light and armoured cruisers and destroyers, or to add the hits obtained on these ships. Unfortunately the number of heavy shells fired at targets other than capital ships cannot be estimated with reliability, and the second alternative must be adopted, though some of the figures are doubtful.

One of the following tables lists hits by heavy shells which are considered to have been made on cruisers and destroyers:

Heavy shell hits on cruisers and destroyers			
Defence	est 7	*Wiesbaden*	est 15
Warrior	15	*Pillau*	1
Black Prince	est 12		
Southampton	1	G86	1
Marvel	1	S35	2
Defender	1		
Total	*c*37	Total	*c*19

The percentages are therefore: British 4480 heavy shells, 123 hits 2.75%; German 3597 heavy shells, 122 hits.3.39%.

The 11in hit on the *Spitfire* from the *Nassau* when they collided, is not counted.

It may be thought that the inclusion of the *Black Prince* unduly favours the German figures, and if this ship is excluded they become – *c*3570 heavy shells, 110 hits, 3.08%.

It is possible in many cases to calculate percentage figures for

Hits obtained by German Battleships and Battlecruisers		
Ship hit	By 1st SG	By German Battleships
Lion	13	—
Princess Royal	6	3
Queen Mary	7	—
Tiger	15	—
New Zealand	1	—
Indefatigable	5	—
Invincible	5	—
Barham	6	—
Warspite	2	13
Malaya	—	7
Colossus	2	—
Defence	3	4
Warrior	—	15
Black Prince	—	12
Southampton	—	1
Marvel	—	1
Defender	—	1
Total	65	57
1st Scouting Group	1670 heavy shells	65 hits	3.89%
Battleships	1927 heavy shells	57 hits	2.96%
less *Black Prince*	*c*1900 heavy shells	45 hits	2.37%

individual ships but differences of visibility, which cannot be assessed, make these figures of doubtful value. It is however instructive to work out the percentage of hits obtained by battleships and battlecruisers, as detailed in the tables above and right.

It is doubtful whether the apparent superiority of the 1st SG is of much significance as they had on the whole better visibility.

These figures indicate that the shooting of the 1st and 2nd BCS left much to be desired as they certainly did not have worse visibility than the 5th BS.

Several of the British ships shot very well for the limited period in which they could see their targets clearly, particularly the *Iron Duke*, with seven hits on the *König* from 43 rounds at *c*12,600yds. For a

Hits obtained by British Battleships and Battlecruisers

Ship hit	By 1st and 2nd BCS	By 3rd BCS	By 5th BS	By 2nd, 4th, 1st BS
Lützow	7	8	4	5
Derfflinger	1	3	3	14
Seydlitz	9	1	7	5
Moltke	1	—	4	-
von der Tann	2	—	1	1
König	—	—	1	9
Grosser Kurfürst	—	—	5	3
Markgraf	—	—	3	2
Kaiser	—	—	—	2
Helgoland	—	—	1	-
Pommern	—	1	—	-
Schleswig-Holstein	1	—	—	-
Wiesbaden	—	2	—	13
Pillau	—	1	—	-
G86	—	—	—	1
S35	—	—	—	2
Total	21	16	29	57

1st and 2nd BCS	1469 heavy shells	21 hits	1.43%
3rd BCS	373 heavy shells	16 hits	4.29%
5th BS	1099 heavy shells	29 hits	2.64%
2nd, 4th, 1st BS	1593 heavy shells	57 hits	3.70%

longer period the best British performance was by the *Barham* and *Valiant*. Their figures cannot be separated, but together they fired 625 rounds and made twenty-three or twenty-four hits (four on *Lützow*, three *Derfflinger*, six or seven *Seydlitz*, four *Moltke*, one *von der Tann*, four *Grosser Kurfürst*, one *Helgoland* giving a percentage of 3.68 to 3.84.

Of the German ships, the best continued performance was by the *Lützow* with an estimated nineteen hits (thirteen on *Lion*, one *Barham*, est. two *Invincible*, est. three *Defence*), from 380 rounds for a percentage

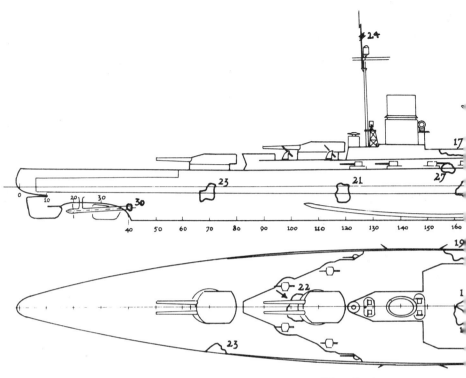

Lützow: *plan based on an official German original showing estimate of hits suffered at Jutland. Hits 10, 12, 13, 21, 23, 25, 28, 29 and 30 were on the starboard side; hits 1, 2, 3, 7, 8, 9, 14, 15, 16, 20, 26, 27 and 31 were on the port side.*

of 5.00, but she had on the whole, better visibility conditions than the *Barham* and *Valiant*. For a shorter period, the *Moltke*'s shooting at the beginning of the action was outstanding.

The German battleships and battlecruisers expended far more ammunition from their secondary batteries, and a considerable proportion of this was at capital ships, while it is believed that none of the twelve British battleships with 6in guns, or the *Tiger*, employed their secondary batteries at such targets. The *Westfalen* which took the greatest part of any of the German ships in the night fighting against destroyers, was only seventh in the amount of 5.9in ammunition expended. There is no record of the total number of medium calibre hits on British capital ships, except that there were three on the *Tiger*, and as far as is known, only one such hit, which disabled a 15in gun in the

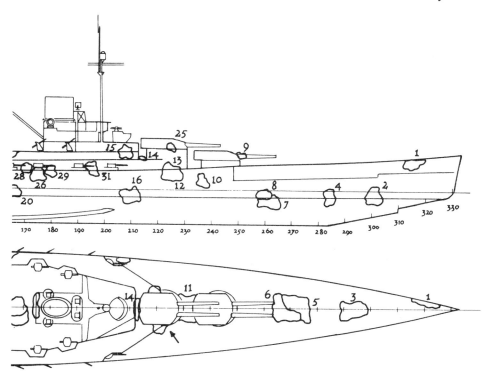

Warspite, was of any importance.

Secondary guns were all in hand-worked pedestal, or in the German navy centre pivot mountings, except that 4 – 6.7in in the *Hessen* were in single turrets with electric training and elevation. The most important guns, the 6in and 5.9in, could fire at 7 rounds or more per minute, and in many German ships, where it was the usual practice to provide an ammunition hoist for each 5.9in gun, this could be maintained, but British ships had fewer or slower 6in hoists, and apart from ready ammunition, the supply was in some instances only capable of providing about 3 rounds per gun per minute, though in the *Canada* the maximum rate was 5½. The ammunition allowance was usually about 150 rounds per gun with extreme figures of 100 and 200, and in British ships nose fuzed HE and common shell were carried for 6in and

British Secondary Ammunition Expenditure		
	6in	4in
Erin	6	–
Iron Duke	50	– –
Royal Oak	84	–
Canada	109	–
Benbow	60	–
Bellerophon	–	14
Temeraire	–	50
Vanguard	–	10
Colossus	–	16
Collingwood	–	35
Neptune	–	48
Marlborough	60	–
Revenge	87	–
Hercules	–	15
Agincourt	111	–
Barham	25	–
Valiant	91	–
Malaya	31	–
Tiger	136	–
Indomitable	–	4
Total	850	192

4in guns, though the *Agincourt* had no common shell originally and the *Canada* TNT filled SAP instead. The German 6.7in had AP and nose fuzed HE, and the 5.9in base fuzed and nose fuzed HE.

The actual bore of the 6.7in gun was 6.795in, and of the 5.9in, 5.87in. The secondary armament ammunition returns were as follows. Ships which apparently expended no rounds are omitted from the British list.

The German figures include star shells of which the *Nassau* fired 1 – 5.9in, *Ostfriesland* 1 – 3.5in, *Thüringen* 2 – 3.5in and *Posen* 3 – 3.5in. The large number of 3.5in fired by the *Westfalen* is interesting, and indicates that such light anti-destroyer guns still had their uses at night, though the British 4in returns show that they were of little value in daylight fighting.

Against oil fired destroyers nose fuzed HE was the accepted German 5.9in shell, but the *Helgoland* at least reported firing nose and base fuzed 5.9in HE alternately at night, in case a more resistant target appeared. For four ships, the numbers of each type of 5.9in HE fired,

German Secondary Ammunition Expenditure

	6.7in	5.9in	3.5in
König	-	c137	-
Grosser Kurfürst	-	216	2
Markgraf	-	214	-
Kronprinz	-	-	-
Kaiser	-	41	-
Prinzregent Luitpold	-	106	-
Kaiserin	-	135	-
Friedrich der Grosse	-	151	-
Ostfriesland	-	101	1
Thüringen	-	115	32
Helgoland	-	61	-
Oldenburg	-	88	30
Posen	-	64	32
Rheinland	-	26	-
Nassau	-	75	-
Westfalen	-	176	106
Lützow	-	c400	-
Derfflinger	-	235	-
Seydlitz	-	450	-
Moltke	-	246	-
Von der Tann	-	98	-
Deutschland	-	-	5
Pommern	-	-	-
Schlesien	20	-	6
Schleswig-Holstein	20	-	---
Hessen	34	-	24
Hannover	21	-	44
Total	95	3135	282

have survived: *Markgraf* 128 nose fuzed, 86 base fuzed, *Kaiserin* 21 nose fuzed, 114 base fuzed, *Derfflinger* 118 nose fuzed, 117 base fuzed, *Moltke* 171 nose fuzed, 75 base fuzed. The *Schleswig-Holstein*'s 6.7in fired HE and no AP.

The only figures found for British secondary guns are: the *Marlborough* 55–6in HE, 5–6in CPC, the *Valiant* 83–6in HE, 8–6in CPC, the *Agincourt* 111–6in HE, the *Vanguard* 5–4in HE, 5–4in Common.

In cruisers 6in and lesser calibres were in pedestal, or in German ships centre pivot mountings, hand-worked except that in the *Falmouth* class self-contained hydraulic training and elevation gear for each

Light Cruiser Ammunition Expenditure

	6in	5.5in	4in		5.9in	4.1in	3.5in
Galatea	13	—	15	Frankfurt	379	—	2
Phaeton	11	—	—	Pillau	113	—	4
Inconstant	7	—	2	Elbing	230	—	—
Cordelia	12	—	3	Stettin	—	81	—
Southampton	155	—	—	München	—	161	—
Birmingham	110	—	—	Stuttgart	—	64	—
Nottingham	136	—	—	Hamburg	—	92	—
Dublin	117	—	—	Rostock	—	c500	—
Falmouth	175	—	—	Regensburg	—	372	—
Yarmouth	160	—	—				
Birkenhead	—	70	—	Total	722	c1270	6
Gloucester	13	—	24				
Calliope	11	—	66	less *Wiesbaden* and *Frauenlob*:			
Constance	—	—	7	includes 2-4.1in star shell fired by			
Comus	6	—	17	*München*			
Caroline	3	—	9				
Royalist	2	—	9				
Chester	—	56	—				
Canterbury	46	—	51				
Castor	26	—	32				
Champion	8	—	15				
Fearless	—	—	3				
Active	—	—	8				
Boadicea, Blanche, Bellona			nil				
Total	1011	126	261				

mounting had been ordered in March 1914, but it is doubtful whether this was fitted at Jutland. The use of power-worked 5.9in mountings had been considered for the later German capital ships, but trials showed that the minimum training rate of 1/32° per second could not be held with sufficient accuracy. The 9.2in and 7.5in were in turrets, twin for the 9.2in in the *Defence* class and otherwise single, with hydraulic training and elevation, and in the twin 9.2in, hydraulic loading rammers.

Individual hoists for each gun were not possible in light cruisers, and apart from ready ammunition, the rate of supply for 6in and 5.9in was about three to five rounds per gun per minute, and usually nearer the lower figure, at least in British ships. The ammunition allowances were 128 per 5.9in and 150 per 4.1in in German light cruisers, as against 150–200 per 6in and 150–250 per 4in in British ships. The 9.2in had 125 and the 7.5in 125–180 per gun.

In the armoured cruisers, AP, Common and nose fuzed HE were carried for 9.2in, 7.5in and 6in, but AP was omitted in British light cruisers, while the German had base fuzed and nose fuzed HE for 5.9in, and three types of HE for 4.1in with internal, nose and time and percussion fuzes.

Anti-aircraft fire was of little importance at Jutland. Most German dreadnoughts and battlecruisers, and the light cruisers of the 2nd SG, had 2–, or in some ships 4 – 3.5in AA guns firing a 22lb shell at 2460fs, while the majority of British capital ships and older light cruisers had 1 – 3in AA firing a 12½lb shell at 2600fs. Most British capital ships and light cruisers also carried some time fuzed shrapnel for their heavy 6in and 4in guns.

The light cruiser ammunition returns are given below. The *Minotaur*, *Cochrane* and *Shannon* fired no 9.2in or 7.5in, and there are no figures for the other armoured cruisers, except that the *Duke of Edinburgh* expended 20 – 9.2in, and there are also none for the *Wiesbaden* and *Frauenlob*.

It will be noted that nine German light cruisers fired more rounds than twenty-six British, which might indicate that a number of the latter were under-employed in the battle.

There are few figures for the different types of shell fired. The *Frankfurt's* 5.9in returns give an expenditure of 96 AP and 283 HE, but it is believed that this should read base fuzed and nose fuzed HE respectively. The *München's* 4.1in fired 91 internal fuze, 57 nose fuze and 11 time and percussion fuze shells, and the *Hamburg's* 49, 37 and 6 respectively. The *Canterbury's* 6in and 4in only fired HE, as did the *Royalist's*, while the *Comus* only used Common shell.

The ammunition allowance was generally 120 rounds per gun in British destroyers, Common shell and nose fuzed HE being carried, while German destroyers had 80 rounds per 4.1in and 100 per 3.5in, both calibres having internal and nose fuzed HE.

It is thought that the total number of rounds actually fired by the British destroyers was about 1700, and by the German 2400.

There were probably some unrecorded 5.9in hits on capital ships, and no estimates can be made for the ships sunk, apart from the *Warrior*.

No estimates can be made for the ships sunk apart from *Elbing*, *Rostock* and the *V27*. An accurate estimate of the number of 9.2in

Recorded hits by German medium and light shells

	6.7in	5.9in	4.1in	3.5in	By Secondary guns of Battleships and Battlecruisers	By Light Cruisers	By Destroyers
Warspite	—	5	—	—	5	—	—
Lion	—	1	—	—	1	—	—
Tiger	—	3	—	—	3	—	—
Warrior	—	c6	—	—	c4	c2	—
Calliope	—	5	—	—	5	—	—
Canterbury	—	—	1	—	—	1	—
Castor	—	?3	?7	—	—	c10	—
Chester	—	c17	—	—	—	c17	—
Dublin	—	5	8	—	—	13	—
Falmouth	—	1	—	—	1	—	—
Galatea	—	1	—	—	—	1	—
Southampton	—	2	c18	—	—	c20	—
Acasta	—	2	—	—	2	—	—
Broke	—	?2	?5	2	?2	?5	2
Garland	—	1	—	—	1	—	—
Marne	—	—	1	—	—	1	—
Moorsom	—	1	—	—	1	—	—
Nessus	—	1	—	—	1	—	—
Obdurate	—	—	2	—	—	?2	—
Onslaught	1	—	—	—	1	—	—
Onslow	—	3	2	—	3	2	—
Petard	—	?3	—	?1	4	—	—
Porpoise	—	1	—	?1	2	—	—
Spitfire	—	?1	—	—	?1	—	—
Total	1	64	44	4	37	74	2

Grand Total 113

7.5in hits on the *Wiesbaden* is also impossible, but it is thought that the total was about 6.

Damage to the armament of capital ships has been mentioned in the detailed descriptions of hits, and serious breakdowns have also been noted if their time was known. In addition the *Vanguard* had trouble with the lock mechanism of her one 12in that had a Holmstrom breech, and one 12in in the *New Zealand* had a badly choked vent which entailed

	6in	5.5in	4in	By Secondary guns of Battleships and Battlecruisers	By Secondary guns of Armoured Cruisers	By Light Cruisers	By Destroyers
König	4	—	—	—	—	4	—
Nassau	—	—	2	—	—	—	2
Oldenburg	—	—	1	—	—	—	1
Rheinland	2	—	—	—	2	—	—
Westfalen	—	—	1	—	—	—	1
Derfflinger	2	—	7	—	—	2	7
Seydlitz	—	?1	1	—	—	1	1
Elbing	1	—	—	—	—	1	—
Frankfurt	2	—	2	—	—	4	—
Hamburg	4	—	—	—	—	4	—
München	5	—	—	—	—	5	—
Rostock	—	—	3	—	—	—	3
Stettin	2	—	—	—	—	2	—
B98	—	—	1	—	—	—	1
G40	1	—	—	—	—	1	—
G41	1	—	—	1	—	—	—
G87	1	—	—	1	—	—	—
S32	—	—	3	—	—	—	3
S50	1	—	—	—	—	1	—
S51	1	—	—	1	—	—	—
V27	—	—	2	—	—	—	2
V28	1	—	—	1	—	—	—
Total	28	1	23	4	2	25	21

Grand Total 52

the mushroom head being shifted. In the *Tiger* the cordite flash door of the right gun loading cage in 'B' turret had to be pinned up, and in the same turret a shell sliding forward caused the right waiting position flashdoor to be unshipped.

In the *Seydlitz* a back-flash occurred in 'A' turret which went down the shell hoists to the working chamber and slightly burnt two men, while three others suffered from gas. A pencilled note in her report states that the force of this was a new experience. One lower shell hoist was put out of action by an electrical failure in this ship, but the other supplied the turret – apparently 'A' – with transfer in the working chamber, and vibration from hits also caused many hoist fuzes to blow. In the *Moltke* a large number of instances of temporary propellant gas poisoning occurred among the turret crews. Smoke and gas were always a problem in German turrets as the cartridge case was extracted into the turret, but it may be that the *Moltke*'s smoke suction gear was inadequate and/or that the routine for getting rid of spent cartridge cases was not observed.

At the end of the daylight fighting eight heavy guns were out of action in surviving British ships, one in the *Warspite*, two in the *Lion* and two in the *Princess Royal* as a result of hits, and three from other causes, one in the *Marlborough* from a premature, one in the *Princess Royal* from a breech mechanism failure, and one in the *Tiger* from the fracture of a valve box and plunger. Of these three, the *Princess Royal*'s gun, and possibly the *Tiger*'s were serviceable again on the morning of 1 June.

The equivalent German figure was ten, four in the *Derfflinger*, four in the *Seydlitz* and two in the *von der Tann*, while there were also two in the *Lützow*. All twelve were as a result of hits. In addition four heavy guns in the *von der Tann* had been out of action for a considerable time during the battle from failure to run-out properly, and the remaining two in this ship were on hand training as the result of a hit. In the *Seydlitz* the power training of one turret broke down at the start of the battle, shortly before the turret was disabled by a hit, and by the end of the day the main training gear for the aftermost turret in the *Seydlitz*, and also in the *Lützow*, had failed as power cables, unwisely run above the armour deck, had been cut. The main training gear of the *Seydlitz*'s fore turret failed after cables had been under water for about 8 hours.

It is often stated that the British rate of fire was slower than the German, and this was probably true for some ships, but the *Lion*'s first five salvos were fired in 2½ minutes, while the *Lützow*'s took 3 minutes. The *Lützow* however fired her first thirty-one salvos in 19 minutes, giving an average interval of 38 seconds between salvos, and obtained six hits on the *Lion*, whereas the latter fired her first twenty salvos in 14½ minutes (interval 46 seconds), and obtained only two hits. There appears to be no record of the number of salvos fired by the *Moltke* in this opening period, but the *Derfflinger* subsequently fired six salvos at the *Queen Mary* in 2 minutes 25 seconds which gives an average interval of 29 seconds. Of British ships the *Marlborough* fired fourteen salvos in 6 minutes at the *Grosser Kurfürst* and the *Iron Duke* nine salvos in 4 minutes 50 seconds at the *König*. The average intervals between salvos were 28 and 36 seconds, and three and seven hits were respectively obtained. The *Lion* also attained the same rate of firing as the *Marlborough* in the 2020 action, but both average range and success in hitting were less.

The above rates of fire for the *Marlborough* and *Iron Duke* were achieved at shorter ranges and times of flight than those for the *Derfflinger* and *Lützow*, which would favour them to some extent. The approximate times of flight were: *Marlborough* 15 seconds, *Iron Duke* 17/18 seconds, *Derfflinger* 21 seconds, *Lützow* 21 to 29 seconds.

The British system of main armament fire control was more advanced than the German. The Director enabled the guns to be trained, laid and fired from a single position, usually the fore-top, as the training angle of the Director and the elevation angle of the Director sight were transmitted electrically to pointers in each turret which were matched with dials driven respectively off the main training arc of the turret and the gun slides. The German Director-pointer, located in the gunnery control tower, gave the correct training angle to the turrets in a similar manner, but the guns were laid and fired individually. There was no range plotting in German ships, whereas the British used the Dreyer table. In this a range clock drove a pencil on moving paper, and readings of as many range-finders as possible were plotted, so that the clock could be kept in step with the mean range by visual inspection.

Otherwise the rate of change of range was determined by mechanical course and speed resolvers such as the Dumaresq, which required an estimate of the target's initial course and speed, and by spotting corrections of the salvos fired. In the German system the rate was determined by these last two methods combined with estimates from the range-finder readings.

The British main armament Director proved its value in the battle, and little accurate firing could have been achieved without it. Only the *Erin* and *Agincourt* still lacked Directors, and the former did not fire a shot from her heavy guns, while the *Agincourt*'s shooting was not among the best of that from the battleships.

In the *Indomitable* whose shooting was at times good, training was usually by Director, but it was preferred to lay the guns individually as in German ships. The *Iron Duke*'s Director had an early type of Henderson gyro fitting which fired the guns at the correct instant in the ship's roll, but the gyro adjusting screw gave out just before opening fire, and the telescope supplied was not good enough optically, so that the Henderson fitting was not used. The 15in ships and the *Canada* each had two Directors, aloft and in an armoured shield on the CT crown, and in the *Barham* the aloft position was used until some defects developed from vibration caused by her own gunfire. This apparently occurred during the 'Run to the South', and her report considered that it would have been better to have reverted to gunlayer firing in this part of the action, as it was difficult to keep up rapid fire with the armoured Director on account of the very small motion of the ship. In the *Malaya* the armoured Director was used initially and the aloft position when it was necessary to use 'super-elevation' fittings, which were only provided for this Director.

In several ships fire was opened before a single range-finder reading had been obtained and the British 9ft RF's were in general inadequate, though the *Iron Duke* reported very good results. The 15ft instruments, which were only in 15in gun ships except for one in the *Orion*, seem to have been better, and the *Valiant* reported that a good plot was obtained at the beginning of the action, though after the first half hour only isolated groups of ranges were available. The *Barham* also obtained good ranges on occasion during the 'Run to the North', though the fall of shot could not be seen. Conditions in the battle were as a rule unfavourable for Dreyer table plotting, and this part of the British fire-control system did not give the results that would have been expected in clear visibility and with longer spells of firing at a particular target. It may be mentioned that the *Lion* and *New Zealand* made range plots, and the former a bearing plot, which appeared to be very good, but in neither case was this reflected in the percentage of hits obtained.

Opinion varied as to whether the control officer should be in the fore-top or in the gunnery control tower. In the *Valiant* conditions were found to be better from the latter position, and the gunnery control tower was also favoured in the *Iron Duke*. The *Benbow*'s report, in particular, complained of the difficulty of getting the Director layer on to the right target, and of getting the spotter on to the same target as the Director, though spotting glass indicators were fitted. Similar difficulties were noted in the *Valiant* whose report stated that some means of direct connection between the Director layer and the Control officer's glasses was urgently needed. In the *Vanguard* a Kilroy 'aid to spotter', by which the spotting glasses could be mechanically connected to the Director, had recently been fitted, and was found to be most valuable, but capital ship targets were not engaged. The *New Zealand*, too, reported good results from an 'aid to spotter' with a bearing receiver from the Director tower and a bearing arc on the spotting glasses, though her shooting was among the worst.

Difficulties were experienced in estimating the inclination of the target, and it was also considered that the 'bracket' method of ranging, in which each salvo was spotted before the next was fired, was too slow, and that a 'ladder' method, as later adopted, should be tried. In this two salvos separated by a known amount, were fired in quick succession and spotted as a pair, and the process continued until first the deflexion and then the range were determined.

The exceptionally small spread of the 15in salvos from the 5th BS was noted by several German ships, and the *G38* also reported the very small spread of a long range salvo from the *Orion*.

The more primitive German fire-control system seems to have worked well, but was inferior to the British. Relatively little could have been accomplished without the Director-pointer, and the principal criticism of this equipment was that the old pattern telescopes, still fitted in many ships, were far from meeting requirements, though the new type telescopes fitted in the *Derfflinger*, gave excellent results, provided the protective glasses were wiped after each salvo from the fore turrets. Other points raised in the *Seydlitz*'s report were the inadequacy of the auxiliary eyepiece provided for the Gunnery Control Officer, the need for power working of the Director transmitter and the advantage of a simple gyro fitting which would allow the target to be found again after rapid alterations of own ship's course, perhaps made in smoke. The *Westfalen*, *Rheinland* and the pre-dreadnoughts were without Director-pointers.

The German stereoscopic range-finders were probably better than the British coincidence instruments in the conditions of the battle, though a larger size than 10ft would have been valuable. No range plot was used and in the *Seydlitz* at least, the range clock was only of value in the earlier part of the action, and firing was continued on readings from the range-finder in the gunnery control tower. Additional communications between the various range-finders and the main control stations were needed, and a range-finder required in the fore-top, though this might entail some reconstruction of the mast.

Control was carried out from the forward gunnery control tower, but the after control was used when visibility was impaired from the forward position. The *Invincible* was sunk when the *Lützow*'s after control was in use. Difficulties were experienced in getting the spotter in the fore-top on to the correct target and in the *Seydlitz*'s report, the fitting of training pedestals reciprocally connected to the Director-pointer transmitter was demanded. In theory the control officer was able to check the Director target through the auxiliary eyepiece, but in

367

the *Seydlitz* this was so little use, that the control officer had to operate the Director-pointer himself. In the *Derfflinger* the spotter's glasses in the fore-top were linked to the Director by 'follow-the-pointer' gear, but the spotter could not transmit in this way to the Director. In the latter part of the battle, the British hulls could be made out from the top when only gun-flashes were visible from the GCT, but by then communications with the fore-top had been cut by splinters. Better protection for these, and reciprocal transmission between the Director and spotting glasses were demanded, though the ideal was to site the Director aloft with a tripod mast as in British ships.

The German time of flight clocks were not very reliable, and in the *Lützow* three units of a newly installed Petravik gyro-sight system ('Abfeuerungs Gerät') were broken by the effect of her own gunfire, but this equipment had not been used in the battle.

The control equipment for the 5.9in guns of German capital ships and light cruisers was well in advance of that for the British 6in, as Director-pointers were used, while there were no Directors so employed in the British navy at that time, though the *Westfalen*, which inflicted most damage on the British destroyers, had no Director-pointer. German searchlights were better handled, star shells were entirely lacking in British ships, and there was also no equivalent to the German night identification system using coloured lights, or to the very effective artificial fog, which was well supplemented by the use of oil fuel smoke.

The events leading to the loss of five large British ships from magazine explosions have been previously described in so far as they are known. The *Invincible*'s 7in turret armour would be pierced easily by German 12in APC at c10,500yds, as would the *Defence*'s 7in or 8in at a shorter range, while the *Black Prince* with $7\frac{1}{2}$in–6in, was virtually unprotected at only 750–1500yds, quite apart from other weaknesses in the two latter ships' armouring. In the *Indefatigable* an 11in shell at c15,500–16,000yds from the *von der Tann*, going through the $\frac{7}{16}$in side plating below the upper deck, could well have pierced the 1in main deck and then the 3in armour of 'X' barbette which extended almost to main deck level. The 7in barbette armour between the main and upper decks, would probably not have been pierced by the *von der Tann*'s guns at the above range, but it might have been holed and hot armour fragments driven in, which could have caused the explosion.

The *Queen Mary* was sunk at 14,400yds and German 12in APC might pierce 9in armour up to c16,000yds or to c17,000yds in the case of a turret face plate where impact would be closer to the normal. The easiest path for a shell causing the explosion of 'A' or 'B' magazines would have been to pierce the 9in face plate of either turret, or else through the ⅝in or ¾in side plating between the forecastle and upper decks, then the 1in upper deck, and finally the 3in barbette base between the upper and main decks, 'A' being more likely in this instance as the barbette was nearer the ship's side (16ft at upper deck level from side to barbette armour). Various other paths are possible quite apart from a shell entering through one of the turret gun ports, or hot fragments from a hit that failed to pierce, causing the disaster.

Though these losses could thus in a sense be attributed to inadequate thickness of armour, there was little that could be done to remedy this in completed ships apart from thickening the turret crowns and additional deck plating in vulnerable positions, and it must be noted that all the British battleships were liable to similar disasters if their turret or barbette armour were holed. Of the 136 barbettes in the four battle squadrons at Jutland, only four, the wing barbettes in the *Colossus* and *Hercules*, had more than 10in max and this thickness of armour might be pierced by German 12in shells up to about 14,000yds. Only the six ships with 15in guns, and the *Agincourt*, had more than 11in on their turret faces. The real cause of the disasters was that the precautions for preventing flash of ignited propellant reaching a magazine were not matched to the behaviour of British charges, though if the British ships had had German charges it is very unlikely that they would have blown up. This was not, however, clear at the time.

It was realised before 1914 that there were two dangers, the first that decomposition of the nitro-cellulose could initiate a spontaneous explosion, and the second that the effect of enemy shells, torpedoes or mines might blow up the ship. The first required that the magazine cases of the charges, and the magazines, should be able to vent to air before a dangerous pressure built up from the ignition of the charge or charges in the case affected, and the second that the magazines should be protected from enemy weapons. Such pre-1914 evidence as there was indicated that the first danger was greater than that of enemy shells causing a magazine explosion, and was best avoided by a strict time limit on the service life of the charges, not exposing them to excessive heat or damp, and great care in manufacture so that certain impurities in the nitro-cellulose, notably traces of sulphate, often derived from pyritic coal dust or cinders, were avoided. The pre-war records of the British and German navies were good in this respect, and though there were spontaneous explosions of 6in charges in the pre-dreadnought *Revenge* in 1899 and in the cruiser *Fox* in 1906, and of 5.9in charges in the

German cruiser *Vineta* in 1903, none of these caused a major disaster to the ship. The Germans learnt much from the *Vineta* incident, and by 1914 had developed a far more advanced propellant than the British.

Other navies had suffered serious losses from spontaneous propellant explosions, the principal incidents prior to 1914 leading to the loss or total wrecking of the following ships – *Maine* (USA) 1898, *Mikasa* (Japan) 1905, *Aquidaban* (Brazil) 1906, *Iéna* (France) 1907, *Matsushima* (Japan) 1908, *Liberté* (France) 1911.

Further disasters occurred between 1914 and the date of Jutland. In the British navy the pre-dreadnought *Bulwark* was blown to pieces in the Medway in November 1914, though it appears that gross carelessness in the treatment of exposed 6in charges and HE shells with live fuzes may have been the reason and not decomposing propellant. The armoured cruiser *Natal* was sunk in December 1915 at Cromarty, and this ship had much dubious cordite on board. In the German navy, the light cruiser *Karlsruhe* was lost 350 miles east of Trinidad from an internal explosion in November 1914. The *Karlsruhe* was extremely unsuited to the tropics as temperatures as high as 76°C had been recorded, and the German Official History remarks that the explosion may have been due to a quantity of lubricating oil thinned with petroleum for use as fuel.

In other navies, an explosion in the old Chilean battleship *Capitan Prat*, which had some very bad cordite in her magazines, was not disastrous to the ship, as the gases of the explosion had an easy vent to air, while the loss of the Italian pre-dreadnought *Benedetto Brin* is said to have been due to a bomb placed in the after magazine.

As far as the effect of enemy shells was concerned, the evidence from the Russo-Japanese War in 1904–5 seemed to show that this danger was not so great. The Russian pre-dreadnought *Borodino* had been sunk at Tsushima by a final magazine explosion after a number of serious ammunition fires, the worst of which broke out as a result of 2–12in hits near the mainmast, about 10 minutes before the final explosion, which occurred after a 12in hit near the foremost beam turret of the 6in secondary armament. Serious ammunition fires or explosions had however occurred at Tsushima in the Russian pre-dreadnoughts *Kniaz Suvarov, Orel* and *Sissoi Veliki* without involving a magazine, and previously in another Russian pre-dreadnought, the *Poltava*, a hit by an 11in howitzer shell at Port Arthur had caused a serious fire in a 6in magazine, apparently involving some 12in charges also, but it had been possible to flood the magazines before disaster occurred.

On the Japanese side a violent ammunition explosion from a hit by an 8in shell destroyed a 6in casemate in the armoured cruiser *Iwate* at the battle of Ulsan. Flames passed down a hoist, but apparently got no further and no magazine was involved. Later at Tsushima in the pre-dreadnought *Fuji*, a 12in shell pierced the shield of the after barbette and burst inside, setting fire to 3–12in charges. A large part of the shield was blown away by the shell burst, and water shooting out of the cut hydraulic pressure pipe to one of the loading rams was of great use in quenching the fire. The *Fuji*'s 12in guns had charges of British type, and it is important to notice the value of a high pressure water source at the site of a propellant fire, and also of free venting to air, both accidentally provided by the shell burst. The *Iwate*'s 6in guns also used British type propellant, but in brass cartridge cases, which would help in limiting the spread of a violent ammunition fire.

Much data is lacking on the fires and explosions in the Russian ships at Tsushima, but the largest fire in the *Kniaz Suvarov*, that in the .*Orel* and also in the *Sissoi Veliki* appear to have concerned the 6in ammunition where the nitro-cellulose propellant charges were in brass cartridge cases, as were those for the *Poltava*'s 6in guns.

The method of ammunition supply to the heavy guns in British capital ships appeared to be reasonably safe in 1914, but no large scale trials with up-to-date turrets had been carried out, and this was the important and blameworthy omission. The magazines were above the shell rooms in all ships, and in the dreadnoughts the magazine crowns were one deck below the armour deck, or two decks below in the *Royal Sovereigns*, where the armour deck rose to main deck level. The crowns of 'Q' magazines in the 13.5in battlecruisers were also one deck below the armour deck, but in the other turrets in these ships, and in all turrets in the 12in battlecruisers, the magazine crowns were at armour deck level, and slightly above lwl.

The magazine doors gave access to the handing room where the charges were placed in the lower hoists which were located in a trunk fixed to the rotating part of the turret. These hoists brought the shells and charges for each gun to the working chamber, where they were transferred to the gun loading cage of the respective upper hoist. Waiting positions for two charges were provided in the working chamber, and for two more in the handing room, and in action there would thus be eight charges in a turret between magazines and guns Flash doors were fitted to the trunk and the cages of the hoists, and the propellant was in more or less closed compartments in all stages of its passage from handing room to gun loading cage.

Unfortunately it was not realised how violently British charges would ignite in a turret fire, and the above flash doors were inadequate, the magazine doors were not flash tight under pressure, and flash had a free path to the handing room via the space between the fixed and rotating turret structures, and possibly via other routes. Also there were no magazine scuttles for passing charges, in fact, the magazine doors would be continuously open in action, and many more charges removed from their magazine cases, or in opened cases, than there should have been. There is a revealing remark, too, in the *Invincible*'s reports on the Battle of the Falklands, stating that the flash doors on the gun loading cages in 'P' turret had been previously removed as the charges occasionally jammed in the cages, and it was easier to clear the jam if the doors were removed. Nevertheless none of this would have been fatal to the ship if British charges had behaved like German ones.

German capital ships varied far more in their arrangements, and in some instances considerable differences existed between the turrets of a single ship. In the 12in dreadnoughts the magazines were below the shell rooms, and the same was the case in the centre-line turrets of the *Nassau* and *Westfalen*, but in the wing turrets of these ships and in all turrets in the *Rheinland* and *Posen*, the magazines were above the shell rooms, as they were in the *Seydlitz* and *Moltke*, in three of the *von der Tann*'s turrets and in the aftermost turret of the *Derfflinger* and *Lützow*. In the other turrets of the two latter ships and in the *von der Tann*'s stern turret, the magazines were below the shell rooms. The crowns of the uppermost ammunition space, whether shell room or magazine, were usually at armour deck level, but they were one deck lower in the wing turrets of all four *Nassau*s, the *Seydlitz, Moltke* and *von der Tann* and in the *Moltke*'s foremost turret.

As a rule German handing rooms were considerably larger than British ones, and in some ships appear to have served as part of the magazine stowage space, while the openings between magazines and handing rooms were not flash tight. In most capital ships' turrets, there was a rotating trunk, and the lower hoists led to the working chamber, but there were separate upper shell and cartridge hoists for each gun, and while the shell hoists delivered the projectiles near the loading trays in rear of and between the guns, the cartridge hoists came up on the outside of the gun cradle trunnions, and the charges slid down open troughs to the loading trays. In the aftermost turret of the *Derfflinger* and *Lützow* the shell hoists ran direct to the gunhouse without a break in the working chamber, though the cartridge hoists were still as described above.

The turrets in the *Nassau* and *Westfalen*, and the wing turrets in the

Rheinland and *Posen*, differed in having fixed hoists and working chambers from which an upper hoist for each gun conveyed both shells and charges to waiting racks between and in rear of the guns, and thence to the loading trays. In the 11in pre-dreadnoughts the tubular pusher hoists ran direct to each gun from the ammunition handing rooms and supplied shells and charges alternately.

In the last of the 12in battlecruisers, the *Hindenburg*, arrangements for all four turrets resembled those in the aftermost turret of the *Derfflinger* and *Lützow*, while in the 15in turrets in the *Bayern*, a single hoist for each gun ran direct from the shell rooms and the handing rooms of the magazines (which were above the shell rooms with crowns at armour deck level) to a position between the guns, and shells and charges were transferred to the left or right ammunition car, which ran on rails across the gun-house, and from which the guns were loaded.

As will be seen less care was generally taken of German charges than British, and there were no noteworthy flash precautions, and it was the practice in 1914 to have supplies of ready charges in gun-house and working chamber.

Experience of major calibre ammunition fires from the effect of enemy shells between 1914 and Jutland was limited to the Dogger Bank action, when there was a very large fire in the *Seydlitz*. In both the *Lion* and *Tiger*, a turret had also been hit during this battle, but no ammunition fire occurred.

In the *Seydlitz* a 13.5in shell struck the aftermost barbette, and burst in holing the 9in armour, driving in red hot armour fragments. These ignited 11in main and fore charges on the transfer rails in the working chamber. The flash shot up into the gun house and ignited the charges there, and down the lower hoists, setting fire to charges in them and in the handing room as well as to some in the magazine. The ignition of the charges was at first comparatively slow, as when the fumes of the burning charges in the working chamber began to penetrate to the handing room one deck below, the crew of the latter opened the bulkhead door, which opened towards the stern, to escape into the handing room of the after superfiring turret. At this moment the charges in the handing room ignited, and flash blew open the connecting door to the after superfiring turret, which opened towards the bows, and passing into this turret ignited charges in the handing room and some in the magazine, and the fire spread to the working chamber and gunhouse.

In both handing rooms the main and fore charges ignited except for some in unopened magazine cases. In the magazines the fore charges in

373

process of transport did so, but apparently not the main charges, even when in opened magazine cases. Altogether sixty-two complete (main and fore) charges totalling over six tons of propellant were destroyed. The main fear seems to have been that the heat of the fire, which melted some of the zinc magazine cases, would explode the shells in the shell rooms below, and not that the magazines would explode, but it was possible to flood the ammunition spaces and bring the fire under control before this occurred.

It is an often repeated error to state that as a result of this fire the Germans introduced flash precautions before Jutland. Actually the principal step taken was drastically to limit the number of charges out of their magazine cases or in opened cases, though too many were still present at Jutland in the *Derfflinger*'s two turrets in which fires occurred. As previously noted, some flash doors were fitted in the *Lützow*, but this was not done in the *Seydlitz* or *Derfflinger* where flash reached the handing rooms, and the hinged flaps on the magazine scuttles were not flash tight in the British sense of the term. It may be noted that at the end of the war, the German 15in turrets were not flash tight by the then British standards.

If the *Seydlitz* had had British charges at the Dogger Bank she would unquestionably have blown up.

The risk to medium calibre charges in armoured ships caused more concern in the British navy between 1914 and Jutland than did the safety of those of the heavy guns. In the 9.2in and 7.5in turrets of the armoured cruisers there were no working chambers, and the cartridge hoists ran direct to the guns, charges for the amidships turrets being first conveyed via ammunition passages to the hoists. For the 6in guns some ships, such as the *Tiger* and the *Black Prince* class, had a hoist to each gun from the ammunition passages, but in others including the *Queen Elizabeth* and *Royal Sovereign* classes the hoists (four in number but a total of eight in the *Canada*) ran direct from the 6in shell rooms and magazines to the batteries. There were no 6in handing rooms and no particular flash precautions. The arrangements in the *Queen Elizabeth*s are of most concern to events at Jutland, and in these ships the 6in magazines and shell rooms were between those of 'B' turret and the foremost boiler room. The four hoists ran from the shell rooms to the battery (upper) deck, and the charges were passed to the shell rooms from the magazines above via open scuttles.

It was the practice to have twelve ready charges per gun in magazine cases which held four each, but at the Dogger Bank battle, the *Tiger* started with twenty ready charges per gun in cases, and a further twenty in the ammunition passages, and this amount was not greatly reduced during the action in which the *Tiger* fired 268–6in shells. In German capital ships each 5.9in gun was in a casemate with an individual hoist, and usually an individual ammunition room containing both shells and charges, though sometimes one ammunition room supplied two hoists and guns. The 5.9in ammunition rooms were located amdiships inboard of the torpedo bulkhead, and usually on two deck levels. No particular flash precautions were taken, and ready charges, apparently sixteen, were stowed in each casemate.

The methods of British 6in ammunition supply would probably not have been dangerous to the ships if brass cartridge cases had still been in use; it was a different matter with charges in silk bags.

At the battle of Coronel there had been ammunition fires and explosions in the armoured cruisers *Good Hope* and *Monmouth*, and it was believed that the former had finally been blown in two. At the Falklands the armoured cruiser *Kent* had had a very narrow escape. A 4.1in shell struck the gun port of a 6in casemate and burst just outside, only flash and small fragments entering the casemate where two or three charges were ignited. The flash of these went down the hoist to the ammunition passage, and but for prompt and gallant action by one of the crew (Sergeant Mayes RMLI), charges in the passage would probably have ignited and the flash of these reached the magazine and blown up the ship.

As a result of this, ships were ordered in early 1915 to report what measures were considered necessary against the ignition of charges in batteries and casemates and along ammunition passages. The danger was only appreciated in a few ships, particularly the *King Edward*s of the 3rd BS where it was possible to look some way up the forward 6in hoist from the magazine. Steel flash covers for the tops of the dredger hoists in all 6in casemates were already being fitted in this class, and were later approved for the *Black Prince* class. Proposals for improvements in the *Emperor of India* were vetoed by the Admiral of the 4th BS (Sturdee), and comments from the *Defence*, where 7.5in turrets were supplied from ammunition passages, have a melancholy interest: 'In this ship the comparative safety of the passages makes the danger less than in many other cases, and with the number of guns to be supplied it is better to accept some risk rather than reduce the rate of supply, which anything of real use in this line must do.'

Serious medium calibre ammunition fires had occurred in German ships. In November 1914, when the battlecruiser *Goeben* was in action with the Russian Black Sea Fleet, a 12in shell struck the 6in armour of a

5.9in casemate and burst on impact or in holing the armour. Heavy fragments of the latter detonated three HE and broke up two AP shells, and this fired 16–5.9in ready charges. Flames entered the magazine which supplied both the above casemate and one adjoining, but did not ignite any charges.

Worse fires occurred in the armoured cruiser *Blücher* at the Dogger Bank battle. This ship had a main armament of 12–8.3in guns in six twin turrets, which in general principles were similar to the 11in turrets in the *Nassau*. Of the *Blücher*'s turrets four were supplied from ammunition rooms containing shells and charges and located below the turret, but the two forward beam turrets were fed from the ammunition rooms of the two after beam turrets via ammunition rails running lengthwise amidships. A 13.5in shell pierced the armour deck and 35 to 40–8.3in charges (each 77½lb) on the ammunition rails ignited in succession. Flash entered both the forward beam turrets via the hoists, and ignited the charges in the working chambers and elsewhere, and very great damage was done, but although a further ammunition fire occurred in the foremost turret, the *Blücher* proved very hard to sink by gunfire and was eventually torpedoed. With British charges she would certainly have blown up.

The *Blücher* was the only ship of her class, but as a result of the fire in the *Goeben*, anti-flash flaps were fitted to the tops of the 5.9in hoists in German ships, and the amount of ready ammunition in the casemates restricted, while further improvements to the hoists were made in some instances.

The need for better magazine flooding arrangements in both navies was shown at Jutland, and in the *König* in particular, as well as in the *Seydlitz* and *Tiger* other magazines or shell rooms than those intended were wholly or partially flooded. In the *Warspite* magazine flooding cabinets on the main deck were wrecked, and were described as useless, handing rooms being recommended for the principal flooding position, while in the *von der Tann* the flooding valves for the aftermost magazines were buried under wreckage. Access to the flooding valves from the weather deck was apparently not provided in either fleet.

Flooding of magazines was very slow in British ships as it was considered that a time not exceeding 30 minutes was satisfactory, and the quickest in any ship was 15 minutes. Sprays which increased the efficiency of the flooding water were fitted in German ships, but not in British, though it was known that Vickers had provided them in the magazines and shell rooms of the Russian armoured cruiser *Rurik* which they launched in 1906.

It is exceedingly doubtful however if any improvement in flooding arrangements would have saved the ships that blew up at Jutland.

After the disasters in the battle of Jutland, measures were taken in British ships to ensure that the flash from charges of the existing type, ignited anywhere in the turret structure, did not reach the magazines, and corresponding precautions were taken for the secondary armament. A description of these measures falls outside the scope of this book, but it may be noted that no work seems to have been done on the different behaviour of British and German charges until about 1920; it was then handicapped by lack of German charges for comparison and ignorance of the exact method of containing the propellant in the charge.

The British propellant in use at Jutland was MD Cordite composed of 30% nitroglycerine, 65% nitrocellulose ($c13\%$N) and 5% petroleum jelly. This was in cylindrical cord form and for heavy guns the diameter of the finished cord was 0.34in. The German propellant was of long tubular grain form, and at the beginning of the war most ships were using RPC/06 of typical composition 23.5% nitroglycerine, 70.5% nitrocellulose, 5% petroleum jelly, 1% sodium bicarbonate. By the time of Jutland, however, this had largely been replaced by RPC/12, the first of the 'solventless' propellants, which did not require the removal of previously added nitrocellulose solvents, and could be made to better dimensional accuracy, as well as being more adequately stabilised. The composition varied slightly being higher in nitroglycerine for smaller calibres, and the nitroglycerine/nitrocellulose (11.7–12.1% N) ratio was adjusted between about 1/2.2 and 1/2.7 with 4–7% Centralite (symmetrical diphenyl diethyl urea), 0.25% Stabilit and 0.25% magnesia. For the 12in gun the external diameter of the tubular grains was 0.71in and the internal 0.315in, which gave a smaller initial surface area per unit weight of propellant than the British 0.34in diameter cord. As far as the safety of the ship in action was concerned the most important differences between British and German charges were as follows.

In the German 12in SKL/50 and 11in SKL/45 and 50 guns, about 75%, and in the 11in SKL/40 all of the charge was in a stout brass cartridge case (12in weight 119lb) which covered the base and nearly all the side of the above part of the charge. The rest of the side and the top were covered by a relatively thin brass cap (12in weight 2.65lb) which volatilised, or was blown out of the gun on firing. The igniter, which contained 7oz coarse grained powder, was at the base of the charge and well protected by the cartridge case.

The remainder of the charge for the 12in and 11in SKL/45 and 50 guns, known as the 'fore charge', had no igniter and was contained in an inner and outer silk bag, which were sewn at the top onto a brass cap. The latter behaved like the main charge cover cap on firing, as did other thin brass parts, present inside the 2 silk bags to give additional mechanical strength.

In contrast to the above, British guns from 12in to 15in had the charge in four equal parts, each of which was in a single silk bag, and each of which had a 16oz fine grain black powder igniter. This last was in a shalloon bag which undoubtedly leaked powder dust over the charge in handling, and at the time of Jutland, the mill-board disks, intended to protect the igniters, were removed in the handing room when using power loading. British 9.2in and 7.5in charges were in two equal parts, and otherwise as the heavy gun charges, except that the igniters contained 8 and 6oz respectively. The 6in guns had the charge in one part with a 2oz igniter at each end, while the German 5.9in had brass cartridge cases, similar to those for heavy gun main charges, with a 1¾oz igniter.

German charges were by no means flash proof when out of their magazine cases, but their ignition was delayed and they burnt relatively slowly, and no dangerous pressure rise occurred from a number of charges violently igniting at nearly the same instant, as occurred with British charges. Thus even in the *Seydlitz* at the Dogger Bank battle, when 62 complete 11in charges were involved in the fire in her after turrets, there was no explosion. There is no doubt that far too great a number of exposed charges were present in many British ships at Jutland, but this was at most only a contributory cause of the disasters that occurred. In the *Lion*'s 'Q' turret the ignition of 8–13.5in charges between magazines and guns, all of which were in hoist cages or authorised waiting positions, would have blown up the ship if 'Q' magazines had not been closed, and very probably would have done so anyway if they had not been flooded, though the total weight of propellant that ignited was only about a sixth of that in the *Seydlitz*'s fire.

The loss of the *Pommern* from explosions following a torpedo hit appears to resemble that of the armoured cruiser *Prinz Adalbert* in the Baltic in October 1915. The latter was hit by an 18in torpedo from the *E8*, which is thought to have caused the middle 5.9in ammunition room to explode, and this was followed by the ship blowing up, it would seem more violently than the *Pommern*. None of the German armoured ships of the pre-dreadnought era had torpedo bulkheads, and their underwater protection was far inferior to that of the German dreadnoughts and battlecruisers. They were known to be liable to such disasters but the considerable alterations necessary to the secondary armament ammunition stowage and supply were not carried out, though wood filling outboard of the magazines gave some slight additional protection.

In point of fact magazine explosions of extreme violence as a result of a torpedo or mine were rare. The only one in an armoured ship in either the Russo-Japanese War or World War I prior to Jutland comparable in violence to that in the *Prinz Adalbert*, was when the Russian armoured cruiser *Pallada* was torpedoed by the *U26* in October 1914.

Magazine explosions occurred in three or perhaps four pre-dreadnoughts in the above period as a result of striking mines – the *Petropavlovsk* and *Hatsuse* in the Russo-Japanese War, possibly the *Bouvet* at the Dardanelles in March 1915 and the *Russell* in April 1916 off Malta, but though all four were lost, none of the explosions was of extreme violence, and this was probably due to the rush of sea water through the large hole caused by the mine, limiting the amount of explosive involved.

Considering next the damage to capital ships that survived the battle, the following hits were made by heavy shells on the turrets and barbettes of British ships:

Turret face: 1 (*Lion* 'Q')

Turret roof: 2 (*Malaya* 'X', *Tiger* 'Q')

Barbette above hull: 3 (*Princess Royal* 'X', *Tiger* 'X', *New Zealand* 'X')

Barbette between forecastle and upper decks: 1 (*Tiger* 'A')

In addition a shell is known to have struck 'Q' turret in the *Queen Mary* c5 minutes before she blew up. This was either on the turret face or forward part of the turret side.

In each case the armour was holed or displaced but in only two hits (*Lion* 'Q' and *Tiger* 'X') did the shell enter, and only in *Lion* 'Q' did it burst properly. This was also the only hit to cause a turret ammunition fire, though this did not occur until a considerable time after the hit, and would have been prevented if the fire party had done their work thoroughly, or if the charges between magazine and gun-house had been returned to the magazine.

The thinner armour on the lower part of barbettes was damaged by the hits on *Princess Royal* 'X', *Tiger* 'X' and possibly to a slight extent

'A', while it was struck by fragments in *Barham* 'B' and *Warspite* 'X', but in no case with serious results. There were two hits on gun barrels (*Princess Royal* 'Q', and *Warspite* 'Y' by a 5.9in) but neither affected the turrets.

For surviving German capital ships and the *Lützow*, the figures were:

Turret face: 2 (*Konig* 'A', *Seydlitz* starboard wing)

Turret side: 1 (*Lützow* 'B')

Turret rear: 1 (*Seydlitz* 'X')

Turret roof: 2 (*Derfflinger* 'Y' *Seydlitz* 'Y')

Barbette above hull: 5 (2 on *Derfflinger* 'A', *Derfflinger* 'X', *Seydlitz* 'X', *von der Tann* 'A')

Barbette between forecastle and upper decks: 1 (*Grosser Kurfürst* 'A': the shell burst close to the barbette before hitting).

The two hits on *Derfflinger* 'A' and that on *König* 'A' were glancing and the armour was only slightly damaged, as was the armour of *Grosser Kurfürst* 'A'. The roof of *Seydlitz* 'Y' was bowed inwards, and in the other seven hits the armour was holed, but in only two (*Derfflinger* 'X' and 'Y') did the shell pierce, bursting in both instances and causing serious propellant fires, the magnitude of which was due at least in part, to there being too many charges in transit between magazine and gun. Less serious fires were caused by each hit on *Seydlitz* 'X' and by that on *Lützow* 'B'. Neither the *Derfflinger* nor the *Seydlitz* had any particular anti-flash fittings, but flash doors limited the fire in *Lützow* 'B' to one fore charge.

In one case (*von der Tann* 'X') the thin barbette base was seriously damaged but no propellant was ignited though practice targets stowed below the turret were set on fire. Gun barrels were hit twice (*Seydlitz* port wing and *Lützow* 'A') with some damage to the turret from the shock of impact and small splinters respectively.

If British propellant charges had been used in the German ships, the *Derfflinger* would certainly have blown up as would in all probability the *Seydlitz*, and possibly the *von der Tann*.

Of secondary armament ammunition fires that in the *Malaya's* starboard battery came near to causing the loss of the ship, and less serious fires occurred in the *Barham, Warspite, Tiger, Colossus, Lion* and *Princess Royal*. In the *König* three hits caused such fires, and there were others in the *Seydlitz, Moltke* and *Schleswig-Holstein*. The hit on the

König below the water line, which completely destroyed one 5.9in magazine and damaged a second, would have caused the ship to blow up with British charges.

The hulls of surviving British capital ships suffered far less damage than the German, and in only three was the water-tight integrity much affected. These were the *Marlborough* from a torpedo hit, the *Warspite* from a shell through the upper edge of the main belt and from three others aft, of which one was on armour, and the *Malaya* from three shells below the water line. In German ships, considering first that part of the hull from the fore barbette to the stern, significant flooding occurred in the *Ostfriesland* from a mine, in the *Seydlitz* from a torpedo, in the *König* from a shell below the water line, in the *Grosser Kurfürst* from two shell hits on the side armour, in the *Moltke* from one hit on the inside of the armour aft and two hits on the main belt, and in the *von der Tann* from a hit aft.

The most serious damage to German ships was, however, from shells forward of the fore barbette, and in the projected German post-Jutland designs for capital ships, the heavy side armour was taken closer to the ends of the hull, and the forward broadside torpedo flat removed. Of the seventy-eight heavy hits on surviving German dreadnoughts and battlecruisers, fifteen or sixteen had their main effect forward of 'A' barbette, and in the *Lützow* it was eight out of twenty-four. For surviving British capital ships the equivalent figures were seven out of sixty-eight, but none of the seven forward was important. The two shells which burst in or near the broadside torpedo flat were the prime cause of the loss of the *Lützow*, and their effect was increased by two other shells below water and, as her draught grew deeper, by the four hits on the weather deck or upper part of the side plating.

Most of the *Seydlitz*'s troubles were due to the effect, as her draught increased, of four hits on the forecastle deck, and one on the upper edge of the forward side armour. Serious flooding was also caused in the *Grosser Kurfürst* by a shell striking the side armour well forward, and in the *Derfflinger* by the combined effect of two shells on the side armour near the bows, and a third on the forecastle side plating further aft.

The damage to the midships part of the above ships in both navies emphasised the importance of the torpedo bulkhead (not continuous between end barbettes in the *Marlborough*) which was only seriously damaged by the shell hit on the *König* and by the combined effect of a mine and too sharp a turn in the *Ostfriesland*, and also of good subdivision and a large pumping capacity. The armour belt should be taken to the main deck at full thickness, and to as great a distance as possible below water. In the forward part the only practicable measures were to make the subdivision and drainage and pumping systems as complete and efficient as could be achieved both above and below the armour deck, unless the displacement was large enough to allow the heavy side armour to be taken near the ends of the ship, as in German 1916–18 designs. Torpedo nets, carried by German ships at Jutland, proved to be a danger in action because of the risk of fouling the propellers if damaged by shells, as pieces of the stowed net trailed in the water. In the British fleet the *Lion* and *Princess Royal*, and it is believed the *Queen Mary*, still had nets at Jutland, but there is no record of their causing trouble.

In the *Lützow* it was considered that the large broadside torpedo flat, which ran across the ship, should have been divided into two, that the ventilation of this flat was unnecessary and dangerous to the ship, and that the forward water-tight door to the flat was of an entirely inadequate and dangerous pattern, while other water-tight doors and hatches below the armour deck should be capable of being more firmly secured. Ventilation ducts should not be led through the principal transverse bulkheads. Compartments above the armour deck in the forward part of the ship should be sub-divided by water-tight bulkheads and doors, and ventilation ducts in the forward part must be water-tight and in all, even the smallest, water-tight compartments, safeguarded by valves sited at the bulkheads, and not in the compartments. Voice-pipes also should have cocks at the bulkheads, and should be seamless. It would appear that the detailed arrangements for water-tightness in the forward part of the *Lützow* were defective, and in post-Jutland World War I German capital ship designs the broadside torpedo tubes, if fitted, were either located amidships or above water.

Other such improvements were mentioned in the *Seydlitz*'s report, and would have applied to most if not all of the German ships. It was considered in the *Seydlitz* that bulkheads should be carried as high as the battery deck without breaks, particularly in the fore part of the ship, and that each section of which there were seventeen, should have a separate ventilation system. Additional reliable fool-proof stationary and portable pumps should be provided, and adequate drainage and pumping systems installed for compartments above the armour deck, and for small compartments below, such as the ship's control room, transmitting stations and switchboard rooms. In the machinery spaces, steam pipes and electrical cables should not be laid along or near the torpedo bulkhead, and attention should be paid to the water-tightness of the 5.9in casemates which should have drainage and pumping systems. The coal-shoot hatches in the casemates should be more firmly secured as they frequently sprang open and dense coal dust caused much inconvenience. The most important defect in the *Seydlitz* appears to have been lack of drainage and pumping for compartments above the armour deck.

The *Derfflinger's* report also emphasized the need for adequate drainage from compartments above the armour deck in the forward and after parts of the ship, and called for better and more reliable portable pumps. Leakage from voice-pipes and ventilation trunks does not appear to have been troublesome in this ship. Heat from the steering engines and their steam pipes made conditions very difficult in the after part, and it was suggested that electric or hydraulic steering machinery should be used in new construction. The *Derfflinger's* mainmast was also excessively heated by gases from the after funnel.

The less detailed British reports emphasise the risks from ventilation trunks, and the importance of water-tight doors being properly secured. All decks particularly the middle deck must be kept water-tight, and it is remarked that 90% of the troubles take place between main and middle deck levels, while the waterline should be considered as at least 6ft above lwl and measures taken accordingly.

Although horizontal protection was weak in all or nearly all capital ships in both fleets, there is no instance of a complete shell penetrating the armour deck in surviving ships, and there are not many of fragments from a burst doing so.

The instances of the latter were: one each in the *Barham, Warspite, Tiger* and *von der Tann* and one, or possibly two, in the *Lützow*. In the *Barham*, where the armour deck was at middle deck level, a fragment went on through the lower deck into the forward 6in magazine, but no harm was done, and in the *Tiger* the base of the shell penetrated the web of the main steam pipe.

Armour gratings gave good service in stopping splinters and debris from reaching boiler and engine rooms, and in the *Lion* the engine room gratings were reinforced with fire bars and wire netting. In the *Marlborough* one boiler room was put out of action by the torpedo hit, and in the *Malaya* oil fuel gradually leaking in, as a result of one of the under-water hits, put a boiler room out of action by the evening of 1 June. In the *Warspite*, the port feed tank was wrecked by the shell which pierced the upper edge of the main belt, and this allowed a considerable amount of sea water to enter the port wing engine room via the fan flat. Similarly, water entered the middle engine room from the main deck which was awash, and the large openings between fan flats and engine rooms should have been capable of being closed and made water-tight.

The ship's control room and foremost oil-fired boiler rooms had to be abandoned in the *Lützow* before she sank, but in the *Seydlitz* the forward boiler room remained in service, though the ship's control room was eventually abandoned. All three oil-fired boilers in the *König* were seriously affected by one of the hits on the casemate armour which damaged the air supply with danger from gas. Smoke and gas caused the *Seydlitz*'s starboard low pressure turbine room to be vacated for a short time, while machinery spaces in some other ships of both fleets were similarly affected to a lesser degree, particularly in the *Derfflinger*, where only gas masks enabled the personnel to remain. The *Markgraf*'s port engine had to be stopped owing to overheated bearings from a bent propeller shaft, possibly caused by a 'near-miss' heavily shaking the ship aft, and the *Kaiserin*'s centre engine was out of action for a little over an hour from a leaky condenser, as was the *Grosser Kurfürst*'s for an hour and three-quarters.

German coal does not appear to have been of such good quality as British, and the *von der Tann* was particularly troubled by stony fuel, and was at one time limited to 18kts by dirty fires. The importance of high speed in both battleships and battlecruisers was much emphasised in German post-Jutland designs.

The *Warspite*'s steering failure might well have caused her loss, and other less serious instances of steering difficulties were caused in the *Invincible* by her helm temporarily jamming, and in the *Lion* by a misunderstood order and by the gyrocompass failure. Steering troubles occurred in the *Seydlitz* and *von der Tann*, and in the latter both steering engine rooms were untenable for 20 minutes from smoke and gas.

There is little evidence on which to assess the quality of German APC shells. There was only one possible hit on British heavy armour, that by the *von der Tann* on the *Barham*'s belt, and the thickness, which varied from 13in to 8in, is not known at the point of impact. The hit was below the water-line, and the armour was only slightly driven in, and in any case the range of c17,000yds was too great for the *von der Tann*'s 11in to pierce even 8in armour.

There were four hits on 9in armour in surviving ships, and in one of these, which was on the *Tiger*'s belt, the 11in shell had little effect, and may have hit at too great a range to pierce. In the *Princess Royal*, 'X' barbette was struck obliquely by a 12in shell at a range of c13,000yds. A large piece of the 9in armour was broken off and driven in, and the shell then went through the 1in upper deck and burst 8ft from impact.

This was a good performance, and so was that by the 11in shell from the *Moltke* which pierced 'X' barbette in the *Tiger*, as although the shell struck near the edge of the 9in armour and failed to burst properly, the range of *c*13,500yds was about the theoretical limit for piercing this thickness by an 11in.

It is at first sight most remarkable that a 12in SAP of the German type could pierce the 9in face plate of the *Lion*'s 'Q' turret at *c*16,500yds and burst inside, but less than half the area of impact was actually in the 9in plate and the balance either in the edge of the 3¼in roof or in the space of the gun port.

Altogether in surviving ships, neglecting an underwater hit on the *Malaya*, and one, probably by a ricochet, on the junction of the 6in and 9in armour in the *Princess Royal*, 7in – 8in armour was pierced once by a 12in and holed but not pierced by an 11in, while one 11in had little effect. Six-inch armour was pierced four times by 12in and twice by 11in, while 3–12in, of which one was SAP and 1–11in, had little effect. Of these hits on thinner armour, the most noteworthy were two by 12in shells which pierced the *Princess Royal*'s 6in side. One at *c*13,000yds struck at 15–20° to the normal and burst 52ft from impact, after inflicting much damage along its path, and the other at *c*15,500yds struck at 25–30° to the normal and burst 5ft from impact in a bunker.

It can be concluded from the above that German APC shell was adequate, as was German SAP, judging from the hit on the *Lion*'s 'Q' turret, and the 1658 hit on the *Barham*, which was probably by a shell of this type.

There is far more evidence on which to assess the performance of British shells, as there were seventeen hits on armour of 10in or over, and seventeen on armour of 9in – 6in, neglecting ricochets, in surviving German ships. It was known perfectly well before the war that British lyddite filled APC was unlikely to pierce heavy armour, and that the best that could be expected at near normal impact was that the shell would detonate in holing the armour with a 'considerable' effect in rear of the plate. It was also known that the shells were likely to break up on striking 6in – 8in armour at about 30° to the normal. What was perhaps not so well realised was the liability of the shell to break up at less oblique impact on heavy armour, and also to detonate, or to burst from a concussion explosion of the lyddite, before it had penetrated far into the plate, so that although the armour might be holed, no shell fragments entered the ship. Pre-war trials also showed that there was little difference in the probable effect of lyddite APC and black powder CPC on armour, and that the latter might be at least as destructive on heavy plates.

Armour	Ship	Shell	Approx. Range (yds)
14in Belt	G Kurfürst	15in	13,000
12in Side	Derfflinger	12in/45	10,000
12in Side	Derfflinger	12in/50	8500
12in CT	Derfflinger	12in/45	12,500
12in Belt	Seydlitz	12in/45	11,000
12in Belt	Seydlitz	12in/45	9500
12in Upper belt	Seydlitz	12in/45	9500
10¾in Belt	Moltke	15in	16,500
10¾in Belt	Moltke	15in	15,500
10½in Side	Derfflinger	12in/50	8500
10¼in Side	Derfflinger	12in/45	10,000
10¼in Barbette	Derfflinger	15in	9000
10in Turret	Seydlitz	15in	19,000

These defects in the British APC were due to the use of lyddite as the burster for which it was quite unsuitable, and to the shells being too brittle, while the fuzes, which had no delay, were also unsatisfactory, and it would seem carelessly manufactured by Woolwich.

Of the seventeen hits on heavy armour, one by a 12in nose fuzed HE and three others in which the shell glanced off can be omitted. Details of the remaining thirteen are given in the table below:

In the Result column, 'effect' refers to that of the shell burst or break up. Armour fragments were usually driven into the ship. It is believed that all the 12in shells listed in the table were APC. It is not known whether the 15in shells that hit the *Grosser Kurfürst* and *Moltke* were APC or CPC, but the 15in which pierced the *Derfflinger*'s barbette was APC, as was probably that on the *Seydlitz*. As will be seen one shell pierced and burst inside, five holed the armour with little or no effect inside the ship from the shell bursting or breaking up, and seven did not hole the armour. All 4–12in shells which holed the armour struck on or close to a joint between plates.

The shell which pierced the *Derfflinger*'s barbette behaved satisfactorily, though the task was not difficult for a 15in. The 2–12in/45 shells that holed the *Seydlitz*'s 12in armour striking at 40° to the normal, gave a remarkable performance which can be explained by weaknesses in the armour close to the plate joints. The 2–12in/45 shells

Result

Not holed. Shell burst on armour.
Not holed. Hit on joint. Shell burst on armour.
Holed. Hit on joint. Shell broke up or possibly burst. Effect outside.
Not holed. Hit 8in from joint at *c*30° to normal. Shell broke up or perhaps burst.
Not holed. Hit at *c*60° to normal. Shell broke up.
Holed. Hit close to joint at *c*40° to normal. Shell broke up or burst. Effect mostly outside.
Holed. Hit close to joint at *c*40° to normal. Shell burst after penetrating small distance. Effect outside.
Not holed. Shell burst on armour.
Not holed. Shell burst on armour.
Holed. Hit on joint. Shell broke up. Effect outside.
Not holed. Shell burst on armour.
Pierced. Hit at *c*10° to normal. Shell burst inside.
Holed. Shell burst. Effect mostly outside.

which hit 12in armour at 11,000–12,500yds would not have been expected to do much damage as the range was too great quite apart from the oblique impact, and it is not certain whether the 15in hits on the *Grosser Kurfürst* and *Moltke* were by APC shells. The other five hits indicate the inadequacy of the British APC as the pre-1914 tests had done.

The failings of this shell, however, are best shown by the hits on 9in – 6in armour. In one case the shell (13.5in 1400lb CPC) was deflected off the armour, and in another a 12in TNT filled CPC struck obliquely and broke up. Of the remaining fifteen shells to hit 2 – 13.5in 1400lb CPC pierced and burst inside, as did 1–15in APC, and the other twelve of which eleven were APC and one either APC or CPC all holed the armour, but 1–15in which hit very obliquely, broke up on the plate, five (2–15in, 2–13.5in 1400lb, 1–13.5in 1250lb) burst on or near the plate surface, the effect of the burst being outside, and six burst in holing, the effect in three (1–15in, 1–13.5in 1400lb, 1–13.5in 1250lb) being partly inside and partly outside, and in three (1–13.5in 1400lb, 1–13.5in 1250lb, 1–12in) inside or mostly so.

In contrast to the rest of these APC shells, the one 15in which pierced and burst inside behaved well, as it struck the *Moltke*'s 8in upper side armour at about 18,000yds, the angle to the normal being probably *c*20°.

The two 13.5in 1400lb CPC shells which pierced, both hit the *König* at 12,600yds, one well below water on the extreme lower edge of the belt (7in) so that only half the hole was in the armour, and the other 8in – 14in from the edge of the 6¾in battery bulkhead which was struck at *c*45° to the normal. Both confirm that within its limits CPC was a good shell.

There was one case in surviving ships of a shell piercing a turret or CT crown. This was in the *Derfflinger* where a 15in APC struck the 4.3in sloping roof of 'Y' turret close to the join with the 3.15in flat roof, and burst on the right cartridge hoist. The range was *c*9500–10,000yds giving an angle of descent of 6½–7°, and an angle to the plate surface of *c*22°. Of other hits an 11in holed the 3¼in roof of 'Q' turret in the *Tiger*, and a 12in made a very small hole in the 4¼in roof of 'X' in the *Malaya*. The 2¾in roof of 'Y' turret in the *Seydlitz* was bowed inwards by a 12in, and a 13.5in glanced off the *König*'s 6¾in conning tower roof.

The effects of each of the above hits, and of other hits on armoured ships, have been described in the chapters dealing with damage to capital ships, pre-dreadnoughts and armoured cruisers in each phase of the battle, and some details of the hits on light cruisers and destroyers are given below.

Calliope. Hit by 5–5.9in from the *Markgraf* at *c*2030. The positions of three hits are known.

1 Burst against breech of port after 4in, wrecking the gun and mounting.

2 Burst near No 2 starboard 4in below the bridge, and put the gun out of action.

3 Pierced upper deck and burst in after dressing station on lower deck.

Canterbury. Hit by 1–4.1in from the *Regensburg* at *c*1810–1815. This internal fuzed shell struck the hull plating aft, passed through 2 bulkheads and the lower deck, and finished unexploded in the fresh water tank.

Castor. Hit by about ten shells, 5.9in from the *Elbing* and 4.1in from the *Hamburg* and *Rostock* at *c*2215.

1 5.9in struck starboard side plating below second 4in and burst inboard, making a hole 4ft × 4½ft in the side. Fire mains, ventilation ducts and voice pipes to the 4in guns were destroyed.

2 Struck starboard side plating forward just above the upper deck, and passed across ship, bursting while going through port side.

3 Burst on forecastle with little damage.

4, 5, 6 Struck bridge, which was extensively damaged, all electrical circuits being cut.

7, 8, 9 Burst on armoured side plating (2in on 1in or 1½in on ½in). Splinters caused damage to after 4in guns and after control.

10 Struck motor-boat, which was completely wrecked and set on fire, so that the ship was lit up.

Chester. Hit by about 17–5.9in shells from the 2nd SG at *c*1740–1750. The positions of eleven hits are known.

1 Burst on port armoured side plating (1¾in on ¾in) on line between CT and bridge, and about 3ft above wl. Plate holed and frames damaged but little effect otherwise. Burst and most of shell fragments kept out. The hole was temporarily repaired but speed was limited to 22kts when the sea rose.

2 Struck upper edge of port armoured side plating (2in on 1in) below No 1 port gun. Side holed above armour, which was virtually unaffected.

3 Holed side plating just forward of third funnel, and a little above upper deck.

4 Burst on port armoured side plating (2in on 1in) just aft of No 3 port gun. Plate holed and frames damaged but little effect otherwise. Burst and most of shell fragments kept out.

5 Burst on starboard armoured side plating (1¼in on ¾in) on a joint between two plates, aft of mainmast and below AA guns. Effect as No 4.

6 Hit on starboard side of bridge.

7 Direct hit on No 1 port 5.5in gun.

8 Struck port side of fore funnel and burst inside, making a hole said to be 6ft × 8ft in the starboard side of the funnel. The tubes of two boilers were slightly damaged by splinters.

9 Burst inside after control, which was completely wrecked.

10 Burst immediately above grating hatches of port condenser room. Machinery undamaged.

11 Hit and bent shield (1½in max.) of No 4 starboard 5.5in gun.

The remaining hits were mostly on the forecastle and upper decks (both ¾in max.) which were holed and splintered in many places, while fittings on both decks were much damaged, and the engine room ventilation trunks wrecked. Many casualties were caused to the crews of the port and two after starboard guns, and gunnery voice-pipes were cut below the forecastle deck. No 1 starboard 5.5in was seriously damaged, and the breech mechanism of No 2 starboard 5.5in was also damaged, in both cases by splinters. One 3pdr AA gun was put out of action, and several local cordite fires occurred, while there were two fires, which were promptly put out, in the ammunition passage, caused by molten metal or burning cordite falling from one of the hoists.

One nose fuzed shell was found unexploded.

Dublin. Hit by 5–5.9in shells from the *Elbing*, and by 8–4.1in from the *Stuttgart* and perhaps *Frauenlob* and *Hamburg* at *c*2235.

5.9in Hits:

1 Pierced side plating above upper deck in line with foremast, and burst 20ft from impact on the upper deck, making a hole 3ft × 4ft. Fires were caused on the upper and lower decks over the forward magazines.

2 Pierced side plating near hit No 1, but changed direction to a fore and aft line and, after piercing four bulkheads, burst 80ft from impact, wrecking the seamen's heads.

3, 4 Both came from the starboard quarter, one bursting on the bulkhead at the end of the forecastle deck, and the other on the W/T trunk. Splinters pierced cabin bulkheading and coal shoots to 90ft from impact.

5 Burst on strong-back of steam cutter's falls with extensive damage in vicinity.

4.1in Hits:

1 Indented armoured side plating forward (1¾in on ¾in) and glanced off.

2 Pierced flash screen of fore 6in without bursting or other damage.

3 Pierced side plating forward and two bulkheads. Did not burst.

4 Burst after passing through chart-house which was wrecked.

5 Pierced side plating abaft fore-mast and burst 10ft from impact, holing forecastle and upper decks.

6 Pierced amidships armoured side plating (2in on 1in) at a joint between two plates, and stopped in a coal bunker without exploding.

7, 8 Burst on cutter's davit with local splinter damage.

Falmouth. Hit by 1 – 5.9in from the *Lützow* at *c*1830. This struck the foremast without bursting and cut voice-pipes to the top.

Galatea. Hit by 1 – 5.9in from the *Elbing* at 1436. This shell which did not explode, struck below the bridge, went through the forecastle and upper decks, and bulged out the armoured side plating (1½in on ¾in) on the far side above the water-line, causing some leakage.

More serious damage was caused by a splinter which broke up the impeller of the port after forced draught fan at *c*1815, so that the after boiler room was out of action and speed limited to 18kts for a time, and to 24kts after temporary repairs, though much oil fuel smoke was made at this speed.

Southampton. Hit by one heavy shell, probably 11in from the *Nassau*, at shortly after 1650, and by 2 – 5.9in from the *Elbing* and about 18 – 4.1in from the *Stettin*, *München*, *Rostock*, and perhaps *Frauenlob* and *Hamburg* at *c*2235. The 11in hit was from port, and the rest from starboard. The positions of fifteen hits are known.

11in Hit:
Struck armoured side plating (1¼in on ¾in) obliquely, abaft mainmast, making a dent *c*4ft long to a maximum depth of *c*9in, and splitting the plating along a line of rivets so that some water entered.

5.9in Hits:
1 Burst on armoured side plating (1¾in on ¾in) just forward of the bridge. The armoured plating was holed, with little damage inboard.

2 Burst on side plating by mainmast. The plating was holed and cabins and bulkheads damaged.

4.1in Hits:
1 Pierced side plating between 1st and 2nd funnels, bursting 6ft from impact, with little damage.

2 Indented armoured side plating (2in on 1in) just abaft 2nd funnel.

3 Indented armoured side plating (2in on 1in) forward of 3rd funnel, and just above lwl.

4 Indented armoured side plating (2in on 1in) in line with 4th funnel, bursting on impact.

5 Pierced side plating aft of fourth funnel, bursting in a cabin with damage to light structures in the vicinity.

6 Struck armoured side plating (2in on 1in) abaft the 4th funnel, and burst on impact. The armoured plating was holed and bulged back about 9in.

7 Indented armoured side plating (2in on 1in) near upper edge and a little aft of Hit No 6.

8 Pierced side plating in line with AA gun, bursting in a cabin with local damage.

9 Pierced armoured side plating (1¼in on ¾in) in line with after searchlights, and burst in a cabin with little damage.

10, 11 Struck near each other aft of Hit No 9, one entering through a deadlight and bursting 6ft from impact in a cabin, and the other piercing the side plating and bursting in the wardroom flat. The ¾in upper deck was bulged *c*5in upwards, the after ammunition hoist trunk holed by a splinter, and considerable damage done to light structures.

12 Pierced side plating right aft and burst in the Commodore's after cabin.

In addition to the above, there were about 6–4.1in hits along the forecastle and upper decks (both ¾in max) from the bridge to abaft the mainmast. These caused many casualties and widespread damage to deck fittings and structures.

Of the armament only 1 – 6in gun and the 3in AA gun were damaged, but casualties to gun crews put the three starboard 6in guns out of action, and most of the crews of Nos 1 and 2 port 6in were also casualties. There were three cordite fires involving a total of twelve charges, and in one the flame passed down the midships hoist leading to the ammunition passage, but got no further. Both after searchlights were wrecked, and the starboard forward one put out of action by damage or by casualties to the crew.

In general British light cruisers withstood 5.9in nose fuzed HE and 4.1in shells without any very serious damage, but the poor protection to gun crews given by open back shields was shown by the high casualties in the *Chester* and *Southampton*. Omitting the 11in hit on the *Southampton*, Hit No 2 on the *Chester*, and the hit on the *Galatea*, the armoured side plating was struck by 4 – 5.9in shells, 8 – 4.1in and 3 either 5.9in or 4.1in. Of these 2 – 4.1in pierced, 4 – 5.9in and 1 – 4.1in holed the plating without piercing and the remainder were resisted. The heaviest (2in on 1in) plating is known to have been struck by seven shells, of which 1 – 4.1in pierced, 1 – 5.9in and 1 – 4.1in holed without piercing and 4 – 4.1in were resisted.

Elbing. Hit by 1 – 6in from the 2nd LCS at *c*2235 in the W/T transmitter room.

The port engine was out of action from a leaky condenser, and speed reduced to 20kts from 1915 to 2309. The ship's loss was entirely due to the collision with the *Posen* at *c*2332. The *Elbing* was struck relatively gently and at an acute angle, estimated in the *Posen* as 20-25°, but was holed to starboard aft. The starboard engine room flooded, the list reaching 18°, and water spread to the port engine room which also flooded, while steam condensed in the pipes to the steering and dynamo engines, so that power steering and lighting failed, though the list was much reduced as the water spread. The ship was in no danger of sinking, but her engines were entirely disabled, and she had to be scuttled at about 0200.

Frankfurt. Hit by 2-6in and 2-4in from the *Canterbury* at 1826-1829.

The 2-6in shells struck the superstructure side, and one of the 4in the superstructure deck, all in line with, or near the mainmast. This was holed and the engine room air shaft much damaged.

The other 4in pierced the hull plating far forward and well above water.

A 4in shell also burst underwater near the stern, and slightly damaged both propellers.

Frauenlob. Hit aft by 6in shells from the 2nd LCS at *c*2235, and a fire started which apparently involved the after magazine, though according to the *München*, it appears to have been soon extinguished.

A torpedo fired by the *Southampton* hit the *Frauenlob* in the port auxiliary engine room, and she capsized and sank in a few minutes.

Hamburg Hit by 3–6in shells from the *Castor* at *c*2215, and by 1–6in from the 2nd LCS at *c*2235.

From *Castor*:

1 Pierced side plating and burst in port side bunker in line with second funnel, and *c*6ft above lwl.

2 Through after funnel without exploding.

3 Burst on port engine deck light. The crew of No 3 port gun were all wounded, and splinters pierced the upper deck.

From 2nd LCS. Burst on reserve signal yard on fore funnel. Splinters caused damage and numerous casualties on the signal deck, bridge and forecastle. The 10ft range-finder and much bridge equipment were put out of action and the fore funnel riddled.

München. Hit by 2–6in from the 3rd LCS at *c*2020–2025, and by 3–6in from the 2nd LCS at *c*2235.

From 3rd LCS:

1 Burst inside the upper part of the after funnel. The air pressure from the explosion tore away and bent part of the casings round the boilers in the after boiler room, which contained the four large boilers, and it was very difficult to maintain steam for full speed, though after 20 minutes of temporary repairs, it was possible to hold 30mm water gauge air pressure as against the usual 60.

2 Burst in port cutter with splinter damage on upper deck.

From 2nd LCS:

1 Probably burst on water near the ship. A splinter entered the conning tower and another put a searchlight out of action.

2 Went through the second funnel and burst on a funnel stay. The starboard range-finder was wrecked by a splinter.

3 Burst on water near the ship. The side plating amidships was holed in sixteen places by splinters.

At the end of this action the helm in the conning tower became almost immovable, and the trouble was not traced to a bent wheel shaft, possibly caused by a splinter from Hit No 1, for *c*2½ hours, during which time the ship was steered from the steering gear compartment.

Pillau. Hit by 1–12in shell from the *Inflexible* at 1758. This shell came from 16° forward of the port beam, and exploded in the officers' watch station below the chart-house. The main effect of the explosion apparently went overboard, but the chart-house was wrecked, the bridge and after end of the forecastle much damaged, and splinters pierced the upper deck and starboard side plating. The lower part of the fore funnel was driven in and holed, and the funnel uptakes of the forward boiler room damaged and torn, as was the starboard air supply shaft to the second boiler room. Flash entered the second boiler room via this shaft, and a fire occurred. All six coal-fired boilers were temporarily out of action, but the *Pillau* could make 24kts on her four oil-fired boilers, and the two boilers in the third boiler room were in operation again at 1900 and the port boiler in the fore boiler room half an hour later, when she could steam at 26kts, though the other three coal-fired boilers remained out.

Except in the 2nd boiler room, the hit was hardly more noticed below the armour deck than the shell bursts in the water round the ship, and electric lighting and order transmission equipment remained intact. The conning tower, *c*20ft from the burst, was little affected.

Rostock. Hit by 3–4in shells from the *Broke* or others of the 4th Flotilla at 2345–2350.

Two of these struck the side plating amidships, causing some leakage into an upper bunker.

The other shell damaged the after searchlight platform.

Hit by a torpedo at *c*2350 fired by the *Contest* or *Ambuscade*. This was running on the surface and hit on the port side just abaft the bulkhead between the two foremost of the five boiler rooms. Both filled, putting the two oil-fired and two coal-fired boilers out of action, but the bulkheads forward and aft of the flooded boiler rooms held tight. The wing and upper bunkers to port of the flooded boiler rooms filled as did those to port of the third boiler room.

As a result of the torpedo hit about 930 tons of water entered the ship giving an increase in draught of 4¾ft forward, a decrease of 8in aft, and a list of 5° to port. The *Rostock* was thus in no danger of sinking, and although the main turbines and steering and dynamo engines temporarily stopped, she was presently able to steam at 13kts for a short time, but serious salting of the remaining boilers, the cause of which was never discovered, allowed only a slow speed to be maintained, and although taken in tow by S54, the *Rostock* had not proceeded more than 20–25 miles by *c*0355 when the *Dublin* was sighted, and it was decided to scuttle her.

Stettin. Hit by 2–6in shells from the 2nd LCS at *c*2235.

1 Pierced side plating just abaft forward port 4.1in and burst *c*10ft inboard. Splinters put one searchlight out of action and damaged the steam pipe to the siren.

2 Struck face of shield of No 4 port 4.1in and put the gun out of action. There was a small hole in the 2in shield and it was deeply bulged and displaced. The shell explosion was not complete, though there were many splinters.

Wiesbaden. It is impossible to estimate the number of hits with accuracy, but it is thought that there were about fifteen by heavy shells (2 by 3rd BCS and 13 by battleships), 6 by 9.2in or 7.5in from the *Defence* and *Warrior* and a number of 6in to 4in hits by the 2nd and 3rd LCS and the *Onslow*.

A torpedo from the last named also hit, apparently far aft, at *c*1815.

Both engines were disabled by a hit from the 3rd BCS at or just before 1800, but the *Wiesbaden* was still able to fire a torpedo after most of the heavy shells and the *Onslow*'s torpedo had hit, and she remained afloat until at least 0145.

The only survivor, Leading Stoker Zenne, made an inspection during the night of as much of the ship as he could reach, and memorised his findings in astonishing detail. The *Wiesbaden*'s hull was divided into 16 sections numbered from the stern to the bows, and in sections 5 to 12 which extended from about the mainmast to the conning tower, only section 10 comprising the foremost boiler room had escaped serious damage. There was apparently some damage and flooding in sections 13 to 16, and though section 4 was little damaged, the stern of the ship was wrecked, it would seem largely by the torpedo which hit in section 2. The first shell to hit the *Wiesbaden*, which put both engines out of action, had hit in section 6 and caused a great escape of steam, and fires subsequently broke out in this section.

One of the *Wiesbaden*'s forward guns had continued firing for a time, but the mountings of Nos 2 and 3 port guns were displaced by the deck being torn up, and No 2 starboard gun was split at the muzzle. The submerged torpedo flat in section 12 was flooded, but some of the torpedoes could still be made out. The second and third funnels were shot away by the *Marlborough* at *c*1905, and the bridge was apparently destroyed, but the masts were still standing, and everything close by the mainmast was undamaged.

The *Wiesbaden*'s list gradually increased to starboard which had been the engaged side, and she sank suddenly and quietly.

It is impossible to estimate the number of hits on the British destroyers that were lost. The *Tipperary, Turbulent, Ardent* and *Fortune* were sunk by 5.9in shells from the *Westfalen* and other battleships, though also hit by some of smaller calibre. The *Tipperary* and *Turbulent* remained afloat for some time, and frequent ammunition explosions occurred in both. The *Turbulent* may have been finally sunk by a torpedo from the *V71*, but she was already in a sinking condition.

The *Nomad* was disabled by a 4.1in or 3.5in shell in the engine room, and the *Nestor* by 2–4.1in in her boilers, but both were sunk by 5.9in from battleships. The *Nomad*'s fore magazine was hit and blew up before she sank, and a fair number of heavy shells were fired at the *Nestor*, though it is doubtful if any hit.

The *Shark*, hit by 4.1in from the *Regensburg* and 2nd Flotilla, and by 3.5in from other destroyers, was disabled, but it is not thought that any 5.9in shells hit, and she remained in action until sunk by a torpedo from the *S54*. The *Sparrowhawk* was not hit by any German shells, but was completely disabled by collisions with the *Broke* and *Contest* and later scuttled.

On surviving British destroyers, the recorded hits were as follows:
Acasta. Hit by 2 – 5.9in shells from the *Lützow* or *Derfflinger* at *c*1820 in the after part of the engine room. Several steam pipes were holed and the steering engine wrecked. The *Acasta* remained stopped for *c*6 hours, and was towed much of the way back by the *Nonsuch*. She was also holed forward and aft at *c*1810, but details are lacking, and it is not known whether the damage was due to splinters.

Broke. Hit by at least nine shells, and bows destroyed in collision with the *Sparrowhawk* at *c*2350. The hits were mostly 4.1in from the *Rostock* at *c*2345–2350, but there were probably one or two 5.9in from the *Westfalen* at this time, and 2–3.5in from the *S53* and *G88* hit amidships with little or no damage at *c*0100. Apart from these last hits, none was abaft the fore funnel. The bridge was badly damaged, the three foremost boilers out of action, apparently from a shell bursting at the base of the fore funnel, and water leaked into the forward boiler room. A speed of 7kts was attained after the battle.

Contest. Not hit but stem broken in collision with the *Sparrowhawk* at *c*2350, and speed reduced to 20kts.

Defender. Hit by 1–12in shell from the 3rd Squadron at *c*1830. This shell, which was a ricochet, struck the ship's side and entered the forward boiler room, lodging unexploded in the ash pit of No 1 boiler.

The boiler room was put out of action with an oil fuel fire, and speed reduced to 15kts, but No 2 boiler was later brought into use again.

Garland. Hit by 1–5.9in shell which struck a boat, during the night action of the 4th Flotilla.

Marne. Hit by 1–4.1in shell from the *Hamburg* or *Rostock* at c2215. This struck the upper deck aft without bursting and with only slight damage.

Marvel. Hit by 1 – 12in shell from the 3rd Squadron at c1815 which struck right forward without exploding with little damage.

Moorsom. Hit by 1–5.9in shell from the *König* or *Grosser Kurfürst* at c1700–1705. This burst in a cabin aft with damage to oil tanks and loss of some fuel.

Nessus. Hit by 1–5.9in shell from the *Grosser Kurfürst* at c0205 which put a boiler out of action.

Obdurate. Hit by 2–4.1in shells, probably from the *Regensburg*, at c1640 which caused little damage. The *Obdurate*'s forecastle 4in burst when fired, apparently at c0330.

Onslaught. Hit by 1–6.7in HE from the *Schleswig-Holstein* at 0213. This completely wrecked the bridge and ignited a box of 4in QF charges.

Onslow. Hit by 3–5.9in shells from the *Lützow* at c1815, and by 2–4.1in from the *Rostock* at c1830. There is apparently no record of the effect of the 4.1in shells, but the 5.9in all holed the ship's side, two bursting in No 2 boiler room and badly damaging the main feed tank, and the 3rd in a cabin aft. The *Onslow* was towed back by the *Defender*, and as the sea rose No. 2 boiler room and after cabins flooded.

Petard. Hit by four shells, 5.9in or 3.5in, from the *Westfalen* at c0035. Speed was reduced to 28kts.

1 On port side of quarter deck, disabled crew of after 4in.

2 Struck ship's side aft and wrecked cabins.

3 Struck upper deck over No 2 boiler room, entered the stokehold and caused a considerable oil fire from a cut pressure-gauge pipe.

4 Burst just short of the ship in line with the first two funnels, and showered splinters over this area.

Porpoise. Hit by at least two shells, 5.9in or 3.5in from the *Posen* or *Oldenburg* at *c*0015. A 5.9in shell hit at the base of the after funnel, and burst the air chamber of the spare torpedo. This blew in the upper deck and holed the main steam pipe. Loss of water left only two of the four boilers usable. A second shell hit on or near the bridge, and damaged the steering.

Spitfire. Collided with the *Nassau* and hit by 1–11in shell at *c*2335, and by a smaller shell from an unidentified ship shortly before. The bridge was wrecked, and the mast and fore-funnel brought down, probably by the *Nassau*'s 11in gun blast, while the upper part of the port hull plating was torn as far as the bridge in the collision, but there was less damage near the water-line, and the third bulkhead held, with three boilers remaining in use.

The 11in shell went through the bottom of the second funnel, and grazed the top of the boiler without exploding, while the smaller shell hit on or near the torpedo davit.

Of the German destroyers that were lost, the *V48*'s machinery was disabled by one or two 4in shells from the *Shark*, and she was then hit by 6in from the 2nd LCS and *Valiant*, and finally sunk by 4in from the 12th Flotilla. The number of hits cannot be estimated in this instance, but the *S35* was probably sunk by 2–13.5in shells from the *Iron Duke*, and the *V27* was scuttled after being disabled by 2–4in shells from the 13th Flotilla in the forward engine room. The *V29* was sunk by a torpedo from the *Petard*, and the *V4* scuttled after an underwater explosion probably due to a mine.

On surviving German destroyers, the hits were:
B98 Hit by 1–4in shell from the *Shark* at 1807. This struck the after twin TT mounting which was put out of action, and brought down the mainmast.

G40 Hit by 1–6in shell from the *Champion* at *c*0330. This struck the starboard side near, but above the water-line, making a hole of *c*5ft diameter, and damaged the after turbine with great loss of steam so that the *G40* had to be taken in tow.

G41 Hit by 1–6in shell from a battleship at *c*1920. This burst on the forecastle, with splinter damage and casualties, and considerably reduced the *G41*'s speed.

G42 Not hit but severely shaken by heavy shells from the *Colossus* and perhaps other ships at *c*1905–1910, so that her condensers developed leaks, and her speed which was only 25kts from trouble with newly fitted feed pumps, gradually fell to 15kts.

G86 Hit by many splinters of a heavy shell from a battleship at *c*1925. This burst to starboard very near the forward part of the ship. Splinters pierced the hull plating and the forward oil tank, and hit the bridge, wheel house and wireless room, as well as putting a torpedo out of action. Some water was made, and the forward boiler fell out temporarily, so that speed was reduced to 25, and later to 27–28kts.

G87 Hit by 1–6in shell from a battleship at *c*1925 which passed through the ship below the bridge without exploding.

S32 Hit by 3–4in shells, the first from the *Shark* at *c*1845, and the others from the 4th Flotilla at *c*2335.

1 Passed through forecastle with little damage.

2 Hit below bridge.

3 Hit in after boiler room and riddled main steam pipe, so that the *S32* had to stop, but eventually proceeded with sea water feed to the Danish coast.

S36 No direct hits but splinter damage from destroyers' 4in at *c*1635–1640 cut control equipment, damaged the muzzle of the midships gun and caused one boiler to fall out for 20 minutes.

S50 Hit by 1–6in shell from 2nd LCS at *c*2055, and by a shell from the 3rd Squadron at *c*0205.

The former pierced an oil tank and entered the forward boiler room, damaging the main steam and oil pipes, and finished unexploded in the stokehold bilge. The forward boiler was shut down and speed reduced to 25kts.

The German shell went through the top of a ventilator without other damage.

S51 Hit by 1–6in shell from a battleship at *c*1930. This flooded the forward stokehold, so that one boiler and the forward steering engine were out of action, and reduced speed to 21kts.

S52 Some unimportant damage by splinters from the battlefleet's heavy shells at *c*1930.

V28 Hit by 1-6in shell from a battleship at *c*1925. This was on the water-line forward and caused a large leak so that the forward magazine was out of action, and speed reduced to 17-19kts.

The above hits on both British and German destroyers show how vulnerable the steam machinery was in these ships.

Although the British were probably more apprehensive of mines and torpedoes from surface vessels than the Germans, they inflicted greater damage with these weapons. The *Ostfriesland* was damaged by a mine, and torpedoes were responsible for some of the damage to the *Seydlitz*, for the loss of the *Pommern, Rostock, Frauenlob* and the *V29*, and in part for that of the *Wiesbaden*. The precise reason for the loss of the *V4* is not known, but it was probably a drifting mine. Of British ships the *Shark* was sunk and the *Marlborough* damaged by torpedoes, and the *Turbulent* may have been finally sunk by one.

The latest British torpedo at the date of Jutland was the 21in Mark II****, which had a range of 4200yds at 44-45kts and of 10,750yds at 28-29kts. The explosive charge was 400lb TNT or Amatol. The earliest versions of the Mark II had a range of about 450yds less at 44-45kts and 750yds less at 28-29kts. It was intended that each capital ship, and each light cruiser with submerged TT, should have two of her outfit of torpedoes with 'extreme range' setting – *c*17,000yds at 18kts – but it is not known how many had actually been converted. The torpedoes carried in the *Canada, Erin, Agincourt, Broke*, and some of those in the *Chester* and *Birkenhead* had reduced performance and/or smaller war heads compared to the standard Mark II, and it appears that some of the latter in capital ships, and possibly in light cruisers, still had the old 280lb wet gun-cotton charges, but the number is not known.

Of German torpedoes, the 23.6in had a 540lb Hexanite TNT charge, and a range of 6550yds at 36kts and of *c*15,000 at 28kts. The latest 19.7in at the date of Jutland, the G7**, had a 440lb Hexanite – TNT charge, and a range of 5450yds at 35kts and of 10,950 at 28-28½kts. Earlier torpedoes of the G7 series had ranges down to 4050yds at 35kts and 9850 at 28-28½kts. It is not known whether any German ships still had the older 19.7in G6D with ranges of 3800 and 7650yds, but the *V6* fired a G7* to scuttle the *V4*. No 18in torpedoes at Jutland had a greater range than 7000yds.

British torpedoes were considered to leave a less visible track than

German ones.

In the daylight action on 31 May, 54 torpedoes were probably expended by the British fleet as follows:

Battleships: 5– *Marlborough* 2, *Revenge* 1, *Valiant* 1, *Malaya* 1
Battlecruisers: 8 – *Lion* 7, *Princess Royal* 1
Light cruisers: 8 – *Nottingham* 1, *Falmouth* 2, *Yarmouth* 1, *Calliope* 1, *Caroline* 2, *Royalist* 1
4th Flotilla: 4 – *Shark* 2, *Acasta* 1, *Ophelia* 1
10th Flotilla: 7 – *Moorsom* 4, *Turbulent* 3
13th Flotilla: 22 – *Nestor* 4, *Nomad* 4, *Nicator* 3, *Petard* 4, *Nerissa* 2, *Onslow* 4, *Moresby* 1

The targets were:

Unit	Number of Torpedoes fired at Unit
3rd Squadron	17
1st Squadron	3
Either 3rd or 1st Squadron, probably 1st Squadron	5
2nd Squadron	1
1st Scouting Group	21
2nd Scouting Group	2
Wiesbaden (disabled)	4
9th Flotilla	1

Hits were obtained on the *Seydlitz* by the *Petard* or *Turbulent*, on the *Wiesbaden* by the *Onslow* and on the *V29* by the *Petard*, which gives a figure of 10.3% hits for the 10th and 13th Flotillas. One torpedo track is stated to have run under the *Nassau* and one under the *S33* but a torpedo leads its track by a distance depending on speed and depth (about 150yds for a 29kt torpedo at 20ft), and it is not thought that the torpedoes did so. All torpedoes fired were 21in with high speed setting in one instance (hit the *V29*), extreme range in four, and long range in the remainder.

In the same period the German fleet probably expended 90 torpedoes:

Battleships 1 – *König* 1
Battlecruisers 7 – *Lützow* 2, *Derfflinger* 1, *Moltke* 4
Light cruisers ?4 – *Frankfurt* 1, *Elbing* 1, *Wiesbaden* ?2
1st Flotilla 5 – *S32* 5
2nd Flotilla 1 – *G104* 1

3rd Flotilla ?15 – *V73* 2, *G88* 5, *S54* 3, *V48* ?5
6th Flotilla 26 – *G41* 5, *V44* 5, *G87* 5, *G86* 4, *V69* 2, *V45* 1, *S50* 1, *G37* 3.
9th Flotilla ?31 – *V28* 5, *V27* 1, *V26* 4, *S36* 2, *S51* 4, *S52* 6, *S34* 1, *S33* 2, *V29* 4, *S35* ?2

The targets were:

Unit	Number of Torpedoes fired at Unit
Battle line (including 5th BS)	34
Battle line or 1st and 2nd BCS	7
5th BS or 1st and 2nd BCS	7
1st and 2nd BCS	19
3rd BCS	10
1st Cruiser Sqdn	2
1st or 3rd LCS	2
4th Flotilla	6
12th Flotilla	1
13th Flotilla	1
To scuttle *V27*	1 (missed)

Hits were made on the *Marlborough* by the *Wiesbaden*, and on the *Shark* by the *S54*. Torpedo tracks, omitting those that were clearly imaginary, were reported to have run under the ship by the *Marlborough, Inflexible, Indomitable* and *Nomad* (2) and the torpedoes are believed to have run under the *Marlborough* and *Nomad*. Two of the torpedoes fired were 23.6in and the rest 19.7in. The settings were not known in every instance but only five at most were short range.

For the remainder of the battle, from nightfall on 31 May onwards, 40 torpedoes were expended by the British:

Light cruisers 2 – *Southampton* 1, *Castor* 1.
4th Flotilla 17 – *Tipperary* 2, *Broke* 1, *Spitfire* 2, *Garland* 2, *Ambuscade* 3, *Ardent* 2, *Sparrowhawk* 1, *Contest* 2, *Fortune* 2. (The *Tipperary*'s last 2 torpedoes, fired to prevent explosion, are omitted.)
11th Flotilla 3 – *Magic* 2, *Marne* 1
12th Flotilla 17 – *Faulknor* 2, *Obedient* 2, *Marvel* 4, *Onslaught* 4, *Maenad* 3, *Narwhal* 2.
13th Flotilla 1 – *Moresby* 1

The targets were:

Unit	Number of Torpedoes fired at Unit
3rd Squadron	?9
1st Squadron and screening light cruisers	17 (it is thought that about 7 were aimed at the light cruisers).
2nd Squadron (at that time included *Nassau*)	?8
1st Scouting Group	1
2nd Scouting Group	2
4th Scouting Group and attached light cruisers	3

Hits were obtained on the *Pommern* by the *Onslaught*, on the *Rostock* by the *Ambuscade* or *Contest* and on the *Frauenlob* by the *Southampton*, giving an overall percentage of 7.5 for the period. Torpedo tracks are stated to have run under the *Markgraf* and *Elbing* and it is possible that the torpedo ran under the *Elbing*. All fired were 21in (one Weymouth in *Broke*) and the settings were 21 high speed, 14 long range and 5 doubtful. Some may possibly have been fired cold by the 4th Flotilla to reduce the initial dive.

The corresponding German expenditure was 22 torpedoes.
Light cruisers 3 – *Frankfurt* 1, *Pillau* 1, *München* 1
1st Flotilla 3 – *G40* 1, *G38* 2
3rd Flotilla 7 – *S53* 1, *V71* 4, *V73* 1, *G88* 1
5th Flotilla 1 – *V6* 1
6th Flotilla 3 – *V45* 3
7th Flotilla 5 – *S24* 2, *S15* 1, *S16* 1, *S18* 1

The targets were:

Unit	Number of Torpedoes fired at Unit
2nd LCS	1
Castor and 11th Flotilla	2
Champion and Destroyers	3
4th Flotilla	8
Turbulent	2
To scuttle *Lützow*	2 (1 missed)
To scuttle *Rostock*	3
To scuttle *V4*	1

One hit may have been obtained on the *Turbulent* by the *V71*, and torpedoes were seen to run under the *Broke, Turbulent* and *Lützow* none of which was under way. One torpedo fired was an 18in and the rest 19.7in. The settings are not known, but were probably all high speed in the destroyers.

For the whole battle six hits were obtained by the British from 94 torpedoes, and only two or three by the Germans from 105 fired at British ships. It is difficult to account for the discrepancy, but defects were observed in the running and depth taking of some German torpedoes, and no night attack was made against the British battlefleet. The few torpedoes expended by the capital ships of both sides and by the British light cruisers should be noted, and in view of the large number of torpedoes carried by these ships, it would seem that more might have been fired.

No submarines took part in the actual battle, though their imagined presence caused concern, thirty reports of supposed enemy submarines being made by British ships between 1535 and 2200 on 31 May, and there were multiple alarms during the German fleet's return on the morning of 1 June. Real and not imaginary submarines had some effect before and after the action, but far less than had been expected. The Germans placed much importance on airship scouting, but except for the *L11* on the morning of 1 June and for anti-submarine patrols by shore based seaplanes, the contribution of any type of aircraft to the Jutland operations was of very little value, and in the case of the *L24* entirely misleading.

Jutland was thus essentially a two dimensional battle, and the last great fleet action that can be so described. The foregoing pages are, it is hoped, sufficiently complete, but a full account can never now be written as too much material has disappeared.

Notes on Sources

THIS BOOK IS based on the reports of ships taking part in the battle, the reports of damage incurred and the findings of committees set up after the battle to study various aspects. There is one published work: *Battle of Jutland, 30 May to 1 June 1916. Official Despatches with Appendices.* Cmd. 1068 (1920), usually referred to as 'Jutland Despatches', which contains most of the British ships' reports and signals, but omits much information that is to be found in the following unpublished material.

1 *Public Record Office*
   ADM 1/8457, 8458, 8459, 8460, 8463.
   ADM 116/1302, 1484, 1485, 1486, 1487.
   ADM 137/301, 302, 1642, 1643, 1644, 1645, 1946, 1973, 2027, 2028, 2029, 2134, 2135, 2138, 2141, 2142. (See Appendix sections 7 and 12)
   ADM 137/383, 626, 1922, 1924, 1925, 1926, 1977, 1979, 2069, 2070, 2075. (information on British submarine movements in the Jutland period).
   ADM 53 Series Ships' Logs (contain little apart from information on proceedings of destroyers).
   ADM 173 Series, Submarines' Logs (important for British submarine movements).
   CAB 45/269. (See Appendix Section 6).

2 *British Library.*
   BM Add MSS 48989 – 49057 (Jellicoe MSS).
   The Jellicoe Papers, edited by A Temple Patterson, have been

published by the Navy Records Society (1966–8), but much vital Jutland material in Add MSS 49014 and 49027 is omitted.

3 *National Maritime Museum*
   i   Repair Drawings of HMS *Tiger* and *Southampton*.
   ii   Papers of Sir Martyn Jerram and Sir Walter Cowan.

4 *Naval Historical Library*
   i   Grand Fleet Battle Orders.
   ii   Grand Fleet Gunnery and Torpedo Memoranda on Naval Actions, 1914–1918. (contains Grand Fleet Gunnery and Torpedo Order No 15 on Jutland).
   iii Projectile Committee. Final Report. This contains drawings and brief descriptions of the most important hits on surviving British capital ships.
   iv   Records of Warship Construction, 1914–18. This contains some notes on damage.
   v   Torpedo School. Annual Reports, 1916 and 1917.
   vi   Various uncalendared MSS.
        (Some of the above are also in the National Maritime Museum).

5 *Papers in possession of Earl Beatty*
   A number of unique ships' reports among the papers of Admiral Beatty.

6 *Papers in possession of Captain SW Roskill*
   Naval Staff Appreciation of Jutland. (Copy held in British Library) BM Add MSS 49042 (Jellicoe MSS). The principal value of this notorious work is the list of deciphered German signals. Most of the rest was reproduced in the published Admiralty *Narrative of the Battle of Jutland*. In the Roskill Papers is a slightly different list of deciphered signals compiled by W F Clarke, who served in Room 40. There is a copy of Clarke's list in the Naval Historical Library (Ca 1982). Others lists of the deciphered signals are in PRO CAB 45/269 and in BM Add MSS 49014.

7 *German Sources*
   Bundesarchiv – Militärarchiv, Freiburg im Breisgau.
        War-diaries and action reports of German ships engaged in the battle of Jutland. These are, in general, far better than the corresponding British reports.

Damage reports of surviving German ships. Many of these are incomplete, but there is a report entitled *Panzertreffer* in the Library of Kiel Arsenal, which gives drawings and detailed descriptions of all hits on armour of 20mm and above in surviving German capital ships.

Some supplementary information is in PRO ADM 137/1644, and in various MSS in the possession of the Naval Historical Branch.

8 *Official Histories*

Some of the information available in the 1920s has since disappeared, and the official histories are thus a necessary source, though to be used with caution.

The German Official History is: *Der Krieg zur See, 1914–1918. Der Krieg in der Nordsee*, vol v by Captain Otto Groos, the navigator of the *von der Tann* at Jutland. (Mittler and Sohn, 1925).

The British official accounts are: Admiralty: *Narrative of the Battle of Jutland* (HMSO 1924) Corbett, Sir Julian S. *History of the Great War. Naval Operations* vol iii, rev ed (Longmans, 1940).

Reproduction of the Record of the Battle of Jutland by Captain JET Harper (1927) Cmd. 2870.

9 *Track Charts*

The German Official History, Corbett and also 'Jutland Despatches' each have a separate case of track charts; those intended to be published with the Harper Record are in the Naval Historical Library. Those of the German Official History are the most useful, though not free from error. The reports of one ship in each fleet, namely the *Lion* and *Derfflinger*, give the turret training angle for each salvo and, where possible, the battlecruisers' courses have been checked by cross-plotting these angles.

10 *Other Printed Sources*

Other published works containing information, apparently not to be found elsewhere, are:

Chatfield, Admiral of the Fleet Lord, *The Navy and Defence*, (Heinemann, 1942)

Dreyer, Admiral Sir Frederic, *The Sea Heritage: a Study of Maritime Warfare*. (Museum Press, 1955).

Fawcett, Lt Commander HW and Hooper, Lieutenant GWW, *The Fighting at Jutland*, unabridged edition (Macmillan, 1921).

Mantey, Vice Admiral E von, *Auf See unbeseigt* (JF Lehmanns

1921). For *Wiesbaden* only.

Scheer, Admiral Reinhard, *Deutschlands Hochseeflotte im Weltkrieg.* (August Scherl, 1920).

Marine Rundschau May 1926. Article by Commander Günther Paschen, gunnery officer of the *Lützow.*

Die Zwei Weissen Volker by Commander G von Hase, gunnery officer, the *Derfflinger* (K F Koehler, 1923) must be used with great caution, as it is frequently at variance with the *Derfflinger*'s official reports.

11 *Ship and Armament Data*

(A) Details of British ships and their armament have been taken from unpublished official sources. The chief are:

   i   Steam Ships of England, 1915–16, 1917–18.

   ii   Records of Warship Construction, 1914–18.

   iii Armament, Gunnery, Hydraulic and Ammunition Handbooks.

   iv Torpedo School, Annual Reports 1912–19.

   v   Technical History Series.

   vi Projectile Committee. Final Report.

The above sources will be found in the Naval Historical Library, and in the National Maritime and Imperial War Museums. Doubtful points concerning ships have been verified from the Ships' Covers and Drawings in the National Maritime Museum. In addition the Ordnance Minutes for 1912–14 (PRO SUPPLY 6/179–184) have been examined for test firings of AP shells.

(B) Details of German ships are to be found in: Gröner, Erich, *Die deutschen Kriegsschiffe, 1815–1945*, (Lehmanns, 1966–7). Additional material is in *Schiffbau* Nr 28–1921, and Nr 40 – 1921, (the latter is by Dr H Bürkner).

Particulars of armament will be found in unpublished material in the Naval Historical Library, and in the Naval Historical Branch. A nearly complete collection of gun mounting handbooks is held in the Imperial War Museum. Much information has been obtained from various sources in Germany through Captain Meusemann.

Marine Rundschau June and August 1961, contains a history of the development of German underwater protection by Professor H Burkhardt. The details given of the scuttling of the *Lützow* are incorrect.

12 *Pre-Jutland Operations*

Details of pre-Jutland operations in the North Sea are to be found in *Der Krieg in der Nordsee*, vols i–v and in the various Naval Staff Monographs (unpublished) in the Naval Historical Library. Additional material on the Dogger Bank action is in PRO ADM 137/305, 1943, 2134, 2135, while damage to British ships in this action is also given in Records of Warship Construction, the Projectile Committee's final report, and the *Lion*'s Cover. Damage to German ships is in *Panzertreffer*.

Details of the loss of the *Audacious* are in Records of Warship Construction and in the Cover for the *King George V* class.

13 *Russo-Japanese War*

Facts concerning the Russo-Japanese War are to be found in the following unpublished works in the Naval Historical Library: Translation of the Japanese Confidential History; Sir Julian Corbett's *Maritime Operations in the Russo-Japanese War 1904–5*; Reports of British Naval Attachés.

Index

A

B

C

D

E

F

G

H

I

J

K

L

M

N

O

P

Q

R

S

T

U

V

W

Y

Z